THE UNNECESSARY SCIENCE

A CRITICAL ANALYSIS OF NATURAL LAW THEORY

GUNTHER LAIRD

The Unnecessary Science: A Critical Analysis of Natural Law Theory

Copyright © 2020 Onus Books

Published by *Onus Books*

All rights reserved. No part of this publication may be reproduced, stored in a retrieval system, or transmitted in any form by any means, electronic, mechanical, photocopy, recording, or otherwise, without the prior permission of the publisher, except as provided for by UK and US copyright law.

Cover design: Onus Books

Trade paperback ISBN: 978-0-9935102-6-7

OB 16/28

CONTENTS

FOREWORD BY BRADLEY BOWEN 1
PREFACE 11
CHAPTER 1: A VERY BRIEF INTRODUCTION TO PHILOSOPHY 21
1.1: Subfields and Important Concepts of the Field 21
1.2: All Greek To Me 26
1.3: Properties 33
1.4: Minds and Materiality 41
1.5: Differentiations – Essences and Existence and Forms and Functions and Angels and Souls, Oh My! 43
1.6: Ethics 50
CHAPTER 2: FALLIBLE FAITH 59
2.1: Christmas Miracles and Easter Inductions 61
2.2: An Induction at Golgotha 72
2.3: The Problem with Miracles 76
2.4: Jews and Muslims and Pagans, Oh My! 89
2.5: Locke was right! 104
CHAPTER 3: CONTRACEPTIVE CAUSALITY 109
3.1: Innocuous Intentions 113
3.2: Contrary and Other Than 119
3.3: The final cause of Fapping 122
3.4: Harems 132
3.5: Gay Marriage is Super, Thanks For Asking 139
3.6: Marriage as an Artifact 144
3.7: Abortion 147
3.8: Aristotle, Infanticide, and Genocide 159
CHAPTER 4: ARISTOTELIAN ATROCITIES 165
4.1: Aristotle and Slavery 167
4.2: Plato and Nazism 175
4.3: Aristotle and Communism 184
4.4: Thomistic Tragedies 191
CHAPTER 5: FALLACIOUS FORMS 199
5.1: Fact and Value 200
5.2: Whose Form Is It Anyways? 211
5.3: Live and Die by the Forms 216
5.4: Putting the Foot Down 227
5.5: The Rewards of Rationality 232
5.6: Euthyphro's Revenge 240
5.7: The Trouble with Transcendentals 246

5.8: The Problem of Evil 253
CHAPTER 6: EXASPERATING EXISTENCE 263
6.1: Abstract Objects..263
6.2: Possible Worlds...271
6.3: Propositions..275
6.4: The Birds and the Bees 277
6.5: Deistic Existence...283
6.6: Essence Is Existence 299
6.7: Act and Potency..308
CHAPTER 7: ACTUAL ALTERNATIVES 329
7.1: Deism...330
7.2: Lovecraftian-Aristotelian Realism 333
7.3: Atheistic Atomism..337
CONCLUSION 345
REFERENCES 351

Foreword

By Bradley Bowen

The Culture Wars are still raging. Abortion rights, gay rights (including the right of same-sex couples to marry), and separation of church and state are still under attack by Catholics and Evangelical Christians. On the other hand, liberals, socialists, humanists, skeptics, feminists, gays and lesbians are still fighting to defend these rights.

Many religious conservatives in the U.S. recognized that Donald Trump was a habitual liar and a womanizer who had no deeply held religious or moral convictions, but they voted for him anyway, because they believed he would put conservative judges on the Supreme Court, and that those judges might well put an end to abortion, gay rights, and separation of church and state, turning back the clock on the liberalization of the USA.

The Culture Wars are primarily a political battle. But if the Culture Wars are ever to end, that will require either an ideological compromise or an ideological victory of one side over the other. Roe vs. Wade was an attempt by the Supreme Court at a compromise between a liberal stance and a conservative religious stance. But Catholics and Evangelicals are clearly unwilling to accept such a compromise, and they still oppose equal rights for gays and lesbians, and separation of church and state. So, one side needs to win these ideological conflicts in order for the Culture Wars to end.

Christianity has been on the decline in Europe, and in recent decades it appears that the USA is following down that path as well. In the late 1970s, about 90% of Americans identified themselves as

Christians.[1] In 2007, about 78% of Americans identified themselves as Christians, and more recently, in 2019, only 65% of Americans identified themselves as Christians. In 2007, about 16% of Americans had no religious affiliation, but 26% of Americans claimed no religious affiliation in 2019.[2] When Catholics and Evangelicals eventually become just another "minority" group in the USA, their reactionary influence will fade away, and liberals, socialists, humanists, skeptics, feminists, gays and lesbians will be able to overwhelm the cultural and political influence of conservative Christians.

Beliefs about sexual morality among Catholics and Evangelicals are based, in part, on the Bible. They are also based, in part, on the teachings and theology of the Catholic church (for Catholics) and of various protestant churches or traditions (for Evangelicals). So, one part of the defense of traditional Christian sexual morality is the case for God, and the case for the truth of the Christian religion.

Many Christians, especially Catholics and Evangelicals, believe that the existence of God can be proven through philosophical argumentation and that the superiority of the Christian religion over other religions can also be proven on the same basis. One such believer is the Catholic philosopher Edward Feser. He attempts to use philosophical arguments, based on the philosophy of Aristotle and of Aquinas, to prove the existence of God, and to show the superiority of the Christian faith over other religions. In his books and blog posts, Feser provides clarification of the philosophy of Aristotle (384-322 BCE) and Aquinas (1224-1274 CE) for a general audience. If someone unfamiliar with ancient Greek philosophy and medieval philosophy wanted to learn about the thinking of Aristotle and Aquinas, Feser's

---

[1] "Religious preference" search, *GSS Data Explorer*, last accessed July 5, 2020, https://gssdataexplorer.norc.org/trends/Religion%20&%20Spirituality?measure=relig_rec

[2] "In U.S., Decline of Christianity Continues at Rapid Pace", *Pew Research Center*, last accessed July 5, 2020, https://www.pewforum.org/2019/10/17/in-u-s-decline-of-christianity-continues-at-rapid-pace

writings would be an excellent choice to help understand these two great philosophers.

Although he was born about 1,800 years before the Renaissance occurred in Europe, Aristotle was the original "Renaissance man". He studied, taught, and wrote on the main areas of philosophy: metaphysics, epistemology (the theory of knowledge), and ethics, as well as on political philosophy. He initiated the systematic study of the structure and rules of reasoning, called logic. Computers are based on logic, so the next time you use a PC, tablet, or smartphone, remember that Aristotle made those devices possible. He also studied, taught, and wrote on natural science, especially on physics and biology. Furthermore, he studied and wrote about rhetoric, the theory of drama, and literature.

Aristotle learned philosophy from Plato at Plato's Academy in Athens and was a teacher at the Academy for many years. Later in life, he taught in the Lyceum in Athens for more than a decade. Like Plato, Aristotle wrote dialogues, and those dialogues were viewed as eloquent by Cicero. But unfortunately, those dialogues did not survive. The works that we have from Aristotle are not very eloquent and are probably lecture notes rather than polished writings intended for a wide audience, but they are filled with interesting philosophical questions, arguments, and insights. If someone wanted to study the thinking of just one philosopher, Aristotle would be an excellent philosopher to choose.

If one is interested in Philosophy of Religion and interested in the question "Does God exist?", there is no greater and more important philosopher to study than Thomas Aquinas. Aquinas is an important philosopher of religion and has been especially influential in Catholic thinking, on the existence of God, on ethics, on metaphysics, and on theology. If someone were to study only one philosopher who argues in support of the Christian faith, Aquinas would be an excellent choice.

This brilliant and prolific theologian was born in Italy and, after the re-discovery of the writings of Aristotle in the West (in the 11th century), made use of the philosophy of Aristotle to develop and defend Christian theology. He studied philosophy and theology in Paris, and then lectured in Paris for a few years, and in 1256 became a full professor. Aquinas went back to Italy for about ten years, and then returned to Paris once again to teach for a few more years. In 1272, he returned to Italy to teach at the University of Naples, and he died there in 1274.

Many Introduction to Philosophy courses have students read a famous passage about the "Five Ways", in which Aquinas presents five different arguments for the existence of God. However, such an introduction to Aquinas can be very misleading. The actual proofs of the existence of God given by Aquinas are much more complex than the simple arguments in the "Five Ways" excerpt. Furthermore, some of the concepts in Aquinas's proofs are technical terms that are not easy to understand. So, reading Aquinas on one's own can be confusing and frustrating. There is a need for a knowledgeable modern philosopher to guide one in understanding Aquinas's proofs for the existence of God. This also applies to other philosophical issues covered by Aquinas, in ethics, metaphysics, and epistemology.

Edward Feser is one such modern philosopher who has studied both Aquinas and the Greek philosopher whom Aquinas greatly admired: Aristotle. Feser is a big fan of Aquinas, and he advocates Thomistic views about the existence of God, and Thomistic views about nature and human beings, and about values and ethics. Feser argues for the significance of Thomist philosophy in relation to modern issues and in making a rational defense of the Christian faith. He is an apologist for Christianity, especially for Catholicism, and he makes no attempt to hide his admiration of Aquinas or his Catholic faith, and that enthusiasm is part of what makes reading Feser interesting and worthwhile.

Traditional sexual morality does not rest entirely on the inspiration and interpretation of the Bible, nor on the authority of any particular Church or theological tradition. If there are problems and weaknesses in the case for God and the case for Christianity (and for a specific version of Christianity), then the Bible and the teachings of a particular Christian church or tradition will not provide sufficient grounds for traditional Christian morality. However, according to conservative religious believers who accept a "natural law" view of morality, one can rationally prove that abortion and homosexual relationships are morally wrong, without having to quote verses from the Bible, or proclamations from the Pope.

One such religious conservative is the previously mentioned professor of philosophy, Edward Feser. According to Feser, if we return to the philosophy of Aristotle, as developed by the Christian philosopher Thomas Aquinas, we will find that philosophy and reason can provide objective answers to questions about morality, including answers about the morality of abortion, contraception, and homosexual relationships. He makes use of Thomist natural law theory of ethics to support traditional Catholic moral beliefs, especially concerning sexual morality. Feser believes there are solid philosophical arguments that support conservative Christian beliefs about morality.

In *The Unnecessary Science,* Gunther Laird raises skeptical objections and challenges to Feser's view that the philosophy of Aristotle and Aquinas can be used to show the superiority of the Christian religion over other religions, and to prove the existence of God. Laird also raises skeptical objections against arguments for traditional Christian beliefs about sexual morality that are based on such philosophy, especially on the "natural law" view of morality promoted by Aquinas and his Thomist followers.

Gunther Laird is a skeptical thinker, and he challenges many of the arguments and conclusions of Feser in support of Christian and Catholic religious and moral beliefs. Laird shows that there are many serious problems and inconsistencies in Feser's defense of Christian theology and Catholic moral beliefs, and also in some of the basic ideas in the philosophy of Aristotle and Aquinas, given Feser's understanding of those ideas.

A significant portion of *The Unnecessary Science* is focused on the conservative Catholic moral views that Feser defends on the basis of Thomistic metaphysics and ethics. So, for those who are not particularly interested in Philosophy of Religion, or the question of the existence of God, there is plenty of interesting and worthwhile discussion here about Thomistic metaphysics and ethics as presented by Feser, and to what extent conservative Catholic morality can be supported on that basis.

Feser is a good guide to help one learn about the philosophy of Aristotle and Aquinas, and Laird is an excellent skeptical guide who can help one to think critically about the Thomist arguments and views presented by Feser, especially in relation to Thomistic metaphysics and ethics and whether they provide strong support for conservative Catholic morality.

There are at least two good reasons why liberals (including liberal Christians, Jews, and Muslims), humanists, socialists, skeptics, feminists, gays and lesbians should be interested in reading *The Unnecessary Science* and learning about Feser's Aristotelian/Thomist case for Christianity and for traditional Christian sexual morality.

First, even if we can eventually overwhelm conservative Christians politically, as their numbers continue to decline, that does not mean that we ought to do so. We (liberals, humanists, skeptics, etc.) should move our country and culture away from conservative Christian beliefs and values only if we have good reason to reject or doubt those beliefs and values. We can be sure of this only if we seriously consider the reasons and arguments that intelligent conservative Christians give in support of their views. Because we value truth and fairness, we have an obligation to consider the reasons and arguments of people like Edward Feser.

Second, although it is true that many conservative Christian believers are closed-minded, and generally not interested in discussing reasons for or against their beliefs and values, there are some conservative Christians who are willing to discuss and debate these issues. If they are presented with clear and compelling arguments against their beliefs and values, many of those Christians will change their minds. I was a teenage Evangelical Christian, and the reasons and arguments of liberals, humanists, skeptics, etc., eventually completely changed my mind.

Sometimes when conservative Christians are challenged with clear and compelling objections, they will become less dogmatic; sometimes they will become less conservative, and over time some will even change their basic viewpoint, and become a liberal, or humanist, or socialist, or skeptic, or feminist, or decide to admit they are gay or lesbian (or bisexual or something else). So, for those conservative Christians who are open to discussing these issues, we should be prepared to present clear and compelling arguments challenging conservative Christian beliefs and values.

One aspect of Laird's skepticism that is admirable and helpful is his frequent use of hypothetical reasoning. Most people tend to focus on the premises of an argument and object to the truth of one or two premises. That is a perfectly acceptable way to criticize an argument, so long as the premise that is challenged is in fact false or dubious.

But there are other ways of criticizing arguments that are often more appropriate and more insightful. The use of hypothetical reasoning can greatly expand one's ability to think critically about arguments. If one grants for the sake of argument the truth of a premise, and then asks "What does this imply?" that can lead to the discovery that the premise actually works against the conclusion that is was supposed to support.

In other words, it is often helpful to accept some, or even all, of the premises of an argument, but then think carefully and deeply about what those premises mean, and what they imply. This often leads to insights about weaknesses or even contradictions within an argument or point of view. This is one of the main skeptical moves that Socrates would make. He would accept a premise or claim of someone, and then, step-by-step, show that this premise leads to a contradiction or to an obviously absurd conclusion. That sort of reasoning is called a "reduction to absurdity" argument.

Gunther Laird's critique of Edward Feser is filled with hypothetical reasoning. It is filled with arguments that accept one or more of Feser's Thomistic assumptions, and then proceed to show that this assumption leads to a contradiction with Feser's conclusion or with some other belief that Feser is trying to promote, or it leads to significant doubt about Feser's conclusion. This, by itself, makes Laird's critique of Feser's Thomistic views worthwhile. Even if you ultimately agree with Feser on an issue and reject Laird's criticism of Feser on that point, you will still benefit from seeing example after example of the use of hypothetical reasoning to think critically about an argument or point of view.

Laird also provides lots of examples of dialectical thinking, which is another important aspect of critical thinking, and of the thinking of Socrates. He does not just raise objections against the arguments presented by Feser; he also considers how Feser would likely respond to the objections. In some cases, there is an extended back-and-forth between Feser's view and Laird's view on a given issue. Such intellectual back-and-forth is necessary to go beyond our ordinary superficial modes of thought, so this is another aspect of Laird's writing that promotes critical thinking about issues of religion, morality, and philosophy.

In *The Unnecessary Science*, Gunther Laird provides an intellectual banquet of concepts, principles, arguments, and skeptical objections concerning religion and morality that draws upon the ideas of two of the greatest philosophers of western thought: Aristotle and Aquinas—as clarified and defended by the modern Catholic philosopher Ed Feser. Laird provides an antidote to Feser's conservative Catholic views: skeptical arguments that will help liberals (and others) to win the Culture Wars. He does this in a way that is user friendly and entertaining, while emphasizing and promoting some key aspects of critical thinking—hypothetical reasoning and dialectical thinking. In this book, you will discover how philosophical thinking going back to ancient Athens still has relevance for how we should think and live in the 21st century.

Bradley Bowen is a formerly professing evangelical Christian. The study of philosophy led Bradley away from his Christian faith. A popular blogger on Patheos, *he has a BA in Philosophy from Sonoma State University (1984), an MA in Philosophy from the University of Windsor (1987) and did further graduate study in Philosophy at the University of California at Santa Barbara earning a C.Phil in Philosophy (1991).*

Preface

In 1991, the first African American member of the Supreme Court of the United States, Thurgood Marshall, decided to retire after a long and storied career as a trailblazer for civil rights. Then-President George H.W. Bush had to make a difficult choice on who to replace him. On the one hand, his Republican supporters wanted a new Justice who would further the Court's rightward trend. On the other hand, Bush Sr. was facing considerable political pressure to prove his attention and sensitivity to the aspirations of his black constituents, since he had received significant criticism for his handling of civil rights affairs at this point in his term. As it so happened, there was a promising black federal judge who also possessed impeccable conservative credentials—nominating this fellow would, from the perspective of the President, both satisfy his conservative backers while demonstrating his willingness to advance Americans of all racial backgrounds to the highest levels of their government. Thus, less than a month after Marshall's retirement, Clarence Thomas would take his seat upon the Supreme Court.[1]

Despite his considerable and accomplished legal career, Thomas's nomination was not without controversy. I refer not to the Anita Hill affair, but to Thomas's *philosophical* commitments which have received much less public attention. Laurence H. Tribe noted that Thomas held some beliefs of dubious compatibility with a secular republic: "judging

---

[1] Andrew Rosenthal, "Marshall Retires from High Court; Blow to Liberals," *The New York Times,* June 28, 1991, https://www.nytimes.com/1991/06/28/us/marshall-retires-from-high-court-blow-to-liberals.html , Maureen Dowd, The Supreme Court: Conservative Black Judge, Clarence Thomas, Is Named to Marshall's Court Seat", *The New York Times,* July 2, 1991, https://www.nytimes.com/1991/07/02/us/supreme-court-conservative-black-judge-clarence-thomas-named-marshall-s-court.html (both last accessed on July 5, 2020).

from his speeches and scholarly writings, [he] seems instead to believe judges should enforce the Founders' natural law philosophy—the inalienable rights 'given man by his Creator'.... He is the first Supreme Court nominee in 50 years to maintain that natural law should be readily consulted in constitutional interpretation."[1]

The words "natural law" might seem familiar to people paying attention to debates of seemingly less immediate importance—arguments between professional philosophers of ethics in the lofty ivory towers of academia. Far below them, within the swamp of various online fora ranging from Twitter to Patheos, atheists and religious believers of all varieties sparring with each other over the rationality or irrationality of the moral tenets preached by various religions—along with religion itself—also refer to the "natural law" tradition. The combatants either attack it as vacuous (in the case of many, though not necessarily all, of the atheists) or hold it up as the most complete and coherent set of ethics ever devised (in the case of many, though certainly not all, of the believers). But as the example of Justice Thomas proves, many people in positions of great power take "natural law" quite seriously, and may influence the lives of millions—for better or worse—because of what they believe natural law entails. Thus, there may be more immediate, practical benefit—if not necessity—in studying that tradition, over and above mere familiarity with what goes on in abstruse academic debates or online trolling.

If you don't live in the ivory tower and/or the darkest recesses of right-wing Twitter, you might be wondering if there's even the slightest bit of hope for understanding the immensely complicated but also

---

[1] Lawrence H. Tribe, "Clarence Thomas and 'natural law,'" *The New York Times*, July 15, 1991, last accessed on July 5, 2020, https://www.nytimes.com/1991/07/15/opinion/clarence-thomas-and-natural-law.html . Also see Anthony Murray, "When Judges Believe in 'natural law,'" *The Atlantic,* January 27, 2014, last accessed on July 5, 2020, https://www.theatlantic.com/national/archive/2014/01/when-judges-believe-in-natural-law/283311/

immensely influential "natural law" tradition. By very great fortune, however, there is a contemporary academic who explains it in terms readily accessible to laymen. Edward Feser, Professor of Philosophy at Pasadena City College, has acquired a reputation as one of the most ferocious *and* most accessible defenders of that tradition writing today. Even reviewers generally critical of natural law appreciate how he "[makes] philosophical argument compulsively readable."[1] Those sharing his respect for the tradition effusively praise him for explaining the most recondite and refined arguments of thinkers such as Aristotle, Leibniz, Augustine, and Aquinas "as thoroughly as possible, in a way that communicates their internal coherence to readers who may have no special formal training in philosophy."[2] While there are many scholars who write within and in defense of the natural law tradition—Reginald Garrigou-Lagrange, David Oderberg, and Gyula Klima, among others, are recommended by Feser himself[3]—most of their work is aimed towards professional philosophers rather than the common public. Edward Feser, on the other hand, has written very extensively for the layman; many of his books, such as *The Last Superstition*, *Aquinas: A Beginner's Guide*, *Locke*, *Philosophy of Mind: A Short Introduction*, and *Five Proofs of the Existence of God* are intended for use by college students and explicitly marketed towards beginners.

    Given all this—the extent of Feser's outreach to the general public outside of academia, his wild popularity among fans of natural law, and the voluminous amount he has written explaining what the natural law

---

[1] Anthony Kenny, "We Have All Been Here Before," *The Times Literary Supplement*, July 22, 2001, last accessed on July 5, 2020, https://www.the-tls.co.uk/articles/private/we-have-all-been-here-before/

[2] David Bentley Hart, "The Exemplary Clarity of the Five Proofs of the Existence of God," *Church Life Journal*, March 1, 2018, last accessed on July 5, 2020, https://churchlifejournal.nd.edu/articles/the-exemplary-clarity-of-the-five-proofs-of-the-existence-of-god/

[3] Edward Feser, *Scholastic Metaphysics* (Scholastic Editions - Editiones Scholasticae, 2014), 7-8.

consists of—anyone wishing to confront the natural law tradition would do well to begin with him. That is precisely the aim of this book.

Feser, as he so often does, explains precisely what the "natural law" tradition is in language you don't have to be a Supreme Court justice to understand. From about the fourth century B.C, in ancient Greece, philosophers such as Plato and his student Aristotle started pondering questions like "what is change?" and "when we say two things share a certain property, what do we mean?" Eventually, the answers they arrived at led them (or at least some of their followers) to conclude that a single, eternal, omnibenevolent, omnipotent, and omniscient God existed, and that this allowed human beings to objectively discern what behaviors were immoral or moral. Centuries later, during the fall of the Roman Empire and the subsequent Middle Ages, Catholics such as St. Augustine and St. Aquinas took another look at the writings of pagan thinkers like Aristotle and Plato and married them to the Catholic religion, concluding that the answers to philosophical questions these Greeks had found also pointed towards the truth of Christianity (and very specifically Catholicism), as well as the truth of orthodox Catholic moral teaching. That meant no divorce, no gay marriage, and no abortion, among other things, along with state sponsorship of the Catholic church and official discouragement (to put it mildly) of atheism.[1] This is the philosophical tradition to which Clarence Thomas belongs, and according to which *Roe vs. Wade* or gay marriage or public denial of a supernatural God overseeing human affairs are all offenses against the moral order and cannot be tolerated by any state, secular or otherwise. Regardless of whether or not the Founding Fathers subscribed to that tradition, its adherents claim it is objectively true and must be upheld even today, centuries after their deaths. As Feser tells us

---

[1] *The Last Superstition*, 27-28, 132. Due to the amount of times I will be citing this book and Feser's other work, henceforth *The Last Superstition* will be cited as *TLS*, *Scholastic Metaphysics* will be cited as *SM, Aquinas: A Beginner's Guide* (Oneworld publications, 2009), as *AQ, Neo-Scholastic Essays* (St. Augustine's Press, 2015) as *NSE*, and *Five Proofs of the Existence of God* (Ignatius Press, 2017) will be cited as *FP*.

in *The Last Superstition*, "the classical theism and traditional morality of Western civilization...ought to be restored to their rightful place as the guiding principles of Western thought, society, and politics, and that, accordingly, secularism ought to be driven back into the intellectual and political margins whence it came."[1]

My objective in this book is precisely the opposite. I hope to at least raise the possibility that Aristotle's arguments for God do much less than Aquinas supposed to prove the truth of Christianity (or any particular religion), indicating that contemporary political secularism still has much to recommend it; that Aristotle's philosophical positions do not buttress Feser's "traditional morality" (and not only with regard to sex) as strongly as the good professor claims; that there is more tension between Aristotle's philosophy and Aquinas's than Feser and other defenders of a continuous natural law tradition let on; and finally, that Aristotle's metaphysics did not even prove the existence of God as indisputably as Feser claims.

This is certainly a lofty goal, particularly since I'm just a not-especially-intellectually-accomplished layman, and I'm going up against a bona-fide professor of philosophy, along with several of his professor friends, and the luminaries of the Western intellectual tradition he claims on his side. But, if I may claim something to my credit, I am well aware of my shortcomings, and in this case, I don't believe I've bitten off more than I can chew. This book will not attempt a full, advanced, philosophical takedown of the natural law tradition or its individual Aristotelian or Thomistic components. Rather, *The Unnecessary Science* will provide a general plan or starting point for such an attempt, highlighting a broad variety of weaknesses and internal tensions (some obvious, some not) within the tradition that can be detected in the writings of its most able modern evangelist. This will allow beginners to attain a basic grasp of philosophical concepts, a familiarity with what they will (hopefully) oppose, and an acquaintance with many books,

---

[1] *TLS*, x.

scholarly articles, and other resources (including blog posts) that can point them towards contemporary and ancient thinkers who have critiqued the natural law tradition even more ably than I. Professional philosophers and those who are already experienced with the arguments surrounding natural law will also find much of value in this text: It covers a very wide range of intellectual ground; even if the basic arguments I have put forth here are not perfect, there is such a broad variety that many scholars might not have heard of several before, allowing such scholars an avenue to do further research and refine and strengthen these arguments in ways I could not.

For that reason, the sorts of sources this book will incorporate might be somewhat more eclectic than one would expect in an academic monograph. In addition to books and articles you could find on JSTOR or at academic libraries, as well relevant primary sources published by reputable organizations online, I will also cite many blog entries and book reviews written by individuals (some anonymous, some not) found across the Internet. There are two reasons to take this approach. First, a good portion of Feser's thought is found not only in his books but also his blog, edwardfeser.blogspot.com. There, he has expanded on much of the content found in *The Last Superstition, Aquinas: A Beginner's Guide*, and his other published work, clarifying, expanding on, and strengthening what he as previously written. To forthrightly address his very strongest arguments would, therefore, require me to address his blog posts as well. The second consideration is this: As we have already established very firmly, the issues raised by natural law theory and its proponents are both relevant and (in some cases) directly impact the lives of people far outside the ivory tower, and if Feser has explicitly directed much of his work towards the general populace, it stands to reason that many laypeople would have come up with their own responses to Feser's arguments. Wisdom should be accepted wherever it is found, and given how insightfully many bloggers and Internet commenters have responded to much of what Feser has written, it is only fair to ensure their voices are heard as far as possible; an undertaking to which I hope I have made a modest contribution.

Given the wide range of non-academic sources I'll be using, I'm sure it will be a relief to learn that this book will not be written in an academic style. While, of course, my argumentation and citation will meet the highest scholarly standards, I have tried my hardest to avoid overwhelming my readers with technical jargon. In places where such jargon is unavoidable, I have bolded important terms where they first appear and explained them in plain language so even lay readers will find advanced philosophical ideas to be at least readily accessible. Additionally, throughout the book, I attempt to maintain a light, conversational tone, and I have peppered it with many jokes and funny asides which will hopefully make at least a few people laugh. Philosophy is notorious for being not only complex but extremely dry and boring, and one of the things for which I admire Feser, particularly in *The Last Superstition*, is how he makes the subject seem entertaining and engaging as opposed to sleep-inducing. However, as Feser himself admits, in *The Last Superstition* this was done extensively through polemics; he spends more than a few paragraphs insulting notorious atheist writers with whom he disagrees.[1] This is not a criticism of his work, as I myself have been known to be even more caustic on occasion. Rather, it is for precisely that reason—to train myself to be more charitable, as many of my friends have advised me to be—I have filled this book with gentle humor that is merely whimsical, at my own expense, or good-naturedly poking a bit of fun at Feser for portions of his work he might have done well to take a little less seriously. In this way, I hope *The Unnecessary Science* will prove to be engaging and perhaps even entertaining without being polemic or overly mean-spirited.

The fun will start from the top and then work all the way down to the metaphysical bottom. Chapter 1, **A Very Brief Introduction to Philosophy,** sets the stage for readers brand-new to the subject. I'll explain the basic concepts needed to understand Feser's arguments, like how we study metaphysics and how philosophers think about things like

---

[1] *TLS*, 25-26.

universals, epistemology, and so on. Chapter 2, **Fallible Faith**, will explore Feser's religious claims. First, I assert that even if metaphysics tells us Christianity is true, it cannot tell us which one of the many branches is. That should be enough to tell us that Christianity might not be indisputably true after all—indeed, the very metaphysics Feser claims for his cause make it much more likely Judaism or Islam is correct. But unfortunately for Jews and Muslims, Aristotelian metaphysics are incapable of making *any* sort of historical evidence "overwhelming," simply due to the contingent, non-deductive nature of historical inquiry. This leads me to claim that no purely rational argument can establish the truth claims of any of the three monotheistic Abrahamic religions. Even worse for Professor Feser, I also argue that traditional Catholic teaching about angels, or *any* metaphysics which allow for the existence of immaterial intellects besides God, make it insurmountably difficult to judge the veracity of any miracle story. One, therefore, cannot rule out any particular religion—even pagan ones—despite the pretensions of classical theistic monotheism!

Without the threat of hellfire, natural law ethical theory might seem much less convincing. Whatever the "objective" definitions of good and bad may be, there's much less direct reason to pay attention to them if you don't have to worry about eternal punishment. Even so, I'll still address these kinds of ethics. In chapter 3, **Contraceptive Causality**, I argue that many "traditional" condemnations of non-procreative sexual behavior have very little force without religious backing, *even if* we accept Aristotle's metaphysics. These discussions form the groundwork for chapter 4, **Aristotelian Atrocities**, which is more historical than philosophical in nature. There, I examine the development and implementation of "modern" ideologies such as Nazism and Communism and conclude they did not depart as much from the "classical" tradition as Feser claims they did. I also argue that the natural law tradition is perfectly compatible with many of the sins Feser rejects, such as abortion and racial chattel slavery.

With all that said and done, the second half of this book plunges into a direct assault on Feser's metaphysics. In chapter 5, **Facetious Forms,** I expand on my historical analysis to explain how and why Aristotelian realism with regard to universals can so easily justify terrible crimes. This chapter points out how even if you accept the existence of Forms, you still cannot evade the is-ought problem Hume described centuries ago, or even form a coherent, broadly binding ethical system based only on adherence to Forms. Needless to say, I also explore the dire consequences this poses for classical theism, particularly with regard to theodicy. Chapter 6, **Exasperating Existence,** critiques many elements of the "classical tradition" on purely logical grounds rather than ethical ones. I explore how Feser's preferred solutions to the Problem of Universals don't really work, and how the distinction between "essence and existence," one of the central Thomist arguments for the existence of God, does not necessarily lead to theistic conclusions. Chapter 7, **Actual Alternatives**, is more or less just what it says on the tin. I endeavor to explain how a variety of alternative metaphysical frameworks (deism, pantheism, and naturalistic atheism) can solve all of the philosophical problems Thomism purports to, proving that Feser's preferred philosophy is certainly not the only game in town, so to speak.

As you may be able to tell from my mention of bloggers, this book owes a great deal to the Internet. Not just in the sense of allowing me to easily access so much information, but also in the sense of allowing me to build a community of like-minded individuals who both shared and encouraged my interest in philosophy. I am first and most thoroughly indebted to Jonathan MS Pearce (and Onus Books), who very kindly agreed to take a chance on publishing this book as well as providing a very keen editor's eye; his advice and suggestions have vastly improved it over the first draft. I met Jonathan through the suggestion of several members of an online discussion group, and quite naturally I am most grateful to the members of "Contra Aquinam Intergalactica" and many commenters of Jonathan's Patheos blog[1] as well. Jonathan also connected me to other members of his blogging network on Patheos, most notably Bradley Bowen[2], to whom I am most grateful for both writing the foreword to this book and providing several additional suggestions for the text. Finally, many commentators on my personal blog and those of the aforementioned bloggers, as well as the subscribers of several Reddit communities, such as /r/philosophy, helped me immensely by pointing me towards books, articles, and other blog posts highly relevant to this project. While none of them directly assisted in the actual writing of this book itself, it would have been much worse without incorporating the sources they suggested, so I am thusly very grateful to Tru, Arensb[3], Camestros Felapton,[4] Jonathan David Garner, Lash Wantonly, InaneDragon,[5] /u/rivka33, and my many sympathetic readers in general. If nothing else, convincing even one person to read the writing of the bloggers and Redditors I have mentioned here would make this book a success as far as I'm concerned.

---

[1] Jonathan MS Pearce, *A Tippling Philosopher*, last accessed July 24, 2020.
https://www.patheos.com/blogs/tippling/
[2] Bradley Bowen, *The Secular Outpost*, last accessed July 24, 2020.
https://www.patheos.com/blogs/secularoutpost/author/bbowen/
[3] Arensb, *Epsilon Clue*, last accessed July 24, 2020.
http://epsilonclue.wordpress.com/
[4] Camestros Felapton, *Camestros Felapton*, last accessed July 24, 2020.
http://camestrosfelapton.wordpress.com/
[5] InaneDragon, *Inane Dragon*, last accessed July 24, 2020.
https://www.patreon.com/inanedragon/creators

Chapter 1: A Very Brief Introduction to Philosophy

1.1: Subfields and Important Concepts of the Field

We all know things, or at least hope we do. Even admitting we know nothing—as Socrates famously did—is, ironically, to claim to know at least one thing. So we then start to wonder: What do we know, and how do we know it? These are the foundational questions of philosophy, at least for our purposes in this book. The sub-fields of philosophy which tackle these questions specifically are **metaphysics** and **epistemology**.

Metaphysics is the study of reality at its most basic level, even more basic than the subatomic particles of primary interest to scientists. A physicist, for example, might study the characteristics and behavior of quarks. But she cannot even begin to pursue that line of research without knowing what the terms "characteristics" (or, as we'll see, "properties") and "behavior" mean and reference. Metaphysics (good metaphysics, anyways) would provide our enterprising scientist with effective, practical definitions of those terms. Indeed, a good metaphysical framework provides working definitions of all the most fundamental concepts in our day to day life—what it means to say a thing exists, changes, or can be categorized.[1]

So, how can we arrive at such a useful metaphysical framework? A reasonable answer might be "by observing the environment around us and basing our worldview upon the evidence we parse." Alas, a sly philosopher might point out that such a task is impossible unless we already have a metaphysical framework to use. No matter how much evidence we gather, or how astute our observations, we cannot make sense of any of them without some idea of how to categorize them, describe their characteristics, and ensure our observations are accurate. Or, in other words, we would be left wondering how we know what we

---

[1] *AQ,* 20-21.

claim to know and whether that knowledge is reliable. **Epistemology** is the study of such questions—the study of knowledge itself—asking how we know what we know and whether our knowledge is reliable.

At the moment, our epistemological concerns revolve around two types of information and two types of reasoning: Empirical (or **a posteriori**) and logical (or **a priori**) facts, and **inductive** as opposed to **deductive** reasoning. Empirical facts are derived from the experiential methods we described above: observing the environment, a given phenomenon, or anything else of interest with our senses of sight, hearing, taste, and so on. For instance, if you were to claim, "it rains a lot in England," and based this claim upon either seeing many showers on your last trip to England, or looking up statistics (observations gathered by many people over time rather than just one) on rainfall in that country, you would base that claim off of knowledge gained through empirical means.

A priori, or purely logical claims, on the other hand, are those we acquire from pure reasoning, with no empirical observation necessarily required. For instance, we can know that all triangles have three sides and all squares have four sides (even if we've never seen a triangle or square with our own eyes) simply by reasoning about what we know a line, or straight side, to be and extrapolating on what shapes formed from lines would look like, just inside our own minds.

These types of facts are often (but *not* always!) associated with inductive or deductive reasoning—that is to say, deriving conclusions from premises or starting claims. Inductive reasoning can lead us from certain starting claims to conclusions about those claims that are probably true, and in some cases almost certainly true, but are generally impossible to prove beyond absolutely any shadow of a doubt. If we know it rains a lot in England, we can say it's very likely to rain there in the summer, perhaps almost certain, but we cannot say it is *absolutely certain* to rain, or that it *must* rain there.

Deductive reasoning, on the other hand, is not probabilistic—it will invariably lead you to correct conclusions so long as your starting premises are correct. For instance, to use the above example, even if someone had (somehow) never seen squares or triangles before, if she knew that all triangles *must* have three sides (no more or less) and all squares *must* have four sides (no more or less), she could conclude with absolute certainty that no triangles are squares and no squares are triangles, simply by extrapolating from the definitions of those terms in her mind. Given the definitions of squares and triangles, there is no way she could be wrong. The only way to escape the conclusion would be to change the definitions of square and triangle—and of course, not many people would be eager to do that!

Such a deductive argument can also be called a **syllogism**. There are two properties we must always keep in mind when evaluating a syllogism: its logical **validity** and its **soundness**. Validity refers to whether or not the conclusion necessarily follows from the premises, but soundness refers to whether or not the premises are actually true. We can demonstrate this by using a syllogism based on, say, famous people we know rather than geometric figures. Let's take Socrates, for instance, and say this:

1: All men have brown hair

2: Socrates was a man

3: Therefore, Socrates had brown hair

If it were true that all men were necessarily brown-haired, then we could not avoid the conclusion that Socrates had brown hair. The above argument is therefore valid. However, we obviously know that all men do not have brown hair. We can have red, black, blond, or other colors of hair. Thus, the above argument is not sound because the first premise on which it is based is not true in reality.[1]

Note, as well, that each claim in the above syllogism is an empirical, or a posteriori fact rather than a purely logical, a priori one. Although deductive reasoning is most often used and associated with a priori claims (such as the geometric definition of squares and triangles), and inductive reasoning more closely associated with empirical claims, one can make deductive arguments based off of empirical claims. After all, we don't know that Socrates was a man based on reasoning off definitions that could have been held purely in our mind—we only know he was because the historical documentation (Plato's writings and so on) tell us he was. And if it were true that all men have brown hair (again, it's obviously not), we wouldn't have arrived at that "fact" based on a priori reasoning about the definition of "man," but rather that all the men we saw around us had brown hair. For the purposes of this book (the terms are used somewhat differently in professional parlance), we can associate deductive and inductive statements with the terms **analytic** and **synthetic**, respectively. Philosophers since Kant have acknowledged four combinations of all the above expressions: Analytic a priori, synthetic a priori, analytic a posteriori, and synthetic a posteriori.[2] We will briefly touch on this subject in Chapter 2, so just keep these distinctions in mind for now.

Hopefully this demonstrates that deductive reasoning is a very powerful tool, but one that must be used very carefully. It's very useful in the fields of logic and mathematics, but can't be used in every

---

[1] Also remember that it is possible for an argument to be true while being logically invalid. For instance, if we were to say, "Some men are Greek, Socrates was a man, therefore Socrates was Greek," we'd be making an invalid argument even though its conclusion is correct (Socrates really was Greek). That *some* men are Greek does not logically entail that Socrates was Greek, because he might have been German or French or something. Only if the argument stated *all* men were Greek would it be valid—though, in that case, it would also be unsound!

[2] Edward Feser, *Aristotle's Revenge: The Metaphysical Foundations of Physical and Biological Science* (Editiones Scholasticae, 2019), 140.

situation. In fact, it can be downright risky when you combine it with empirical, a posteriori starting claims; for instance, nothing about the definition of England entails "raining a lot," we only know it does from empirical experience, so it's much harder to construct an airtight deductive argument about what its weather will be like. We would have to content ourselves with inductive, probabilistic descriptions of how the weather would *probably* go. And even in real-life situations where deductive reasoning can apply, the cautious scholar must always make sure her arguments are both valid and sound.

But, fundamentally, you must first utilize deductive arguments before you can even begin to understand real-life situations, at least according to philosophers like Edward Feser. They claim that deductive argumentation is necessary to arrive at a useful metaphysics which would allow us to make sense of any empirical observation.[1] It just so happens that this metaphysical framework also necessitates the existence of an omniscient, omnipotent, and omnibenevolent God, which Feser and Aquinas reasoned was the Christian (specifically Catholic) God. This, more or less, is what is called **classical theism**: A belief in God based on a metaphysical framework initially conceived of by the ancient Greeks, most notably the aforementioned Aristotle. Not all classical theists are Christian—Aristotle obviously wasn't, having died centuries before Christ was born—and not all Christians are

---

[1] I should note here that, as far as I can tell, Feser considers metaphysical reasoning to be the combination of empirical starting claims and non-probabilistic, deductive reasoning I warned about above. As he says on p. 83 of *TLS*, "metaphysical arguments...take obvious, though empirical, starting points, and try to show that from these starting points, together with certain conceptual premises, certain metaphysical conclusions follow necessarily." However, Feser would probably argue that he's on safer ground to combine deductive reasoning with empirical claims because the empirical claims he's concerned with are so general they might as well be *logical, a priori* claims. For instance, we only know change occurs through experience, even if only in our own minds, but (so Feser would say) this experience is so universal that it might as well be an a priori postulate, like the definition of a square or triangle. For the purposes of argument in this book, we'll concede that point to him.

classical theists. But since Edward Feser made most of the arguments we'll be critiquing here, we must first understand what Catholic classical theists believe and why they do so, in order to successfully refute their arguments.

In the interest of fairness, I must note that these arguments may seem obtuse, needlessly complicated, and even weak, but some of the blame is mine, not Feser's. I am essentially condensing several chapters across several books Feser has written into a single introduction—I simply don't have time or space here to explain every concept or address every objection as thoroughly as he did. This summary, as brief as I could make it, is simply intended to provide the reader with the bare-bones philosophical background necessary to make sense of classical theism. Don't worry, though: Once my new students are armed with this foundational knowledge, I'll be re-visiting all of these concepts in much greater depth in the subsequent chapters of this book, and I'll be addressing the more varied, specific, and subtle explanations Feser might complain I'd missed here.

1.2: All Greek To Me

With that out of the way, let's begin with the pre-Christian philosophers. Imagine you lived in ancient Greece, circa 480 BCE. Life wasn't exactly pleasant back in those days—you had Athenians killing Spartans, Persians invading regularly, and nothing nicer to wear than a drafty old toga. But on the plus side, some of these Greeks had plenty of free time to work on metaphysics. Several of them concentrated much of their effort on some of the questions we discussed earlier: What is change? And how does it relate to the world?[1]

They came up with some pretty strange answers. According to a couple of them—Parmenides and Zeno—the truth was that change did not exist at all, that nothing actually changed, despite what our senses tell us. Parmenides noted that change could reasonably be defined as an

---

[1] *TLS*, 28-29, *SM* 31-33, *FP*, 17-20, *AQ*, 9-10.

object, creature, or some living thing starting off as something and ending up as something else. For instance, we say a caterpillar changes into a butterfly because it starts off as a fat, worm-like little thing and then (given enough time and food) ends up as a lovely flying creature. But what causes this transformation? If we say the caterpillar exists (that is to say, it is "a being"), something else must be responsible; it assumedly can't just change itself or change for no reason. But the only alternative to a being—so Parmenides said—was a non-being. And a non-being is non-existent, simply nothing. So there could be nothing causing the caterpillar to change into a butterfly—in fact, nothing that could cause anything to change at all. Parmenides concluded that all change was an illusion, and if our senses told us otherwise, they were lying.[1]

Zeno came to the same conclusion in a slightly different manner. Let's imagine our hungry little caterpillar has spotted a tasty leaf four inches away from him, and inches his way towards it. But to get halfway to a leaf four inches away, he must first reach the halfway point, which is two inches away. To get there, he must reach another halfway point, just an inch away. And to even traverse that trifling distance, he must first move half an inch, which itself requires him to move a quarter of an inch, and so on, ad infinitum. This is called Zeno's "dichotomy paradox:" That local motion is impossible because traversing a finite distance necessitates traversing an infinite number of smaller distances. The same applies to any other sort of change: For Mr. Caterpillar to turn into a butterfly, he has to eat (let's say) a hundred leaves, but first has to eat fifty, then twenty-five, and so on, ad infinitum. Thus, Zeno agreed with Parmenides: Change is impossible, regardless of what we think we see with our own eyes.[2]

Aristotle thought all of this was wrong—not just due to the empirical evidence we can see all around us, but for entirely deductive reasons as well. Using nothing but reason alone, one must conclude that

---

[1] *TLS*, 30-31.
[2] *TLS*, 31, *SM*, 32.

Zeno and Parmenides had fallen victim to what is called **retorsion**. Retorsion refers to an argument that refutes itself, or one that undermines its own starting assumptions. In the case of Parmenides and Zeno, it is that the very act of reasoning implies change of some sort—going from one state to another. Even without looking at any empirical evidence—even if the reasoner was just a brain in a tank—in her own mind, a philosopher would go from thinking about Parmenides' argument, to evaluating it, and then finally to concluding whether it is right or wrong.[1] In other words, through the process of deductive reasoning, the philosopher's mind started at one state, moved to another, and ended up in a different final state—it changed. Thus, the argument that nothing changes must be wrong, because the very act of making it and evaluating it refutes it.

What did Aristotle provide in response? The theory of actuality and potentiality. He believed that Parmenides was simply wrong to hold that the only alternative to "being" was "non-being." Potentiality was another alternative, and one that could ground a much more workable metaphysical framework. Return again to our caterpillar: He exists as a hungry little worm-like creature, or, in other words, he is *actually* a caterpillar. Parmenides could see no way he could possibly be a butterfly, but Aristotle held that there was something that could influence our little friend despite not existing in the same sense at the same moment. Namely, the fact that the caterpillar was *potentially* a butterfly. For Aristotle, the ways anything potentially could be—caterpillars, coffee, rubber balls, whatever—occupy sort of a middle ground between existence and non-existence, which is how he could claim that existing things could change without asserting that change could come from non-existence or non-being.[2]

Now, for Aristotle, there was no such thing as an "infinite" number of potentialities. Any actual thing—that is to say, anything that exists in some way or another—is potentially a certain number of ways and not

---

[1] *SM*, 32.
[2] *FP*, 18-19, *SM*, 32-33, *TLS*, 53-54.

others. So, Mr. Caterpillar is potentially a butterfly, or, if he's unlucky, potentially a meal for a hungry bird. But he is not potentially a dog or a rock or a philosopher. No matter what you do to him or how many leaves you feed him, when he makes his little chrysalis, a dog or a rock will never pop out, and he will never do any sort of philosophy, unless maybe if you ask Franz Kafka. The same applies to any other object in our experience. A cup of coffee might be actually hot and bitter, but it is potentially cool (if you leave it out for a while) and potentially sweet (if you put a lot of sugar into it). It is not potentially blood or radioactive fuel, because nothing you do to it will ever make it capable of conveying nutrients or powering a reactor. A red rubber ball (to use Feser's favorite example) might be potentially blue (if you paint it) or squishy (if you hold it over a flame), but it has no potential to bounce to the moon or follow someone around by itself.[1]

That's a start, but not enough to reach a good metaphysics of change. First, note that while caterpillars, coffee, and rubber balls are "mixtures" of actuality and potentiality, their actuality is (so to speak) "more important" in a sense. A caterpillar can't potentially be a butterfly unless it actually is a caterpillar, as a non-actual, or non-existent caterpillar can't become anything—not a butterfly, nor a meal for a bird, since our feathered friends can't feed themselves on imagination! Similarly, a cup of coffee must be actual in the first place before we can say it is potentially hot or cold or sweet, and a rubber ball must be actual before we can say it is potentially red or blue or gooey. The astute reader will note that when I say these things are "actual," I could also just be saying "they exist." This will be an important point in future chapters, but for now, the important takeaway is that potentiality is dependent upon actuality. Contra Parmenides, potentialities do exist in a certain sense (they're not just nothing or non-being), but actual things, or actuality, exist more directly. And, according to Aristotle, while nothing can be purely potential (since any potentiality depends on an actuality of at least some sort), it is not incoherent to say something is purely

---

[1] Ibid.

actual—though that, again, is a point we'll return to at the end of this section.[1]

With that established, Aristotle can complete his metaphysics by explaining how change is regulated. It is true that caterpillars which can potentially be butterflies, or red rubber balls which are potentially blue, don't simply become these things by themselves, or at random. Their potentialities are actualized by other things. A caterpillar's potential to be a butterfly is actualized by the nutrients and energy in the leaves he eats, a red rubber ball's potential to be blue is actualized by someone painting it blue, and its potential to be squishy and gooey is actualized by fire (or some other source of actual heat). Of course, anything that actualizes something else's potentialities must be actual itself, since imaginary fire or imaginary leaves can't have any effect on an existing rubber ball or caterpillar. So, we can summarize Aristotle's metaphysics by noting that A: Change exists and one cannot coherently deny this, B: due to the fact that non-being is not the only candidate for changing existing things, "potentiality" can do that, and C: any potentiality needs to be "actualized" by something that already is actual.[2]

According to Aristotle, and Edward Feser, and classical theists generally, if you accept the basic metaphysics behind this account of change, you must inevitably accept the existence of God. Once again, this argument might seem somewhat weaker here than it originally did; Aristotle delves into this subject much more extensively in his *Metaphysics*, and Feser offers considerably more detailed summaries in each of his books. Rest assured we'll be revisiting these subjects later on, and also addressing Feser's responses to the objections you're probably already thinking of. But a brief overview before we get into the specifics is useful.

For these thinkers, the actualization of potentials can be seen not just in obvious, every-day changes, like caterpillars turning into

---

[1] Ibid.
[2] Ibid.

butterflies or coffee being heated up, but even in the changes underlying those changes. Again, take the example of a cup of coffee being heated up. It can't just heat itself up, or turn hot for no reason—in other words, its potential to be hot can't actualize itself. It needs something actual, something existent, to heat it up. There are many choices—a fire, or the heating coils on an electric stove—but they have to be actual, existing fires or actual, existing heating coils. But even that isn't enough, as fire doesn't just appear out of thin air, and heating coils don't spontaneously heat. Something is required to actualize those potentials—friction or a chemical reaction turns wood or gas from potentially aflame to actually aflame, and an electric current turns an inert coil into a heated one. But what actualizes those? When you get that deep you have to start looking at the laws of physics—laws of chemical reactions are why you can get a fire under certain circumstances, and the electromagnetic force is why electrons zip from atom to atom, producing the heat of an electric coil. Yet even those base physical forces require the actualization of potentials—the electromagnetic force might "potentially" be something else (weaker or stronger, which would change whether or not an electric coil could produce heat), which implies even these basic physical forces need something to actualize them.[1]

Thomists claim we can't have an "explanatory regress"—that is to say, we can't just explain the laws of physics by referring to an even deeper law, which would require a deeper law, and so on, ad infinitum. For the purposes of argument and the interests of saving time, let's say they're right. So, given what we have discussed about the laws of physics potentially being different, thinkers like Aristotle, or more specifically, his successors (since everything we know about the laws of physics would only be discovered centuries later) would say they involve certain potentialities being actualized. What could possibly actualize those? It would have to be something that was "purely actual," something with no

---

[1] *TLS,* 90-91, *FP,* 22-23. To be fair, Feser might contest the way I'm using the phrase "laws of physics," but that's a more specific debate about the philosophy of science and the general point I'm making about actualizing potencies is the same one he made in *Five Proofs*.

potentialities at all. This "purely actual" thing would have to be eternal. It would never have come into existence, but would simply exist eternally and necessarily, since coming into being involves a potentiality being actualized (for instance, a butterfly comes into being because the nutrients in leaves actualize that potentiality in a caterpillar). It also couldn't be changed at all, and would be entirely unchangeable, because change involves actualizing potentials, and anything with potentials wouldn't be purely actual. It would also be omnipotent, because if it actualizes the laws of physics it must be able to exert control over them—like a flame or an electric coil exerts control over the temperature of a pot of coffee (or, more literally, the person who starts the fire or turns on the stove, since that actor would be actualizing the potential of the flammable materials or the electric coil). If such a being could control the laws of physics, it must be able to do just about anything—send a meteor to destroy a city by changing the laws of gravity for a bit, raining fire from the sky by momentarily changing the chemical circumstances under which flame is produced, and so on.[1]

Eternal and omnipotent? It's easy to see why guys like Aquinas, and then Edward Feser and friends, would look at Aristotle's metaphysics, which require something that's "Pure Actuality," and then conclude that Pure Actuality must also be God. But how did they arrive at the other divine properties? How did they conclude that the omnipotent Pure Actuality must also be intelligent (omniscient, in fact) and good (omnibenevolent, in fact)? There are several other divine characteristics asserted by classical theists (God being simple and absolutely unitary), but those are only directly relevant in chapter 2, so we can leave them aside for now. To understand why Mr. Pure Act must be all-knowing and all-good in addition to all-powerful, we have to stick

---

[1] *TLS*, 96-97, *FP,* 30-33. Again, this isn't exactly the argument Feser uses, but a very simplified one to illustrate his general line of reasoning. We'll come back to this in much more depth when we discuss miracles in chapter 2. It is also important to note, and we will return to this later, that God's omnipotence "does not extend to logical impossibilities," such as creating round squares, because there is no such thing as a power to do what is logically contradictory (see *FP* 208-209).

with the Greeks a little longer—just long enough to pay Aristotle's teacher, Plato, a visit. After that, it's off to Roman Africa to say hello to Saint Augustine, and then we'll end up in medieval Italy, cooling our heels with Saint Thomas Aquinas. These three guys attempted to figure out—through metaphysics—how we could define characteristics shared by a variety of different things, how we could define things at all, and the implications those matters have for the field of ethics. As we'll see, the answers to those questions imply that God has intelligence and goodness, at least according to the classical theists.

1.3: Properties

So, thanks to Aristotle, we have a metaphysical framework that can account for change. Now we need one for characteristics, or as they're called among philosophers, **properties**. As you'll recall, properties such as color and shape are the other thing we were wondering about at the beginning of this chapter. They are reasonably known as particular traits and attributes possessed by a given object that help define it. Our friend the caterpillar has the properties of color (let's say he's green), shape (a worm-like body), and size (let's say he's about an inch long). These properties help us distinguish him from other things, like our rubber ball. The rubber ball has the same categories of properties—color, shape, and size—but different types of those properties. Its color is red rather than green, it's shaped as a sphere rather than a worm, and let's say it's three inches in diameter instead of one inch long.

We must be careful, however, because even though the caterpillar and the rubber ball might be distinguished by the kinds of properties they each have, many objects in the real world have both their general categories (colors, shapes, and so on) and their specific kinds of categories in common (being green in particular, or round in particular). Leaves, for instance, are also green, so you might say they share the property of "greenness" with caterpillars. Billiard balls are also round, so you might say they share the property of "roundness" with rubber balls.[1]

These sorts of properties—color, shape, size, and other things that can be common across a variety of objects that are still very different from each other—are what philosophers like Edward Feser call "**universals.**" In the metaphysics he, Aristotle, and Aquinas adhere to, such universals are also **abstract**. "Abstract" means these properties exist in a general rather than a specific sense, and can be defined without reference to any other particular feature a concrete, material object may have. We notice that both a leaf and a caterpillar have something in common (greenness) while ignoring their other material features (size, shape, being an insect rather than a plant). Going even further, we can talk about (and reason based off of) these universals without referring to *anything* material at all—we need only keep their proper definitions in mind, which makes them "objects of thought." You and I would be able to discuss and think about the color green without thinking of any specific, material green object (caterpillars, leaves, whatever)—thus why they're called "universals." Additionally, while any green object may be green in a material sense—it has a certain pigmentation, or reflects light in a certain way—"greenness" itself seems to be immaterial. You can see particular green things, but you can't see greenness considered as a general characteristic, you can only think of it. Needless to say, you can't smell it, taste it, or touch it, either! Thus, these kinds of things seem to be objects in a sense, but not material—so philosophers call them "**abstract objects.**"[2]

This also applies to things like propositions, numbers, and "possible worlds." Recall our earlier example of the philosopher who was just a brain in a jar, and how she could reason to true conclusions about Socrates if she only knew the definitions of certain terms—that if he was a man, he was necessarily mortal, and similar relationships between those terms. This is what philosophers call a **proposition**: "statements

---

[1] *FP*, 87-88.
[2] Ibid.

about the world, always either true or false, which are distinct from the different sentences we use to express them."[1] Like universals, propositions seem to be true in a general, immaterial sense rather than just specific, material ones. For instance, the proposition "Socrates was mortal" is true and remains so centuries after Socrates' body rotted away and every material trace of him has disappeared. Indeed, the fact that he's gone proves the truth of that proposition, because if he was still hanging around in our material world today, he would probably be immortal![2] Numbers are also the same way, at least according to this view. We can talk about mathematics in relation to material things (if you have two apples and add another pair of apples to them, you now have four apples), but it seems to be the case that mathematical truths are immaterial and "necessary," in the sense that they could not be otherwise. Even if all material things went out of existence, wouldn't it still be the case that 2 + 2 = 4, or that triangles have three sides?[3] For these reasons, propositions and mathematic principles are also considered to be abstract objects.

Given all this, how can we make sense of universals, propositions, numbers, and other abstract objects? As Feser asks, "Are they merely objects of human thought—purely conventional entities, sheer constructs of our minds? Are they merely useful fictions? Or might they after all really be material things, but of some more exotic kind than the ones we've considered so far?"[4] The position that abstract objects are merely "useful fictions" is called **nominalism**, and the position that they exist, but are conventions of the human mind, is called **conceptualism**. Feser's own position, in contrast to these two, is **realism**: that abstract objects truly do exist, and they are neither reducible to any material

---

[1] Ibid.
[2] *FP*, 88-93.
[3] *FP*, ibid., *TLS*, 41.
[4] *FP*, 97-102.

thing or collection of material things, nor mere products of the human mind.[1]

At this point, I must beg the reader's indulgence for two small asides. The first is a historical one, without which some of the later topics we bring up might be confusing. According to Feser's account, conceptualism and nominalism can both be traced back to another medieval thinker named **William of Ockham**. While this fellow is known for "Ockham's Razor," or the principle that the simplest explanation is the best one, Feser states that Ockham was absolutely *not* a proto-rationalist, but rather the opposite! According to Ockham, since God is omnipotent, His Will could not be constrained by *anything*, including Essences. So Ockham concluded that there really was no such thing as mind-independent Essences (or universals generally) at all, and that the only reason we detect similarities in anything we encounter or see any regularity in the world around us was simply and only the will of God. Indeed, for Ockham, divine revelation was the only way we could really know anything at all. He even thought it was theoretically possible for God to command us to do absolutely *anything*—rape, murder, hating God, listening to Carrot Top, whatever—and it would therefore be good.[2] Some alert readers might be thinking this is very similar to **divine command** theory, which states that the goodness or badness of any action is determined by whether or not God wills it. You'd be exactly correct. We'll be discussing ethics in relation to God in much greater depth later on, so I mention Ockham now to give you a heads-up on the material.

Now, Feser is certainly a devout soul, but he has no time for conceptualism, or denial of realism with regard to universalism, even if attached to Catholicism (Ockham was also a clergyman). Ironically enough, for the purposes of this book, I would be happy to *concede* that position to him. The second thing I wanted to note is this: I will be operating under the assumption that Feser is correct, and that realism

---

[1] Ibid.
[2] *TLS*, 168-169.

(Aristotelian realism, at least) is true and nominalism and conceptualism are false. However, I would be remiss if I did not mention that the subject is *far* more controversial than Feser lets on. He spends a great deal of time in *The Last Superstition*, *Scholastic Metaphysics*, and *Five Proofs* defending realism against its competitors (and, in the first book at least, excoriating Ockham), but several philosophers have constructed formidable arguments for those competitors in recent years.[1] Indeed, according to a survey published about a year after *The Last Superstition*, only 40% of professional philosophers were Platonist or otherwise leaning towards realism—if the argument was as settled as Feser thinks, most of his colleagues have not gotten the memo.[2] Still, I have chosen not to engage that debate for two reasons. First, the "problem of universals" is one of the most complex and intractable in philosophy. To do justice not just to realism but nominalism, conceptualism, and other forms of anti-realism would easily be another book in itself, and one longer than the already-hefty one you're reading now! Second, to generously concede to Feser so much—to assume his preferred realism is true and then fight him "on his own ground," so to speak—makes the dismantling of his position that much more thorough. It would be easy enough to simply note that nominalism or conceptualism cut the legs out from under Thomist philosophy generally, but exploring how realism does not give Thomism much of a leg to stand on in the first place is an even more revealing display of its weaknesses. Thus, I must make very clear that the realist arguments in the rest of this book are *not* intended as an endorsement of realism or

---

[1] Jonathan MS Pearce, *Did God Create the Universe from Nothing? Countering William Lane Craig's Kalam Cosmological Argument* (Onus Books, Kindle Edition, 2016), locations 731-784, Richard E. Hennessey, "Universals in Feser's The Last Superstition. A Neo-Aristotelian Alternative to Realism in the Theory of Universals." *After Aristotle*, January 21, 2015, last accessed July 5, 2020, https://afteraristotle.net/2015/01/21/universals-in-fesers-the-last-superstition-a-neo-aristotelian-alternative-to-realism-in-the-theory-of-universals/

[2] David Bourget & David J. Chalmers, "What do philosophers believe?" *Philosophical Studies* 170 (3):465-500 (2014). The referenced study specifically can be found here: https://philpapers.org/surveys/results.pl (last accessed July 5, 2020)

to imply that realism has triumphed over the alternatives in the view of most philosophers.

With that out of the way, let's continue our discussion of realism with a brief overview of its history. Plato is generally considered to be the man who came up with realism, or at least offered the first known defense of it in the *Phaedo*, *Republic*, and *Parmenides*. Since abstract objects could not be material, and they could not exist in human minds alone, Plato believed they existed in a sort of "Third Realm." The various universals we see around us—the greenness of any particular caterpillar or the roundness of any particular ball—merely participate in the "Form of Green" or the "Form of Roundness," which both reside in the Third Realm (and we'll return to the term "form" shortly, in section 4 of this chapter). Unfortunately, this had plenty of problems of its own. For instance, if abstract objects like "greenness" or "roundness" were just floating around in a kind of Platonic heaven, how could they have any influence on the material world? And if material things merely "participate in" the Forms of whatever universal properties they have, do those Forms themselves participate in further Forms somewhere in the Third Realm?[1]

Aristotle attempted to surpass his teacher and address these issues. **Aristotelian Realism** holds that universals like colors, shapes, sizes really do exist independently of us—we didn't just make up greenness or roundness, as nominalists might have it—but that they only exist objectively inside the objects which possess them, and that it is only human minds that abstract them and consider them as universals. To paraphrase Feser paraphrasing Aristotle, greenness exists in particular material caterpillars and leaves, roundness exists in particular rubber balls and billiard balls, but the human intellect isolates these properties from the specific objects which possess them and

---

[1] *FP*, 96-105, *TLS*, 31, 273n6.

considers them abstractly on their own, thus regarding greenness or roundness as universals.[1]

Alas, even Aristotle's realism is not entirely satisfying. For instance, it seems unable to deal with propositions and numbers. As mentioned above, the proposition "Socrates was mortal" is true even after he no longer exists in the material world. Similarly, relationships between numbers and other elements of mathematics would seem to exist independently of the material world. There is also the matter of possible material worlds. For instance, Feser notes that if the no material world existed, it would be possible for some material objects to come into existence (the material universe coming out of nothing, let's say). There are also fictional creatures that do not exist in material reality but do exist in our minds and could possibly be brought into existence—there are no specific material examples of unicorns and Tolkien's orcs, but perhaps we could genetically engineer them if we wanted. What grounds those possibilities? Since Aristotle's brand of realism requires abstract objects like universals to always be present, or "instantiated in" at least one material object, it seems unable to grapple with other abstract objects that seem to exist only potentially materially, or independent of material things altogether.[2]

If even Aristotle and Plato couldn't solve what philosophers call "the problem of universals," who could? Saint Augustine of Hippo—at least if you agree with Feser. Augustine was born in 354 A.D. in the city of Thagaste, which is now Souk-Ahras in Algeria. By his own admission, he was a very impious youth who spent most of his time getting up to no good before converting to Christianity at the age of thirty-two, largely thanks to the patient example of his mother.[3] Aside from putting him on

---

[1] *TLS*, 61.
[2] *FP*, 97-102.
[3] Augustine, *Confessions,* translated by R.S. Pine-Coffin (Penguin Books: 1961), 19-21, 32-50. The grievous sins Augustine details himself committing are things like stealing apples, going to the theatre, and getting worked up over Greek myths.

the straight-and-narrow, Augustine's newfound religion helped him concoct a solution to the issues raised by both Platonic and Aristotelian realism. Abstract objects had to exist somewhere, but not in material things, since they would exist even in the absence of a material world. They could not exist in some Platonic heaven, because otherwise, they wouldn't be able to influence material things. The God of the Bible, however, created the material world, and was described in the text as all-knowing as well as all-powerful. Thus, Augustine concluded that all abstract objects existed in God's mind, a suggestion which combined the strengths of both Aristotle and Plato's theories. The divine mind, like Plato's heaven, was independent of specific material objects; but since it obviously belonged to an all-powerful God, it was more able to influence the material world than an inert third realm would be. Much like Aristotle did, Augustine acknowledged abstract objects had to exist mentally in some way, but a divine mind existed necessarily, everlastingly, and independent of the material world, allowing it to ground completely immaterial objects like numbers, propositions, and creatures that could possibly exist but do not.[1]

It's not hard to see why classical theists would have thought the Divine Mind also belonged to the eternal, unchanging, uncreated Being of Pure Actuality. It's not unreasonable—at least at first glance—to believe an omnipotent being would also be omniscient, and a metaphysical framework that solves the problem of change and the problem of universals with a single Being is pleasantly parsimonious. But not everything has been fully explained just yet. Must the Divine Mind necessarily be immaterial? To understand why, we must at last pay a visit to the middle ages.

These may not seem so bad to us today, but nobody ever accused Augustine of being insufficiently melodramatic.
[1] *FP*, 103-105.

1.4: Minds and Materiality

Saint Thomas Aquinas looms large in the thought of Edward Feser and other "natural law" philosophers, even today. Thus, our last order of business in this introduction, before we can begin a critique of this tradition, is to go over the metaphysical arguments Aquinas made in books such as the *Summa Theologica*. Being both very smart and very Catholic, Aquinas synthesized the Platonic, Aristotelian and Augustinian ideas discussed above, combined them with his reading of the Bible, and drew conclusions from the resulting mélange that explain why his intellectual descendants condemn homosexuality, abortion, religious pluralism, and the other trappings of "modernity" as much as they do.

We're not quite ready for his ethical theories yet, though—we must spend a bit of time explaining why he thought that intellectual activity is necessarily immaterial. According to Aquinas, all animals, including human beings, are capable of apprehending individual material objects and their associated properties via the five senses. Both people and dogs can see a rubber ball and react to it based on its color, or the sound it makes when bouncing, or its smell, or its taste (hopefully a dog playing catch would know more about this than his owner). However, dogs are incapable of understanding any of these characteristics as abstract universals. They cannot (at least as far as Aquinas knew) comprehend or reason upon redness, bounciness, or being rubbery, though they can be trained (as Pavlov managed to do) to react in the same way to similar stimuli.[1] Since universals—along with numbers and propositions—do not exist materially and are independent of any given material thing, Aquinas concluded that the intellectual activity of human beings, unlike the purely instinctive behavior of lower animals like insects or rote responses to stimuli like those of dogs, cats, and birds, must be immaterial. In fact, he believed *anything* capable of grasping abstract objects must be immaterial, and the more objects it

---

[1] *AQ,* 143-149.

could grasp (i.e. the smarter it was), the less material it would be. Since God, as Augustine established, grasped all abstract objects, He is the smartest being in existence, and must therefore be immaterial—the most immaterial of all things, in fact.

Now, one might argue that the abstractions of redness, triangle, and other universals do have a material basis—patterns of neurons firing in our brains. Contemporary classical theists like Feser, however, hold that this is self-refuting. According to them, whatever neural patterns may be associated with any given universal could not *represent* that universal unless there was already a mind to interpret them as such. Feser uses the example of writing to illustrate this point. The word "triangle," just written out here, symbolizes both the concept of triangularity and the pronunciation of the word. But on its own, "triangle" is just a meaningless bunch of pixels on a computer screen (as I write this) or blots of ink on a page (as you read this). If you were to show that word to a non-English speaker, it would be meaningless to them unless you translated it into their language, and if you were to show the word to a pigeon, ant, or some other non-sentient animal, it would never be anything but meaningless to them. What applies to pixels and ink would assumedly apply to electrochemical signals in brain: they would require a mind to actually signify anything. Thus, the mind itself cannot be reduced to neural patterns in the brain or any other material "symbol," and must be immaterial, making the human mind immaterial. And what applies to the human mind would apply to any other mind, which means that God's mind (and by extension, God Himself) must be immaterial.[1]

The curious thing about this argument is that it might seem to imply the mind is actually separate from the brain, or the body itself, in some way. It will hopefully not come as a surprise to find out that Aquinas—and by extension, Feser, and many other prominent natural

---

[1] *TLS,* 231-242. Again, to be fair to Feser, it's not just classical theist and natural law types who believe in the immateriality of the human intellect. John Searle, an atheist philosopher, has also argued for the same position.

law theorists, believe that the mind can actually exist without the body, or without any material mooring at all. Catholics such as Feser certainly believe in the existence of the soul, which persists after the body has died, and angels, which are entirely immaterial beings. But, as readers will note, classical theists also claim that God is the supreme immaterial being. So how can they distinguish between an immaterial God and equally immaterial souls and angels? According to Feser, it's the fact that God's existence simply is His Essence, while angels are immaterial Essences conjoined with existence, and souls are the Essences of material human beings which also have to be conjoined with existence.[1] What the hell does any of that mean? Read on to find out.

1.5: Differentiations – Essences and Existence and Forms and Functions and Angels and Souls, Oh My!

I'd wager these peregrinations are getting as tiresome for you as they are for me, dear reader, but just try to stay awake for a little longer. Once I explain the classical idea of Forms, we'll finally be ready to jump into natural law ethics.

As previously mentioned, natural law theorists tell us that certain properties, such as greenness and roundness, are universals in a general sense (that is to say, they cannot be reduced to any given material thing or collection of material things). But what are they in a *specific* sense? There has to be a difference between greenness and roundness. And, as mentioned previously, figuring out what those differences may be—how to categorize properties, in other words—is the business of metaphysics.

We can immediately say that greenness is the state of being green, and roundness is the state of being round. Okay, but now we have to ask what the difference is between "green" and "round." That shouldn't be too hard: Green is a color, and round is a shape. But what is "green" and what is "round," when each characteristic is considered as a color and shape specifically? After all, there are many other colors and many other

---

[1] *AQ,* 15, 28-29.

shapes. How does one distinguish green from red or blue, and round from triangular or rectangular?

At this point, the dictionary is as good a place to go as any. We are told that "green" is the intermediate color between blue and yellow, and is associated with certain wavelengths of light. To be round is to be sphere-shaped, and a sphere is a three-dimensional circle, or in other words, a body in which every single point of its surface is the same distance from its center.[1] Hooray! That would seem to answer the question we had at the beginning of this section. How can we tell what green is, and what distinguishes it from other colors? The fact that it's a mixture (which differentiates it from pure blue, pure yellow, and other mixtures such as purple, which is blue and red) and associated with certain wavelengths of light (other colors have different wavelengths). How can we distinguish roundness from triangularity or rectangularity? Round things are defined by their surface points being equidistant, while triangular or rectangular things are defined by having three or four sides (respectively), their interior angles adding up to certain sums, and so on. Huzzah! Now we'll never have to worry about getting all these things mixed up.

Even better, we've just found what Plato, Aristotle, Aquinas, and their intellectual descendants called the "**Form**" of these things. A Form, (or an Essence), is what defines a thing and distinguishes it from everything else. The specific wavelengths of light associated with green define it and distinguish it from other colors, and the equidistance of all points on its surface from its center defines a sphere and distinguishes it from other shapes.[2] Now, it's not just colors and shapes that have

---

[1] "Green," Dictionary.com, 2019, https://www.dictionary.com/browse/green (July 5, 2020), "Round," Dictionary.com, 2019,
https://www.dictionary.com/browse/round (July 5, 2020).

[2] *TLS,* 31-35, *AQ,* 16-24. Essence, Form, and Nature each connote slightly different things in the most technical usage, but the distinction isn't important in this context, so here we will use the terms interchangeably. I should note here that I am capitalizing all these terms in my own text, though leaving them uncapitalized when directly quoting from other authors, to differentiate the specifically

Forms. According to natural law adherents, *everything* has a Form. Concepts (there's something that defines justice and distinguishes it from tyranny), artifacts (there's something that defines a PlayStation 5 and distinguishes it from a Game Boy), and even living things (there's something that defines a human being and distinguishes her from a squirrel or jellyfish).[1]

In the case of living things, natural law theorists often use the terms "soul" or "Nature" in place of "Form." Aristotle drew a difference between "immanent" and "transeunt" causation (we come back to this in Chapter 5), which means that he believed living things are capable of a sort of self-motivation (even if only growing and taking in nutrients) that inanimate objects are not. To him, the Forms of all living things—plants, animals, and humans—were Souls, with plants having the lowest sort of soul which allowed them to do nothing but grow, animals having a higher soul that incorporated physical activity, and humans having the highest soul that allowed them rational thought (more on this very soon).[2] Second, in reference to "Nature," they draw a difference between artifacts which have no inherent tendency to come together in the way they do, and "natural" creatures which arise from processes inherent in nature itself. Finally, in reference to animals specifically, people like Feser use the term "Form" to refer to the physical characteristics and "dictionary definition" of an organism, and "Nature" to refer to those things in addition to behavior, growth and development, and in the case of humans, morality, attitudes, and beliefs.[3] We'll come back to all of

---

philosophical terms from the common verbs and adjectives which denote different things.
[1] Ibid. As you can imagine, there's also a debate over whether or not these Forms, Essences, or Natures really exist. That debate is similar to and influenced by the one we saw with universals, and Realists, Nominalists, and Conceptualists generally share the same attitudes towards Forms as they do towards universals. As mentioned earlier, for the purposes of this book, we'll accept Feser's view that realism with regard to Forms is true.
[2] *AQ,* 134-38, *TLS,* 125-127.
[3] Ibid.

these concepts when we get to critiquing natural law ethics in chapters 3 and 4, but just try to keep them in the back of your head for now. At the very least, it'll help explain why Feser's ethical tradition is called "Natural" Law.

At the moment, there are just a few more things we have to establish before moving on to ethics. Essences and Natures are considered universals, since our minds are capable of understanding what it is about (to take one example) squirrels that makes them squirrels, even if we can't see any squirrels at the moment, or even if squirrels should go extinct. Thus, everything mentioned above with regard to universals—their immateriality, their existence in the mind of God, and so on—applies to Natures as well.

However, some Essences are also immaterial in an individual sense. The Essence of a human being, for instance, would be what distinguishes us from other things and defines us. So, what is the definition of a human being? The definition, or Essence (or Form, or soul), of a squirrel might be "A furry rodent with a bushy tail" and the same for a spider might be "An eight-legged arthropod with fangs." So perhaps we could say a human being might be "A two-legged hairless primate." But remember, as we said above, living things can also be distinguished by their behavior. A fuller description of the Form of a Squirrel might therefore be, "a furry rodent with a bushy tail *that eats nuts and lives in trees*, and the Form of a Spider might be "an eight-legged arthropod with fangs *that spins webs to capture prey.* So, in that case, we have to wonder: What makes human beings behaviorally distinctive?

Aristotle, Aquinas, and Feser would say that it is our capacity for abstraction, or, in other words, our rationality. This is why the traditional definition of human being, at least according to natural law theorists, is "rational animal," and for our purposes, an updated definition might be "a two-legged primate that *reasons and uses abstract thought.*" But, as readers will recall from the previous sections, rational activity is immaterial—in order to understand or talk about any kind of abstraction, whether universals, numbers, or propositions, we need to grasp them apart from any particular material example of any of them. And it is (ostensibly) no good to say that such rational activity can be reduced to neurons in the brain, as any physical substrate would need a mind to interpret it.

So, if the Form, or soul, of a human being involves abstract thought (like the soul of a spider involves spinning webs, or the soul of a squirrel involves gathering nuts), the human soul must be immaterial in a way no other Form or soul is. Indeed, Feser takes this to mean that any individual human soul is, in fact, *independent*, to some extent, from the body it inhabits. A soul (a type of Form) is that which makes a human being a human being. As described above, the human soul—the "abstract reasoning" bit of it—cannot be reduced to any physical part of the human body. But it must influence the human body in some way, because human beings move and act in conscious ways based on our ability for abstract thought. A squirrel or spider, being entirely material, might only react to stimuli on an instinctive level (a shadow on the ground evokes a flight response, without any thought involved, for instance). On the other hand, according to Feser, human beings can think about abstract objects (Green things are beautiful, or two plus two equals four) and then take action based on those abstractions (I'm going to paint my house green, or show off my awesome arithmetic skills to all my friends). From this, philosophers like Feser reason that if the soul of a human being can influence the body despite not being a part of the body, it can exist on its own without the body. Thus, according to them, the traditional Christian belief of human souls existing after death is not a mere superstition like ghosts or ectoplasmic spirits. It is, rather, a logical and rigorous extension of Aristotle's metaphysical principles.[1]

---

[1] *TLS*, 126-128, *AQ*, 137-38. The behavior of squirrels and spiders is, again ostensibly, entirely instinctual—they don't really "understand" what they're doing—so their souls, and all animal souls, are considered to be entirely material, which makes them lower than our souls.

The same applies to the angels we read about in the Bible, which many Christians (particularly Catholics like Feser) believe still play roles in human life today. As (again, supposedly) demonstrated above, we human beings have a Form or soul that can exist even after the destruction of our physical bodies. However, they are still connected to our physical bodies from the day of our conception, and are only released from them when we are, well, released from our mortal coils. Since God, the omniscient and omnipotent Being of Pure Act, created us, flesh and soul, there seems to be no reason He could not simply create a disembodied soul and skip the whole "flesh" part. This is precisely what Aquinas thought angels were, and what people like Feser claim they are today. Entirely immaterial Forms created by God, but which have intelligence and the ability to impact the material world (like the human soul can influence the human body—this is why the Form of an angel is a type of living soul, as they have more capacity for action than just geometric Forms or artifacts).[1]

It seems like we've answered the question of how immaterial souls and angels might be proven to exist, but we're still not sure about how they can be distinguished from other immaterial things. The answer to that lies in the magic word "exist." Neither human beings nor angels existed eternally in and of themselves, even if we could argue that human souls would spend an eternity in either heaven or hell, and angels can live forever. Even if they could exist eternally into the future, they did not always exist in the past—they had to be created by God at one point or another. This means they are combinations of potency and act—they all moved from potentially existing to actually existing. Their potential for existing had to be actualized by something (which would, of course, be God, Mr. Pure Act). Thus, human souls and even angels are

---

[1] Edward Feser, "Cartesian Angelism," *Edward Feser,* July 29, 2017, last accessed on July 5, 2020, http://edwardfeser.blogspot.com/2017/07/cartesian-angelism.html , archived at http://archive.is/vE3Hz. Also see *SM,* 190-191, *AQ,* 28-29.

distinguishable from (and inferior to) God, who did not have to be created by anything and has simply existed forever.[1]

All this is another way of saying that "everything except for God has an essence distinct from its existence." To fully understand this curious turn of phrase, let us again think about the Forms of physical properties like color and the soul of certain living things. The Form of the color green is "a combination of red and blue, or the color evoked by light with a wavelength of 495-570 nanometers." The Form (or Essence, or soul) of a squirrel is "a furry rodent with a bushy tail that eats nuts and lives in trees." By grasping their Forms, we can grasp what it means to be green or a squirrel, and what distinguishes them from other things.

Just knowing their Forms alone, however, does not allow us to know whether or not the color green or squirrels exist. For instance, if the laws of physics were different, perhaps light would not produce the color green, or any other color at all. If evolution had taken a different path, perhaps squirrels as we know them would have gone extinct (that is to say, passed out of existence) years ago, or never have come into being at all.

Thus, Aquinas concluded that everything—the color green, light, squirrels, nuts, trees, people, angels, absolutely everything—needed something to conjoin their Essences with existence. What could do such a thing? It would seem to be a being whose Form just was its existence. But such a being, one whose Form could be summed up in just one word, would be completely and utterly without potencies, since it could not have failed to exist, and it could not be anything other than just existence. In other words, it would be Pure Actuality, and that, according to the natural law guys, is just another term for a single, omniscient, and omnipotent God.[2]

So, we have established that God is all-powerful and all-knowing. Most of us know, though, that God is all-good as well. What does that

---

[1] *AQ,* 24-30.
[2] *AQ,* 28-30, *TLS,* 121-128.

mean? In fact, what does it mean to be "good" in the first place? To answer those questions, we can finally take a look at natural law ethics.

1.6: Ethics

Just as with his metaphysics, Aquinas's ethics drew heavily from Plato and Aristotle—which makes sense, because they are based upon the metaphysics we've spent so much time exploring above. The two fields of philosophy are distinct, though, even if they are (for natural law theorists) highly interrelated. Metaphysics, as we will recall, is the study of reality in order to understand what's out there and how it can be categorized. What we have found is that anything that's out there can be categorized into various Forms and related to each other through propositions held in the wholly immaterial mind of God, which we can reason through logically as well as empirically with our own semi-immaterial minds. So that's the information we have to work with. **Ethics** is the study of what we *should* do with that information—or, in other words, the study of morality. Pretty much everyone wants to be a good person and avoid doing evil, unless you're some kind of anime villain. But what is good? What is evil? And how can we form a workable theory of morality even if we understand those definitions? The job of the ethicist is to answer those questions, and philosophers like Feser, taking up the torch passed to them by Aquinas, Augustine, and Aristotle, think they're up to the task.

To understand why, we must take a closer look at the Forms. The Form of a triangle, as we'll recall, is to be a figure with three straight sides and whose angles add up to 180 degrees. Now, try to draw one as quickly as you can on a piece of paper with nothing but a pencil. More likely than not, it won't be a perfect triangle. In fact, it would probably seem very sloppy—the lines are probably uneven and squiggly, the sides might not fit together properly or even be conjoined, and so on. So try again, but this time draw your triangle slowly and carefully, with the aid of a ruler. More likely than not, your second triangle will look much nicer than the first. Its sides will be straighter, its corners nice and closed, and so on. Perhaps you've still made some small mistakes, and nobody can draw an absolutely perfect triangle (since there will always be microscopic irregularities caused by the material of the pencil and paper), but it's a safe bet your triangle will be a *better* triangle than the first. In fact, according to Feser, "it would be perfectly natural to call [the first triangle] a *bad* triangle and [the second triangle] a *good* one."[1]

This (supposed) insight forms the basis of natural law ethics. Remember, ethics attempts to find workable definitions of the words "good" and "evil" (in this case, a type of badness can be used to understand a more direct kind of evil we're supposed to avoid). It seems that the Greeks who came up with the theory of Forms also managed to find useful (according to the Thomists) definitions of good and bad: "Good" means "to adhere closely to the definition or standards entailed by a given Form," and "Bad" means "to deviate from the definition or standards of a given Form."

Interesting definitions, but how can geometry tell us anything about human beings? Well, recall from the previous sections that *everything* has a Form. Not just triangles or squares or circles, but caterpillars, spiders, and of course, people too—and for living things, as you'll recall from the previous sections, we often speak of their Natures rather than just their Forms. So if a "good" example of something is one that adheres closely to its Nature, we could say that a "good" spider or caterpillar is a little creepy-crawly that adheres closely to the standards entailed by the Nature of the Spider or the Nature of the Caterpillar. That would be having eight legs and spinning webs (for the spider) or being worm-like and eating lots of leaves (for the caterpillar). By the same token, "bad" means deviating from one's Nature, so a spider that lost some of its legs, or a caterpillar that doesn't eat leaves and starves to death would be bad.[2]

If we apply this reasoning to human beings, we find that a good human is one who adheres to the Nature of Man (which is to be a

---

[1] *AQ*, 176-77, *TLS*, 36-37.
[2] Ibid.

rational animal), and a bad human is one who deviates from it. This supposed truth, according to Feser, provides a guide for how human beings *should* behave, fulfilling the purpose of any useful ethical theory. All human beings strive for what they perceive to be good and avoid what they perceive to be bad. Even evildoers (again, except for maybe the crappy ones from cheap anime or videogames) act for what they *think* is good. A thief steals because he desires the good of money or material wealth, or a murderer kills because he thinks the death of his victim will provide him some good (the satisfaction of revenge, an insurance policy, whatever).[1]

But with an understanding of the Forms, it's possible to arrive at an *objective* definition of good and bad. After all, to paraphrase Feser, it would be silly to consider it mere personal preference that a good triangle has three straight sides and a bad one does not. The goodness or badness of a triangle is objectively and indisputably entailed by what it is. The same applies to caterpillars, spiders, and people—their Natures are matters of objective fact, which means they can be objectively said to be good or bad depending on how well they adhere to those Natures. The truest, most over-arching definition of good is to adhere to one's Nature, and bad to deviate from it. Thus, the "goods" of ill-gotten gains (for the thief) or revenge (for the murderer) are actually false and illusory. The *real* good to which they should aspire is adhering to the nature of a rational animal, and that precludes crimes like theft or murder.[2] We can, at long last, understand why this system of ethics is called the **natural law Theory**. It's not based on the vague idea that anything "natural" is good, or that we should all go back to nature in the sense of the environment around us. That would imply "unnatural" things like bicycles or eyeglasses were bad, which would be (obviously) silly. It is rather extrapolating an understanding of Forms to the analogous concept—Natures—in living creatures.[3]

---

[1] Ibid.
[2] *TLS,* 137.
[3] *TLS,* 133.

That's all nice as far as it goes, but even the sympathetic reader might still be left with some questions about natural law. For instance, where does God come into all of this? Given how much we've talked about Mr. Pure Act in the preceding sections, surely He ought to show up in this one? Give yourself a pat on the back, dear reader, you're exactly right. But to understand how, we once again have to back up a bit, yet again look at the Forms, and take a small detour to the Four Causes.

Remember what we discussed with the rubber ball? It adhered to a certain Form (the Form of Roundness), and also had several actualities and potentialities (being actually red and solid while being potentially blue or gooey). According to Aristotle, another way of thinking about all these properties is to categorize them as four separate causes. The first two causes encompass the physical properties we've discussed. The ball's **material cause** is what it's made out of, which in this case is rubber. The ball's **formal cause** is how it's shaped or what Form it adheres to, which in this case is sphericity. But have we explained everything about the ball? Aristotle thought not, and his intellectual descendants from Aquinas to Feser agreed with him. They believed and still believe that an object's **efficient cause** and **final cause** are also important. The rubber ball's efficient cause would be what brought it into being, but the term refers to any actualization of potentiality. In this case, what actualized the ball's potential to exist (in other words, what made it) would be the actions of the workers at the Acme ball factory. And the most important cause of all would be why the ball was made in the first place. Its final cause, which can be considered as its purpose or function, would be to provide amusement to children as a toy. The final cause, or **telos,** in the original Greek, is the most important one of all, according to Feser. Though modern philosophers have mostly abandoned Aristotle's idea of final causality, Feser holds that it is actually impossible to make sense of anything without reference to final causes, even natural objects like stones, matches, or the moon.[1]

We'll come back to that idea, in future chapters, but for now we'll look at how final causality relates to ethics and gets us to God. Yet again, Aristotle believed that what was true of objects with regard to their Forms was also true of living things with regard to their Natures. Spiders and caterpillars have material causes (being made out of bug flesh), formal causes (having eight legs or a worm-like body), efficient causes (being born from spider or butterfly eggs), and final causes (having the function of eating bugs or leaves). Human beings are no exception, and since our formal cause would be "rational animals," it would seem our final cause would be rational activity. Or, in other words, our function is to reason.

The perceptive reader will have already figured out that this is another way of talking about natural law ethics. If it is a matter of objective fact that any given object has a function, it is objectively true that a "good" example of an object will fulfill its function, and a bad one will fail to do so, just like a good object will adhere to its Form and a bad one deviate from it. Therefore, a caterpillar that fulfills its function of eating leaves is good (and will become a lovely butterfly), while a caterpillar that fails to do so for whatever reason (bad luck, genetic defect, whatever) will be a bad one. If we look at human beings the same way, a good human being is one who reasons well, and a bad one reasons poorly. Since everyone wants to achieve good and avoid the bad, our ethics should revolve around reasoning well, and anything that involves reasoning poorly is merely an illusory good and ought to be rejected.[2]

So, what does reasoning well entail? Recall that rationality and reasoning involve grasping Forms and other universals (which are immaterial) and drawing conclusions from them. This is perhaps just a long-winded way of saying that reasoning and exercising rationality is

---

[1] *AQ,* 16-23, *TLS,* 62-72.
[2] Ibid.

pursuing truth. But according to natural-law theorists like Feser, God is the ultimate underlying reason for why *anything* is true. All Forms, propositions, and abstract objects reside in His mind, so He is the reason anything we understand about them would be true. He also perpetually conjoins the Essences (or Forms, or Natures) of things to existence (a topic discussed in depth in Chapter 6 of this book), so we couldn't know anything was true at all unless He was doing the work to keep them in existence. Thus, God consists of the ultimate truth, which means that if the final cause of human beings is to pursue truth, our ultimate final cause is ultimately to pursue God.[1]

As an aside, this moral theory provides another reason why God would have to be purely good as well as purely actual. Aquinas believed the words "good, actual, powerful, true, real, beautiful," and so on actually referred to the exact same thing, only in different senses. He called them the "transcendentals" and said they were **convertible** with each other. So saying God is "purely actual" would be the same thing as saying He is "purely good," which would also be saying He is pure beauty, pure existence, pure power, and so on.[2] We'll come back to the idea of convertibility in chapter 5, but just keep it in mind for now.

Anyways, we're now left with the question: how to pursue God? That would seem to be the purview of religion, and we can't tell which religion is correct. The Hindus say one thing, the Muslims say another, and of course Catholics like Feser and Aquinas think they have the answer. Even Aristotle would disagree with all of them, since he came up with his version of God independently from Muslim, Hindu, and Christian philosophers. What makes Feser think that Catholicism is the best choice for pursuing God, and every other choice, even that of Aristotle, incorrect?

As it turns out, historical analysis combined with "pure reason," in Feser's words from *The Last Superstition*. Pure reason, as we have

---

[1] *AQ*, 143.
[2] Ibid., 33-36.

ostensibly discovered above, tells us that there must be an eternal, unchanging, omniscient, and omnipotent God ruling over the universe. If there weren't, we would not be able to explain change or abstract objects. And since this Purely Actual Being is omnipotent and created and sustains the entire universe, He would be capable of performing any kind of miracle. Raising someone from the dead, or coming back to life Himself, would be well within His capabilities. In light of this philosophical background, "the evidence for Christ's resurrection can be seen to be overwhelming." So, if God exists, something like the Resurrection could happen, and the weight of the historical evidence says it did, so Christ was most likely who He said He was. Since God is all-good, He would never lie, which means that the words of Christ (in the New Testament) and the traditions Christ came to fulfill (from the Old Testament) are all true. In other words, the Bible is divinely inspired and true, which would mean that Christianity is the one true faith, and Catholicism, having been passed straight down from Christ to Peter to the present day, is the truest branch of it.[1]

Naturally, this would entail that the moral claims of the Bible are true. Stealing, murder, and adultery are out, but so are many other things—homosexual behavior (Leviticus 18:22), abortion (because babies are supposedly "knit in their mother's wombs"), and any kind of non-procreative sex (some Christians interpret Onan's death in Genesis 38 as punishment for masturbation). However, according to Feser, one of the advantages of natural law theory is that it provides secular justifications for all these injunctions, which even non-Christians ought to find convincing. Aristotle, for instance, believed homosexuality was wrong (he compared it to "eating dirt") based entirely off of his analysis of the "function" of human sexual activity.[2] The very short version, which, as always, we'll revisit later in much greater depth in chapter 3, is this: We've established that "good" and "bad" can be understood in relation to a given object or organism's Form and/or function. However,

---

[1] *TLS*, 154-156.
[2] Ibid, 50.

this applies to body parts as well. Eyes have the function of seeing, so a bad eye would be one that doesn't see well. Human sexual faculties are the same way—penises, testes, and so on, have the function of reproducing (aside from urination in the case of the penis), so a man who could not impregnate a woman would have a bad set of reproductive organs. Maybe his testes aren't producing sperm (infertility), maybe his penis can't grow erect (impotency); whatever the case may be, our guy is in a tough spot. But just as an organ that can't fulfill its function is a bad organ, mutilating or misusing an otherwise healthy organ so it can't fulfill its function is a bad action, under Aristotle's natural law theory. Since the function of the sexual faculties is ultimately to reproduce, using condoms to stymie that function is metaphysically bad. The same applies to homosexual sex, masturbation, and even oral sex, as those are non-procreative and thus contravening the function of reproductive organs. Abortion is even worse, since it is a contravention of that function *and* the murder of a human being. According to natural law theory, a fetus is not a potential human, but an actual human that happens to have unrealized potentialities.[1]

Whew! It seems we're all the way back to actuality and potency—that is to say, *metaphysics*. Hopefully this chapter has given you a sense of how these abstruse philosophical debates directly influence ethical issues we encounter today. We've learned the difference between metaphysics and epistemology, explored the metaphysics of Parmenides and Zeno and explained how Aristotle's metaphysics, in contrast to theirs, accounted for change. As a bonus, we also learned about Aristotelian realism with regard to properties and other universals and abstract objects (called Forms or Essences), along with the arguments for the immateriality of the mind that are entailed by Aristotelian realism. Finally, we saw how Aristotle's successors brought together all these metaphysical concepts to argue for the existence of a single God (the Christian one, for Feser), as well as the immorality of abortion and

---

[1] *TLS*, 133-134, 147-150, *AQ,* 185-186.

homosexuality (among other things) in the ethical realm due to the Aristotelian doctrine of final causality.

Given that abortion, non-procreative sex, and irreligion generally seem to be progressively more acceptable in modern Western societies, you might expect that natural law theorists believe we're living in pretty wretched times. You would, of course, be correct. Feser doesn't mince words: He describes contemporary society as a "cesspool," salvageable only because we have not *entirely* abandoned all vestiges of Aquinas and Aristotle's natural law tradition. In fact, Feser goes even further:

> *Abandoning Aristotelianism, as the founders of modern philosophy did, was the single greatest mistake ever made in the history of Western thought...It is implicated in the disintegration of confidence in the rational justifiability of morality and religious belief...and [the] intellectual and practical depersonalization of man that all of this has entailed, and which in turn led to mass-murder on a scale unparalleled in human history.*[1]

Anyone even mildly familiar with 20th-century world history can guess which mass murderers Feser refers to: "[Abandoning Aristotelianism] led to a debasement of man the most brutal realizations of which were Nazism and Marxism."[2]

Ouch. Nobody can really deny that Hitler and his ideology were responsible for the worst atrocities in living memory, and the crimes of the communist regimes are nothing to sniff at, either. So, is Feser right? Are we bound to accept natural law ethics and metaphysics, lest our societies devolve into the murderous chaos that Nazi Germany and Stalinist Russia exemplified? And is Christianity, specifically Catholicism, really the only alternative to ideologies like those?

Keep reading, and I think you'll find that the answer is a resounding "no."

---

[1] *TLS,* 224, 51. Italics in the original.
[2] Ibid., 222.

Chapter 2: Fallible Faith

The theology and metaphysics of the previous chapter may have been a bit dry and boring, and I cannot blame you, dear reader, if you have fallen asleep. Fortunately, this one will be much more exciting. Here, we'll use the metaphysics we've just discussed to evaluate the competing claims of Judaism, Christianity, and Islam, and even Greek and Norse polytheism too. Holy wars always get the blood flowing, though thankfully, in this case, the phrase is figurative rather than literal.

Dr. Feser is quite confident his side has won these philosophical Crusades, which I suppose is a good thing considering how well the real-life ones went.[1] As described in the previous chapter, since metaphysics is fundamental to making sense of the world (even more fundamental than science or empirical inquiry), Feser first establishes that the existence of change also necessitates the existence of a being that itself is unchanging, eternal, omnipotent, and responsible for all the physical laws[2] in the universe—God, in short. And since only a being like that could manipulate physics in such a way as to perform the miracles attributed to Christ, it follows that Christ really was God, and that, therefore, Christianity is true.

At first glance, it may seem odd that Feser spent so much time and so many words (remember, the previous chapter on metaphysics was a summary of several whole books) on establishing the existence of a supreme God through logical argument. After all, if you heard a burning bush talking to you, or saw a Jewish guy coming back to life after being crucified, wouldn't that be proof enough that the supreme deity exists?

---

[1] There's obviously a reason they call it Istanbul rather than Constantinople, these days, and everyone knows it, even if They Might Be Giants didn't get the memo.
[2] Again, Feser has some reservations about the idea of "physical laws," but the term is used here simply for brevity.

Why would you need to set up your metaphysics first before getting right to the miracles and concluding that Christianity must be true?

Well, according to Feser, without those metaphysics, there's no way to discern whether or not you're truly witnessing a miracle. In an essay on his blog titled "Signature in the Cell," he points out that any kind of miracle could plausibly have a mundane explanation *unless* you already know beforehand that God exists. For instance, let's say someone discovers "Made by Yahweh" imprinted on every cell in a human body. Would that prove that the God of the Bible existed? No, because it's possible the scientist was hallucinating, or that it was placed there by a "cabal of Christian biotech whizzes," or the whole thing was a strange joke that some playful aliens were pulling on the human species. The only way anyone could perceive such an event as a genuine miracle proving the existence of God would be if they already had "independent reason" to believe in God. And it just so happens that Aristotle's metaphysics provide an irrefutable independent reason to believe in God.[1] In other words, without Aristotle, there is no particular reason to believe in Christ; but with Aristotle, we can say for certain Christ's miracles really were divine and that Christianity is therefore true. His metaphysics provided the foundation upon which the Thomists have built an impregnable bulwark of faith.

On closer inspection, it seems to me that the Thomist fortress is nowhere near as secure as Feser claims. In this chapter, I shall argue the following points: First, even if we accept an Aristotelian sort of Christianity, there is no way to ascertain which variant of Christianity is true. Catholicism, the various Orthodox churches, and Protestants all make mutually contradictory claims to be the true heirs of Christ, and all of them acknowledge His miracles. Naturally, this makes creating a universal, coherent religious framework (not to mention a moral one) quite problematic. I will then explain how Aristotelian metaphysics

---

[1] Edward Feser, "Signature in the Cell," *Edward Feser* (blog), July 26, 2014, last accessed on July 5, 2020, http://edwardfeser.blogspot.com/2014/07/signature-in-cell.html , archived at http://archive.is/bXg76 on February 15, 2018.

themselves are of little use in verifying *any* particular claim *any* religion has made: Ascertaining whether or not a miracle actually occurred is a matter of history and empirical observation, and any historical argument by nature cannot be as ironclad as a metaphysical or logical proof. For that reason, even if we believe in the Aristotelian God, it is impossible to make *deductive* conclusions (with the absolute certainty attending to reasoning based on a priori premises, as in mathematics or formal logic) on whether or not an event that seems like a miracle actually was caused by any divine or supernatural being. Finally, since Aristotelian metaphysics allow for the existence of immaterial entities such as angels and demons (according to Thomists), it is impossible to figure out deductively, as Feser would prefer, whether or not any supposed miracle was the work of God or a less powerful but still immaterial "Form conjoined to an act of existing"—that is to say, an angel, some other kind of supernatural being, or even a demon.

I bring these arguments together to demonstrate that, far from buttressing the foundations of Christianity, Aristotelian metaphysics severely *undermine* it vis-à-vis the claims of Judaism and Islam. Indeed, since any miracle attributed to Christ could actually be trickery from an angel or demon (if Aristotelian metaphysics are true), Jews and Muslims have even stronger grounds to deny His divinity! Worst of all, Aristotelianism cannot even entirely refute polytheism—allowing for the existence of immaterial minds means Hellenic and Norse paganism, among others, are compatible with the existence of a single Purely Actual Being. I conclude by illustrating how these problems with Feser's particular brand of Aristotelianism severely undermine the "traditional" ordering of morality and politics he prefers.

2.1: Christmas Miracles and Easter Inductions

To be fair to Dr. Feser, my summary of his arguments on the Resurrection has been slightly simplified. I'm sure the most astute of my readers have already come up with one objection: "Don't lots of religions have miracles, too? Why should we believe in Christianity over all the others?" Feser has a response in *The Last Superstition:*

> [I]f a monotheistic religion's claim to be founded on a divine revelation is going to be at all credible, that claim is going to have to rest on a very dramatic miracle.... The resurrection surely counts as such a miracle, for there are no plausible natural [as opposed to divine] means by which a dead man could come back to life. What does Islam have to match this? Muhammad's 'miracle'...is the Qu'ran itself. This is...rather anticlimactic, especially given that the contents of the Qu'ran can easily be accounted for in terms of borrowings from Jewish and Christian sources. Jewish miracle claims are going to be the ones familiar from the Old Testament...but Christians accept those too, so even if their historicity were verified, they could not make the case for Judaism over Christianity specifically. Moreover, the direct eyewitness evidence for these miracle stories is more controversial than the evidence surrounding the resurrection. All things considered, then, the one purportedly revealed monotheistic religion which can appeal to a single decisive miracle in its favor is Christianity.[1]

All well and good. But even if Christianity stands triumphant over Judaism and Islam (and a wide variety of other monotheistic religions Feser doesn't mention, like Zoroastrianism or the Yazidi faith), as well as all other polytheistic religions,[2] that is still not as much of an accomplishment as Feser might like. For all the variety of the world's non-Christian religions, there are enough sects and divisions within Christianity itself to give all of them put together a run for their money. Is Catholicism the big one? Of course. But—and this is such common knowledge I suspect I hardly need a citation—there's no shortage of little ones. Protestantism is nothing if not prolific: It has given us Lutherans, Anglicans, Episcopalians, Presbyterians, Quakers, Amish, Baptists, Methodists, Pentecostals, and Pietists, to name just a very few. There are also Messianic Jews, Mormons, and Christian Scientists, along

---

[1] *TLS,* 160.

[2] Perceptive readers will note that at first glance a sort of pantheism which holds an eternally-existing universe itself as Pure Act might be compatible with Aristotelian theology, but according to Feser, any solution to the problem of universals necessitates a God with an intellect who is also distinct from the universe, ruling out such an alternative. See *FP* 15, 235, 247.

with a fair number of dead sects, such as the Arians and the Cathars. Even the Holy Mother Church Herself has a few tears in her seamless garment. There exists a branch of traditionalist Catholicism called **sedevacantism**, which holds that all the Popes since the Vatican II council have been heretics and therefore not true Popes![1]

It would be far beyond the scope of this book—and far beyond your humble narrator's abilities—to take a side with any one of these various sects. I bring them up only to highlight the weaknesses in Feser's position, as cumulatively revealed in *The Last Superstition, Aquinas,* and *Five Proofs for the Existence of God.* A reasonably fair summary of the argument threading through each of those books is this: *The philosophical tradition running from Aristotle to Aquinas to Feser himself can give the world coherent answers to religious questions with a very high degree of certainty.* It's easy to see why such an argument might be compelling. If it were correct, we would have quick, ready-made answers to life's most important questions, such as which religion is true (Christianity), where morality comes from (the Christian God), and how to determine right and wrong (following or disobeying the tenets of Christianity).

But, alas, it would only be an effective, convincing argument *if* Christianity were a singular, undivided entity. Since Christianity most certainly is not a monolith, the supposed advantages of Aristotelian theology are beset by a host of problems at least as severe as those it ought to have overcome. Classical theism tells us that a single religion, out of thousands upon thousands, is true! Hooray! Wait, that religion itself has hundreds upon hundreds of sects. Drat. At least the Resurrection allows us to "rationally evaluate" each of them, right? Oh, wait, they all acknowledge the Resurrection. Double drat. Aristotelian

---

[1] Mary Jo Weaver and R. Scott Appleby, eds., *Being Right: Conservative Catholics in America* (Indiana University Press, 1995), 257-258. For further explanation of what sedevacantists believe, see Michael W. Cueno, *The Smoke of Satan: Conservative and Traditionalist Dissent in Contemporary American Catholicism* (Johns Hopkins Press, 199), 114-120.

ethics tell us the highest instantiation of morality, indeed human reason itself, is to worship God! Hooray! Wait, how do we discern what constitutes proper Christian worship? The Catholics, Mormons, and Adventists all have very different ideas about that. *Triple* drat!

I believe that many "Drats!" would tax the patience of most sensible people. But perhaps all is not lost for the intrepid Dr. Feser. He might argue that all branches of Christianity are valid in some way. In one blog post, Feser compared Catholicism to a healthy dog, Eastern Orthodoxy to a dog with its tail cut off, and Protestantism to a dog without a tail and missing one leg.[1] The implication is that while Catholicism might be the most complete way of fulfilling the purpose of man (worshipping God), Orthodoxy and Protestantism are not entirely unsatisfactory and do represent some degree of success in the endeavor (Feser doesn't deal with salvation in that post, and we won't either). Unfortunately, there are at least a few Protestant sects who are nowhere near as sporting.

Take, for instance, the Seventh-Day Adventists. In 2015, Feser wrote an article examining their beliefs in the context of Dr. Ben Carson's bid for the presidential nomination of the Republican Party. After reading through several articles about the sect's founder, as well as a statement of beliefs contained on an Adventist website, Feser concluded that the Adventists believed Catholicism was not merely incorrect but outrightly evil. He quoted the Adventist scholars Denis Fortin and Jerry Moon, who said that Ellen G. White, founder of Adventism, believed the "'Church of Rome' is the 'Apostate Babylon.'" Feser then quoted Adventists.org, which said "world religions—including the major Christian bodies as key players—will align themselves with the forces in opposition to God and to the Sabbath."[2]

---

[1] Edward Feser, "Canine Theology," *Edward Feser* (blog), January 3, 2016, last accessed on July 5, 2020, http://edwardfeser.blogspot.com/2016/01/canine-theology.html , archived at http://archive.is/eIOmJ on February 20, 2018.

[2] Edward Feser, "Should a Catholic vote for Ben Carson?" *Edward Feser* (blog), December 11, 2015, last accessed on July 5, 2020,

The Catholic Church, of course, would be one of those anti-God forces, with the Seventh-Day Adventists being the ones in keeping with God's will.

The Adventist position, too, is not entirely unmerciful—they admit that "many Roman Catholics are brothers and sisters in Christ." It is obvious, however, that their views on morality, man's duty to God, and which religion is true are incompatible with Catholicism, and many other Christian denominations as well. While some individual Catholics might be saved, the Catholic Church as a whole will set itself against God during the End Times. This has some rather dire implications for Feser's argument. Both Catholics and Adventists would be able to accept the Thomistic line of reasoning that says

A: Change is real, therefore God exists,

B: Christ's Resurrection is real, therefore Christianity represents God, so therefore

C: The purpose of human life and the highest fulfillment of human reason is to adhere to Christianity.

But Catholicism and Adventism have mutually incompatible definitions of "adherence to Christianity." Catholicism asks its adherents to go to Mass on Sundays and pay homage to the Church as an institution, which is supposed to be divinely inspired as well. Adventists say that this is all wrong, that Catholicism is itself actually evil, and that

---

http://edwardfeser.blogspot.com/2015/12/should-catholic-vote-for-ben-carson.html#more archived at http://archive.is/NzQBB on February 20, 2018. The book from which Feser draws his information is Denis Fortin, Jerry Moon, *The Ellen J. White Encyclopedia* (Review & Herald Publishing, 2014), 319-320. The statement of Adventist belief comes from the General Conference of Seventh-Day Adventists Administrative Committee, "How Seventh-day Adventists View Roman Catholicism," *Adventist.org*, April 17, 1997, last accessed on July 5, 2020, https://www.adventist.org/en/information/official-statements/statements/article/go/0/how-seventh-day-adventists-view-roman-catholicism/24/ archived at http://archive.is/p0QnJ on February 24, 2018.

adherence to Christianity means worshipping God on Saturday above all else, as well as avoiding "earthly" popes, Bishops, and so-called churches, which are actually servants of evil. How can the "classical tradition," based as it is off Aristotle's metaphysics, tell us which of these competing views is correct?

It seems to me the "classical tradition" cannot carry out this task no matter how much Dr. Feser wishes it could.[1] While he has not written much specifically on the subject, we can come up with some ideas of how he might respond by teasing out some of the implications in his essays and looking at how Catholics have traditionally argued against Protestantism.

The easiest route Feser might take would be to simply dismiss opposing brands of Christianity as merely false at the face of things. For instance, in his article on Ben Carson, Feser told us that Adventist beliefs are "simply nutty" and "crackpot stuff."[2] But Feser did not give any especially compelling reason to agree with him, at least on his own terms. Aren't Christianity's claims in general "nutty?" As fedora-clad atheists never tire of telling us, the story of a "Jewish zombie" dying for the sins caused by some guy eating an apple a long time ago sounds pretty wacky.[3] But Feser would say we're simply obligated to believe it due to "metaphysics." Fine, but the Adventists could say the exact same

---

[1] Feser has attacked several Protestant doctrines, such as *sola scriptura* and theistic personalism, but so far as I know has not written any articles or monographs specifically comparing Catholicism to Protestantism. See Edward Feser, "Craig on Divine Simplicity and Theistic Personalism," *Edward Feser* (blog), April 15, 2016, last accessed on July 5, 2020, http://edwardfeser.blogspot.com/2016/04/craig-on-divine-simplicity-and-theistic.html and Edward Feser, "Feyerabend on Empiricism and Sola Scripture," *Edward Feser* (blog), July 13, 2015, last accessed on July 5, 2020, http://edwardfeser.blogspot.com/2015/07/feyerabend-on-empiricism-and-sola.html . However, Feser has written one essay touching upon his conversion to Catholicism rather than Orthodoxy or Protestantism, which we will discuss soon.

[2] Feser, "Should a Catholic vote for Ben Carson?"

[3] A brief Google search for the phrase "Cosmic Jewish Zombie" should be a more than sufficient citation for this.

thing. If we know for certain that God exists, and if we know for sure Christ was divine (as proved by His resurrection), we know for sure He is pure Good and would never lie, and therefore everything He told us is true. If He said the Catholic Church was aligned with the evil Whore of Babylon, well then, we are simply metaphysically obligated to believe it.

Feser would undoubtedly reply to this with a bit of Biblical **exegesis**, which is the art of interpreting and discerning the true meaning of a given text, usually religious ones such as the Bible. He would tell us that Christ never mentioned anything about the Whore of Babylon, as that term is found only in the Book of Revelation, written by someone else. He might go on to argue that it is impossible for the Catholic Church to be aligned with the evil forces of the end times, as Catholicism's influence has historically been good rather than evil, its charitable and evangelical works in keeping with Christ's commandments and therefore good in both the vernacular sense (kind and benevolent) and the metaphysical sense (fulfilling the function of humanity, which is obeying God).

Indeed, these two methods—exegesis and historical inquiry—are how Feser might argue for the truth of Catholicism above all others. It is typically how Catholics have defended the Faith against Protestants. For instance, Peter Kreeft has pointed out that the authorities of the Catholic Church were the ones who codified the Bible in the first place, so if an Adventist, Baptist, or anyone else is going to trust the Bible, they might as well trust the Church. Devin Rose has claimed that since, in Luke 10:16, Christ said of His apostles, "whoever listens to you listens to Me," the Catholic Church those Apostles founded would also have divine remit, since "nowhere does Jesus say that at some point he would abandon his Church...or that the authority he had given his leaders would be revoked."[1]

---

[1] Peter Kreeft, *Catholics and Protestants: What Can We Learn from Each Other?* (Ignatius Press, 2017), 37-38, Devin Rose, *The Protestant's Dilemma: How the*

Again, this is all well and good. I'm neither an expert in Biblical exegesis nor a historian of Christianity, so I wouldn't be able to tell you if these guys are right or not. However, I do know just a little bit about the historical method, and I can tell you that history is a less-than-ideal ally for metaphysics. This is because metaphysical arguments are deductive, and can be known with certainty, while historical arguments are inductive, based on the gathering of empirical data, and therefore only probabilistic. In other words, any historical argument, no matter how seemingly ironclad, has a possibility of being wrong.

Review what we discussed in Chapter 1. A deductive argument based on a priori claims might go like this: "All triangles have three sides (no more or less), all squares have four sides (no more or less), therefore no triangles are squares." The conclusion of the argument is completely inescapable given the definitions of the terms "triangle" and "square." There is no contingency to be found. On the other hand, take a historical argument, such as "The assassination of Franz Ferdinand by Gavrilo Princip caused World War I." This is a true historical fact—Archduke Ferdinand was shot by Princip on the 28th of June, 1914. But it is still entirely contingent: There is no characteristic inherent in Franz Ferdinand that necessitated he die on that day, no characteristic in Gavrilo Princip necessitating he assassinate anyone, and no inherent reason that act would have caused World War I—something else might have been the spark that set the tinderbox of Europe aflame.[1]

Reformation's Shocking Consequences Point to the Truth of Catholicism (Kindle edition: Catholic Answers Press, 2014), location 152.

[1] The nature of historical inquiry is a truly massive subject and not one that can be satisfactorily examined in this book, but interested readers a very strongly encouraged to take a look at least some of the many essays and monographs which have attempted to do so. See Richard Evans, *In Defense of History* (W.W. Norton and Co., 2000), 19-22. Evans describes various changes in the Western study of history over the course of the early modern period to the twentieth century, and in his discussions of various attempts to turn history into a science, he notes that the historical enterprise is even *less* capable than the hard sciences of producing universally reliable results through inductive means. Evans summarizes the great

The same concerns apply to any historical defense of the Catholic Church. If Feser wants to argue that the Catholic Church could not be the evil Whore of Babylon described in Biblical prophecy because no evil institution would do so much good, he will be making a historical argument. The words "Catholic Church" describe an institution, and do not entail that institution will necessarily do good (unlike Socrates being a man necessarily entails his being mortal). Even if we agree with Feser that the Church has generally been a force for good, that would be a contingent fact, not a necessary one, and therefore up for debate. Adventists could recite a long list of Catholic cruelties (the Inquisition, the troubles in Ireland, and of course, the sexual abuse of children) to prove that the Church really is evil. Thus, no matter how certain we might be that Christianity is true through deductive metaphysical reasoning, we cannot judge between the multitudes of bickering Christian denominations the same way.

Feser might argue that there is such a deductive argument to be made for Catholicism being mostly if not entirely good, and therefore on God's side (during the Apocalypse or whenever). Recall the exegetical argument of Devin Rose, that Christ gave His authority to the apostles. If Christ was God, then the apostles must have His approval, which means the Church they founded could not possibly be evil—it would be a metaphysical absurdity on the level of saying Socrates was not mortal. Feser offers some more specifics in another essay published in late 2019: "revelation [i.e the Bible itself] would be ineffective unless there is some 'moral person' or ongoing institution that can interpret it authoritatively. But such an institution is run by persons in the ordinary sense, and where these persons disagree, [it] cannot function unless

---

European historian George Trevelyan on page 21: "Nobody was ever going to unravel scientifically the mental processes of twenty million Frenchmen during the Revolution of 1789. Nor could interpretations of this event be arrived at by a mere process of induction. The causes and effects of the Revolution could never be known scientifically like the causes and effects of some chemical reaction, nor could they be grounded on discoverable laws like the law of gravity or the second law of thermodynamics."

there is some chief executive with authority to break any deadlock. In short, divine revelation, to be effective, requires something like apostolic succession and a papacy." [1]

But both exegesis and authority fall prey to the problem of induction as well. There is nothing in Luke 10:16, where Jesus tells Peter that "the gates of Hell will not prevail" against his church, that necessarily entails that the church of the apostles is the same as the present-day Catholic Church. Very many Christian denominations claim to be the heirs of the apostles—the Orthodox Church does, and the Presbyterian theologian Robert Lewis Dabney believed Presbyterianism to be the most accurate approximation of how the apostles lived.[2] A Seventh-Day Adventist could argue that the Catholic Church is actually a false usurper of the teachings of the apostles, having branched off from the true faith centuries ago, and that the Adventists are the true heirs of Peter, the true unpolluted apostolic church against which Hell has never prevailed.

In fact, the points Feser himself brought up perfectly illustrate these inductive issues. He tells us that we need a "chief executive" to properly interpret the Bible. Now, that "chief executive" (the Pope) got his authority from a chain that starts at Peter, who was divinely and thus infallibly appointed by Christ (i.e God Himself). But who's in charge of making sure *every single one of those appointments* is actually legitimate? Let's say that, I dunno, around a thousand years ago, some sneaky conspirators assassinated the "true" heir of Peter, and either duped or bribed the Cardinals into selecting a non-Peter approved stooge to sit on his throne. This would obviously break the line of

---

[1] Edward Feser, "The God of a Philosopher," in Brian Besong and Jonathan Fuqua, *Faith and Reason: Philosophers Explain Their Turn to Catholicism* (Ignatius Press, 2019), 50-51.

[2] Robert Lewis Dabney, "The Attractions of Popery," in *Discussions of Robert Lewis Dabney,* Volume III (Southampton, Great Britain: Banner of Truth Trust, 1982), 362-363. As he said, "We believe that the Christianity left by the apostles to the primitive church was essentially what we now call Presbyterian and Protestant."

apostolic succession and thus negate the (anti) Pope's authority to interpret the Bible, and indeed, the truth of the Catholic Church itself. How could Feser prove *deductively* that this never happened?

There may be historical reasons to doubt such a thing ever occurred. Devin Rose, for example, says that Protestants have been unable to give any specific date (just "sometime before the fifteenth century," as I implied) for when the Catholic Church became corrupted and distinct from true Christianity, which means there is no real reason to take vague claims of corruption or Petrine discontinuity very seriously.[1] That may be so, but once again, *historical* arguments are inductive rather than deductive, and based on empirical, a posteriori claims that could very possibly be false as opposed to entirely logical, a priori claims that are necessarily true. Simply because one cannot give an exact, specific date for an event occurring does not mean it did not occur, especially since any historian can tell you that a great deal of documentation ends up getting destroyed over the centuries. Jesus never said to Peter, "your true heirs will call themselves Catholics and will preserve My teachings infallibly for eternity." If He did, that might have solved a lot of problems, but as it is, biblical exegesis unfortunately cannot provide any certain answers as to which Christianity is correct. There is nothing inherent in the text of the Bible itself that mandates Catholics are necessarily the Church founded by (and on) Peter—and thus, no way to conclusively disprove the claims of Presbyterians or Adventists or Mormons or any of the other various sects of Christianity through ironclad, deductive means. Aristotle's legacy, alas, is much less clear and clean than we would like.

---

[1] Rose, *The Protestant's Dilemma,* locations 152-220.

2.2: An Induction at Golgotha

Even more troubling for those of Feser's philosophical bent is how the preceding arguments severely undermine the case for the *Resurrection itself.* The Resurrection—and, in fact, every miracle associated with Christ, ranging from curing diseases to banishing Legion—was a historical event, and could be proven to have really happened only through the historical method. No matter what "metaphysical background" may inform any analysis of His life, and even if the historical evidence for His death and subsequent return to life seems "overwhelming," we cannot really be *absolutely certain* it occurred.

This is not a subject on which Dr. Feser has written to any great extent. Understandable, since he is a philosopher rather than a historian of religion. But in *The Last Superstition*, he is kind enough to direct his audience to further reading. What, precisely, constitutes the "overwhelming" evidence for the Resurrection? According to Feser's endnotes, it can be found in several books written by the apologist William Lane Craig.[1] I have neither the time nor space to go over Craig's claims with a fine-toothed comb, but I can provide a brief summary in order to illustrate the points I'm making here.

In *Reasonable Faith,* Craig argues that the four Gospels of the New Testament are generally reliable documents, and therefore the Resurrection they describe most probably happened. According to him, the writing style is consistent with first-century Jewish vernacular, meaning the authors of the Gospels most likely came from Jesus's Jewish community or were very familiar with it. Additional proof of the Gospel's reliability comes from the fact that so many subsequent authors, ranging from men such as Barnabus and Clement all the way up to Eusebius in 315 A.D., regarded them as reliable. Third, the Gospels were so well-

---

[1] *TLS*, 283, endnote 15.

organized so soon after their creation that it seems very likely they were reliable historical documents.[1]

Since the Gospels bear all the hallmarks of good historical writing of that time period, if the Resurrection they describe did not actually happen, their authors must have either been deceived or were deceivers themselves. Craig draws on several other Christian apologists to argue that neither option can be correct. The authors of the Gospels were intelligent and reasonable men, unlikely to be fooled, and so many other people witnessed the events they described that a mass hallucination would beggar belief. Indeed, a mass hallucination could not have made Christ's body disappear from His tomb. Thus, the only option left is that the Gospel authors were lying, and that is quite unlikely as well. Several of the authors were tortured and killed for their religion—why would they die in the name of Christ unless they truly believed He had returned to them?[2]

Yet again, all well and good—since I'm not a scholar of Jewish culture and history, for the purposes of argument we can take Craig's word on all this. But the very act of relying on historical analysis like this severely weakens Feser's arguments for both Catholicism in particular and Christianity in general in two important ways.

First, take another look at the excerpt from "The God of a Philosopher" we discussed just at the end of the previous section. As Feser said, "revelation would be ineffective unless there is some 'moral

---

[1] William Lane Craig, *Reasonable Faith: Christian Truth and Apologetics, Third Edition* (Crossway Books, 2008), 333-340. Feser used the first edition of the book, published in 1994, but to be as fair as possible I looked Craig's latest edition, which responded to some criticisms he had received over the years.

[2] Craig, *Reasonable Faith*, 335-40. Richard Swinburne takes these arguments and uses something called Baye's Theorum to come up with a probability of the Resurrection being true, which he calculates at 97%. Aside from the mathematics, he marshals the same historical evidence as Craig, so I didn't repeat it here, but interested readers are directed to *The Resurrection of God Incarnate* (Oxford University Press, 2003).

person' or ongoing institution that can interpret it authoritatively." But why does this only apply to "revelation" alone? Wouldn't we also need some sort of authority to provide the correct interpretation of the *historical context* surrounding a supposed revelation, which is necessary to conclude that a purported revelation is what it says it is? In that case, who died and made William Lane Craig (or Swinburne, or any other scholar of Biblical history) king—I mean, Pope? Why should we believe Craig or any other apologist isn't simply lying straight through his teeth, and that all of his historical claims about the Gospel authors being intelligent, honest, and so on are actually false, meaning that the Bible wouldn't be reliable at all?

    Feser would probably say that Craig and/or Swinburne (at least) are honest and honorable men who can be trusted to tell the truth. Far be it from me to gainsay that, but curiously enough, neither of those two fellows are Catholic—Craig is a perplexed Protestant and Swinburne is an obstinate Orthodox.[1] If they are trustworthy—or in other words, "authorities"—with regard to the authors of the Gospel, why should we assume they are any less trustworthy with regard to the Gospels themselves? If we trust Craig or Swinburne's historical analyses, why shouldn't we trust them when they would (assumedly) tell us that Catholicism is wrong and Protestantism or Eastern Orthodoxy is right? In other words, Feser's argument for Catholicism based on the doctrine of apostolic succession seems quite arbitrary. We need some reliable authority to interpret the Bible, which Catholicism provides in the form of direct succession from Peter. But we don't need any similar successors holding divine authority to judge that the Bible itself is an accurate

---

[1] Swinburne says he has been Orthodox "since 1995" on his faculty website, last accessed on July 5, 2020, http://users.ox.ac.uk/~orie0087/ , and according to Bishop Robert Barron, Craig is Protestant. See Robert Barron, "An Evening with William Lane Craig," *Catholic World Report,* January 23, 2018, last accessed on July 5, 2020, https://www.catholicworldreport.com/2018/01/23/an-evening-with-william-lane-craig/

historical account (as Craig, being Protestant, assumedly inherited none of Peter's authority). Why might that be?

Leaving aside denominational conflicts, the second problem we encounter is that all this historical debate relies primarily on inductive reasoning based on empirical claims, not deductive reasoning based on a priori ones. Even if Craig and Swinburne were Catholic themselves, all the evidence for the reliability of the Gospels they marshal is entirely contingent. Craig's conclusions may be very likely given with regard to such evidence, but they are not absolutely, necessarily entailed by the evidence. The Gospels have an authentic writing style? Perhaps outsiders who had spent a lot of time in Judea had learned to mimic it perfectly. The authors of the Gospels were intelligent men and wouldn't have been fooled by an illusion? Intelligent people do occasionally fall for hoaxes or suffer from delusions. The authors couldn't have been liars because no-one would die for a lie? That's hardly certain. Some might prefer a painful death to the humiliation of being proved a fraud, and many people throughout history have died for odious causes. Craig, Swinburne, and assumedly Feser, might say that these possibilities are so unlikely that we should prefer their alternatives. But "unlikely" is not the same as "impossible."

In fact, the divergence between deductive and inductive proofs of God and Christianity (respectively) should make us very suspicious of the latter. It's important to remember that in almost all of his published work aside from "The God of a Philosopher" and *The Last Superstition*, Feser is consciously non-denominational. As he says in *Five Proofs*, "God's existence can be rationally demonstrated by purely philosophical arguments." But if that is actually so, it seems to me that "purely philosophical theists" like Aristotle have a significant head up over all the other theists.[1] Aristotle's arguments have two things going for them: First, they're deductive and thus possessed of a degree of certainty where historical arguments are not, as we discussed above. Just as importantly,

---

[1] *FP*, 15.

however, they're *universal*. They rely on absolutely no specific knowledge or "historical context" *at all* and are completely available to absolutely anyone, anywhere in the world and in any period of history. Theoretically, a Native American warrior living in the Hudson valley during the 10th century AD and an Egyptian farmer on the banks of the Nile in the 10th century BC could have reached the exact same conclusions Aristotle did *solely by observing change in the world around them*. Needless to say, neither man would require any sort of "authority" to reach those conclusions. Revelation, on the other hand, is far, far less ecumenical. Only a very small group of Jews in a very small part of the Roman Empire during a very small, specific timeframe could have possibly witnessed the miracles of Jesus Christ and received His revelation. And even that wouldn't be enough—they would require someone like Peter to properly interpret it after Christ had left. This is all very puzzling if, as Feser claims, God's existence has been obvious to most people (philosopher and layman alike) throughout history.[1] Why would God make Himself so well-known to humanity in general, but choose a certain revelation (both the event of the Resurrection *and* its accurate description in the Gospels) that is necessarily closed to the vast, vast majority of humanity across both time and space? This implies that the specific revelation of Christianity (and the even more specific revelation of any particular denomination thereof) is not exactly essential. One starts to think that even if we can be sure that God exists, we should be much more suspicious of any supposed miracle, including a Resurrection—which means we should be suspicious of Catholicism and Christianity in general.

2.3: The Problem with Miracles

Indeed, even closer examination can tell us that the deductive *as well as* the inductive evidence for the Resurrection is much weaker than Feser lets on. As usual, he himself might have given us some good reasons to doubt the Aristotelian background for it. I can demonstrate this by

---

[1] *FP.*, 300-305.

means of yet another analogy, hopefully more amusing for the lack of depressing subjects such as World War I.

Let us imagine that one day, mysteriously, the body of Elvis Presley disappears from his grave in Graceland, Tennessee. The media flocks to the area, the King's fans are in an uproar, the FBI is dispatched to figure out what happened to it, and the nation descends into general chaos. Just before the nuclear bombs start flying, Elvis suddenly reappears! Dressed in his finest sparkly threads, his black hair waxed and mussed into a perfect pompadour, his skin as healthy and radiant as it was when he first came on stage, he casually strolls into a local Denny's at 5 AM in the morning and orders a milkshake. It's not a busy night, and there are only thirteen people there, including the staff. But none of them can deny it—the King has returned! They crowd around him, begging for his wisdom, and he tells them that he was resurrected by God to return peace, love, and rock-and-roll to this benighted world. He must return to heaven very soon, he says, but once he does, they must start a new religion called "Elvisism." He's a bit vague about its tenets, but it mostly revolves around listening to his songs at least once a week. With those words of wisdom dispensed, he stands up and casually saunters away as if nothing had happened, and when his audience desperately runs outside to follow him, they find out he's gone! There's no proof he was ever even there...except for a recording the cashier had made on her smartphone, which is irrefutable evidence of what he did and said. She uploads it on YouTube, gaining over one billion views in less than six hours, and soon everyone in the world is convinced of the inescapable truth of the new religion. The nuclear strikes are called off, all the world's great religions are swiftly abandoned, and Planet Earth is soon united in peace and harmony under the soothing tunes of the greatest musician who ever lived, now proven to be divine as well.

If such an event were to take place—if the corpse of Elvis were to disappear, and someone who looked just like him appeared soon after, would Dr. Feser abandon Catholicism and embrace the hip-grinding ways of his new savior? I rather suspect not. Like any good skeptic, Dr.

Feser would point out that a multitude of explanations besides divine activity could explain these shenanigans. Some mischief-makers stealing Elvis's corpse and hiring a look-alike to fool the dupes at Denny's, for instance.

But wait! Don't we know for sure it would be an act of God? After all—to once again review Feser's reasoning—we know that change exists, which means that a single unchangeable Being exists, which also must be omniscient, omnipotent, and omnibenevolent. Since that Being can control the laws of physics (and can also reunite souls with bodies), He could have brought Elvis's corpse back to life, thus allowing the King to get his shake at Denny's. That means, as Feser might say, "His miraculous resurrection puts a divine seal of approval on what He said," which of course would mean that Elvisism would be true.[1]

Given that line of reasoning, would Feser relent and join the Church of Elvis? I still suspect not. Feser would probably say, "Well, simply because the existence of Pure Act makes miracles *possible*, it doesn't follow that any strange happening or bizarre event is *necessarily* a miracle. Perhaps they're elaborate hoaxes which will be revealed given enough time and investigation. Or perhaps there are scientific explanations, like will'o'the'wisps being proven to be marsh gas, that we haven't discovered yet. But simply believing in Pure Act doesn't mean I have to believe every trick someone might pull over me."

Reasonable enough, but couldn't you say the same for Christianity? As I have described above, there are "natural" explanations for the miracles attributed to Christ, simply due to the nature of historical inquiry. It is true that the existence of Pure Act makes Christ's miracles possibly true, but that does not make the evidence "overwhelming." Otherwise, any random person could claim to be a

---

[1] *TLS*, 156.

dead celebrity, or have risen from the dead, and point to "overwhelming" evidence on their side.[1]

Feser might try and refute this by saying that given their different historical contexts, it is far more likely Christ's Resurrection would be divine than Elvis's. After all, Christ was known for many miracles in addition to coming back to life, and in any case it would have been harder to pull off such a hoax back in the days of Roman Judea, since any grave robber would not have had the aid of machinery to break in or any technology which could help hide his presence. But two problems remain with this solution. First, even if it is *unlikely* that anyone could break into the tomb and steal Christ's body in ancient times, it is not *impossible*. Perhaps someone bribed some guards or soldiers near the tomb to assist them with the scheme, for instance, and the subsequent reappearance of Christ was, if not a mass hallucination, a look-alike that fooled the audience. It may be *unlikely* that anyone could disguise themselves as Christ, but given the number of people who can pass for Elvis today, it is hardly impossible that there was at least one person in ancient Judea who resembled Jesus enough to trick a grieving, emotionally-distraught audience. Of course, this is assuming the testimony of the Gospels is entirely accurate—very many scholars have looked at the Biblical account and found more than a few reasons to be skeptical.[2] But either way, it is far from certain that the Resurrection

---

[1] For more problems with the Resurrection, see the paragraph on Ockham and miracles at Arensb, "The Last Superstition: Hedonism Killed Aquinas," *Epsilon Clue*, November 21, 2016, last accessed on July 5, 2020,
https://epsilonclue.wordpress.com/2016/11/21/the-last-superstition-hedonism-killed-aquinas/

[2] My most excellent editor has done an excellent job rounding up a selection of these theories on his personal blog. See Jonathan Pearce, "Easter Round-Up: Everything You Need To Know About The Resurrection (Skeptically Speaking)," *A Tippling Philosopher*, April 20, 2019, last accessed July 5, 2020,
https://www.patheos.com/blogs/tippling/2019/04/20/easter-round-up-everything-you-need-to-know-about-the-resurrection-skeptically-speaking/

happened exactly the way Scripture tells it, which means that it is far from certain Catholicism (or any other branch of Christianity) is true.

The second problem is that even if we were to discard all other mundane possibilities and insist that the body of Jesus disappeared from His tomb, and that He really did appear before a large audience, including the authors of the Gospel, there are other non-mundane, non-divine explanations for the event. I can think of two in particular: Aliens and angels.

I am being deadly serious here—these suggestions are absolutely not jokes or intended to be dismissive. I bring them up because they illustrate some of the issues with the Thomistic metaphysical system, issues even Feser himself is aware of and has brought up in good faith before. Indeed, he has written on the matter at some length, in another blog post titled "Christians, Muslims, and the Reference of 'God.'" Feser offers (in his view) a counterfactual:

> Suppose it turned out that there is no such thing as a cause of everything other than himself who is one, eternal, immaterial, necessary, omnipotent, omniscient, perfectly good, etc. But suppose also that there really was a powerful being who sent Moses to deliver the Law to Israel, who sired Jesus and sent him as a prophet, who imparted preternatural powers to him and to the apostles so that they might found a Church, etc. But suppose that this powerful being was an extraterrestrial and that the events recorded in the Bible were all caused in something like the way Erich von Däniken describes in Chariots of the Gods. Suppose this extraterrestrial called himself "the Father" and that he had two lieutenants who called themselves "the Son" and "the Holy Spirit." Would this be a scenario in which Christian theism turns out to be true? Of course not, and (I hope!) no Christian would say so. It would be a scenario in which atheism is true.[1]

---

[1] Edward Feser, "Christians, Muslims, and the reference of 'God,'" *Edward Feser* (blog), December 28, 2015, last accessed on July 5, 2020,

Feser, of course, is definitely not an atheist. Immediately after, he points out that atheism is "metaphysically impossible," for the reasons summarized in chapter one of this book. Thus, he concludes that a powerful being really did guide Moses and incarnate as Christ, but this was the omnipotent Supreme Being of classical theology rather than merely a powerful extraterrestrial.

Unfortunately, it seems to me that Feser doesn't quite understand the extent to which his choice of example here undermines his other religious arguments. The fact that a single, all-powerful Being exists does not mean various lesser beings, who are nonetheless more powerful than human beings, necessarily do not exist. Indeed, Feser admits such beings may exist (angels, who as we heard in chapter one are immaterial). So why couldn't superior material beings exist, such as the Vulcans from Star Trek? Our pointy-eared friends had long since mastered faster-than-light travel by the time some drunkard on Earth was playing around with it, according to the movie *First Contact*. A species like the Vulcans, if it existed, could easily be responsible for the supposedly inexplicable-by-natural-means miracles of Christ.

Say there was an incredibly advanced space-faring species from, I don't know, Proxima Centauri who sent out an anthropological expedition to the far end of the Milky Way in our year 0 A.D (their year 70358 Blargsmap). For whatever unfathomable alien reason, they learn the local language and send down an extremely advanced android or psionic clone to Bethlehem, perhaps numbered JC-01. JC performs many amazing feats which seem incredible but are actually the result of miniature anti-gravity generators or special psionic brain waves. When Roman soldiers hear of this, they attempt to kill JC, but the android also has extremely advanced self-repair capabilities. Within three days, JC appears to have "resurrected" and busts his way out of his "tomb." He

---

http://edwardfeser.blogspot.com/2015/12/christians-muslims-and-reference-of-god.html

appears before the human followers he has gained before being beamed up to his mothership, which promptly returns to Proxima Centauri.

In such a scenario, Feser would say Christian theism is false, since the "miracles" attributed to Christ were merely artifacts of super-advanced technology rather than actual suspensions of the natural order which only Mr. Pure Act could orchestrate. But such a scenario would *also* be compatible with the existence of a Purely Actual Being. Nothing about it denies the existence of a single, subsistent Existence underlying everything else in existence. It merely requires the existence of an intelligence greater than man's, which is hardly metaphysically impossible. How would first-century Judeans, even educated ones like the authors of the Gospels, distinguish between genuine miracles and technological wizardry that appeared miraculous? And how could we today, living millennia after the events, judge which explanation is more probable than the other?

I can think of two ways Feser might respond to this quandary. First, he might argue that human beings are the only sentient life in the universe, and that no technological means exist to create convincing facsimiles of the Biblical miracles. But there is little evidence for either of these assertions. Nowhere in the Bible does it say *only* man was created in the image of God (that is to say, with the power of reason). If Mr. Pure Act created a universe with billions upon billions of stars with even more billions of planets orbiting them, there is no Scriptural reason He might not have granted sentience to some other species on some far-off world.

Indeed, at least one of Feser's colleagues acknowledges this possibility. David Oderberg is a Thomist philosopher and apparently a good friend of Feser's, judging from the lavish praise Feser has given him.[1] In his monograph, *Real Essentialism* (which will feature quite

---

[1] *SM*, 5, 9. The book is dedicated "to my [Feser's] dear friend David Oderberg," and Feser hopes it "complements" Oderberg's *Real Essentialism*, and "certainly has not

heavily in future chapters of this book), Oderberg brings up the idea of rational animals other than *Homo Sapiens*. He makes the point that living organisms should be considered "human" if they are capable of abstract reasoning like we are, and that "human-ness" is a metaphysical category rather than a biological one.[1] All well and good—for full disclosure, I agree with him, though not for Thomist reasons. Unfortunately for Feser, if we allow for non-human rational animals, or "ranimals" in Oderberg's words, we must also allow for the possibility that some of those ranimals may be considerably more intelligent and technologically adept than we are. There is no reason to believe they would not have been able to fool even educated first-century Judeans, given the progress people living today have made in fields such as holographics and robotics. And while it may be exceedingly unlikely for intelligent life to evolve, given the immense size of the galaxy it is not an impossibility. If we say there is only a one in a billion chance for any solar system to harbor an advanced civilization, in a galaxy containing one hundred to four hundred billion stars, there may be a hundred to four hundred other civilizations around us. It is possible at least one of those civilizations developed faster-than-light travel along with a sense of humor quirky enough to pull one over on some hapless Jews a little over two thousand years ago.

Second, Feser might try to argue that Mr. Pure Act would somehow prevent the aliens from fooling Earthlings as is the case in my example. But what reason would God have for doing that? As is obvious from everyday experience, God does not often intervene when human beings lie to each other. If someone tells a falsehood or attempts to conduct a hoax, it is up to us to ferret him out; there are few examples of mysteries being solved by divine revelation. Even when it comes to lies about God, God Himself seems content to leave them be. Being a good Catholic, Feser would ostensibly think that Protestant faith-

---

surpassed it." To paraphrase St. Paul, no man hath greater love than he who lays down his own book for his friend's.

[1] David Oderberg, *Real Essentialism* (Routledge, 2007), 100-103.

healers or snake-handlers are lying when they claim to have been blessed by God or speak with Him personally.¹ Yet God has not apparently done much to prove the falsity of their dubious "miracles." So then why would we expect God to save us from the falsehoods of a more advanced alien species?

Equally problematic to Feser's argument for Christianity is the existence of angels. I should note that Feser *hates* it when people make fun of angels, as can be seen in his rather testy reply to Richard Oerter, who laughed at Feser's hypothesis that inertial motion could be caused by angels.² Rest assured, to reiterate what I said earlier, there will be no jokes here. I'll treat the subject with the very utmost seriousness.

A brief refresher: Since Aristotle's Theory of Forms implies that anything capable of grasping and reasoning upon universal Forms must be immaterial, it also seems to be the case that something immaterial, like the human mind or soul, can exist independently of the material parts in which it seems to reside, such as the brain. Thomists take this to imply that entirely immaterial beings can exist as well—namely, the angels of Biblical lore.

What purpose do these angels serve, and how do they interact with the world? In his article, "Mind-Body Interaction: What's the Problem?" Feser describes Saint Aquinas, in the *Summa Theologiae*, "[comparing] the way an angel moves a physical object to the way the moon causes tides in the sea.... The relationship between an angelic intellect and any body it might move, then, is somewhat like the

---

[1] Feser mockingly references "snake handlers in Kentucky" on page 160 of *TLS*, so it's safe to assume he doesn't believe they've been given divine approval.
[2] Edward Feser, "Oerter on Inertial Motion and Angels," *Edward Feser* (blog), January 7, 2013, last accessed on July 5, 2020, https://edwardfeser.blogspot.com/2013/01/oerter-on-inertial-motion-and-angels.html, archived at http://archive.is/6diAL on February 24, 2019.

relationship between a puppeteer and the puppet it moves (only without strings, of course)."[1]

Feser's woes continue, for he seems unaware that this description undercuts the epistemological basis on which we can judge the Resurrection to have really occurred. The astute reader will notice that Feser provides little specific detail on how the angels can actually manipulate physical objects and what the limits of that manipulation are. If they are like puppeteers who can practice their art without strings, it stands to reason they can do so much more deftly than even the most skilled human puppeteer and with virtually any size and type of 'puppet' conceivable. Which means that angelic activity—rather than divine action—might explain the Resurrection. Perhaps an angel, or a group of angels, opened the way to Christ's tomb, levitated out His body (like a puppeteer with a puppet, just without strings), and showed it off to the Apostles. Perhaps the angel or angels manipulated light to make it seem as if Christ was radiant and as perfectly healthy as if He had not died at all and manipulated the air around the audience to make it seem as if He were speaking. Or perhaps these immaterial beings simply manipulated the brains of the Apostles directly, making them hallucinate that Christ had returned from an empty tomb. Without any clear definition of what the angels can and cannot do in relation to the material world, any seemingly miraculous event can be attributed to them rather than God, thus falsifying the Christian (or any other) religion.

Now, Feser has also written that "a miracle in the strictest sense could not be caused even by an angel, since it is a suspension of the order

---

[1] Edward Feser, "Mind-Body Interaction: What's the Problem?" *Edward Feser* (blog), September 17, 2016, last accessed on July 5, 2020, http://edwardfeser.blogspot.com/2016/09/mind-body-interaction-whats-problem.html

to which even angels are subject."[1] Thus, in this view, Christ's Resurrection could not have been caused by an angel because actually bringing someone back from the dead would be an obvious "suspension" of what we know to be the laws of physics (or what Feser would call the way things generally are). But the same epistemological concern I raised with aliens applies here as well: There seems to be no way to discern between a genuine miracle and a merely apparent miracle. Just as Jesus might have possibly been an android with incredibly advanced self-repairing capabilities, the Resurrection might also have been an illusion created by angels or some other kind of immaterial being, since nothing about these "Forms attached to an act of existence" seems to preclude them from being able to fool material creatures in such a way. Perhaps one spirited away Christ's corpse, and another took his form to fool the crowds. How would such a trick be any violation of any order to which an angel is subject? If Feser is referring to the material laws of physics[2], an angel would not be bound to such laws because an angel is not made of atoms or photons or any other physical substance.

It is true that angels are servants of God, and thus presumably would not lie or play tricks on humans. But what about the aforementioned other kinds of immaterial beings? Feser, at least, genuinely believes in the evil version of angels—demons. In a rather striking passage from the *Routledge Handbook of Contemporary Philosophy*, Feser informs us that "[c]lassical theists like Aquinas do, as I have said, affirm the existence of unusual powers...which may be described as 'magical' in the looser sense of being intelligible in themselves, but beyond the abilities and/or understanding of human beings. Demonic interventions in the ordinary course of things would

---

[1] Edward Feser, "Pre-Christian Apologetics" on *Edward Feser* (blog), May 16, 2014, last accessed on July 5, 2020, http://edwardfeser.blogspot.com/2014/05/pre-christian-apologetics.html
[2] Again, Feser believes that laws of physics are more like a description of the various natures of things, but I say "laws of physics" here simply for brevity.

be an example."¹ Scary stuff, certainly. But just what sort of power do these demons have? According to Feser, they are "fallen angels" who "wish ill" upon human beings who decide to consult them.² Given that these demons are apparently fallen angels, it stands to reason they are immaterial beings who have similar powers as true, holy angels. This leads us to an even more frightening possibility: That the miracles attributed to Christ were actually hoaxes perpetrated by demons to fool the people of Judea. Perhaps His body was actually "puppeteered" by some dark spirit, or perhaps demons possessed the minds of all the witnesses to the Resurrection, fooling them into thinking He had returned. Without some explanation of how demonic powers operate, and how they differ from angelic powers (if at all), the case for Christ is as much a case for a supernatural evil intervention as it is for Christianity.

That is certainly a blasphemous argument, and I shudder to make it. It is, however, an honest argument, and one better men than me have made in sincerity. A Roman anti-Christian philosopher named Celsus accused Jesus of merely being a magician or sorcerer, playing a trick on gullible people.³ These accusations were so widespread that Aquinas himself had to address them in the *Summa*. According to the version of it on the *New Advent* website (on which Feser also relies), Christ could not have performed His miracles by demonic power because He had often banished demons, and "the devil does not work against his own kingdom."⁴ But if a group of demons was working together, it is possible that some of them may have pretended to work against Christ, so that false miracles would fool His audience (for instance, if the demon

---

[1] Edward Feser, "Religion and Superstition" in Graham Oppy, ed., *The Routledge Handbook of Contemporary Philosophy of Religion* (Routledge 2015), 197.
[2] Ibid., 198.
[3] Celsus and R. Joseph Hoffman, trans., *On the True Doctrine: A Discourse against the Christians* (Oxford University Press, 1987), 66, 99.
[4] Thomas Aquinas, *Summa Theologiae,* third part, question 43, *NewAdvent.org,* 2017, last accessed on July 5, 2020, http://www.newadvent.org/summa/4043.htm

possessing the unfortunate man in Gethesmane just "pretended" to have been banished by Christ).

If that's a little too horror-movie for my tender audience, what about other sorts of immaterial beings? The interesting thing about the Aristotelian allowance for such entities is that it leaves the door open for a veritable bestiary of spooks and spirits. The Bible might say angels exist, but it never says other kinds of "intellects without matter" do *not*. Muslims, for instance, believe in a sort of spirit called a Jinn, which is neither good nor evil but apparently has the ability to choose, like humans do.[1] Anime fans can tell you all about supernatural beings such as the scary-looking Shinigami from *Death Note* or the nature spirits of *Princess Mononoke*. Though obviously given particular appearances and abilities for the sake of entertainment, these anime characters are based on entities recognized in traditional Japanese religion, which appeared and acted on the world in the same way Feser says angels would.[2] Perhaps one of these spirits manipulated Christ or played a trick on His followers.

In order to refute this sacrilegious anti-apologetic, Feser would have to explain why Jinns, Shinigami, or any other kind of immaterial being aside from angels and demons do not exist or would not be able to play such a trick on mankind. If he could not, he would have to explain how these creatures would be *metaphysically* unable to work together and fool human beings into thinking Christ was working against them while actually serving them in reality. Aristotle's metaphysics would seem to offer little help here, since he came up with the idea of immaterial minds in the first place.[3] In fact, regardless of

---

[1] Amira El-Zein, *Islam, Arabs, and the World of the Jinn* (Syracuse University Press, 2009).
[2] Michael Dylan Foster, *The Book of Yokai: Mysterious Creatures of Japanese Folklore* (University of California Press, 2015), 29, "Yokai as Presence."
[3] As Bradley Bowen has pointed out, one could go even further and say that an Aristotelian allowance for immaterial intellects makes it impossible to justify historical claims about such entities. Historians rely on empirical investigation of material traces to verify claims made by people from the past—if some general

whether or not one believes in disembodied intellects such as angels or demons, Aristotle's metaphysics may actually provide an irrefutable argument *against* the divinity of Jesus Christ—especially if you were to ask Muslims and Jews.

2.4: Jews and Muslims and Pagans, Oh My!

Of the three great Abrahamic monotheisms, Christianity is the least monotheistic, at least at first glance. The whole thing with the Father, the Son, and the Holy Spirit sounds more like three Gods than One. As you might expect, your humble narrator is very far from the first person to notice this. Jewish counter-apologists have concentrated on the apparent paganism of Christian theology for centuries. The great Jewish sage Maimonides—no intellectual slouch or fanatic hack, judging by how Feser always includes him in lists of great classical theists—accused Jesus of "[interpreting] the Torah in a manner that would lead to its total annulment."[1] More recently, Jewish apologists such as Samuel Levine have claimed that Christians misinterpret Old Testament references to God, and that traditional Jewish teaching has always held that God is One and only One and could never be a Father, Son, and Holy Spirit.[2]

Muslims, on the other hand, consider Christ a genuine prophet, and would take great exception with the negative view of Him taken by the intellectuals mentioned above. However, many have also viewed the

---

from antiquity stated that a battle occurred in a certain location, for instance, historians will look for concrete evidence of that battle in that location, like skeletons, discarded weapons, and so on to verify that he was telling the truth. Immaterial beings, however, regardless of whether they're angels, demons, or God Himself, would not leave behind any material traces that would allow historians and archaeologists to judge whether or not any account of their activities was accurate. Thus, if the Gospels describe a lot of supernatural activity, there's no way for historians to ascertain which immaterial entities, if any at all, were involved in those events.

[1] Moses Maimonides and Abraham S. Halkin, trans., *The Epistles of Maimonides: Crisis and Leadership* (The Jewish Publication Society, 2009), 98.
[2] Samuel Levine, *You Take Jesus, I'll Take God: How To Refute Christian Missionaries* (Hamoroh Press, 1980), 57-59.

Christian conception of His divinity as not merely wrong but blasphemous. According to the Qu'ran, Jesus was indeed born of a virgin, but never actually died; the holy book states "they [the Jews] killed him not, nor crucified him, but so it was made to appear to them." It explicitly denies Christ being the son of God Himself, saying in Surah 9, "the Christians call Christ the son of God...they but imitate what the Unbelievers of old used to say. Allah's curse be on them: how they are deluded away from the Truth...(they take as their Lord) Christ the son of Mary, yet they were commanded to worship but One God: there is no God but He."[1]

Needless to say, neither the Jewish nor the Muslim interpretation is compatible with what Feser takes to be the one true revealed religion. Recall that Feser said

> ...if a monotheistic religion's claim... is to be at all credible, that claim is going to have to rest on a very dramatic miracle.... The resurrection surely counts as such a miracle...what does Islam have to match this? Muhammad's 'miracle,' the Muslims tell us, is the Qur'an itself. This is, shall we say, rather anticlimactic...Jewish miracle claims are going to be the ones familiar from the Old Testament...but Christians accept those too.[2]

This sounds reasonable to me—all the talk about the "Judeo-Christian" tradition does seem to indicate some degree of harmony between the two, and in reference to Islam, I've read the Qu'ran, and nothing about it struck me as beyond the capabilities of a modestly accomplished writer of fanfiction. But the trouble comes when we compare that quote to Feser's rationale for believing in Christ's miracles in the first place: "when interpreted *in light of* [Aristotelian

---

[1] Abdullah Yusuf Ali, trans., *The Holy Qu'ran* (Wordsworth Editions Limited, 2000), Surah 19:20 (page 247), 4:157 (78), 9:32 (147).
[2] *TLS*, 160-161.

metaphysics], as it should be, the evidence for Christ's resurrection can be seen to be overwhelming."¹

Jews and Muslims would say exactly the opposite: Given Aristotle's metaphysics, the evidence for Christ's resurrection *cannot be believed*. Recall in Chapter 1 we mentioned in passing how Pure Act (i.e., God) must be absolutely simple and absolutely unitary in addition to being omnipotent, omniscient, and omnibenevolent. The reason for this, according to Feser himself, is that any being composed of parts, even metaphysical parts, is contingent in some way, because there always has to be something keeping the parts together. Material beings like us are composed of physical parts (arms, legs, heads) joined together, metaphysical parts (rationality and animality joined together), and our very act of existing (again, refer back to chapter 1: since our Form is just "rational animal" and says nothing about existence, God must conjoin our Essence to existence). Pure Actuality, however, would be just subsistent Existence—His Essence is His Existence, nothing more and nothing less.² Unfortunately for Feser, the Trinity would seem unable to fit that definition. If God's existence just is His Essence, absolutely and completely unitary and simple, how can there be three parts of Him? It seems that Muslims and Jews could unanimously call upon Aristotle to declare that the absolutely singular God cannot be composed of a Father, a Son, and a Holy Spirit—though they would probably start fighting over whether or not Christ was a genuine prophet or a lunatic, malicious magician, or something else.³

To be fair, this is old news to Catholics. Aquinas made many attempts to reconcile Aristotle with the Trinity. For instance, in the *Summa Theologiae*, the Angelic Doctor claimed that the word "person,"

---

[1] Ibid., 155.
[2] Ibid., 108-109.
[3] Arensb, "The Last Superstition: The Unmoved Mover," *Epsilon Clue,* October 28, 2016, last accessed July 5, 2020, https://epsilonclue.wordpress.com/2016/10/28/the-last-superstition-the-unmoved-mover/

when referring to God, applies to "a relation as subsisting in the divine nature," that is to say, God's Essence.[1] This is, to put it mildly, an unintuitive line of reasoning, but even under a close and sustained analysis we can see that Aquinas fails to make a convincing case for the "Person" of Christ being compatible with the doctrine of divine simplicity.

In Question 30, Article I of the *Summa Theologiae,* Aquinas reasonably and fairly addresses the most obvious objections to his position. In Objection 1, he admits that the word "person" refers to individuals, so if there were three "persons" in God, He would have to be composed of three individuals, in which case He would obviously not be simple, that is to say, not composed of any parts. To get around this, Aquinas claims that the word "person" means something different when referring to God than it does when referring to people we meet in our everyday lives. As he said, "this word 'person' signifies in God a relation as subsisting in the divine nature [God's Essence or Form]."[2]

What could that possibly mean? It would be easy enough to simply dismiss this as incomprehensible nonsense, but in the interests of good sportsmanship we are ought to at least look at what Aquinas is saying a little more closely. He further explained that "The definition of "person" includes "substance," not as meaning the essence, but the "suppositum" which is made clear by the addition of the term 'individual.'"[3] Words like 'suppositum' may seem hard to grasp at first (and we'll talk about the word "substance" at more length in upcoming chapters), but given the metaphysical framework we discussed in chapter 1, we can make the attempt. Recall the description of Essences: Types of universals which

---

[1] *AQ,* 33-35, Thomas Aquinas, *Summa Theologiae,* third part, question 43, *NewAdvent.org,* 2017, http://www.newadvent.org/summa/1030.htm , Thomas Aquinas, *Summa Theologiae,* third part, question 43, *NewAdvent.org,* 2017, http://www.newadvent.org/summa/1028.htm#article1, last accessed July 5, 2020.
[2] Thomas Aquinas, *Summa Theologiae,* third part, question 43, *NewAdvent.org,* 2017, last accessed on July 5, 2020, http://www.newadvent.org/summa/1030.htm
[3] Ibid.

define and distinguish individual things that instantiate them, but which cannot be reduced to any particular individual thing. For instance, the Essence of a squirrel is what makes a certain furry rodent with a bushy tail a squirrel, but that Essence would still exist even if every bushy-tailed rodent disappeared. "Suppositum" is the word Aquinas used to refer to an "individual thing," or, more technically, "individual existence." That is to say, if you went outside and saw a squirrel hanging out in a tree or in your front yard, that individual squirrel would be a "suppositum" that instantiated the Essence of Squirrel-ness. This "individual existence" would be responsible for whatever non-essential or "accidental" characteristics of the particular squirrel you see (for instance, location—being on a tree or in a yard, or physical size—being fat or thin), but it would still instantiate an Essence that, as a universal, cannot be attributed to any individual or particular squirrel, yet exists in common to all of them and would exist even if every individual squirrel died.

Thus, when Aquinas says, "the definition of 'person' includes 'substance,' not as meaning the Essence, but the 'suppositum,'" he means that all three Persons in the Trinity—The Father, the Holy Spirit, and Jesus Christ, share a single Essence, in a (very roughly) analogous way as a squirrel in the branches of a tree, a squirrel hanging on to its trunk, and a squirrel digging for nuts at its roots all share a single Essence of Squirrel-ness, despite being three distinct suppositums (individuals). The Essence of Squirrel-ness itself is still a singular, unified thing, irreducible to any of the individual squirrels, which means that Essence is simple and non-composite. By this reasoning, then, if we consider the Father, the Son, and the Holy Spirit to be "suppositums" that instantiate the Essence of God, that Essence itself is not composed of parts, thus preserving divine simplicity.

Unfortunately, even if this elaborate argument might be plausible with regard to the Father and the Holy Spirit, it completely falls apart when we think of Christ Himself. If any given individual or "suppositum" instantiates a Form or Essence, it cannot possess characteristics that directly contradict that Essence. It is easier to understand this by using geometrical objects rather than animals as examples. If you make a particular toy triangle out of plastic, a "suppositum" that instantiates the Essence of triangularity, it can possess certain "accidental" characteristics—being red, or of a certain size—but it cannot possess certain others, like being curved or having four sides. If it possessed the latter characteristics, it would not be a triangle but rather a plastic sphere or plastic square.

God, as we will recall from our introduction, also has certain necessary characteristics as a result of His Essence. He is immaterial and unchangeable. Thus, any individual "suppositum" instantiating that Essence would also have to be immaterial and unchangeable. Jesus Christ, however, was neither. As my friend Arensb has pointed out, Jesus undoubtedly underwent change in *every sense.* He went from actually being in Mary's womb and potentially a baby to an actual baby which could potentially be a carpenter, and lo and behold, that potential was eventually actualized. Christ changed constantly in terms of location—He started out in Bethlehem, walked over to Galilee, and then marched all the way to Jerusalem. And, of course, His greatest miracle was obviously a change. He started out alive, died, and then came back to life. If Pure Act is, by necessity and in terms of its Essence, immutable and unchangeable, how could it also be a real, material person who changed so much over the course of His life? It is almost certain that Aristotle would find Aquinas's defense of the Trinity absurd, and Jews and Muslims would agree.[1]

Feser might try to get around this by playing some Aristotelian word games. As he admitted to the *Dartmouth Apologia*, "The case of the Incarnation raises unique issues of its own, since...we have the added complication that the Son takes on a body, which has material parts and so forth. But of course it must be kept in mind that simplicity applies in

---

[1] Arensb, "The Last Superstition: The Unmoved Mover."

the first place only to Christ's divine nature, not his human nature."[1] But the analysis we performed in our previous paragraph just now implies that Christ could not possess both a divine Nature, or Essence, and a human Nature. Once again, individual things can possess or instantiate different Essences at the same time if and only if those Essences are compatible. Thus, a plastic triangle can simultaneously instantiate all the Essences of triangularity, redness, equilaterality, and plastic-ness, because color, size, and shape do not necessarily contradict each other. Any individual triangle *cannot* instantiate square-ness or circularity at the same time, since an object cannot simultaneously have three sides *and* four, or a polygon with straight sides cannot simultaneously have curved sides, and so on. Since the Nature or Essence of humanity entails that we are material, changeable beings (that is to say, rational *animals*), it is logically impossible for any given individual thing (suppositum) to share both that Essence and a Divine Essence, which is immaterial and unchangeable.

If Feser would deny this, and claim it is still somehow possible for God to unite an Essence (His Own) with another Essence (humanity) with incompatible properties, he would have to explain why it would be impossible for God to do the same with other Essences, like creating a round triangle that possessed both triangularity and circularity (or to use the peculiar jargon, establish a "Hypostatic Union" between something with the Essence of triangularity and the Essence of circularity). But as we will recall from our introduction to metaphysics, Feser tells us that God's omnipotence does not extend to logical impossibility. So we must conclude that Christ Himself represents a logical impossibility, something even God could not bring into being. Unless, of course, Christ was merely human, perhaps a sorcerer, as Celsus claimed—which would obviously render Christianity false.

---

[1] Edward Feser, "Is Ancient Philosophy Still Relevant? Rediscovering Aristotle, Aquinas, and Classical Theism: an interview with Edward Feser," *The Dartmouth Apologia,* Spring 2016, last accessed July 5, 2020, http://augustinecollective.org/rediscovering-aristotle-aquinas-and/

But what about Christ's miracles? Isn't the evidence for those supposedly overwhelming? A response to this apologetic comes from an unexpected source—David Oderberg. He believes, and it's safe to say Feser does too, that metaphysics is "not the handmaid of science; rather, it is *itself* a science—indeed the queen of the sciences." The subsequent implication is that the metaphysician should be able to play a part in scientific inquiry; even if scientists observe something, he or she has authority to say "however it happened, it could not have been like *that*."[1] If this is true, it would seem that historians (who are even less able to make accurate predictions than scientists[2]) would have to bow before metaphysicians as well. And if those metaphysicians happen to be Jewish or Muslim, Feser and Oderberg are in deep trouble indeed. Someone like the Jewish Maimonides or the Muslim Avicenna might laugh and say, "It doesn't matter how reliable the Apostles may have been, or how unlikely it would be that they were hallucinating. Even if they had recorded the whole thing on video, it still wouldn't matter. Metaphysics tells us with absolute certainty that God cannot change. Thus, Christ could not have been God: However the events associated with Him might have happened, they could not have happened like *that*."

Perhaps Feser might argue that all that apparent change was merely an illusion, and it only *seemed* like Christ had many potencies being actualized because our puny, material brains are incapable of understanding the true operations (and grandeur) of the Triune God. This position is called **mysterianism**. Feser *might* say it is actually a natural consequence of Aristotelian metaphysics. To again refer back to chapter 1, Aristotle and Aquinas believed that the less material something is, the more intelligent it was. Humans are less material, or more immaterial, than dogs or cats, which means we're smarter. However, angels are even less material, making them smarter than us, and God doesn't even need to have His Existence conjoined with His Essence, making Him omniscient. This implies there are limits on what

---

[1] Oderberg, *Real Essentialism*, xii.
[2] Evans, *In Defense of History*, 19-25.

any given being is able to know. God knows everything, while angels can know less, and human beings, even the smartest among us like Einstein or Hawking, in principle cannot truly comprehend God's Nature, since human scientists are still material compared to God's complete immateriality.[1] Thus, it might be possible that Christ, considered as a human being, only appeared to have His various potencies actualized. It might not seem that way to us, but a more intelligent, immaterial being could figure it out.[2]

This strikes me as even more problematic for even more reasons. First, it seems to do terrible violence to the assumedly profound meaning of Christ's life, death, and revival. If we can watch our Savior die before our very eyes—see the nails driven into His flesh, watch Him bleed, hear Him cry, "My God, my God, why have You forsaken me," feel the earth shaking as He passes, and then watch Him rise triumphantly from the empty tomb three days later—if we can watch all that, and subsequently say "Christ did not *really* undergo any changes," then what was the point of it all? How would it be any indication of God's love and empathy for us, or a genuine victory over sin? For Christianity to have any merit, the story of Christ must be real—it would be powerless if Christ was merely pretending or acting out all of His experiences, if He did not genuinely suffer with us. Indeed, as I said earlier in this chapter with regard to similar claims, most Christians, Catholic and Protestant alike, would consider it blasphemous to say Christ did not really suffer, die, and rise. But to say it was all merely an illusion seems dangerously

---

[1] Edward Feser, "Trinity Sunday," *Edward Feser* (blog), June 7, 2009, last accessed on July 5, 2020, http://edwardfeser.blogspot.com/2009/06/trinity-sunday.html
[2] I should make here two small clarifications. First, 'mysterianism,' as Feser notes, was originally coined as a defense of naturalism, but as he also says in "Trinity Sunday," it (supposedly) works as a defense of trinitarianism, so I ascribe this belief to him. Secondly, as implied, in the original blog post Feser is discussing the Trinity as a whole rather than Christ specifically. However, I thought it was very likely he would have deployed mysterianism to account for the apparent incompatibility of an unchanging, immaterial God Incarnating as a changing, material man.

close to such blasphemy, even if that illusion was necessitated by the limitations of our minds.

A second important consideration is that mysterianism, broadly interpreted, is actually an extremely poor defense of the Trinity—or any seemingly outlandish religious doctrine, really. In "Theology and the analytic posteriori," Feser tells us that not all analytic a priori (as you'll recall from chapter 1, analytic statements are deductive and a priori statements can be known through pure reasoning rather than empirical investigation) can actually be known a priori, and must be demonstrated by experience, whether through teaching or something else. [1] For instance, we can know that "all bachelors are unmarried" without ever having met a bachelor just from the definition of "bachelor," making it an analytic a priori statement. However, we would first have to know that definition, and we're not born with the knowledge—we'd have to look it up in a dictionary or have someone tell us, and that's an empirical, or a posteriori, way of gaining knowledge.

Now, Feser argues that the Trinity is also an analytic a priori proposition, and

> If we had a perfect grasp of the divine essence, we would see that the claim that God is three Persons in one divine nature is as necessary and self-evident as "All bachelors are unmarried." But in fact our grasp is so imperfect that we cannot arrive at knowledge of this claim even through indirect natural means, through philosophical arguments, as we can with "God exists." We need supernatural assistance. This assistance comes via a divine revelation backed by miracles, and in particular via the teaching of Christ. And that is something we know about only *a posteriori*.[2]

---

[1] Edward Feser, "Theology and the Analytic a Posteriori," *Edward Feser* (blog), June 10, 2020, last accessed on June 20, 2020, http://edwardfeser.blogspot.com/2020/06/theology-and-analytic-posteriori.html

[2] Ibid.

It is safe to assume Feser would apply this reasoning to other apparently contradictory elements of his confession, such as an immaterial, immutable God becoming a material, mutable man. Unfortunately, it seems to me that Feser's mysterianism completely hamstrings his apologetics, primarily because of the severe disanalogy between the propositions "God is Three Persons in One" or "Jesus was both God and Man" and "All bachelors are unmarried." In the latter case, even if we must empirically determine the definitions of "unmarried" and "bachelor" by looking at a dictionary with our own eyes, *once we have* those definitions it is obvious the proposition is "necessary and self-evident." But even if we understand the definitions of "One" and "Trinity," there is no way we can come to the conclusion that $1 = 3$, and if we know that God absolutely cannot change, we cannot make sense of Him moving from place to place or dying and rising.

Thus, Feser would fall back to mysterianism and claim that our material-brain-limited minds are incapable of comprehending how $1 = 3$ in God or how Pure Act could stroll from Galilee to Gethsemane, and we have to take it on faith. But what justifies faith? "Revelation backed by miracles." But how do we know those miracles were actual miracles as opposed to illusions? We only have *a posteriori* historical evidence, and for the reasons I have given in the preceding sections, there is *no way* to bridge the gap between that and analytic a priori propositions. Feser's argument would require some sort of "divine revelation" espousing the proposition that "Jews living 2000 years ago would never lie or be mistaken, and demons and/or aliens could never trick such people either." Aside from the fact that we obviously don't have such a "revelation," even if we did, how could we tell *that* revelation would be true? A posteriori historical evidence...which would require yet another revelation to assure its verity. In other words, Feser's attempt to bridge the gulf between synthetic a posteriori evidence and analytic a priori propositions via "divine revelation" simply leads us into an endless regress with no conclusion.

This illustrates another problem with mysterianism: It seems tailor-made for hucksters and conmen to exploit the rest of us. What might Parmenides, the silly fellow who thought change was impossible, think of all this? If Feser wants to say that all the change Christ experienced was merely an illusion, why wouldn't Parmenides say that all the change we seemingly see all around us is also an illusion? The charge of retorsion is of little use here. Feser says that we must accept change at least with regard to the mind, since going through the process of evaluating an argument is itself a sort of change. But how could a philosopher be certain his perception of his own mind is accurate? Perhaps the "changes" involved in evaluating an argument and then coming to a conclusion are illusory, merely reflections of an underlying entity that did not actually change at all. If we believe our own minds are changing, that is only an illustration of their limitations, just as it is only a demonstration of their limitations that we can believe the God-man changed when He died and subsequently rose.

Another way to demonstrate this would be to quote directly from Feser's most recent book, *Aristotle's Revenge*. According to Feser, Parmenides "must show that he is *not* implicitly committed to the premise [i.e, that the very act of claiming change is illusory is itself an example of genuine change]. That is to say, [Parmenides] needs to give some account of how it is possible for him to so much as entertain his skepticism [of change] given that change does not exist."[1] Well, mysterianism provides Parmenides just such an account. He could say, "I know the very act of making an argument against change seems to imply that argument is wrong, but it only *seems* to imply that, and doesn't really do so. We just can't figure out how because our minds are just too limited. But Reason tells us change is impossible, so disregard whatever I seem to be implying right now and embrace the mystery." This doesn't seem terribly different from a Christian saying, "I know the very act of dying and then coming back from the dead implies that Christ

---

[1] *Aristotle's* Revenge, 87. The brackets are mine, to clarify precisely what and who Feser is talking about.

underwent change and therefore could not be the Unchanging Changer, but it only *seems* to imply that, and doesn't really do so. Our minds are just too limited to figure out how someone could die and come back to life without changing, but Faith tells us it happened, so just disregard the implications of the Resurrection and embrace the mystery."

That might be a bit too much to swallow, even for people unsympathetic to Feser. All right, so maybe mysterianism can't save Parmenides. But it can easily rescue many other religious beliefs, most notably one Feser said Aristotle crushed: Polytheism. Take, for instance, the Mormon sect. Feser has written that they are actually polytheistic, not truly monotheistic as Christians are supposed to be. Apparently (according to Feser, quoting an article from the priest Luis Ladera), Mormons believe that God the Father is from another planet who sired Jesus Christ through a union with the Heavenly Mother, another alien. Since these are apparently separate beings and obviously not Single, Indivisible, and Simple Existence Itself, the Mormons must worship at best little-g gods, and not the actual Sustainer of the Universe Himself.[1] But, as you will recall, the exact same could be said of Jesus Christ. Since Christ lived, died, walked around, and changed, He could not have been completely unchangeable Pure Act. So Feser must fall back to mysterianism and claim that Jesus really wasn't changing, we just aren't capable of comprehending what truly happened back in Galilee. But then Mormons could do the *exact same thing*. An anti-Catholic Mormon apologist might say this:

---

[1] Edward Feser, "Christians, Muslims, and the Reference of God," *Edward Feser* (blog), December 28, 2015, last accessed July 5, 2020, http://edwardfeser.blogspot.com/2015/12/christians-muslims-and-reference-of-god.html . I should note, however, that the Mormons have also heard these arguments before and maintain they are true Christian monotheists. See the article "Mormons, Polytheism, and the Nicene Creed," *Fairmormon,* last accessed July 5, 2020,
https://www.fairmormon.org/answers/Mormonism_and_the_nature_of_God/Polytheism#Question:_Are_Mormons_polytheists_because_they_don.27t_accept_the_Nicene_Creed.3F

"If the Book of Mormon says God is actually some alien from planet Z, and a female alien from the same planet, and that Jesus Christ was literally their son sent into Mary's womb, that doesn't mean the Church of Latter-Day Saints is wrong. It simply means our limited human intellects are too pathetic and puny to understand how Pure Act can simultaneously be all these things at once."

Mormons do have the attested miracle of Jesus Christ *and* the miracles associated with Joseph Smith (the founder of Mormonism[1]) to back up their religious claims, and according to Feser himself, historically attested miracles are proof of a divine seal of approval. So, if Mormonism has God's seal of approval, it must be true. If Mormon doctrine seems to contradict God's status as a singular Being, Pure Actuality, the flaw is not in the doctrine but in our inability to truly comprehend it. Mischievous Mormons could easily marshal the doctrine of the Hypostatic Union to their defense: Perhaps the Divine Essence is unified with the Essences of all the space aliens in the Mormon pantheon, despite their seeming incompatibility with it, the same way it is unified with the Essence of Man in Christ, despite how the Essence of Humanity entails being changeable, material, and so on. Strange as it may sound, God the Father, the Heavenly Mother, the Holy Spirit, and Jesus Christ really are Pure Act, and we simply have to take it on faith that they are the same Being.

Getting shown up by the Mormons would be embarrassing enough, but even worse for Feser, genuine old-school *pagans* could use the same, or a very similar argument the Mormons did. A Hellenic Greek could say, "Zeus, Athena, and the rest of the Greek pantheon really are just expressions of Aristotle's singular God, and they only appear to differ in personalities, gender, and other characteristics because puny

---

[1] For instance, the miracle of Joseph Smith's supposed translation of the golden tablets and his vision of the angel Moroni. See W. Paul Reeve and Ardis E. Parshall, eds., *Mormonism: A Historical Encyclopedia* (ABC-CLIO, 2010), 81, 191.

human minds cannot truly comprehend the true nature of the divine."[1] And even if that defense might be too strained for Feser, the Aristotelian allowance for immaterial intellects provides them with yet another. The pagans could concede that the gods of their pantheon were not different aspects of the singular God, but that they still existed as immaterial intellects superior to humanity in knowledge and power. In other words, Zeus, Athena, and all the rest would occupy a similar metaphysical position as angels in Catholic theology. Indeed, according to the classicist Richard Bodeus, this is actually what Aristotle did. Bodeus argues that Aristotle was less of a monotheist than Feser makes him out to be, and that the Stagirite believed in the Greek gods, who he saw as benevolent "immortals" influencing Greek society.[2] Various other pagans, such as Norse believers in Odin and Thor, could make similar arguments. Considering the extent to which Feser relies on Aristotle to make an open-and-shut case for monotheism and Christianity, the "great" philosopher's openness to polytheism should make him more than a little worried.

 The only way Feser could wriggle out of the Mormon or the pagan's grip would be to dispute the truthfulness of Joseph Smith's accounts, or those of the Greeks. But that would be a historical argument, not a metaphysical one, and as I have shown above, history is a trickier business than metaphysics. If Feser wishes to keep his mysterian doctrine, he pays dearly for it, and even if we were to reject it, he would still pay an equally high price for clinging to Aristotelianism—

---

[1] "Pure Act" in this case might be something like Oceanus, a god who gave birth to Zeus and Hera and supposedly held up the entire world, like Feser says God is supposed to conjoin Essence and existence. Or perhaps "Chaos," the universal void from which all things come, yet which has always existed independent of anything else.

[2] Richard Bodeus and Jan Garret, trans., *Aristotle and the Theology of Living Immortals* (State University of New York Press, 1992). I am indebted to Reddit user /u/HippeHoppe for directing me towards the intersection of Aristotelianism and Hellenism.

at least from the standpoint of arguing for the Christian God above all others.

2.5: Locke was right!

Feser's arguments for Christianity are more than merely philosophically significant. They are part of his larger project, social conservatism, which means (in his view) they imply society and politics should be organized in certain ways and not others. If those arguments are incorrect, and I think I've proved above they just might be, Feser's attempts to counter what he sees as the ills of modern, pluralistic liberal society will be that much weaker. We can catch a clear glimpse of Feser's vulnerabilities if we take a close look at his criticisms of John Locke.

John Locke was an 17th-century British philosopher whose arguments for individual liberty and religious toleration provided the foundation for the political culture most of us living in Western countries take for granted today.[1] As you might surmise, Feser isn't a big fan of the "religious toleration" bit. I'm not saying he's one of those "Deus Vult" lunatics, or that he thinks "heretics" ought to be burned at the stake or anything similar. As evinced above, he apparently respects Protestants and Jews like William Lane Craig and Maimonides, so he at least puts in an effort to keep from looking too much like a would-be Torquemada. But Feser does believe Locke made critically weak philosophical arguments for religious toleration, even if he might accept them for practical reasons.

According to Feser's book on Locke (which is also its title), Locke was a Protestant Christian, but he was not entirely, unshakably certain Christianity was true. He believed human beings "can know that God exists, but not much more than that; so government should not tolerate atheism, but it should tolerate all sorts of other and more specific disagreements over religious doctrine. Here again, Locke would be taking a position that is far from neutral, and one that favors

---

[1] Edward Feser, *Locke* (Oneworld Publications, 2007), 1-4.

Protestantism over Catholicism, the latter of which makes fairly strong claims about what is knowable in matters of religion."[1]

Those "fairly strong claims" would be what we have discussed above: The Aristotelian argument for change entails we can know God exists with absolute certainty, therefore the evidence for Christ's miracles is overwhelming, therefore Christianity (specifically Catholicism) is true. But as we have also discussed above, Aristotelian metaphysics necessarily entail none of Feser's conclusions (and by extension those of the Catholic Church), and in fact undermine several of them. Protestants, Muslims, Jews, and even pagans can use Aristotle's metaphysics to shore up their own religious positions. Locke's "epistemological modesty"[2] with regard to religion is thus rather well-founded. Thomists like Feser consequently have little right to demand any given government, or society as a whole, support Catholicism. Since metaphysical arguments cannot objectively and irrefutably prove Catholicism to be true, it is quite reasonable for secularism to be the reigning principle of any government, treating all religions neutrally rather than showing favoritism to any one of them.

We can base this conclusion quite firmly and securely on not just the study of history and political science but the *philosophical* considerations explored throughout this chapter. As we have discussed, neither Aristotelian metaphysics nor "the verified miracle of the Resurrection" can tell us which of the very many Christian denominations is the right one. Then we reviewed the difference between logical deduction and induction, and discovered that the historicity of any given miracle relies on historical induction rather than

---

[1] Ibid., 157-159. Locke, of course, makes many other arguments and Feser attempts to rebut them, but most of that deals with the practical methodology of religious toleration and not the metaphysics which are the subject of the present discussion. Interested readers are directed towards Karl Popper's famous essay, *The Open Society and Its Enemies* (Princeton University Press, 2013), particularly the "paradox of tolerance" mentioned in the endnotes of page 581.
[2] *TLS*, 177.

deduction, meaning that even a deductive Aristotelian proof for God cannot prove the truth of Christianity or any other religion (monotheistic or otherwise, as it happens), and in fact makes Christianity less likely to be true. Thus, we end up on John Locke's side rather than Edward Feser's: Since philosophical argument alone can't tell us much about the truth of any given religion, it would probably be best to tolerate all of them, at least as long as they don't mandate flying planes into buildings or human sacrifice or whatnot.

Disappointing for Feser, surely, but not the end of the world for him. In light of this understanding, Catholics might be obligated to tolerate Protestants, Muslims, Jews, and pagans (and even atheists, for reasons we'll get into in chapter 7), but all those groups are obligated to tolerate Catholics as well. Nothing in this chapter entails that Catholicism *must* be false, only that it might *possibly* be. I suppose that would limit the force of Locke's revenge—he was, shall we say, not the biggest fan of Catholicism.[1] Even so, the fact that we moderns are philosophically obligated to be even more tolerant than our predecessors does not really seem to make the doctrine of religious tolerance incoherent or self-defeating. As Feser himself has admitted, no philosopher, even a "great" one, fully works out the implications of his philosophy, and it is often left to his successors to correct his mistakes.[2] Thus, even as his bid for religious supremacy has been foiled, Feser can rest easy knowing that his own faith is safe from similar predations, and its defenders cannot easily be accused of hypocrisy or inconsistency.

Far, far more distressing for Feser would be the revelation that natural-law Thomism can provide no better answers in the realm of

---

[1] Feser, *Locke,* 152-154. In at least some of his writing Locke argued the subversive nature of Catholicism rendered it an intolerable threat. However, Feser does note that later in life, Locke at least implied it might be practical to tolerate certain Catholic beliefs as well, so long as foreign actors such as the Pope did not try to interfere in another country's governance.

[2] *SM,* 7-8.

morality than religion. One of the supposed benefits of this philosophy, according to Feser, is that (thanks to Thomism's Aristotelian foundations) it can provide reasonable moral guidance even in the absence of any particular religion. You don't have to be Christian or Muslim or any other religion to figure out that non-procreative sexual activity is wrong, for instance. As Feser tells us, if the final cause of our sexual faculties is procreation, it is objectively immoral to "frustrate" their purpose, and you can arrive at this conclusion without even looking at a holy book—logic alone will do the trick. Less pruriently, Feser also claims that only the Aristotelian tradition can provide an objective basis on which to condemn things like racial chattel slavery or mass genocide: Only if human beings have a certain final cause as rational animals can any of those evils be condemned as objectively frustrating that cause. As we will see, however, absolutely none of this is true. The "classical tradition," when examined closely, cannot coherently condemn all forms of non-procreative sexual activity, and could even justify abortion under some circumstances. And an examination of the historical record will see that tradition *justifying* terrible crimes like slavery and genocide, not preventing them.

Chapter 3: Contraceptive Causality

How could one justify traditional Christian sexual morality if one cannot be entirely certain Christianity is true? Skip back to Chapter 1 for more details, but a quick recap: Aristotelian metaphysics tells us that everything we see in the world has certain regularities, or final causes. For instance, a match regularly produces flame when struck, rather than lilacs or ice or any other random thing, and the only explanation for this (so Aristotle and Feser would say) is that matches are "directed towards" producing flame. Or, in other words, the production of flame is a match's "final cause:" the reason for its existing, its proper function, the purpose for which it was made (in the Acme match factory or wherever). And according to Feser, any match that failed to fulfill that function or purpose would be a "bad" match. After all, wouldn't it be natural for us to call a match that failed to catch, or produced only a small flame, bad or defective in some way? By the same token, a match that caught easily and produced a nice warm flame—that is to say, fulfilled its function efficiently and well—would be a "good" or even a "perfect" match. There is supposedly nothing subjective or vague about these value judgements, they are simply objective statements of fact.[1]

Since everything has a final cause and a corresponding "objective" standard of goodness and badness, living creatures are in that sense no different than matches. Where they differ, according to the natural law tradition to which Feser belongs and Aristotle begun, is that they have a multiplicity of "functions," so to speak, and can objectively be called "good" and "bad" depending on how they carry out those functions overall. Feser's favorite example is that of a squirrel. A squirrel is the sort of creature whose final causes include scampering up trees, avoiding predators, burying nuts, and being four-legged and bushy tailed (these last characteristics are more properly called part of its Form, but Form

---

[1] *TLS,* 238, 290, 43, 139, *AQ,* 174-178.

and Function are closely related in Feser's view anyways). We would naturally call a squirrel who deftly climbed trees and buried nuts a "good" or "healthy" squirrel, and one who had lost its legs or tail, or "ate toothpaste" or just "lay spread-eagled on the freeway" an "unhealthy" or "bad" one, and these would simply be objective assessments.[1] Notice, too, that each individual characteristic given here can be "good" or "bad" on its own—the respective goodness or badness of one body part does not necessarily affect the others. For instance, the Aristotelian might look at a squirrel that had four healthy feet but ate toothpaste rather than nuts and say, "this squirrel's locomotive faculties in particular are 'good,' since its four healthy feet fulfill the function of moving it up trees, but his digestive faculties in particular are 'bad,' because by consuming toothpaste rather than nuts they contravene (or "frustrate," to use Feser's preferred term) their function of nourishing the squirrel."[2]

Human beings are no exception to this. While (in the Aristotelian view) we are "rational animals," every part of our physical bodies has its own function (final cause) and thus its own standards of goodness or badness. Our legs are good or bad to the extent they allow us to walk, our digestive systems are good or bad to the extent they

---

[1] *TLS,* 36-40, 137-142.

[2] Also notice that there seems to be some slippage in the use of the term "final causality." At first, Feser uses it to describe physical phenomenon that are both deterministic *and* neutral with regard to any sort of well-being, since they involve inanimate objects. A match will *invariably* produce fire if struck given the proper physical conditions—if it does not, it is because of specific forces or materials acting on it, such as being wet, or struck in space where there's no oxygen to burn. Any failure to do so is only "bad" from *our* perspective, because the match itself doesn't care about fulfilling a final cause of any sort, and indeed its failure to do so is actually a "regularity" in itself. Soon after, Feser looks at animals and applies the same reasoning to them, despite their behavior and health being merely probabilistic rather than completely reliable, and being *consequentially* significant to them rather than merely neutral. As far as I've been able to tell, Feser never addresses this inconsistency at length in *any* of his books or blog entries, so I doubt it's a problem caused only by hasty summary. I will focus a great deal on it in Chapter 5.

nourish us, and so on. As it happens, the sex organs of human beings are no exception. Their final cause is "procreation," as Feser puts it. And while he admits they also have other functions (such as urination for the penis), *in reference to sex*, the standard by which they should be judged is procreation. For example, a man who could still urinate with his penis but could not impregnate a woman with it (due to sterility, injury to his sperm ducts, or whatever) would have a "good" excretory system but a defective or "bad" reproductive system, since in the former sense the penis fulfills its final cause, but in reference to the latter it does not. Genetic defect or injury has "frustrated" its proper function.[1]

So now we understand that certain sorts of maladies can make our sexual faculties "bad" in a thin sense. But what makes homosexual behavior, extramarital sex, contraceptive sex, and abortion *morally* bad? After all, if a man were sterile or suffered an injury that rendered him so, we would consider him unfortunate, but we would not say he did anything wrong. By the same token, a woman who suffered a miscarriage would earn our sympathy rather than scorn. How do we go from "having a damaged reproductive system is bad" to "non-procreative sex and abortion are morally wrong?" The answer lies in the difference between states *involuntarily inflicted* upon someone and *rationally chosen activities*. As mentioned earlier and touched upon in Chapter 1, Aristotelians believe humans are rational animals, meaning we can understand Forms and reason concerning them. The purpose of doing that (i.e., our final cause) is ultimately to understand and act on the Form of the Good.

Thomists believe *that* Form is the Christian God, but as described in the last chapter, there's no way of knowing whether or not the story of Christ was real. Thus, when it comes to ethics, the Thomist might retreat to secular, objective, Aristotelian natural law, and say that understanding and acting on the Form of the Good entails figuring out what is good (i.e., what fulfills the final cause) for each individual thing,

---

[1] *TLS*, 141-151, *AQ*, 179-188.

such as our individual body parts. This means ensuring our legs are used to walk, our digestive system used to nourish us, and, of course, our reproductive organs used to reproduce. These are actions we choose using our rational faculties (our minds), and since our minds are how we engage our "highest" final cause, that makes freely choosing to fulfill the final causes of our lower functions morally good instead of good in a thinner sense. But the opposite also obtains. Using condoms, or masturbating, or having gay sex, or getting abortions, all turn our procreative faculties "non-procreative." Thus, they are instances of the rational mind choosing what is "objectively" bad (frustrating the function of its own body parts), which makes such actions moral failings rather than mere misfortunes, since injury and disease (such as sterility in men or an unintended miscarriage) are inflicted by chance rather than chosen by rational actors.[1]

There's a bit more to it, given how humans specifically reproduce. Since our babies are so helpless, they need the presence of both a mother and a father to survive. This indicates (according to Feser) that the final cause of our reproductive organs is not just procreation but procreation *within a male-female pair bond*.[2] This obviously rules out masturbation, homosexual behavior and contraception, and in fact makes them *gravely* immoral rather than just somewhat immoral. Unlike, say, misuse of our digestive systems or legs, reproduction is how new humans are formed and families are the basis of society, so any misuse of any faculty relating to them harms society as a whole. Abortion is even worse, because in addition to "frustrating" a woman's reproductive faculties, the destruction of an embryo or fetus counts as

---

[1] Ibid.

[2] In this view, the only reason sex is even pleasurable at all—the "final cause" of its fun, you could say—is to A: get people to make more babies, and B: bond one man and one woman—Feser's term for the latter function is "unitive;" in his words, "the *procreative* end of sex points, in human beings, given their rational nature, to a *unitive* end." See *NSE*, 394.

the destruction of an actual human being (not just a potential one), i.e., murder.[1]

We will explore what Feser means by "actual human" at the end of this chapter, but for now, suffice it to say that I believe these ethical conclusions are unwarranted, *even if one accepts their metaphysical underpinnings*. Here, I will not make the slightest attempt to "deny the reality" of final causation.[2] Instead, I will argue that the final causes of our reproductive organs are not what Feser says they are, and there are many sensible estimations of their functions that render traditional natural law sexual ethics incoherent, inconsistent, or both. I will begin by demonstrating that Feser's definition of the phrases "intending to actively frustrate" and "contrary to an entity's final cause" severely vitiates any sanction upon non-procreative sex. I will then show how the existence of wet dreams illustrates that male sexuality is not *solely* procreative in its purpose (indicating masturbation and contraceptive sex might be okay after all). I build on this analysis to prove that "basic facts" about male and female reproduction "point towards" polygamy, not monogamy, and also imply that abortion and even infanticide are morally licit under some circumstances (a position with which *Aristotle himself* would agree). With regard to male homosexuality, I argue it is plausible that gay men instantiate a separate Form and thus possess a different (sexual) final cause than straight men, meaning "sodomy" is not necessarily a contravention of the purpose of their sexual faculties. We can then end the chapter with the conclusion that natural law provides an unsatisfactory foundation for the traditional sexual morality it is supposed to reify, which also points to its weakness as a general ethical framework.

3.1: Innocuous Intentions

One can't accuse Feser of being particularly humble—he thinks the conclusions he's drawn with regard to sexuality are "blindingly

---

[1] *AQ*, 185, 138-142.
[2] *TLS*, 265.

obvious."[1] Needless to say, the many, many critics of natural law would beg to differ. One of their most common objections is this: If using an organ or bodily faculty for some other purpose than its final cause or function is wrong, then a whole host of innocuous activities are wrong. Wouldn't chewing gum count as frustrating our gustatory or digestive faculties, since gum is not nourishing? Wouldn't using our hands to walk frustrate their "intended" function of manipulating objects? Wouldn't using earplugs frustrate the function of our sense of hearing? Wouldn't using deodorant, or holding one's breath, or using a lactation machine "frustrate" the intents behind those ongoing functions? No, no, no, and no, exclaims Feser. In his essay, "In Defense of the Perverted Faculty Argument," we can find several reasons why these objections do not hold.[2] Feser explains that his favored Aristotelianism

> ...does not entail that a faculty F cannot have more than one natural end, and neither does it entail that it cannot be good for A to use F for an end other than E. For 'different from E' and 'other than E' do not entail 'contrary to E.' Nor does it entail that we have to use F at all... The premise says only that if A is actually going to use F, then even if he uses it for some reason other than E, it cannot be good for him to use it for the sake of actively frustrating the realization of E.[3]

Thus, chewing gum does not "actively frustrate" the ends of our digestive faculties, because merely chewing it doesn't do any lasting harm to our ability to nourish ourselves (assuming we spit it out before eating, of course). Wearing earplugs would be permitted because even if they diminish our hearing in particular, they protect it from being damaged by loud noises or allow us to sleep at night. This actually *facilitates* the final cause of this faculty in the long run, since it would be an even graver, more obvious "frustration" if one were to go deaf due to excessive noise or loss of sleep. Hands are "general-purpose" tools, so using them to walk would not frustrate their final cause, which is

---

[1] *TLS,* 143-144.
[2] Edward Feser, "In Defense of the Perverted Faculty Argument" *NSE,* 406-407.
[3] *NSE,* 399, 406.

multifaceted. And finally, in the case of perspiration and lactation, "there are crucial differences between...*an individual deliberate act* of using a bodily faculty and...an *ongoing and involuntary physical process.*" Since we sweat or generate milk in a "general," ongoing sense, individual and temporary actions such as breast pumping do not frustrate their function. However, since sex is a "specific, individual event," every ejaculation must have at least the possibility of ending in procreation. Since the intent of contraception is to reduce that possibility, and since homosexual sex and masturbation do not allow it at all, knowingly undertaking those activities is wrong.[1]

One problem with Feser's argument here, which other critics have noted, is that natural law would seem to condemn heterosexual sex between infertile people, even within marriage, or even in a fertile couple when the woman is pregnant! Feser addresses this as well, saying "[f]oreseeing that a certain sexual act will in fact not result in conception is not the same thing as *actively altering* the relevant organs [i.e., attaching a condom or diaphragm to one of them] or the nature of the act [same-sex intercourse, masturbation, bestiality, etc.] in a way that would make it impossible for them to lead to conception even if they were in good working order."[2] That would seem to wrap things up nicely for the natural law theorist, but the perceptive reader can see it raises even more problems in the attempt of solving one.

Is "actively altering" the sex act always inherently wrong? There seem to be several scenarios when most people would say it is morally licit. Imagine a loving heterosexual married couple where one partner, through no fault of his or her own, has contracted a venereal disease. Perhaps, through great misfortune and shockingly lax procedure, one of them received a tainted blood transfusion, or an untrained nurse at a hospital took a blood sample with a re-used needle rather than a new, sterile one. Afterwards, the afflicted partner insists they use condoms whenever they have relations, in order to keep the disease from infecting

---

[1] Ibid., 406-407.
[2] Ibid., 400.

the other. This would obviously also prevent conceiving any children, but since the disease would then pass on to the couple's offspring, public health demands their nest remains empty. Under the circumstances, then, it would be a hard sell to condemn the couple for using at least one form of contraception, if no others.

Feser might argue that the pair would be morally obligated to remain celibate until the infected partner has been cured, or indefinitely if the disease is non-curable. But this would strike most as both draconian and impractical. If such a couple would be denied the joys of parenthood due to an unfortunate incident they could not foresee nor be blamed for, it seems manifestly unjust to compound their misfortunes by forbidding them to have sex, especially when a simple technological solution would allow them that small pleasure. More likely Feser would allow them an exception based on their intent. They may be "actively altering their relevant organs" with a condom, but since their intent was to protect the healthy partner rather than "frustrate the function" of the act per se, the endeavor wouldn't be morally wrong.

Unhappily for Feser, this would seem to lessen, if not entirely negate, the moral wrongness of other kinds of non-procreative sex. When a man masturbates, he is not necessarily consciously intending to "frustrate" the end of his sexual faculties. He might be overcome with lust, desperately lonely, or just looking for a little fun, but those sorts of direct intentions would seem to be morally neutral rather than good *or* bad, using Feser's definitions of good and bad as facilitating or frustrating a bodily function. The same applies to homosexual behavior. Two men having sex might be lustful, looking for fun, or looking to bond, but not necessarily *consciously intending* to "frustrate" the function of their faculties, even if they would be able to "foresee their behavior would not lead to conception." If it is licit for a couple to "actively alter the sex act/relevant organs" if their intentions are praiseworthy, it ought to be licit for a couple to do the same if their intentions are merely neutral. The only time non-procreative sex would be truly "bad" in Feser's sense would be if it were undertaken *for the explicit purpose* of contraception—a man using a condom or having same-sex intercourse for no other purpose than to prove he could, or a man masturbating even when given the opportunity for sex with a willing and eager partner. Those are apparently the only situations which fulfill Feser's criteria for moral wrongness, "[using one's sexual faculties] for the sake of *actively frustrating* the realization of [their ends]."[1] Given the rarity of such situations, a blanket condemnation of non-procreative sex in general seems unsustainable.

Or does it? Feser believes that "[a]n act can in fact actively frustrate the end whether or not one has such frustration consciously in view, just as an act can in fact be free of such active frustration whether or not avoiding such frustration is consciously in view."[2] But even with this consideration, Feser's argument remains unconvincing. First off, it would seem to disregard the importance of intent in moral action. It is fairly uncontroversial that an act can be morally better or worse due to its intention. If you run a man over with your car because you hate him, you've obviously committed an evil act, but if you run him over accidentally, you're less culpable, and if you run him over because he himself is doing evil (carrying out a mass shooting, say), you have actually done good. If we can agree on that, we can agree that gays and lonely straights are not committing quite as much evil as Feser might have it, so long as their intents are mere pleasure rather than spitefully frustrating final causality for the sake of it.

More importantly, though, Feser's views on sexual stimulation imply the importance of intent in sex, if only on practical grounds. He spends some time defending natural law theory against charges of prudishness, saying, "as long as it does not result in premature ejaculation, manual and oral stimulation of the genitals does not involve

---

[1] *NSE*, 399.
[2] Edward Feser, "Foundations of Sexual Morality," *Edward Feser*, February 7, 2017, comment at February 10, 2017, 9:40 AM, last accessed July 5, 2020, http://edwardfeser.blogspot.com/2017/02/foundations-of-sexual-morality.html

using them in a way that is *contrary to* their natural function."[1] Not to put too fine a point on it, but this is easier said than done. Passionate lovers are not known for fastidiously modulating the intensity of their foreplay to make absolutely certain the lucky man's payload is not launched a millisecond too soon. Feser would have to forbid such shenanigans entirely if he really believed non-copulatory ejaculations were a very grave moral failing. If not, he would have to accept that unfortunate premature ejaculations in such a context would be morally acceptable (if not laudable) because they were unintended accidents caused by the throes of passion. But that would simply be excusing a supposedly immoral act by virtue of the innocent intentions of the actors, which would also condone masturbation and same-sex intercourse.

There is one other argument concerning the general psychology involving sex that deserves a bit of attention. A pair of authors Feser cites in his essay, Gerard Bradley and Robert George, have come up with a supporting argument for Feser's thesis on the particular moral import of sex. They say:

> Chewing gum, rocking in a chair, and taking a walk are examples of "innocent pleasures." The pleasure they provide is effortlessly integrated with larger projects (such as concentrated thinking), and for most people these activities present no hazard to any aspect of the person's well-being. (Chewing or smoking tobacco, by contrast, presents a different sort of case, not because these activities are disintegrative, but rather because they may imperil physical health.) The important point is that in the activity of chewing gum, no existential separation of the bodily self and the consciously experiencing self is typically effected [sic]. In that activity, the body is not typically commandeered into the service of a project that is fully and accurately

---

[1] Ibid., 401.

described (and, thus, morally specified) as producing pleasure, whether as an end in itself or as means to other ends.[1]

For these two, it seems that sex is particularly problematic because it involves a sort of "high," a disassociation of mind and body (you literally forget about everything else when having sex). Yet many leisure activities also involve this disassociation. If you go to a theme park, for instance, you'll achieve such a "disassociative high" when riding a roller coaster, since the sheer speed and sensation of the ride prevents you from thinking about anything else. If you watch a very scary horror movie, you are "disconnected" from your rationality because you will be so absorbed in the show that you think the monster is actually in the theater with you (which is why you jump when something frightening happens even though you "rationally" know nothing on screen is real). If sex is metaphysically significant because it disassociates you from your reason, these things would have to be equally significant. But I doubt George or Bradley or indeed Feser would say so.

3.2: Contrary and Other Than

All this nitpicking over intentions and mental states is bad enough, but the shortcomings of natural law theory can be even more clearly seen in a close examination of Feser's terms "other than" and "contrary to." Feser offers a longer semi-formal syllogism that summarizes his general argument, and its most important premise is probably this:

> If a faculty F [in this case our sexual Faculties]... by nature exists for the sake of some end E [opposite-sex unity and procreation], then it is metaphysically impossible for it to be good... to use F in a manner **contrary to E**.[2]

---

[1] Bradley, Gerard V. and George, Robert P., "Marriage and the Liberal Imagination" (1995), *Journal Articles*, Paper 878, p. 317, http://scholarship.law.nd.edu/law_faculty_scholarship/878

[2] "The Perverted Faculty Argument" in *NSE*, 403-404. The italics are Feser's, the bold and brackets are my addition for emphasis and clarification. The full premise

However, given Feser's allowance for innocuous activities such as chewing gum and walking on one's hands, he would probably agree with this:

If a faculty F exists for End E, it is *morally neutral to use it in a manner that is merely other than/different from E.*

So now we come to the question: What, precisely, distinguishes "other than" or "different" from "contrary to?" Feser offers some hints in *The Last Superstition*. There, he tells us that holding some carpentry nails in one's teeth would not frustrate the "chewing functions" of one's mouth, but vomiting up food so as not to gain weight *would*.[1] Judging from this example, it seems that Feser thinks using a faculty for the *exact opposite* of its end/final cause/function is what constitutes a moral wrong. Food is made to go *in* the mouth, but vomiting sends it *out. In* and *out* are exact opposites, or antonyms. On the other hand, holding nails in one's mouth has no specifically antagonistic relation to ingestion. In fact, we could say that "holding" is merely an instance of "not-putting-in" or "un-putting-in," while vomiting is more severe—it's "putting-out," which would be *anti*-putting-in, or *opposite*-putting in. This would be what Feser means by "contrary to."

Given what we have now learned, perhaps we could restate this step in Feser's syllogism as such:

If a faculty F (in this case our sexual Faculties) exists for End E (opposite-sex unity leading to procreation), it is wrong to use it in a manner *that is anti-E, or the opposite of E,* but morally neutral to use it in a manner *that is merely not-E, non-E, or un-E.*

With regard to procreation, we would therefore conclude that it is wrong to use our sexual faculties for an anti-procreative purpose, or for

---

mentions "rational agents," but that particular distinction is irrelevant to my critique of the argument.

[1] *TLS,* 148.

the opposite of procreation, while it is licit to use them for a merely non or un-procreative purpose.

What would "anti-procreative" be? The definition of "procreation" is to give or create life. Anti-procreation, the opposite or antonym of procreation, would be destruction—*taking away* life, giving *death*, or actively *killing*.

And when we understand this, it becomes apparent that masturbation, contraceptive sex, and same-sex intercourse *are merely non or not-procreative, rather than anti-procreative (deadly)*. It is obvious that while masturbation and homosexual activity may not result in life, they do not in and of themselves take it away either. And while contraception might *prevent* a new life from being generated, to prevent life from forming is a different thing from actively destroying life—prevention and destruction are not synonyms, which means that prevention is not the antonym, or opposite, of procreation. *Therefore, homosexuality, masturbation, and contraception are, under an Aristotelian ethical framework, morally neutral.* To argue otherwise, Feser would have to establish how those non-procreative acts actually run specifically counter and contrary to the aim of procreation (the generation of new life), rather than simply preventing it (at worst).

Does this mean that *any* kind of sexual activity would be morally licit? Not at all. Sex that results in death or physical harm *would* be death-bringing rather than life-bringing, or in other words "anti-procreative" and thus wrong under the light of both common sense and Aristotelian teleology. Intentionally spreading STDs, or engaging in a great deal of unsafe sex for the sake of spreading disease, would be consciously anti-procreative. Especially violent, brutal sex practices (such as rape, obviously) carried out for the sake of injuring a participant, or which intentionally conclude with the death of a participant, would also obviously be condemned under this interpretation.[1] Contrary to Feser's triumphant tone in much of his writing, then, it seems that there is a middle ground between pure sexual libertinism and a blanket ban on all sexual activity outside of heterosexual marriage. Maintaining this middle ground does not at all necessitate abandoning the Aristotelian framework which Feser claims is indispensable.[2] But the problems Aristotelianism poses to Feser's sexual morality do not stop there.

3.3: The final cause of Fapping

Making things worse for Feser is the dubiousness of several premises on which the natural law argument relies. In particular, his assumption that ejaculation is a specific event, rather than the culmination of an ongoing process, is questionable. The existence of wet dreams—embarrassing as those may be to discuss—would seem to indicate that there is an ongoing, general nature underlying the exercise of male sexual faculties. For many men, if not most, wet dreams are a common occurrence, particularly during puberty but often throughout one's life. The technical term for them is "nocturnal emission," and as you can probably tell from the name, they involve a male climaxing to orgasm and ejaculating while he sleeps, usually while in the throes of a sexually-stimulating dream.[3] Given the prevalence of this phenomenon, it would be quite a challenge for Feser to argue wet dreams are caused by any sort

---

[1] It should be noted that this alternative interpretation of Aristotelian ethics would still condemn bestiality. The practice is often dangerous to either the animal (for small creatures) or the human, so there is no reason we need open ourselves to charges of libertinism from Feser.

[2] It is also worth noting that at least one of Feser's fellow Thomists agrees with me exactly on this point. As John Skalko says (regarding Feser's essay) in *Disordered Actions: A Moral Analysis of Lying and Homosexual Activity* (Editiones Scholasticae, 2019), 261-262, "Feser relies upon an unclear account of *contrary use* and *other than* use, which is either ad hoc or cannot grant him the conclusion he desires." Not that Dr. Skalko's arguments against homosexuality are that much better—we will briefly address them soon.

[3] Dan Brennan, "Wet Dream FAQ," *WebMD*, December 5, 2017, last accessed on July 5, 2020, https://teens.webmd.com/boys/wet-dream-faq#1

of disease or genetic defect. They seem to be a perfectly normal aspect of naturally functioning male sexual faculties. So, what can they tell us about the "final causes" of those faculties?

Apparently, that non-procreative ejaculations do not actually represent any sort of final-cause-frustration, and arguably instantiate the opposite. According to Feser, "[i]f we consider the structure of the sexual organs and the sexual act as a process beginning with arousal and ending in orgasm, it is clear that its biological function, its final cause, is to get semen into the vagina."[1] Additionally, "[m]ale sexual arousal is of its nature *woman-oriented*...realization of the natural end [final cause] requires connecting emotionally as well as physically with *another person*. Masturbatory acts involve the active taking of the process of arousal to a climax that does *not* involve another person, and thus turns it against its natural end."[2] But nocturnal emissions are incapable of getting semen anywhere near a vagina; in almost every relevant respect they are essentially masturbatory. The teenager or man is aroused to the point of climax and ejaculates, but at the behest of whatever phantasms run through his head at night, not any actual partner. Needless to say, the only things he "bonds" with are his bedsheets, and he has a very low chance of successfully procreating in such a situation. The only reason Feser might—*might*—not call wet dreams a horrible moral failing and further proof of the degeneracy of modern society is that they're mostly involuntary, and that the plurality (at least) of men "unfortunate" enough to have them are not "actively" choosing to do so.

Alas, that's not enough to salvage Feser's argument. The true threat of wet dreams to the natural law project lies in what they imply about the *telos* of sexual climax and ejaculation. As mentioned above, nocturnal emissions are so common (and apparently have been

---

[1] *TLS*, 144.
[2] *NSE*, 403. Remember, Feser also believes that this "emotional connection" also requires at least the possibility of procreation to keep from frustrating the final cause of sex, so he is also condemning contraceptive and homosexual sex in this passage.

throughout history[1]) it would be absurd to attribute them to any sort of disease or defect. Yet they involve what clearly is, by Feser's reasoning, a "frustration" of what he considers our "natural ends." The only conclusion we can draw is that Feser has to be incorrect somewhere. Either the "natural end of the human male's sexual faculties" is not purely procreative, *or* that arousal-leading-to-climax events which are non-procreative are not *always* wrong, in the sense that "Mother Nature" (as Feser puts it in *The Last Superstition*)[2] occasionally intends for us to ejaculate even when procreation is impossible under any circumstance.

It is no good for Feser to argue that nocturnal emissions are harmless because they're not actively chosen for (i.e., *unintentional*). I am making a more general, *metaphysical* point about what nocturnal emissions tell us about the *final causality* involved in the human male's "sexual faculties." Many of our basic physical processes are unconscious. Most of the time, we do not really choose to breathe or blink, for instance. However, it is obviously morally licit to take conscious control of both activities and use them even when instinct would not impel us to, such as blinking quickly intentionally, or doing breathing exercises. By the same token, since non-procreative ejaculation will in most cases happen eventually and unconsciously at night, there seems to be nothing invidious about "taking charge" of the process consciously and bringing it to a climax a few hours early rather than during sleep. Any form of non-procreative sex, whether masturbation, "sodomy," or contraceptive sex, would seem to fulfill the same natural function wet dreams apparently do—they just allow the man to have some fun in the process, and also keep him from dirtying his pajamas and bedsheets.

Make no mistake, wet dreams do seem to serve some function, which further undermines the natural law position *even if we accept Aristotelian teleology*. According to the *Handbook of Evolutionary*

---

[1] David Brakke, "The Problematization of Nocturnal Emissions in Early Christian Syria, Egypt, and Gaul," *Journal of Early Christian Studies* (vol. 3, no. 4, 1995), 419-460.
[2] *TLS,* 143.

Psychology, sperm produced in nocturnal emissions (and masturbation) tends to be "older and less competitive, and...noncopulatory ejaculations increase the number of younger, highly-competitive sperm ejaculated at the next copulation."[1] Another possible benefit is that nocturnal emissions stimulate the involved muscles and hydraulic structures, providing them a sort of "workout."[2] Again, as has probably been hammered home to the point of annoyance by now, natural law ethics are based around "functions" and their fulfillment or frustration. If an event fulfills a natural function of the faculties which carry it out, that is by definition good. Since non-procreative ejaculations apparently fulfill legitimate natural functions relating to our sexual faculties (clearing out old sperm and strengthening the relevant muscles and hydraulic structures of the penis), they are in that sense good.

All this, by the by, is enough to mostly demolish the arguments against homosexuality most recently (at the time of this writing) put forward by Jonathan Skalko, whom you may remember from a footnote at the very end of the last section. Skalko, another Thomist like Feser (though much younger in academic terms; *Disordered Actions* is his first book), attempts to defend the fourth premise of one of Aquinas's arguments against homosexuality: "that the natural end of the use of the reproductive members is the generation and education of offspring."[3] I will pass over some of Skalko's stranger asides (such as a paragraph on duck, weevil, and octopus penises) to simply note that wet dreams imply, if not the falsity, the incompleteness of Aquinas's premise. Non-procreative ejaculations, as said above, serve legitimate natural functions that can actually assist in "generation" in the long run (again, getting rid of old sperm and strengthening the penis), so the fact that masturbation and homosexual activity involve non-procreative

---

[1] Todd Shackelford, Aaron Goetz, et. Al, "Human Sperm Competition," in David M. Buss, ed., *The Handbook of Evolutionary Psychology, Volume I: Foundations* (Wiley, 2015), 431.
[2] Paul Martin, *Counting Sheep: The Science and Pleasures of Sleep and Dreams* (Thomas Dunne Books, First Edition, 2004), 137-138.
[3] Skalko, 205-206, 208.

ejaculation does not, under the Thomistic logical framework, necessarily make them contrary to the "end" of the "reproductive members."

Ironically enough, a thought experiment chosen by Feser in 2006 does an excellent job of supporting the above argument. Writing in response to Alexander Pruss on the *Right Reason* blog, Feser placed an emphasis on the "positive steps" taken in non-procreative intercourse, which makes them different from mere infertile sex. As he says,

> …there's also no circumstance forcing anyone, say, to ejaculate within a rectum either, the way circumstances do in fact force infertile couples from conceiving. So the cases are obviously different. You have to take a positive step to ejaculate within a rectum, but not to be infertile. Compare the car example again: A car is "for" driving on streets, not for crashing into the garage door. You have to take a positive step to do either one — either to get the car to fulfill its telos or to get it to act in a way positively contrary to its telos. But you do not have to take a positive step in order to keep it from acting in accordance with its telos when you start the car knowing, say, that it will run out of gas in 30 seconds. It won't fulfill its telos in that case, but not because of any positive step you've taken. It's not analogous to crashing it into the garage.[1]

The examples I have given above rob this thought-experiment of any power, at least in my opinion. First, as thinking of the couple inadvertently contracting an STD demonstrates, it is sometimes morally licit to take a "positive step" (using a condom) that results in contraception. Second, Feser's analogy does not really hold because crashing into a garage door is, in some hopefully obvious ways, the *opposite* of a car's function of driving on a road. Such a crash would damage the vehicle and render it less able to do what it should, while

---

[1] Edward Feser, "Reply to Sullivan on natural law," October 31, 2006, comment from Edward Feser on November 2, 2006, last accessed via the Wayback Machine on July 5, 2020, http://web.archive.org/web/20071014120434/http:/rightreason.ektopos.com/archives/2006/10/reply_to_sulliv.html#comment-29349

there is nothing *inherent* to homosexual, masturbatory, or contraceptive sex to prevent or hinder the "abuser" from having procreative sex in the future. In other words, such practices are merely *non*-procreative as opposed to *anti*-procreative. Third, as I just said not even a page ago, non-procreative ejaculations *do* serve a function of their own, so non-procreative sex can be seen as merely one way of facilitating that function, making it morally permissible. No matter how hard he tries, it seems like Feser will have to find some grounds unrelated to frustrating a legitimate natural function if he wishes to condemn non-procreative sexual behavior.

More fun can be had in the writings of Thomas Aquinas himself. In a brief section in the *Summa* concerning "nocturnal pollution," Aquinas said that unintentional actions during sleep are not sinful in and of themselves, so wet dreams would not be proof of immorality.[1] But given what we have established above on the legitimate function of non-procreative ejaculation, the position Aquinas held on non-procreative sex in general becomes much less tenable. In another section of the *Summa*, Aquinas decreed that "in matters of action it is most grave and shameful to act against things as determined by nature."[2] As it so happens, non-procreative ejaculation is apparently part of the nature of our sexual faculties, not in the general sense of something that happens in nature, but in the sense Aquinas meant of an organ's normal functioning and purpose. Human males are "supposed" to get aroused and ejaculate on a fairly regular basis *regardless of whether or not they will actually procreate*. Thus, "actively" ejaculating in non-procreative contexts is merely exerting a degree of human control on what natural processes will bring forth anyways, not "perverting the fundamental

---

[1] Thomas Aquinas, *Summa Theologiae,* second part of the second part, Article 5, NewAdvent.org, 2017, last accessed on July 5, 2020,
http://www.newadvent.org/summa/3154.htm#article5. Aquinas seemed to believe that nocturnal emissions could be the result of sinful actions, such as eating too much during the day, discussing prurient subjects, or even demonic activity, but these can be dismissed as artifacts of the Angelic Doctor's scientific ignorance.
[2] Ibid., Article 11.

nature" or "frustrating the function" of anything, at least not in any especially significant way, and therefore is not a severe subversion of "nature's" purposes.

Since Aquinas is too dead to defend himself, perhaps Feser might take up the slack by arguing in terms of the general habits or attitudes encouraged by non-procreative sex. Given that nocturnal emissions are associated with dreams, they are less likely to have any lasting impacts on the psychology of the dreamer. After all, don't most people live life relatively unaffected by their dreams (aside from extreme cases, like constant night terrors)? Being visited by buxom lasses in your sleep might mean you wake up with wet sheets, but you probably won't have many strong memories of the experience, meaning your general behavior will not be severely affected. Masturbation, same-sex activity, and contraceptive sex, on the other hand, take place in one's conscious, waking hours and strongly imprint themselves in the memory. This argument is implied in Feser's critique of masturbation and pornography, which he says "can seriously distort one's ability to find sexual fulfillment in an [opposite-sex] spouse."[1]

The key word there is *distort*. As I would say I proved above, non-procreative acts are not inherently bad in and of themselves because non-procreative ejaculations are "supposed" to occur in the natural order of things on occasion. Feser is left with a less binding prudential, consequentialist rationale for the immorality of such activity: Non-procreative sex is bad *so far as* it "distorts" one's sexual orientation (i.e., makes one less likely to pursue procreative sex). But in that case, a blanket Thomistic condemnation of non-procreative sex becomes much less reasonable than a more moderate approach of looking at things on a case-by-case basis, because not everyone reacts to sexual stimuli the same way and not every man or woman will necessarily be overcome by their appetites. If someone gets addicted to masturbation or finds their sexual tastes twisted, that would be bad on both a natural law and

---

[1] *NSE,* 409.

common-sense appraisal. But if a normal man simply masturbates occasionally, suffering no long-term ill-effects and still maintaining healthy relationships with women in his life, it is hard to see how his sexuality has been "distorted" under Feser's definition. If a couple grew "addicted" to condoms and never made love without them, that *might* be unfortunate, but if they simply used contraception occasionally until they were sure they were ready for children, that would certainly represent only a minor "distortion" of the proper state of affairs, if any at all. And, lastly, a man or woman exclusively addicted to homosexual activity might be degraded (in Feser's view, not my own, as we will soon see), but a bisexual who has a few same-sex flings before settling down and producing offspring in a heterosexual marriage has apparently maintained a general orientation that fulfills his or her final causes.

A more apt analogy would be with sports or exercise: Human sexual faculties need to be maintained through regular ejaculations even when they're not being "used," just like a football player or steelworker will need to work out at the gym in order to maintain his muscles, even when they're not being used in his job. But exercising to the point of injury, or going to the gym instead of the plant or the football field, would be a dereliction of duty and thus bad. By the same token, non-procreative sexual activity would be licit if undertaken in moderation, but illicit if taken so far as to injure or permanently twist those faculties.

As an aside, perceptive readers will note here that I've said nothing about lesbians so far. This is because lesbianism is so obviously immune to the natural law critique of homosexuality that it would be unsporting to bash Feser over the head with it. Unlike male orgasms, which are always accompanied by the emission of semen, nothing as obviously "procreative" is associated with the female orgasm, women can climax from a notoriously wide variety of stimulations, and can also orgasm whether or not they get pregnant. Thus, it's rather difficult (to say the least) for guys like Aquinas or Feser to tell gals like Sappho or Ellen DeGeneres that tribadism or oral sex are somehow frustrating the function of anything.

One might argue, as a very last resort, that the fact that gays and lesbians statistically seem to have poorer outcomes on a variety of metrics is proof that homosexuality is necessarily contrary to the *telos* of something, whether one's sexual faculties or human flourishing in general. This is the tack Skalko takes in *Disordered Actions*; he spends several pages quoting studies from various journals of public health to conclude that "homosexual activity seems to be linked with an increase in all sorts of mental disorders and problems."[1] The problem here is that nasty public health statistics can be used to "prove" quite a lot of things. For instance, white men and Native American men are several times more likely to commit suicide than black or Asian men, with middle-aged white men having the highest rates.[2] If Skalko would argue that a greater risk of suicide indicates there is something wrong with homosexuality, the same reasoning would "prove" that there is something wrong with being white or Native American. I somehow doubt middle-aged white guys like Feser and Skalko would enthusiastically endorse that conclusion.

It is also true that the negative outcomes associated with homosexuality and bisexuality could be attributed to the discrimination historically experienced by those demographics (a problem Skalko and Feser are unlikely to solve, as their position would further alienate non-heterosexuals from the rest of society). Skalko might deny this, saying "higher rates of societal acceptance and legalization of same-sex unions haven't led to decreased rates of minority distress."[3] The scholars he cites (such as Mark Regnerus) might have come to that conclusion, but others have not—Danish researchers found that the legalization of gay marriage in Sweden and Denmark was followed by a steep decline in suicide rates.[4] Skalko and Feser would, of course, say that correlation is

---

[1] Skalko, 88-94.
[2] American Foundation for Suicide Prevention, "Suicide Statistics," 2020, last accessed on July 5, 2020, https://afsp.org/about-suicide/suicide-statistics/
[3] Skalko, 92-93.
[4] Rachel Savage, "Suicides fall with gay marriage in Sweden, Denmark as stigma fades," *Reuters*, November 19, 2019, last accessed on July 5, 2020,

not causation, that non-LGBT people are still better off psychologically, and so on, and so forth. An excursion into sociology and epidemiology would be even further beyond the scope of the present work, so I will leave such a debate for another day. I merely wish to drive home the point that Feser and Skalko's condemnations of non-heterosexual behavior are based on very shaky philosophical *and* empirical ground.

For our purposes, we can conclude this analysis by directly addressing a challenge Feser offers to his critics:

> A genuine counterexample to the perverted faculty argument's key premise would have to involve an action that *both* involved the *active frustration* of the natural end of a faculty and yet which was *in no way* contrary to what is good for us, not even in a minor respect. I submit that there are no such counterexamples, and that there could not be any given an Aristotelian-Thomistics metaphysics of the good.[1]

Really, now? I can think of one quite quickly: Providing semen samples for doctors to test. On many occasions, hospitals will need to look at your sperm to determine your health. For the most part this is done to gauge fertility—they'll see how quickly your little guys swim, whether they're well-shaped or malformed, and so on—but semen can also be used to diagnose several very serious health problems, like prostate cancer.[2]

Needless to say, the process of acquiring these samples "frustrates their end." You *have* to masturbate into a cup or carry out coitus interruptus and ejaculate elsewhere; they cannot simply take some fluid out of a vagina you've "properly" ejaculated in because that would lead to impurities in the sample. The only way to acquire a proper sample is

---

https://www.reuters.com/article/us-nordics-lgbt-health-trfn/suicides-fall-with-gay-marriage-in-sweden-denmark-as-stigma-fades-idUSKBN1XO010

[1] NSE, 409.

[2] Catharine Paddock, "Prostate cancer diagnosis may be more accurate with semen test," *Medical News Today*, June 9, 2014, last accessed on July 5, 2020, https://www.medicalnewstoday.com/articles/277949.php

absolutely non-procreative ejaculation. And since this is obviously "in no way contrary to what is good for us," (diagnosing infertility will get it cured, "restoring" the sexual faculty, while diagnosing cancer will let you live longer, and so on) it seems I've found just the counterexample Dr. Feser is looking for.

But if he would prefer a misdiagnosis for prostate cancer merely because Aquinas might disapprove, I see no reason to stop him. It would be his funeral, not mine, and it need not be anyone else's, either.

3.4: Harems

It seems difficult, to say the least, for Feser to insist that Aristotelian metaphysics condemn all forms of non-procreative sex considered in and of themselves. Thomists are known for their persistence, though, and I doubt the preceding pages would be enough to make Feser or any other modern-day Thomist give up. Unwilling to let go of either Aristotle's teachings or those of the Magisterium, these fellows might try to keep both by claiming the "final cause" of our sexual faculties is the maintenance of society as a whole rather than the procreation of individuals. Indeed, in *The Last Superstition,* Feser explicitly says:

> The teleology or final causality of sex thus pushes inevitably in the direction of at least some variation of the institution of marriage, and marriage exists for the purpose of generating and nourishing offspring not only biologically but culturally. Everything else is subordinated to this in the sense that it wouldn't exist without, and loses its point without, the overall procreative end. Sex is pleasurable, but only because this is nature's way of pushing us into doing what is necessary for procreation; husbands and wives often feel great affection for one another, but this tendency is put in them by nature only because it facilitates the stability of the union that the successful generation and upbringing of children require.[1]

---

[1] *TLS,* 144.

The implication here is that marriage is the bedrock of society—without it, civilization as a whole would degrade. As Feser notes, human children "are utterly dependent on others for their needs, and for a very long period. This is [also true] of the moral and cultural needs they have... They need education in both what is useful and right, and correction of error."[1] This would be a daunting task for only one person, especially the mother, since pregnancy is such a burden. Fortunately, "nature ordains" fathers to take care of their children, but fathers are also loath to take care of other people's, and "generally speaking and notoriously, jealous of the affections of the women they have children with, sometimes to the point of being willing to kill the competition."[2] Thus, heterosexual monogamous marriage for the purposes of raising children would be the true final cause of sex, because, without it, fathers would either not care for children at all or would be constantly doubting if their children were really theirs. This would result in children not receiving the support and instruction they need to survive, which would obviously result in our entire species going extinct after a while. Under this line of reasoning, any kind of non-procreative sex is inherently "distortive," eroding the foundations of marriage and by extension civilization itself.

This position is still untenable for several reasons. First, what Feser considers "blindingly obvious" biological facts do not really point towards "traditional" monogamy. Consider the preceding discussion: Wet dreams occur in the absence of any sort of loving relationship, much less marriage. If the "the teleology of sex" actually did point towards marriage rather than anything else, men would not regularly go through the process of arousal to climax by themselves. But to keep from belaboring a point already made, let us pretend for a moment that wet dreams do not exist. *Even if* they did not, the "obvious biological facts" would *still* point to something other than monogamy, namely *polygamy*.

---

[1] Ibid., 143.
[2] Ibid.

If Edward Feser is an expert biologist, he has chosen to keep that knowledge entirely to himself—virtually all of the "biological" examples in all of his books consist of basic facts any high-schooler who has ever been to sex-ed would know. "Nature makes it very difficult to indulge in sex without procreation," Feser helpfully informs us. "There is no prophylactic sheathe issued with a penis at birth, and no diaphragm issued with a vagina... [the final cause of the sexual organs and the sexual act] is to get semen into the vagina. That is why the penis and vagina are shaped the way they are.... The organs fit together like lock and key.... All of this too is blindingly obvious."[1]

Given all this, one hopes Feser is aware of another very, very "blindingly obvious" biological fact: women get pregnant and men don't. In fact, it's "blindingly obvious" that one man can get very many women pregnant at virtually no cost to himself. Perhaps this might come as a surprise to the Sage of Pasadena, but even a married man's "sexual faculties" do not cease functioning when his wife gets pregnant. A woman might be able to have only one child every nine months or so, but a man remains fertile and can happily sire children with other women, constantly, while each one is busy baking the bun in her oven. This is even apparent in the nature of sperm and eggs: Men produce literally *trillions* of sperm over the course of their lifetimes, while women produce only a few hundred (at most) egg cells.

This is all very puzzling if Nature and/or God intended humans to be monogamous. One would expect semen production to shut down over the course of a wife's pregnancy (perhaps triggered by hormones). Or perhaps men might produce limited numbers of sperm proportionate to a woman's relatively tiny supply of eggs. But none of that actually obtains in reality. It rather seems that men are "designed" to be very promiscuous, and the teleology of our sexual function is to spread our seeds far and wide. Feser might say that male jealousy necessitates monogamy. But it only necessitates "monogamy" on the

---

[1] Ibid., 142, 143.

part of women, not men. If a group of women were having sex with a group of men, trouble would surely be afoot. But if they were all "taken" by a single man, he will have no doubts at all about the paternity of the very numerous offspring (as Feser says Nature intends) he will sire with all of them and will therefore have no qualms about supporting all of them. It seems that "the teleology or final causality of sex," as ascertained from "blindingly obvious biological facts," "pushes inevitably" towards a system where a single man monopolizes a harem of several women, however many he can afford—perhaps four at maximum for the Muslims, but even more for members of other religious or cultural traditions. This is precisely what they call polygamy.

Now, Feser can allow this much: "the natural law approach to sexual morality can be seen to entail that polygamy and divorce, while historically permitted within some otherwise conservative religious contexts, are suboptimal at best and in practice usually positively immoral."[1] But in light of the previously described biological facts, it is precisely the other way around—*monogamy* is "suboptimal at best." Impregnating multiple women is clearly a natural function of the incredibly prolific sperm-production capabilities of the male sexual faculties. Mandating monogamy would force that awesome capability to go mostly to waste, which would at least hinder, if not outright contravene "nature's intentions." And since adhering to nature's intentions—the final causes of things—is the foundation of Aristotelian morality, it is monogamy, not polygamy, which is actually immoral. At least if we rely on the apparent teleology of our sexual faculties considered under a biological light.

So, then, perhaps we should not consider them purely in terms of their biology and physical operations. Perhaps we should think about what system is most suitable for our society as a whole. Feser would have to concede that the physical facts of human sexuality do point to polygamy: If he's going to look at "obvious facts" like the penis "fitting"

---

[1] Ibid., 151.

into the vagina, he cannot ignore the equally obvious fact that the penis can "fit into" many different vaginas. Very well then, he might say, look at the ramifications this would have from a societal and demographic perspective. Given a relatively equal distribution of men and women, it would be impossible for a single man to maintain a harem of more than one woman without leaving a corresponding number of other unfortunate men "high and dry," so to speak. Such an arrangement would lead to an underclass of angry, disgruntled men with no children and no stake in society, and some incentive to overthrow it. In order to avoid such an unhappy outcome, monogamy would be preferred.[1]

While Feser has never made this specific argument in his own words, I do believe it is a fair approximation of one he would make. In a post at the long-defunct (saved only by the grace of the Wayback Machine) *Right Reason* blog, he said "a focus on the mechanics of the penis alone might suffice to tell us that its biological function is to get semen into a woman's vagina, it is the larger social context within which human beings operate that tells us just how many women at a time nature intends, and specifically that it intends just one."[2] Again, it would be improper to put words in Feser's mouth, but in the absence of anything lengthier he has written specifically on sociology or culture, it seems fair to surmise that avoidance of the aforementioned demographic issues would probably be what he means by a "larger social context."

---

[1] See Valerie M. Hudson and Andrea M. den Boer, *Bare Branches: The Security Implications of Asia's Surplus Male Population* (MIT Press, 2004), 209. Although the authors concentrate on sex-selective abortion, they also note polygamy in Chinese society historically contributed to a scarcity of marriageable women for a portion of the male population, leading to these "bare branches" to engage in dysfunctional behaviors as well.

[2] Edward Feser, "Reply to Sullivan on natural law," *Right Reason*, October 31, 2006, accessed July 5, 2020, archived at
http://web.archive.org/web/20071014120434/http:/rightreason.ektopos.com/archives/2006/10/reply_to_sulliv.html

If so, we have arrived at the second problem with his approach: "social context" is almost always shifting and subjective, not objective and eternal as Feser would like metaphysical arguments to be. At the time and place of this writing (2020 in the United States), we live in a relatively peaceful era with a relatively equal distribution of men and women among the populace. But this was not always so, and it will not necessarily always be so. For instance, imagine a hunter-gatherer society where men had to go out and hunt large, dangerous animals (such as bears or wolves) for food, or defend their hunting grounds from other hostile tribes. A number of men would always die in such risky endeavors, which (assuming the women stayed back to tend to children or gather plants and small animals) would result in a population with few men and many women. In such a "social context," monogamy would be impractical, at least from the standpoint of maintaining the tribe's number. It is very hard to see how polygamy would in any way be "suboptimal." It would rather seem like the *most perfect* instantiation of the *telos* of the human sexual faculties, at least for as long as such a perilous state of affairs held.

Thankfully, things are better today. So wouldn't that mean traditional monogamy is the optimal arrangement right now? After all, when men aren't dying disproportionately on the hunt or in war, there's about one man for every woman, so monogamy would seem to be tailor-made to keep all of us happy. Well, not necessarily. Feser's argument seems to rely almost entirely on the presumption that women are entirely helpless without a man around. As he said in *The Last Superstition*:

> Mother Nature has put a fairly heavy burden on women…. She has also put a fairly heavy burden on children too, given that unlike non-human offspring they are utterly dependent on others for their needs…. So, nature's taking its course seems to leave mothers and offspring pretty helpless… if there weren't someone ordained by nature to provide for

them. But of course there is such a person, namely the father of the children.[1]

This all sounds very high-minded, but a few moments of thought should make us rather suspicious of it. Is it really impossible to raise a child without a father around? Difficult, to be sure, but it can be done. Single motherhood is quite a challenge, and it may be true that children of single mothers are more afflicted by a host of maladies, but there is no shortage of men or women who have managed to grow up and become well-functioning members of society despite the lack of a father figure in their lives.

And even if being raised by one woman is a one-way ticket to tragedy and dysfunction, what about the many alternatives that still don't involve the biological father? Perhaps the mother of a pregnant girl could step in to help rear her grandchild. Perhaps the baby could be given to an orphanage—I somehow doubt Feser would claim Catholic priests and nuns do a bad job of raising foundlings merely because they're not biologically related to any of them. Or society as a whole, spending tax money on welfare programs, could step in to replace the function of the absent father. Or children could be taken away from their biological parents and raised by the state, as was the case in ancient Sparta (and proposed by Plato, by the by[2]). Needless to say, none of these choices would be very attractive to Feser. With the (possible) exception of Catholic orphanages, he would probably declare all of them to be suboptimal at best, expensive boondoggles that only produce more dysfunction at worst. Unfortunately for him, he would have to prove that with *evidence*—he would have to cite papers from social scientists and criminologists demonstrating that biological fathers do a better job

---

[1] *TLS*, 143.

[2] According to Plato in the *Republic*, when the children of the best men and the best women are born, ""they'll be taken over by the officials appointed for the purpose," ensuring that "no mother knows her own child," so that the best specimens in society would have as many children as possible without sowing dissention amongst themselves. See Plato, trans. G.M.A. Grube, *The Republic*, 2nd Edition (Hackett Publishing, 1992), 134-36.

than grandmothers or priests or anyone else in keeping their kids from crime and poverty.

This illustrates the weakness of his position: He cannot figure out what the proper "social context" for sex is based on objective, irrefutable metaphysical argumentation, he must go through the trouble of inductive empirical inquiry. And, as established in the first chapter, such inquiry is always a risky business. Who knows, perhaps sometime in the future, the "social context" of mankind will be such that one of the above alternatives, such as communal state childrearing, proves superior to the nuclear family. In that case, the *telos* of sex would point to that alternative—thus debilitating Feser's blanket condemnation of "non-heterosexual-pair-bonding-marital-sex."

3.5: Gay Marriage is Super, Thanks For Asking

If nonprocreative, even non-marital sex was licit, what other implications would that have for society? If there were nothing wrong with homosexual activity, and if the optimal structure of marriage might change over time, could that indicate gay marriage would be permissible, perhaps even laudable? Feser would most likely protest, but using the very metaphysical framework he insists we must, it is possible to prove that same-sex marriage is legitimate.

Feser seems to believe that just about everything has, or participates in, a Form, because Forms are absolutely essential (heh) to making sense of the world in any meaningful way (so the theory goes). A Form is what "defines and distinguishes" any given object or concept from anything else and is also what gives rise to and explains the distinctive characteristics and/or operations of that object. Given this, it seems reasonable to assume that gays and lesbians participate in the Form of Homosexuality, which differentiates them from heterosexuals. After all, there is obviously something that defines these groups, and their distinctive behavior (anal sex, Broadway, whatever) operates in a regular, non-random fashion that distinguishes them from other groups such as heterosexuals or asexuals.

This is where it gets interesting, and rather uncomfortable for Aristotelians like Feser. If gay people have their own particular Form, it also stands to reason that what is good for them may actually be different than what is good for heterosexual people. After all, the good, in the sense of fulfilling one's function, is different for creatures with different Forms. To re-use Feser's favorite example, it is good for a squirrel to scamper up trees and nuts, but it would starve if it tried to visit many flowers and eat pollen. A bee, on the other hand, is a good bee to the extent it visits flowers and gathers their pollen, and a bad, sickly bee if it buzzes around trees all day and attempts to bring nuts larger than it is back to the hive.

Given this understanding, perhaps what is bad for people like me and (assumedly, given his six children) Dr. Feser is actually good for homosexuals, given their different Forms. The final cause of our *heterosexual* sexual faculties may be to procreate, yes. But perhaps the final cause of a *homosexual's* sexual faculties is something different, like social bonding. There is nothing in this assessment that specifically contradicts Aristotelian metaphysical thought. No denial of realism, final causality, or Essence. Merely the postulation that a certain group might have a slightly different Form than the rest of us and therefore a different final cause with regard to one of their faculties. It is no more inherently unbelievable than the idea that bees and squirrels, possessing different Forms, would also have different final causes concerning their digestive faculties. If Aristotle thought differently—comparing homosexuality to "eating dirt," as Feser reports[1]—then it is only because the Philosopher did not have as good a grasp on the Fabulous Form of Homosexuality as we do now.

This is very good news for advocates of gay marriage. According to Feser, "the metaphysics underlying natural law theory entails that marriage is, not by human definition, but as an *objective metaphysical fact* determined by its final cause, inherently procreative, and thus

---

[1] *TLS*, 50.

inherently heterosexual."¹ *Heterosexual* marriage might be (though, as evinced by the above discussion of polygamy, this is debatable), but perhaps *homosexual* marriage has a different final cause, namely strengthening social bonds between homosexual individuals. This is a reasonable supposition, given the understanding that homosexuals themselves have different final causes (with regard to sex). So, if homosexuals have their own Forms and final causes, and same-sex marriage has its own Form and final cause, there is no reason to take Feser seriously when he says "[t]here is no such thing as 'same-sex marriage' any more than there are round squares."²

His analogy, as we can see, is flawed. Homosexuals themselves do not instantiate an obviously self-contradictory Form like "round squares" would. Since the existence of homosexuals as a distinct category with its own Form is not an obvious logical contradiction, there is no reason same-sex marriage would be either. If Feser wishes to insist that the word "marriage" can *only* refer to heterosexual procreative bonds, fine. He can call gay marriages "civil unions" if he likes. But whatever his choice may be, he is merely using different words for two different actual existing things, like different words describe four-sided polygons and three-sided ones. It therefore seems as silly to call same-sex unions "metaphysical absurdities" as it would be to put triangles at the same level of metaphysical absurdity as "round squares."

At least it would be so if homosexuals truly did instantiate their own Forms. But perhaps they do not. Isn't homosexuality merely a behavior, or a preference for a certain behavior? We wouldn't say people who simply do different things or partake of different hobbies have different Forms. For instance, we could note some people enjoy baseball and others enjoy football, but we wouldn't say "football fans" and "baseball fans" have different Forms. Well, actually, we would and should, as the very existence of the two terms attests. If Forms really do exist, as Feser and his natural-law friends would say, anything that exists

---

¹ *TLS*, 149.
² Ibid.

and can be distinguished in any way from any other existing thing has a Form. Given that there is clearly some difference between football fans and baseball fans, they must instantiate Forms in some way. This would remain the case (at least according to David Oderberg) even if there were some sort of "vagueness" in the definitions, such as how one can be a fan of both baseball and football.[1] In the same way, there really is a Form of Homosexuality distinct from the Form of Heterosexuality, even if some people participate in both to certain extents (namely bisexuals) or no extent (people who feel no sexual attraction or arousal at all, namely asexuals).[2] Thus, some Form of same-sex union could plausibly exist and serve a legitimate purpose, regardless of whether one calls it marriage or something else.

The sticking point then becomes whether or not any legitimate purpose could attend to nonprocreative, same-sex relationships as a whole. As established above, the existence of wet dreams would seem to indicate that non-procreative ejaculation can serve a legitimate purpose, but that purpose (clearing out old sperm and strengthening the relevant muscles) itself points towards procreation. In other words, it might be morally licit to masturbate or have oral or anal sex, but only "in preparation" for copulatory sex, so to speak. Since a homosexual couple who married would ostensibly never procreate in that manner (barring something like sperm donation or in-vitro fertilization), wouldn't same-sex marriage discourage them from doing so and thus be immoral and illegitimate from the perspective of long-term final causes?

Not necessarily. Given a homosexual orientation, it may be the case that gay men and lesbians would simply be incapable of copulating in a procreative manner. If a man cannot be aroused by a woman, he will be unable to maintain an erection and ejaculate in her vagina, and a

---

[1] Oderberg, *Real Essentialism,* 226-227.
[2] It should be noted that people have perceived a distinct "homosexual" identity of some sort in many times and places, going as far back as ancient Rome and the medieval Islamic world. See Michael Ruse, *Homosexuality: A Philosophical Inquiry* (Blackwell, 1988), 18.

woman wholly unattracted to men would be unable to tolerate intercourse with one long enough for insemination to take place. According to Feser, this would mean that gays and lesbians are "defective," in the same sense as someone with a clubfoot.[1] I obviously don't endorse this line of thought and find it quite distasteful, but going along with it can highlight the flaws in Feser's reasoning.

Imagine someone with a clubfoot having the afflicted limb removed and replaced with a fine prosthetic leg, made out of wood or plastic or some other material. The leg isn't as good as a real one might be, but it allows the unfortunate person to walk around better than they otherwise would have. Would Feser say it is "metaphysically incoherent" to call the artificial limb a "leg," despite being a piece of wood or plastic rather than a real one grown of flesh and bone? Probably not, unless he was feeling very nitpicky, and, even then, he wouldn't argue that the use of a false leg to approximate (even if not fully) the function of a real one would be morally wrong. But in that case, same-sex "marriage" can be seen as an approximation (however incomplete) of heterosexual marriage rather than any kind of "metaphysical absurdity." Gays and lesbians may, by dint of genetics or some other biological factor, be "unfortunate" if they cannot conceive children via intercourse. Same-sex marriage, however, could at least allow them to enjoy the unitive aspects of marriage if nothing else, just as an artificial leg could allow a clubfooted person the pleasure of walking, if not all the functions of a full leg (such as running, jumping, and so on).

Feser would respond by saying gays and lesbians already can marry—someone of the opposite sex.[2] But this is obviously suboptimal to say the very least, because while gays and lesbians can easily be friends with people of the opposite sex, by definition they can only *intimately* unite with others of the same sex. Forcing them into opposite-sex marriage would be as foolish as replacing the damaged clubfoot in our example with an actual leg taken from someone else that was

---

[1] *TLS*, 37, 134.
[2] Ibid., 149.

eventually rejected by the patient's body. In that case, the artificial approximation would be preferable. Similarly, in the case of gays and lesbians, an "artificial approximation of marriage" (civil unions, if Feser would like) would be preferable to the "real thing" (opposite-sex marriage) which would irritate and be unfair to both partners.

3.6: Marriage as an Artifact

This is, ironically enough, a rather legalistic way of looking at marriage, relying on very fine-grained disputations about the specific Forms and final causes of things. I'd say this would be expected of a good Aristotelian, but Feser would probably argue that marriage is too personal a matter to be left *entirely* up to cold philosophy. That sounds plausible on a surface reading of things, but I'm not so sure it holds up under sustained thought. Catholicism and other religions may regard marriage as a holy sacrament, but looking at it philosophically, marriage seems to be a very good example of an **artifact**. And I do not use that word in a derogatory sense, not at all. I rather use it in the exact same way Feser would—in opposition to "**substances**." I imagine this might be a bit confusing for new readers, so a brief digression is in order.

Feser, summarizing Aristotle, says "a natural object is one whose characteristic behavior—the ways in which it manifests either stability or changes of various sorts—derives from something intrinsic to it. A non-natural object is one which does not have such an intrinsic principle...only the natural objects out of which it is made have such a principle." The example Feser uses to differentiate the two would be of a plant vine and a hammock made of plant vines. The vines are natural objects in that they have certain characteristics, such as growing up trees and taking in nutrients, on their own. Those characteristics "flow from" their Essence. A hammock, on the other hand, has no such inherent tendencies on its own. It must be constructed artificially from vines (or other natural objects) by human beings. The vines don't display any of the particular characteristics of the hammock (such as shape or being comfy to lie in), and the only reason the hammock does is that it has been constructed in such a way by human beings, solely to serve human purposes. The technical Aristotelian-Thomistic (hereafter referred to as "A-T") term for natural objects like vines would be "substances," and the term for artificial objects constructed by humans, such as hammocks, would be "artifacts."[1]

This is significant because only substances have teleologies or final causes which are ethically important. We can give artifacts whatever purposes we like—for instance, the final cause of a hammer is to drive nails, but there is nothing wrong with using one as a paperweight, because hammers are artifacts, products of human convenience, and can be used for whatever we wish. On the other hand, something like a vine has an intrinsic teleology, towards absorbing water and nutrients in this case, and preventing it from doing so would be bad and lead to its death—bad from the vine's perspective, at least, perhaps not so bad for someone who wanted to prune it away from his garden.

What does any of this have to do with marriage? Well, it seems to me that marriage is a perfect example of an artifact—a cultural one, not a physical one—rather than a natural substance with its own teleology independent of human desires. As illustrated in the preceding section, the optimal type of marriage is entirely dependent on an ever-changing social context. At our present moment, monogamy might be the best arrangement, but in the past, polygamy was. This would seem to indicate that marriage is a created thing, a form of social technology human beings employed to solve changing cultural and demographic issues, much like we would use any other tool. In a hunter-gatherer environment, there was a surplus of women compared to men, so polygamy was instated. In modern times, the gender ratio is equal, so we shifted to monogamy. In other words, marriage might have a Form, but its Form is of an artifact, so it has no inherent teleology of its own. This means we can define it however we wish for whatever purposes we choose. The comparisons to geometry Feser loves (such as his equating same-sex marriage to round squares) are entirely fallacious. Geometric

---

[1] *SM*, 164-165.

objects such as squares and circles are substances of a sort, in that they (assumedly) exist independently and have their own Forms that we discover rather than invent. But for the reasons I have already described, marriage is obviously something human beings invented to solve distinctly human problems. It makes no sense to say we "discovered" any metaphysical or logical truths about marriage because marriage is entirely contingent upon human beings and our ever-changing "social context."

What applies to the artifact of marriage in relation to the final causality of sex also applies in its function within society as a whole. The proper Form of any artifact is also contingent upon the conditions in which it operates: A car (a tool built by human hands) suited for long stretches of highway would need to be modified in order to drive on rough, uneven terrain or through mud and high water. Given that marriage is an artifact, and (to simplify the history somewhat)[1] has indeed been modified from the polygamy of King Solomon's day to the monogamy Catholics claim to prefer, why should it not be modified further? To repeat what we have discussed once more, Feser argues that the final causality of sexuality points to procreative monogamy, which would imply that marriage exists for the sake of producing and rearing children. But even if that were true, it would provide no reason to refrain from modifying our conception of marriage to suit present-day circumstances. As one blogger has noted, the world has billions of people in it, more than enough to ensure there is no need to procreate as much as possible—indeed, such profligacy could actually threaten the continued existence of humanity as a whole if Earth's carrying capacity is exceeded.[2] In such a context, procreative marriage appears to be as

---

[1] The worldwide history of marriage is actually much more complex than a straight line from polygamy to monogamy; I rely on that simplification here only for reasons of space. See Stephanie Coontz, *Marriage, a History: How Love Conquered Marriage* (Penguin Books, 2006) for a lucid introduction of how the institution evolved across several geographic regions following the introduction of agriculture.
[2] Mike Doolittle, "Metaphysical Bigotry," *The A-Unicornist*, https://www.theaunicornist.com/2014/09/metaphysical-bigotry.html, April 16,

unnecessary and possibly self-destructive as a race car taken from an open road and put into a mountainous hill would be. It is therefore eminently reasonable for us rational animals to change marriage from a fundamentally procreative institution to a companionate one, allowing for "sterile" same-sex marriages or the use of contraceptives in heterosexual ones. That is no more a metaphysical absurdity then attaching a new set of wheels to one's car so that it operates in different environments. If Feser disagrees, he would have to metaphysically demonstrate that marriage has the Form of a substance rather than an artifact. Considering how much marriage has changed over time for entirely practical and legitimate reasons, that's a pretty tough task.

3.7: Abortion

The human beings themselves who are getting married would, of course, have Substantial Forms rather than being mere artifacts. Our existence as human beings must necessarily precede our construction of artifacts, because if we had not evolved through natural processes as living creatures with intrinsic principles of operation, there would be no-one around to build cars and hammers and all other kinds of artifacts. But when, precisely, do humans acquire that Substantial Form? As discussed in Chapter 1, Thomists like Feser believe the Form of human beings is

---

2015, last accessed on July 5, 2020. Commenters on a different blog, *Just Thomism* have responded to this line of argument by saying it could also lead to celibacy rather than contraception and gay marriage, see James Chastek, "Analogous to the Vestigial," *Just Thomism,* https://thomism.wordpress.com/2015/04/16/analogous-to-the-vestigial/ , comment #2 from "Peter" on April 17, 2015, 2:50 PM, last accessed on July 5, 2020. I would reply this *could* be an argument for celibacy, if the existence of rugged terrain was an argument for abandoning a car altogether and walking on foot rather than modifying its wheels. Given that marriage is an artifact and that there is nothing necessarily wrong with non-procreative sex, why should we deny anyone the "unitive" benefits of the institution while tamping down on the procreation?

that of a rational animal.[1] But small children are not very rational, babies even less so, and a newly-fertilized zygote not at all. Are these organisms therefore less than human? No, says Feser, and this is why he considers abortion a morally hideous crime even worse than murder.

According to modern Thomists like Feser (but *not* Aristotle or even Aquinas, as we will soon see), even a fertilized zygote is an actual human being—it simply hasn't realized its potentialities yet. What could that possibly mean? Return to chapter 1 if you need a refresher on act and potency, but if you're ready, we can look at Feser's example in *The Last Superstition*. He asks us to imagine an Acme rubber ball sitting in a cabinet. Remember that the ball is actual in some ways (red, round, and solid) and potential in other ways (blue and gooey); those latter potentials could only be actualized by something else, like a person painting it or heating it. However, Feser notes that the ball also has certain potential *behaviors* in addition to potential physical properties like shape or color. The ball is *potentially* rolling down a hill or bouncing around—it just needs someone to remove it from the cabinet and get it going. Also note, however, there are potencies it doesn't have—the ball is not potentially producing light or boiling water. This is because these actualities and potencies "flow from" the Essence or Form of a rubber ball—if it possessed a different Form it would have different potencies. Something that could potentially produce light or heat simply would not possess the Form of a rubber ball—it would instead instantiate the Form of a light bulb or kettle or something else.[2]

So, if a thing's potencies flow from its Form, that implies we can tell what its Form is from its potencies. Looking at a zygote, it would seem that the tiny thing can "potentially" reason. After all, assuming it doesn't get aborted or miscarried, it will eventually grow into a boy or girl who will eventually start to reason. It might not be doing so *yet*, but

---

[1] Note here that I am only being generous by accepting the idea that the "Substantial Form" of human beings is that of a rational animal. See chapter 5 for further discussion on this subject.
[2] *AQ*, 138-141, *TLS*, 128-129.

it has the potential to do so, just like a rubber ball sitting in a cabinet might not be rolling or bouncing *yet*, but has the potential to do so. And if having the potential to roll around at some point in the future (merely needing someone to take it out) tells us that the object in the cabinet has the Form of a rubber ball, then having the potential to reason in the future (merely needing a few years to grow) tells us the zygote in the womb has the Form of a rational animal. But to have the Form of a rational animal is to simply be a rational animal, or a human being with a soul. Thus, "a zygote is...an *actual* human being...just one that hasn't yet fully realized its inherent potentials," which would make abortion the destruction of an actual human being, i.e., murder.[1]

Feser goes on to say that anyone who thinks zygotes are merely inhuman clumps of cells (such as Sam Harris) "might want to ignore the importance of this distinction, but that it *is* a genuine distinction cannot rationally be denied."[2] Actually, and ironically, it seems to me that pro-lifers of Feser's bent are guilty of glossing over some pretty important distinctions themselves, and can find far less support than they'd like in the metaphysics of Aristotle.

Let's take a closer look at the idea that zygotes possess the Form of a human being rather than any other. Feser makes a very big deal out of this, saying "a soul is just the form—the...structure, organizational pattern—of a living thing, an organism, and the human organism, as we know from modern biology, begins at conception."[3] But at least at first glance, this seems like a very strange position. A zygote has a vastly different structure and organizational pattern from a fully-grown human being. Zygotes are tiny and incapable of independent existence, humans are large and capable of living on their own, humans have distinct body parts while a zygote is just one mass, and of course, humans can think while zygotes can only absorb their mother's nutrients. By Feser's *own definition* it seems obvious that an adult

---

[1] Ibid.
[2] *TLS,* 129.
[3] Ibid., 128.

human being instantiates a different Form, which would mean that zygotes might not actually be human and thus fair game. This is where the potentials are supposed to come to Feser's rescue. He claims:

> ...the features essential to human beings...being able to take in nutrients...to think [and in my example, to have different body parts], and so forth—are not fully *developed* until well after conception. But that doesn't mean that they aren't *there*...Rationality, locomotion, nutrition, and the like are present even at conception...as inherent potentialities...[this] doesn't even mean "potential" in the sense in which a rubber ball might potentially be melted down and made into something else, e.g. an eraser. It means 'potential' in the sense of a capacity that an entity already has within it by virtue of its nature or essence, as a rubber ball *qua rubber ball* has the potential to roll down a hill even when it is locked in a cabinet somewhere. And in this sense a zygote has the potentiality for or "directedness toward" the actual exercise of reasoning...that a rubber ball doesn't have, that a sperm or egg considered by themselves don't have.[1]

The most obvious problem with Feser's argument, in my view, comes with the example he uses right at the very end of that paragraph. How, precisely, could a zygote be much more "directed toward" becoming a rational animal than an individual egg or sperm cell could? This might sound strange to you and me, dear reader, but it shouldn't sound strange to Dr. Feser. As we will recall from nearly all of the preceding pages, one of his major hobbyhorses is the idea that our sexual faculties "are directed towards" the production of more human beings. If that really were the case, then every egg cell, at least, would be an actual human being. Feser himself would say that the only reason eggs exist is to create new human beings; if we didn't have sex (say we reproduced by budding or parthenogenesis), we wouldn't have those egg cells. That means the egg's final cause is to become a human being, which also means it is "directed towards" human rational activity, it just "hasn't yet fully realized that inherent potentiality." The only thing the

---

[1] *TLA,* 129.

little egg needs to realize that potential is a little help from a little sperm, followed by nine months in mommy's tummy. What makes the egg's situation *metaphysically* different from the zygote's? The only meaningful distinction between an unfertilized and fertilized egg, *in terms of the potentialities towards which they are directed,* seems to be the split second when the sperm hits the egg. Unless Feser can provide some account of why that exact moment represents a tectonic shift in the "directedness" of the egg cell, he would be forced to concede that a mere unfertilized egg is an "actual human, just one waiting to actualize its potentials" in the same way a zygote is.

Might that tectonic shift be a matter of chromosomes? One of the points for a zygote having its own distinct Form (that is to say, being a unique human being instead of a mere part of one, like some skin cells) is that it has its own distinct set of genes, different from those of its mother. The egg has an X chromosome from the mother, the sperm carries either the father's X or Y chromosome, so when they come together, the resulting girl (if an X-sperm created an XX zygote) or boy (for an XY zygote) would have a distinct genetic blueprint that differed from both of the parents. But on closer thought, this is not the whole story. Both eggs and sperm have distinct "blueprints" *by themselves.* There are always slight variations in the single chromosome of the sperm and eggs created by the father and mother—these gametes are never just clones or identical templates, so to speak, the way cells of other body parts are. Even without a background in biology, this can be easily understood by thinking about siblings. If every egg cell and every sperm were exactly alike, every male and female child of a single couple would be identical to his or her brothers or sisters, because the exact same X and Y chromosomes would be creating them. In reality, of course, that's not the case—except for identical twins (which are two people made from a single egg), there are always little differences among fraternal siblings. This is proof that each individual egg and sperm has a slightly different set of genes, which means they really do possess genetically distinct Forms, in the sense of being distinguished and individuated from others of their general type. Given their "directedness towards" becoming human beings, they would therefore seem to be actual human beings in the same sense a zygote is. But even Feser would admit this would be absurd.

Similar problems arise with Feser's conflation of a certain substance being "intrinsically directed towards" a certain thing (in this case, a rational animal) and *actually being* that thing. To again riff off of one his favorite examples, imagine a glass of water sitting at room temperature. That water is "intrinsically directed" towards becoming ice at cold temperatures. There is something *inherent to* water that gives it the "potential" to be cold and solid—if it were to remain a liquid at 0 degrees Celsius, or turn into violets, or explode or anything like that, it would not really have the Form of water and therefore would not actually *be* a sample of water. But the fact that a glass of water has "iciness" as a potentiality does not mean it actually is a block of ice until the temperature has lowered and it has actually frozen.

Imagine how silly it would be if you asked a waiter at a restaurant for some ice in your lemonade and he instead brought you a glass of water along with it, his excuse being, "well, this water is an *actual* block of ice, just one that hasn't fully realized its inherent potentials." I somehow suspect even Edward Feser would have a tough time tipping the guy extra for being an astute Aristotelian. Unhappily for the pro-lifers, the same reasoning applies to zygotes. There may be something intrinsic, a potentiality or blueprint "directed towards" rationality in a zygote, but only in the same sense that there is something intrinsic, a potentiality or blueprint "directed towards" ice in water. Until that potential is actually realized, it seems as silly to treat a zygote as an actual human being as it would be for a waiter to treat a glass of lukewarm water as an actual block of ice.

Aristotle's doctrines of "primary actuality" and "secondary actuality" are of little help to Feser here. Earlier in *The Last Superstition*, Feser describes the distinction as such:

Since you are a human being, you are a rational animal; because you are a rational animal, you have the power or faculty of speech; and because you have this power, you sometimes exercise it and speak. Your actually having the power of speech flows from your actually being a rational animal; it is a 'secondary actuality' relative to your being a rational animal, which is a 'primary actuality.'

What this means is that "the zygote, given its nature or form, has rationality as a 'primary actuality' even if not yet as a 'secondary actuality.'"[1]

The key phrase there is "given its form." We can agree that a zygote has a "primary actuality" of rationality *only if* we agree it is an actually rational animal in the first place. But as the examples given above should hopefully show, it is far from obvious that a precursor to a rational animal *actually is* a rational animal itself. That being the case, if the zygote possesses a different Form, even if it has the potential to become a rational animal, it does not in and of itself have rationality as a primary actuality. The example of the block of ice comes to mind again: Ice has the "primary actuality" of being cold and solid, and also has the secondary actuality—that is to say, an ability that flows from its primary actuality but is not necessarily always expressed—to cool a drink. Any block of ice will have this power even if it isn't in a glass of lemonade. But it must be frozen into a proper block first—a glass of lukewarm water does not have the primary actuality of iciness and therefore no secondary actuality of a capacity to cool. Only when the water has been given the Form of ice through freezing, and only when a zygote has been given the Form of a rational animal (a soul) through gestation and birth, can either be said to actually be icy or rational.

Admittedly, there may be a disanalogy here: The zygote is a living thing, whereas a glass of water would be an inanimate object. Doesn't the zygote have some inherent principle of growth *and* operation that makes it different from water, which only has a principle of operation

---

[1] *TLS*, 56.

and no inherent tendencies of growth or autonomous behavior? This is most likely the argument that the Thomists John Haldane and Patrick Lee would use, and Feser relies quite heavily on their analysis to buttress the ones he gives in *Aquinas* and *The Last Superstition*. On closer inspection, however, a sharp-eyed reader can see that Haldane and Lee's arguments are not entirely airtight either.

The pair tells us that "the case of foetal development involves an intrinsic principle of natural change in a single substance. This change involves the internally directed growth toward a more mature stage of a human organism, and so the cause of this change, the embryo itself, is already human." According to the authors, an embryo can be said to be "internally directed" thanks to its "epigenetic primordium." The term derives from two words: "the 'primordium' [is] 'the beginning or first discernible indication of an organ or structure', while 'epigenetic' is used to mean 'being developed out of without being preformed.'"[1] Since this primordium—the first discernible indications of organs which will gradually develop as part of a final cause—is present only after the sperm hits the egg, that moment of conception can be considered the moment at which a new human being is formed (or Formed, or ensouled, whichever you like).

But at the same time, Lee and Haldane also mention, "In mammals, even in the unfertilized ovum, there is already an 'animal' pole (from which the nervous system and eyes develop) and a 'vegetal' pole (from which the future 'lower' organs and the gut develop)."[2] This would seem to fulfill the criteria of an epigenetic primordium: The first discernible indications of organs, which are not pre-formed but will develop naturally after they have made contact with a sperm cell. Since one of these blueprints, so to speak, is of the nervous system, the individual egg could be said to be "directed towards" the rationality associated with that nervous system. That would mean an

---

[1] John Haldane and Patrick Lee, "Rational Souls and the Beginning of Life (A Reply to Robert Pasnau)," *Philosophy* 78 no. 4 (2003), 537.
[2] Ibid.

unfertilized egg would be an actual human in almost the same way Feser, Haldane, and Lee say a zygote is an actual human. But, again, this seems absurd.

Absurd, they might say, because an unfertilized egg contains no *inherent principle of growth*. An egg without a sperm attached to it will just sit there until it's eventually flushed out (a process, I hear, that causes quite some inconvenience every month). An egg combined with a sperm, however, has its own unique genetic blueprint *and* something that makes it start to divide and grow in size. Since

> ...there is no extrinsic agent responsible for the regular, complex development, then the obvious conclusion is that the cause of the process is...the embryo itself. But in that case the process is not an extrinsic formation, but is an instance of growth or maturation, i.e., the active self-development of a whole, though immature organism which is already a member of the species, the mature stage of which it is developing toward.[1]

This would be convincing...if Haldane and Lee hadn't forgotten about a very important extrinsic actress indeed: The zygote's mother. A zygote is not really like an adult cat or dog or squirrel or other animal Feser uses as examples of natural substances or animal souls.[2] A grown, independent animal is capable of taking in nutrients, reproducing, and carrying out all its other behaviors (barking, meowing, burying nuts, whatever) on its own volition and does not necessarily rely on any other entity to do it for them. In other words, these animals operate entirely according to their intrinsic principles, though bad fortune (such as predators or local famine) can frustrate these principles. A zygote, on the other hand, relies entirely on its mother's body to carry out its distinctive operations. It first must attach itself to the uterus before it will grow, and none of the "epigenetic primordia" it contains will ever

---

[1] John Haldane and Patrick Lee, "Aquinas on Human Ensoulment, Abortion and the Value of Life," *Philosophy* 78, no. 02 (2003), 271.
[2] *TLS*, 121. The specific term Feser uses is "sensory soul," but that's not relevant to the discussion at hand.

actually become the organs (much less the rationality) they "point towards" unless the mother's body provides it nutrients and proper direction 24/7 for nine months.

In a meaningful sense, while a zygote may be "directed towards" growing in that it possesses a certain genetic blueprint conducive to that end, the little thing is not actually growing itself. Rather, the mother's body is actively stuffing nutrients into it and moving the process along. It does not seem to be an intrinsic principle of the zygote that spurs its growth, but the extrinsic action of the body in which it is found. If zygotes really did possess some intrinsic principle as Haldane, Lee, and undoubtedly Feser hold, they would be able to nourish themselves and grow into little rational animals entirely on their own. But as we all know, this is impossible—a zygote separated from its uterus in some way will quickly wither and die. Even if there were some way to keep it alive—an artificial womb from *Brave New World*, for instance—that womb would still be providing nutrients and direction for the organism's growth. There would still be an extrinsic, external agent responsible for the changes the zygote experiences, it would just be an artificial, science-fiction agent rather than a natural mother.

Neither is it any good to say the "blueprint," the full set of chromosomes (with two being XX or XY) contained in a zygote constitute the "intrinsic principle," at least if merely having an "intrinsic principle" that is not yet fully realized makes an entity of the same type as a fully-grown example. As mentioned earlier, an unfertilized egg contains a sort of blueprint for the nervous system all on its own, it merely needs a handsome, dashing sperm to complete the blueprint and begin the next step of the process towards which it is "directed." If the Thomist Trio wishes to say a zygote is an actual rational animal that is just waiting to realize its potentials after nine months and with the aid of many nutrients, we can say an unfertilized egg is an actual rational animal that is just waiting to realize its potential with the aid of a single sperm, nine months, and many nutrients. As Feser might say, an incomplete or damaged blueprint is still a blueprint, and the half-chromosomal-load of a human egg certainly counts as an incomplete blueprint.

Equally problematic is the word "blueprint," as a blueprint itself contains no intrinsic principle that can be actualized without the aid of an external actor. Imagine you give a builder the blueprints for a house. It would be silly for either you or him to act as if the blueprint itself were an actual (if incomplete) house, because the blueprint is merely providing a set of instructions. The builder must provide the materials and do the work of building a house, even if the blueprints are directing him in a sense. By the same token, the zygote's distinct chromosomes serve as a blueprint for a unique human being, but that human being does not exist yet. Only when enough time has passed and the mother's body has provided enough nutrients (she is the builder in this case) can we really say a new human has come into being.

Under Feser's own lights, then, a consistently Aristotelian outlook makes abortion more, not less, justifiable. When we accept three important Aristotelian views (Realism [that things in the world actually have mind-independent Essences or Forms], the idea that a thing's potentialities tell us what Form it instantiates, and the idea that substantial Form is determined by an inherent principle of growth), we find that since a zygote lacks inherent (as opposed to externally-powered) growth, it does not truly possess the potentialities associated with the Form of a human, and thus is not truly a human. Consequently it does not possess a right to life all humans do. I would say that's a hefty metaphysical argument pro-choicers could add to their arsenal.

We are then left with one more problem: Where, precisely do we draw the line between a merely proto-human zygote and a fully human child? It is a very important question, at least to guys like Feser: If zygotes really aren't rational animals, then it would be acceptable to destroy them, but since children really are rational animals (just immature ones), we can't simply kill them. Aquinas thought that growing proto-humans took on the full Form of Humanity (that is to say, their souls) at about forty days into development, but this was due to the primitive knowledge of embryology available to him at the time. Given that the Form of Man is being a rational animal, an ethics based on Forms seems to entail that any human-seeming organism would only be truly human once it began to demonstrate rational activity. But as we all know, babies aren't very rational, so this would imply the absurd conclusion that infants and toddlers weren't really human (and that abusing or killing them would be less morally severe).[1]

In order to avoid this conclusion, Feser, Lee, and Haldane had to resort to the concept of "epigenetic primordia" and the assertion that a zygote containing a blueprint directed towards being a rational animal (eventually) counted as having an intrinsic principle—making it an example of an actual rational animal, merely an immature one. But, fortunately, even under my own riff on an Aristotelian framework, where zygotes are *not* rational animals, it is possible for me to maintain that newborns are fully human and deserving of rights.

The key lies in the intrinsic principle of growth and behavior mentioned earlier in relation to animals. We have established that zygotes do not possess this principle because their growth and development is dictated entirely by an external actor (the mother's body). However, when a baby leaves the womb, loses the umbilical cord, and takes the first breath out in the world, he or she *gains* that intrinsic principle. Yes, it is true that babies and toddlers are just about completely helpless, and that they need to be fed and cleaned by external actors to avoid starving to death (which obviously entails they are entirely un-rational). But even though babies are helpless, they are not *as* helpless as a zygote, embryo, or fetus. Babies are capable of manifesting behaviors all on their own and exerting *some* control over their environment, even if only in a very thin sense of crying loudly to get someone to notice them. Their independent actions evince a sort of intrinsic principle influencing the world around them, analogous to the way a dog barking or a cat meowing for food evinces an intrinsic,

---

[1] *AQ,* 141.

independently-operating behavior influencing the world, which tells us those things are dogs or cats. A proto-human, however, cannot influence anything in that way. Even a developed fetus, no matter how much it kicks or rolls around in the womb, cannot change the chemicals of the uterus surrounding it, nor how many nutrients the uterus provides it. We can say the fetus's principle of growth is extrinsic, located in the mother's body, while the newborn's principle of growth is intrinsic, rooted in its own behaviors (even if they only serve to get others to feed it). Since the Thomists require a "blueprint" pointing towards rationality (which babies certainly have, given they'll grow to be at least somewhat rational in a few years), *and* an intrinsic principle propelling growth towards that goal, babies fulfill both conditions, while zygotes have only the former. So it is demonstrated that we can justify abortion on Aristotelian-Thomistic grounds without *necessarily* condoning infanticide.

3.8: Aristotle, Infanticide, and Genocide

Distressingly, Aristotle and Plato *did* condone infanticide, and that seemingly murderous act is morally licit under some circumstances given a consistent reading of their metaphysics. Even Feser would admit this; he once noted "they [Plato and Aristotle] did not condemn infanticide when done for eugenic reasons."[1] Perhaps the Greeks did not believe humans actually became humans (in terms of instantiating the Form of a Rational Animal) until they actually began to show evidence of rational activity, which would be about when small children learn to talk. But even if Aristotle believed children were actual rational animals and therefore innocent human beings, he could still justify killing them based on what Feser identifies as **the principle of totality.**

---

[1] Edward Feser, "Why Allow Abortion but Not 'Same-Sex Marriage?'" November 6, 2008, last accessed on July 5, 2020,
https://edwardfeser.blogspot.com/2008/11/why-allow-abortion-but-not-same-sex.html

This principle states that it is occasionally morally licit for a rational creature to frustrate the final causes of one of its body parts or faculties, or even annihilate them (which would otherwise be very bad) if doing so is necessary to preserve the health of the whole organism. For instance, the purpose of the legs is to walk, so doing anything that would prevent them from walking would be immoral under most circumstances. However, if the limb has been wounded and needs a temporary cast, or even worse, if it were gangrenous and needed to be amputated, the Thomist would allow those actions on the basis that living is a higher final cause for the whole organism than walking is for the legs alone. Cutting one's legs off for no reason, however, *would* still be an immoral act on the Aristotelian view.[1]

This principle is necessary to prevent Aristotelianism from falling into legalistic absurdity under the guise of principled scrupulosity. Since Aristotelianism does not judge actions as good or bad based on the effects they actually have in the real world, but rather on whether or not those actions are in keeping with abstract standards (Forms or final causes), a consistent Aristotelian would otherwise have to condemn amputating diseased limbs or cancerous organs, or certain kinds of "harmful" behaviors that serve obvious long-term purposes (like surgery, which involves the otherwise objectionable practice of cutting someone open). The principle of totality would seem to rescue the Aristotelians, and by extension Thomists, from having to bite that particular bullet. But it also opens up a rather glaring hole in the practical exercise of their ethics.

If an individual may occasionally frustrate the final causes of his or her individual faculties for a higher final cause (rational life as a whole), would it not also be acceptable to frustrate the final cause of an individual (considered as a human being) if it would benefit a higher final cause—namely, safeguarding social health as a whole? After all, many of Feser's arguments imply that the final cause of our sexual

---

[1] *NSE*, 399.

faculties (procreation) is itself subordinate to another, higher final cause; he explicitly states that sexual acts are far more significant morally than chewing gum or cleaning one's ears because procreation "[concerns] the maintenance of the species itself."[1]

If we accept that proposition, we must also accept the fact that procreation is not the only contributing factor to the maintenance of the species. Its total population, the resources it consumes in relation to those available to it, and the average health of its members all must also be taken into account as well. And when we include them in our analysis, we find that not only abortion but *direct infanticide* can be justified by the Principle of Totality. If a child were born with Down's Syndrome or some other severe defect, he or she would be a drain on the resources available to the community while offering very little to help them survive. And if a certain country, or even the entire planet, is becoming overpopulated, culling even healthy children might be permitted if it would reduce the population to more manageable levels and prevent total ecological collapse on either the local or planetary level.

Feser, of course, would be horrified. "Murder is a very grave frustration of our final cause as rational animals," he would say. "Since innocent human beings have a right to life by virtue of being human beings, any other human who would take it away, even from young children who are not exercising rationality *yet* but will in a few years, is obviously contravening the purposes of his highest faculties (his rational ones)." But remember the Principle of Totality—cutting off a gangrenous leg frustrates the function of our locomotive faculties, but can be excused because it preserves the life of the entire organism. Likewise, killing innocent children is an obvious frustration of our rational faculties most of the time, but is licit if done to preserve the strength of the species or secure the long-term health of its environment.

---

[1] *TLS,* 149.

Feser might say this sounds like a consequentialist argument—utilitarians (in Feser's view, anyhow) say it is acceptable to commit an evil act if some greater good is produced. But the argument I provide here is not based on the measurement of utility, it is rather entailed by a decidedly non-consequentialist interpretation of Aristotelian final causality. If the parts of an individual are metaphysically subordinate to his whole, so much so that doctors can destroy them in order to secure his life, then the individual himself ought to be metaphysically subordinate to the society or species of which he is a part, so that innocent, not-yet-rational children, at least, can be destroyed in order to secure the safety and prosperity of the whole.

It is difficult for Feser to avoid biting this bullet, given his overall philosophical orientation. He could argue that the individual is the highest final cause of all, so to speak, and while parts of an individual may be sacrificed for his benefit, the individual himself can never be sacrificed for any reason unless he has done something to deserve it. But how would one square this with Feser's talk of "maintaining the species" in *The Last Superstition*? If individual human beings were not subordinate to something else, not directed towards a larger entity they were a part of, then sexual sins would be no more serious than any other kind of sin. Since Feser seems to believe that the needs of society as a whole make certain transgressions more serious than others, it is not a humungous leap to assume that the needs of society as a whole can sometimes outweigh the inherent rights of a human being, simply because human beings, even considered as rational animals, are still "directed" to a higher end—that of preserving their society and/or species.

Once again, however much he might complain, Feser could not deny this anti-Thomistic argument, and the other ones we have discussed, stand on firm *philosophical* ground. As we have seen, the "natural law" case against non-procreative sexual behavior is far from clear-cut. We first explored how the difficulty of discerning an individual's intentions makes it very difficult to accuse him or her of "actively" frustrating the final cause of sex, and that under the definition of "frustration" as "using a faculty contrary to its purpose," homosexual activity and masturbation are actually licit. This is further supported by how non-procreative sexual behavior (nocturnal emissions in males) can actually assist sexual functioning in the long term. Extending on that discussion, we find that Feser's "traditional" morality is very hard to defend, even on his preferred metaphysical ground: The "facts" about human sexuality indicate that marriage is just a tool we can define any way we like, that polygamy is actually more in keeping with the "final cause" of sexuality than monogamy, and of course, that abortion (and arguably even infanticide) can actually fulfill, not frustrate, the final cause of preserving the species as a whole in the long run.

This line of thought would seem to have some terrifying implications. If infanticide is sometimes acceptable for the sake of the species, why wouldn't adult humans be fair game? If maintaining the quality of the species is a higher end than any individual's well-being, why would it not be acceptable to cull individuals, or even entire groups of individuals, if those groups—Jews or blacks or Slavs or whomsoever—can be labeled "inferior" in some way? This is, after all, what Feser claims to be one of the major knocks against modernity, "the intellectual and practical depersonalization of man...which has in turn led to mass murder on a scale unparalleled in human history."[1]

Most unfortunately for Feser, the arguments provided above should show that Aristotelianism can provide very little defense against that sort of depersonalization. In fact, a historical analysis in addition to a philosophical one can demonstrate how Aristotle's ideas could actually *contribute* to it. If the fruits of modernity are slavery, racial strife, and industrialized mass murder, Aristotle could have planted their seeds as easily as Ockham or Descartes.

---

[1] *TLS*, 151.

Chapter 4: Aristotelian Atrocities

Modernity—defined here as non-teleological, post-Aristotelian ways of thinking about morality—has a very bad rap in certain quarters these days. We ended the last chapter with Feser blaming it for a "depersonalization of man" that lead to industrialized mass-murder. You might want to say the Sage of Pasadena was being melodramatic, but we can't dismiss his charges that easily. Other famous philosophers have made similar points, albeit in considerably more measured tones. Alasdair MacIntyre, for instance, has said that "the dominant moral culture of advanced modernity...[is] one of unresolved and apparently unresolvable moral and other disagreements."[1] In MacIntyre's view, throughout most of European history, an Aristotelian moral framework provided common ground for evaluating moral claims with a reasonable amount of objectivity. In its absence, various competing moral theories, ranging from the Utilitarianism of Mills to the Communism of Marx to the brutal racial nationalism of Hitler could find no basis to prove themselves over their alternatives except through shrill shouting matches (at best) or the outright use of force at worst.[2]

On first thought, this critique may seem to have some bite. After all, it isn't as if the past few centuries have been especially peaceful, at least in absolute terms. African Americans endured shocking misery as slaves in the United States up to 1865, an unhappy condition ended only through an earth-shattering Civil War that was (and remains) the single bloodiest conflict in American history. World War I saw unprecedented death and destruction across all of Europe, and twenty years after it ended, World War II would become the *most destructive conflict in human history*.[3] As terrible as the wars themselves may have been, the

---

[1] Alasdair MacIntyre, *After Virtue,* 3rd ed. (University of Notre Dame Press, 2012), ix.
[2] Ibid., ix-x, 1-2, 6-12, 204-225.
[3] Anthony Beevor, *The Second World War* (Little, Brown, and Company, 2012), 780-782. One could argue that other periods, such as the Mongol expansions or the

suffering caused to civilians was even more hideous: The Nazi regime industrialized mass murder with its gas chambers and crematoriums, and, during and afterward, Communist governments in Russia, China, and Cambodia (to name just three) killed millions in purges and famines. Such a tally of horrors is enough to shake the faith of even the most fervent optimist.

Given all this, it is perhaps understandable that Feser might try to find some safety in Aristotelianism. Even if, as the preceding chapters have demonstrated, classical Aristotelianism cannot tell us much about religion or sexual morality, perhaps it could provide at least a serviceable and (most importantly) objective set of general moral guidelines. If absolutely nothing else, Aristotelianism tells us that human beings have a certain teleology (rational activity) and actions can be indisputably good or bad considered in light of that teleology. Thus, unlike any other moral system—Mills' utilitarianism, Kant's deontology, Hobbes's social contract theory, whatever—Aristotelianism can objectively condemn things like racial chattel slavery, racial genocide, or genocidal class warfare as contrary to human teleology.[1]

Alas, this chapter will demonstrate that Feser's hope is entirely unfounded. First, we will explore how Aristotelianism provides no inherent condemnation of racial chattel slavery, and that Aristotle's teachings provided a great deal of defense for the practice in the American South. Then we turn to Hitler's Germany, examining how Nazi philosophers enthusiastically embraced Aristotle's teacher, Plato, even if they were less fond of Aristotle himself. Finally, we end with a look at Communism, learning how Marx borrowed a great deal from Aristotle as well as the "modern" philosophers Feser loathes. We will see how the atheistic regime of the Soviet Union was not actually anti-Aristotelian in the sense Feser would claim, and that even in the absence

---

European conquest of the New World, ended up with higher death tolls, but those took place over a longer span of time and did not end with the deployment of entirely new brands of weaponry (nuclear bombs).
[1] *TLS*, 218-220.

of belief in God or any other kind of immaterial being, Soviet agents responsible for mass torture and starvation justified their actions on grounds very comprehensible to Aristotle's teleology, which can be understood apart from his theology.

4.1: Aristotle and Slavery

The first sin of historical obfuscation over which I will take Feser to task can be found in *The Last Superstition*. He claims that,

> ...the existence of natural law entails...many other rights (such as a right to personal liberty that is strong enough to rule out chattel slavery as intrinsically immoral – the claim made by some that natural law theory would support slavery as it was known in the United States is a slander).[1]

He expounds on this point in an endnote, saying

> That one human being can literally own another as his property, or can kidnap another and make him a slave, or that some races are naturally suited to being enslaved by others, are notions condemned by natural law theory as intrinsically immoral. It is true that natural law theory has traditionally allowed that lesser forms of "slavery" could in principle be justified. But what this would involve is a prolonged period of servitude as a way of paying off a significant debt, say, or as punishment for a crime.... Even so, natural law theorists have tended to see the practice as too fraught with moral hazards to be defensible in practice; and the suggestion that the legitimacy of racial chattel slavery as it was known in early American history follows from natural law theory is, as I say, a slander.[2]

A thorough study of American slavery proves Feser very wrong. Indeed, I would argue that claiming anyone who sees a connection between natural law and American racial slavery commits slander *is*

---

[1] *TLS*, 147.
[2] Ibid., 283. Feser makes almost exactly the same point in his blog. See Edward Feser, "Walters on TLS," *Edward Feser,* January 14, 2009, last accessed July 5, 2020, http://edwardfeser.blogspot.com/2009/01/walters-on-tls.html

itself a slander. As we will see, going back in history to Aristotle himself, and then looking at his biggest fans in the U.S, there is ample evidence in the historical record to support such a connection, and honest, reasonable people can very, very easily assert it exists.

Given Aristotle's importance to the natural law tradition, if it is true that slavery would be "condemned by natural law theory as intrinsically immoral," one would expect Aristotle to have condemned it. But this is not the case—precisely the opposite. The late, great historian of slavery, David Brion Davis, in his equally great, comprehensive study of slavery in the Western world, did not allow Aristotle to escape his probing analytical eye:

> The natural slave, according to Aristotle, could have no will or interests of his own; he or she was merely a tool or instrument, the extension of the owner's physical nature. In an important passage that deserves to be quoted in full, Aristotle makes explicit the parallel between the slave and the domesticated beast: 'Tame animals are naturally better than wild animals, yet for all tame animals there is an advantage in being under human control, as this secures their survival...by analogy, the same must necessarily apply to mankind as a whole. Therefore all men who differ from one another by as much as the soul differs from the body or man from a wild beast (and that is the state of those who work by using their bodies, and for whom that is the best they can do)— these people are slaves by nature, and it is better for them to be subject to this kind of control, as it is better for the other creatures I've mentioned...[A]ssistance regarding the necessities of life is provided by both groups, by slaves and domestic animals. Nature must therefore have intended to make the bodies of free men and slaves different also; slaves' bodies strong for the services they have to do, those of free men upright and not much use for that kind of work, but instead useful for community life.' While even Aristotle admitted that sometimes 'slaves can have the bodies of free men' and that free men could have 'only the souls and not the bodies of free men,' he could nevertheless conclude, in an argument that would have immeasurable influence in Western culture, that 'it is clear that there are certain people who are free and

certain who are slaves by nature, and it is both to their advantage, and just, for them to be slaves.' While slaves in antiquity could usually be recognized by clothing, branding, and collars, and other symbols, the millennia-long search for ways to identify 'natural slaves' would eventually be solved by the physical characteristics of sub-Saharan Africans.[1]

Looking at a little more of Aristotle's work, however, things get even worse for Feser's assertion. Again, Feser claims classical natural law theory justifies slavery only in "the much less harsh form of servitude involving a prolonged obligation to labor for another as payment of a debt, punishment for a crime," etc. But this is in direct contradiction to what Aristotle, assumedly a founder of the classical natural law tradition, believed. As the Philosopher states,

> We have next to consider whether there are, or are not, some people who are by nature... for whom slavery is the better and just condition, or whether the reverse is the case and all slavery is contrary to nature. The issue is not difficult... The relation of ruler and ruled is one of those things which are not only necessary, but also beneficial; and there are species in which a distinction is already marked, immediately at birth, between those of its members who are intended for being ruled and those who are intended to rule.[2]

This quite obviously to justifies slavery as a lifelong condition, based on some "distinction" evident from birth, not as a temporary punishment for some crime.

It is curious that Feser chose not to mention this. He would certainly be aware of Aristotle's *Politics*, given his expertise on Aristotle generally, and would therefore be aware of Aristotle's condoning of

---

[1] David Brion Davis, *Inhuman Bondage: The Rise and Fall of Slavery in the New World* (Oxford University Press, 2006), 33-34. Davis is citing here Thomas Wiedemann's *Greek and Roman Slavery* (Routledge, 1981), 18-19. You can see the quote is accurately represented for yourself by checking out Aristotle, *Politics*, trans. Ernest Baker (Oxford University Press, 1995), 16-17.

[2] Aristotle, *Politics*, trans. Ernest Baker (Oxford University Press, 1995), 15.

slavery. Maybe Feser did not want to weaken his argument by making Aristotle look bad, but then one could accuse Feser of, if not dishonesty, then at least less-than-forthrightness. I don't think this is the case, however, because a criticism of Aristotle would have led Feser to a defense of Christianity specifically (rather than the "Philosopher's God" generally), which is what he would have wanted to do as a Catholic. Later in *Inhuman Bondage*, Davis praises many Catholics for their opposition to slavery. Gregory of Nyssa (the great Catholic saint and theologian) was the first person in all of antiquity to condemn slavery in and of itself (though some Stoics and Cynics were also, well, cynical about the institution).[1] Lamentably, St. Aquinas didn't go as far—according to Davis,

> Aquinas emphasized that the institution [slavery] was contrary only to the first intention of nature, but not to the second intention, which was adjusted to man's limited capacities in a sinful world. Aquinas still thought of slavery as occasioned by sin, but he made it seem more natural and tolerable by identifying it with the rational structure of being, which required each individual to accept, along with old age and death, the necessity of subordination to a higher authority.[2]

While obviously not as forcefully antislavery as St. Gregory, Aquinas nonetheless identified the institution as an undesirable necessity in a fallen world rather than a simple result of nature. Since Feser defends not just Aristotle's God but Aquinas' more particular Catholic God, he would have done well to note how Aquinas was actually more advanced in morality than his predecessor.

Unfortunately, this embryonic antislavery impulse would not blossom within Christendom for many centuries. During that time, Aristotle provided a very strong ground for proponents of American racial slavery to stand on; as noted by many historians of the institution. To quote one of them, Marek Steedman:

---

[1] Davis, 34-35.
[2] Ibid., 55.

...race naturalized slavery not simply by casting slaves as an inferior, but as specifically fitted for a domesticated, childlike dependence.... The true slave, incapable of full rationality, could at best follow directions.... *Were it true*, he [Aristotle] suggests, *that 'a good man is born of good men,' and implicitly, that noxious creatures are born of noxious creatures, then it would be possible to justify the enslavement of the children of slaves.*[1]

Given this understanding of Aristotle, it was easy indeed for Southerners to reconcile his philosophy with their peculiar institution. Chattel slavery of blacks was perfectly consistent with an Aristotelian conception of natural law. Even if both blacks and whites were human (and the popularity of 'polygenesis' theories in the antebellum South made this by no means an uncontested proposition), it just so happened that black humans had a different "Essence" than white humans: The former were congenitally endowed with less reason and virtue than the latter, who, being noble, begat noble children. This meant that blacks were congenitally fated to serve whites, who were congenitally fated to rule—in short, a perpetual system of racial slavery. One can see this 'directly from the horse's mouth,' that is to say, in a veritable panoply of primary sources. Just listen to Professor Thomas Roderick Dew in "The Pro-Slavery Argument" (authored with several other influential Southerners, such as senator James Henry Hammond of South Carolina). He told us:

> Aristotle, the greatest philosopher of antiquity, and a man of as capacious mind as the world ever produced, was a warm advocate of slavery—maintaining that it was reasonable, necessary, and natural; and, accordingly, in his model of a republic, there were to be comparatively few freemen served by many slaves.[2]

---

[1] Marek D. Steedman, *Jim Crow Citizenship: Liberalism and the Southern Defense of Racial Hierarchy* (Routledge, 2012), 31-35. The italics are mine.

[2] William Harper, Thomas Roderick Dew, et. Al, *The Pro-Slavery Argument: As Maintained by the Most Distinguished Writers of the Southern States* (New York: Negro Universities Press, 1968), 306.

Listen as well to the Southern Literary Messenger, a proslavery periodical widely read among educated men in the South, which posted many articles proving slavery was natural in the Aristotelian sense. In a passage that sounds eerily similar to something Feser might have written, an anonymous author declared:

> …to Aristotle, one of the most profound of the philosophers of antiquity, we confidently appeal, and with more confidence, because in this iron age of utilitarianism, his material philosophy, fortified with all the powers of the 'greatest, wisest, meanest of mankind,' has been preferred to the spiritual sublimity of the divine Plato. Aristotle has expressly declared, that 'in the natural state of man, from the origin of things, a portion of the human family must command, and the remainder obey; that the distinction which exists between master and servant is a distinction at once natural and indispensable; and that when we find existing among men freemen and slaves, it is not man, but nature herself, who has ordained the distinction.[1]

To be fair, Aristotle did not say exactly the same things Dew and The Southern Literary Messenger did. As S. Sara Monoson has pointed out:

> Aristotle dismisses body type as a reliable indicator of free or slave by nature even though natural slaves will be especially suited to hard physical labour. As a matter of fact, he acknowledges, 'Slaves often have the bodies of freemen.' Moreover, it does not even occur to him to consider skin colour as a useful sign. He does not trust physical markers much at all."

---

[1] "Thoughts on Slavery, by a Southern," The Southern Literary Messenger, Vol. IV, No. 12, Richmond, VA, Dec. 1838, 739. This primary source is available for free here:
https://play.google.com/books/reader?id=_E4FAAAAQAAJ&printsec=frontcover&output=reader&hl=en&pg=GBS.PP1

She goes on to note that many Southerners relied on mistranslations of Aristotle's writing or read their own biases into him.[1] Unfortunately, the Stagirite cannot be let off the hook so easily. Some Southerners did engage Aristotle directly on his own points—Monoson gives George Frederick Holmes as an example. It seems that Holmes explicitly admitted Aristotle did not claim blacks were naturally suited to slavery—but then claimed this was merely because Aristotle did not have as much experience with blacks as 19th century Southerners did, and if he had, he would approve of racial chattel slavery! Holmes told his readers that "the distinct functions of different races in the onward march of human progress promises to be recognized as the principle axiom of historical science" and of course, predictably, the 'function' of the black race (in the Aristotelian sense Feser tries to defend) would be to serve.[2]

Even then, I suppose, Aristotle needs some defense. You could say that Holmes still failed to appreciate many of the nuances in Aristotle's position; Monson argues that he certainly did. She points out that:

> Aristotle himself never marshals the ubiquity of slavery through history and cross-culturally as evidence of its roots in nature and justice. Instead, Aristotle insists on the logical separation of these issues.[3]

Since Holmes claimed the widespread usage of Africans as slaves meant that Africans were "naturally" slaves, Aristotle would likely disagree and tell Holmes that neither physical appearance nor common usage were sufficient to mark an institution like slavery as "natural" in the "natural law" sense.

---

[1] S. Sara Monoson, "Recollecting Aristotle: Pro-Slavery Thought in Antebellum America and the Argument of Politics Book I" in Richard Alston, Edith Hall, and Justine McConnell, eds., *Ancient Slavery and Abolition* (Oxford University Press, 2011), 265.
[2] Ibid., 270.
[3] Ibid., 271.

But once again, we can't let Aristotle off too easily. Monoson tells us that Aristotle believed,

> ...a different observable form of activity—endurance of despotism without resentment—as a good sign that faulty deliberative capacities, and thus slavish natures, are widespread in a population.[1]

Surprise surprise, slaveowners "found" this trait amongst blacks. Proslavery literature abounded with descriptions of how happy blacks were to be enslaved. It was nonsense, of course—many Southerners took slave songs as proof slaves were "happy" when in fact the songs were about how miserable they were and how they longed for freedom; many slaveowners also whipped their slaves if the unfortunates acted too miserable (a literal case of "the beatings will continue until morale improves"). But the line of reasoning Southerners used was valid under Aristotle's reasoning about slavery—it just wasn't "sound" (it was empirically false).

I have demonstrated, I hope, the two main thrusts of my argument, specifically to refute Feser's attempt at defending Aristotle. To review: Feser claimed that natural law theory, originated by Aristotle among others, condemned slavery as "intrinsically immoral," and that it is slanderous to claim American racial chattel slavery could have possibly been legitimized by natural law theory. As the scholars I've quoted above prove, however, Aristotle never condemned slavery as a whole on natural-law grounds, instead saying it could be justified under certain conditions. And while American slaveowners weren't one-hundred-percent correct in their readings of Aristotle, they still used him enthusiastically to justify their regime. It is, therefore, not at all a "slander" to say that the natural law tradition, exemplified by Aristotle at least, could be and has been used to justify racial chattel slavery.

---

[1] Ibid., 266.

4.2: Plato and Nazism

Most people (or at least those reading a book like this) would consider an acceptance of slavery to be a knock against Aristotelian philosophy. At the very least, it has been an embarrassment to many famous Aristotelians. The aforementioned Alasdair MacIntyre, for instance, has argued that modern-day Aristotelians ought to rescue Aristotle's own philosophy from its founder: "failure to reject Aristotle's social prejudices not only would have made Aristotle's whole system of political, social, and moral thought irrelevant to the vast majority of humankind but would, in fact, have condemned his system to incoherence."[1] Given the enthusiasm with which antebellum slaveholders embraced Aristotle—something Edward Feser said was a "slanderous" charge—one might possibly expect the Sage of Pasadena to be at least slightly less enthusiastic about him, or willing to accept the big man of the natural law Tradition was wrong about more than just science.

It is quite possible Feser would be, but then again, many other right-wingers are probably not as sporting—perhaps, should they ever read this book, other conservatives would conclude that racial chattel slavery is actually wise and just, and only degenerate moderns would have any problem with it. In fairness, I think it's unlikely in Feser's case—to his credit, he has good taste in music,[2] and would probably be hesitant to claim geniuses like John Coltrane or Miles Davis were actually nothing more than hewers of wood and drawers of water. But not everyone can appreciate the finer points of jazz, and the sorts of conservatives who can't tend to be the sorts who would have fought for the Confederacy if they had the chance.

---

[1] Alasdair MacIntyre, *Ethics in the Conflicts of Modernity: An Essay on Desire, Practical Reasoning, and Narrative* (Cambridge University Press, 2016), 86.
[2] Edward Feser, "Pop Culture and the Lure of Platonism", *Edward Feser* (blog), September 6, 2010, last accessed on July 5, 2020, https://edwardfeser.blogspot.com/2010/09/pop-culture-and-lure-of-platonism.html

Even so, while the less refined sort of conservative might be willing to forgive Aristotle's acceptance of racial slavery, such people would probably still maintain it's possible to go too far with the racism thing. Genocide and mass sterilization, to take two examples, would probably be too extreme for even the most die-hard right-winger, at least one concerned with keeping himself off law-enforcement watchlists. Thus, when talking to such people, Feser would likely still maintain that "the classical tradition" would condemn Nazism and its "industrialized mass murder," and that only those "in the company of Plato, Aristotle, and Aquinas"[1] could coherently condemn it.

I am afraid that would be news to the Nazis themselves. Feser at least implicitly blames their misdeeds (and those of the Communists, to whom we will attend in the next section) on modern, non-Aristotelian philosophical concepts like "Darwinian reductionism."[2] However, though the Nazis certainly took a great deal from modern scientific thinking of the late nineteenth and early twentieth centuries (such as American eugenicists and race theorists—Feser's attacks on modernity may be overblown but by no means entirely off the mark),[3] they did not at all forget or dismiss older thinkers, most notably Plato. And it is important to note here that while Feser and Thomists in general consider themselves closer to Aristotle, they believe Plato laid the foundations for the "classical tradition" as a whole. Feser credits Plato for coming up with the concept of Forms in the first place along with the notion of a transcendent, immaterial grounding for the entire

---

[1] *TLS*, 220.
[2] Ibid., 223.
[3] See James Q. Whitman, *Hitler's American Model: The United States and the Making of Nazi Race Law* (Princeton University Press, 2017) for an extensive description of the ways American eugenicists such as Lothrop Stoddard and Madison Grant provided a "scientific" inspiration for the Nazi regime's sterilization and euthanasia policies. However, Whitman also notes that American Jim Crow laws and the extermination of the Native Americans provided considerably more direct and obvious inspirations for Nazi racial laws and their plans to exterminate the populations of Eastern Europe for "living space" (*Lebensraum*).

universe; as he said in *The Last Superstition*, "we see in Plato the first detailed formulation in Western thought of the themes that would persist and be developed further in the classical philosophical tradition, from Aristotle to Augustine to the Scholastics."[1]

It is difficult to tell whether or not Hitler himself had any genuine interest in that classical tradition—as historian Ian Kershaw has noted, Hitler's secretive personality and deceitful, self-aggrandizing tendencies make it more difficult than one would expect to reconstruct not only the events of his life but its intellectual tenor: his philosophical interests, influences, and leanings.[2] Publicly, at least, Hitler evinced a great deal of admiration for the ancient Greeks. Their "monumentalism" influenced his architectural plans, in *Mein Kampf* he declared that his present-day struggle "encompasses both Greece and Germanness together," praised the Spartans for their "unsullied racial state," and often compared himself to Pericles.[3] But it is less clear how seriously he read (much less understood) philosophers such as Plato and Aristotle. Despite this, contemporary readers are not entirely without means of understanding Nazism's philosophical groundings. This ideology did not rise solely upon Hitler's back: there is a wealth of evidence from

---

[1] *TLS*, 38.
[2] Ian Kershaw, *Hitler, 1889-1936: Hubris* (W.W. Norton, 1999), xiv. One of the ways scholars have attempted to gain more insight into the dictator's mind (aside from his published writings) is through the various books he owned through his life. The historian Timothy Rydecker has written a fascinating intellectual biography of Hitler by surveying various libraries which acquired some of Hitler's books following World War II, but Rydecker notes that the fragmented and incomplete nature of these collections (much of Hitler's personal library, along with his other belongings, was destroyed during the war) makes it very difficult to produce a complete and comprehensive sketch of Hitler's intellectual makeup and by extension his philosophical views, positions on metaphysics, and other such matters. See Timothy Rydecker, *Hitler's Private Library: The Books That Shaped His Life* (Alfred A. Knopf, 2008), xvi-xvii.
[3] Richard Wolin, "Fascism and Hermeneutics: Gadamer and the Ambiguities of 'Inner Emigration'" in Anson Rabinbach and Wolfgang Bialas, eds., *Nazi Germany and the Humanities: How German Academics Embraced Nazism* (Oneworld Publications, 2014), 115-124.

various propagandists, theorists, academics, and other functionaries inside of or supporting the Nazi party which can be used to understand its relationship to the "classical tradition." What did such people say?

The craftsmen of the Nazi educational curriculum certainly thought they were in the company of Plato, and indeed, that all good Germans ought to be. Teenagers in Hitler's Germany read Plato extensively in various secondary school courses, and Nazi educators thought they should read more. One teacher at a gymnasium (an equivalent of an American high school), Adolf Rusch, declared that Plato was "the teacher of the German man" and the perfect antidote to a spirit of "outrageous individualism" which threatened the well-being of the German race as a whole. German history books of the 1930s portrayed Plato as "a central figure in the Nordic resistance to the racial, intellectual, and moral decadence of the Athenian city-state" and "the final torchbearer of Nordic Hellenism." A letter from a schoolteacher to the Nazi Ministry of Education gushed that "the active Nordic spirit found its most sublime expression in Plato's philosophy."[1]

Secondary and high school teachers found ample backing for their Platonist sympathies in the highest echelons of German academia. Werner Jaeger, one of the most accomplished German Hellenists of the 1920s and 30s, advanced a new school of philosophical interpretation called the "Third Humanism." Jaeger concentrated on the political aspects of Plato's writing. He held that the *Republic's* "celebration of Spartan virtues such as 'breeding' and 'rank,' along with its characterizations of the 'guardians' as a biologically superior warrior caste" provided a plan for twentieth-century Germans to replace the degenerate, decaying Weimar Republic with an authoritarian replacement and "succeed politically where Plato, in his ill-conceived efforts with the tyrant Dionysos at Syracuse, had failed."[2] Though he was not a Nazi himself, and indeed fled to the United States in 1936 to escape

---

[1] Johann Chapoutot, *Greeks, Romans, Germans: How the Nazis Usurped Europe's Classical Past* (University of California Press, 2016), 196-198, 438.
[2] Wolin in Rabinbach and Bialas, 115-124, Chapoutot, 106.

them, Jaeger had nothing but sympathy for the Nazi attacks on individual autonomy and self-expression.[1] In 1933 he published an article in the journal *Volk im Werden*, edited by a member of the Nazi Party named Ernst Kreick, defending a particularly authoritarian method of humanistic inquiry as exemplified by Plato in the past and Nazism in the present. Jaeger castigated the bloodless humanism of the Enlightenment as misguidedly concentrating on "the aesthetic and formal education of the sole individual," which overlooked the fact that any human being was a "political creature...a social being that existed within a state." It was only this atomized and politically degraded humanism that was "incompatible with the intellectual historical presuppositions of National Socialism." Whatever his other complaints about the National Socialist system may have been, he believed in the Nazi dream of turning its youth into citizen-soldiers whose physical and mental bodies were turned entirely to the service of the state, and believed in this precisely because of its affinity to the society pictured in Plato's *Republic*.[2]

Many other German classicists of this era shared Jaeger's sentiments, and they were even more enamored with the Nazi project.

> As the Plato scholar Kurt Hildebrandt observed, "the Greek doesn't bind himself to God and the world as an individual; he becomes a man through and by virtue of his belonging to the State." The notion that by themselves individuals count for naught but only achieve fulfillment by virtue of the greater sense of purpose transmitted by the state was one of the precepts that encouraged classicists, as well as humanists of all stripes, to greet the advent of the Third Reich with open arms.[3]

But it was among would-be "racial scientists" that Plato's ideas found their most receptive audience.

---

[1] Helen Roche and Kyriakos Demetriou, eds., *Brill's Companion to the Classics, Fascist Italy, and Nazi Germany* (BRILL, 2017), 224.
[2] Chapoutot, 106.
[3] Wolin in Rabinbach and Bialas, 118.

Hans Friedrich Karl Guenther was arguably the father of academic "race science" inside Nazi Germany. He published many books and articles under the auspices of an early Nazi recruit, Julius Friedrich Lehmann, until the 1930s, when he hitched his wagon to the rising star of the Nazi political movement. He had never managed to attain any academic position until the German state of Thuringia elected a National Socialist state government, at which point they lobbied the University of Jena to create a new "chair in racial science" and offer it to him specifically. Guenther happily accepted and formally joined the party in 1932, accumulating a number of awards for his work defending and disseminating Hitler's ideology, such as the Goethe medal for art and science and the Golden Party Badge.[1] If the party thought Guenther was the father of race science, Guenther thought Plato was its grandfather. He wrote an entire book titled *Platon als Hueter des Lebens*, or *Plato: The Guardian of Life*, praising the classical philosopher for being so conscious of "the laws of heredity and selection;" Guenther explicitly called Plato a precursor of "Gobineau, Mendel, and Galton" (whose ideas Guenther utilized to justify his theories of Nordic supremacy) and a clear-sighted proponent of the doctrine of human inequality. Looking at Plato's segregation of human souls into gold, silver, and bronze, Guenther believed the philosopher was anticipating Nazi theories of racial difference, the highest type of human naturally being Nordic, and of course, the only type worthy of both ruling and doing philosophy.[2]

In this way as well, Guenther found in Plato a staunch defender of Nazi eugenics. Though he did not go so far as to directly prescribe murder, Guenther was happy to advocate for "sterilization" of "weak individuals" to secure the health of the polity. Other Platonists, however, were nowhere near as "merciful;" Kurt Hildebrandt recommended the destruction of those deemed to be weak because "leniency [towards a degenerate individual] would appear to Plato to be

---

[1] Chapoutot, 26.
[2] Ibid, 200, 223.

a cruelty against the people seen as a whole."[1] This seems to be almost word for word a restatement of the ugly argument for eugenics I provided at the end of the previous chapter: Hildebrandt would almost certainly say that Plato acknowledged the "principle of totality," which meant he would condone the abortion or even infanticide of individuals if removing them improved the "health" of the state as a whole.

All this is not to blame Plato for the crimes of Nazism—indeed, Feser could take some vindication in the knowledge that pro-Nazi classicists often misread the philosopher in important ways. As Wolin also notes, Jaeger's movement emphasized the study of Plato's political thought rather than his cosmology and metaphysics, which Feser might say the classical tradition held in higher regard.[2] And as Johann Chapoutot notes, "Nazi racism hermetically sealed people into the airtight bubble of their race, while for Plato, every individual with the proper qualities must be deemed worthy and eligible for entry into the castes of warriors and philosopher-kings."[3] Feser and other Thomists, like John Skalko, would argue that the maintenance of innocent life and/or personal freedom is itself the proper end of any social organization, so killing the innocent to maintain a state is utterly self-defeating.[4] I'd be the last to argue with any of that. But even so, the fact that Nazi exterminationism could so readily hijack a progenitor of the natural law tradition should cast some doubt on Feser's argument for it.

To again summarize a line of argument threaded through *The Last Superstition*, the consequence of rejecting "classical metaphysics"—rejecting the idea of formal and final causality—as Hume and Hobbes did, is to forfeit any claim to objective morality. Such people have

---

[1] Ibid., 202-203.
[2] Wolin in Rabinach and Bialas, 117.
[3] Chapoutot, 201-203.
[4] Skalko, 281-282, Edward Feser, "The Socialist State as an Occasionalist God," *Edward Feser* (blog), February 15, 2020, last accessed on July 5, 2020, http://edwardfeser.blogspot.com/2020/02/the-socialist-state-as-occasionalist-god.html

"nothing to say" to a group of sociopaths such as the Nazis "[seeking] to remake society in their image...The Platonist, Aristotelian, or Thomist can say that such people are behaving in an inherently irrational and objectively wicked manner, given human nature."[1] But the quotes from Nazi Germany's most famous philosophers, antiquarians, and classicists do little indeed to assure anyone that the "classical tradition" provides much defense against Nazism. Men such as Werner Jaeger, Hans Guenther, and Kurt Hildebrandt might have been less concerned with Plato's metaphysics, but they never completely repudiated those metaphysics either. Indeed, they would have argued that the Nazi vision of society was actually in keeping with the objective reality of human nature, and explicitly did so. Hans Guenther wrote openly that human beings are political animals by nature, which meant they are directed towards upholding the health of the polity as a whole rather than individual well-being, which would mandate "the elimination of all sick or deformed children, the extermination of all who are unfit for life."[2]

    We can certainly say, as Chapoutot does, and as Feser and Skalko likely would, that Guenther is misinterpreting Plato here, and if he (along with Jaeger and Hildebrandt) had truly understood him, they would have opposed rather than supported the Nazis. But if the failure of these philosophers was in *misinterpreting* Plato rather than simply ignoring him, Feser's advocacy for the "classical tradition" over its modern alternatives becomes much less convincing. He tells us that abandoning that tradition "is implicated...in the intellectual and practical depersonalization of man...which has in turn led to mass murder." Now, in fairness to Feser, he does admit that "non-intellectual factors" also contributed to that depersonalization, in some cases more significantly.[3] But Guenther, Hildebrandt, and Jaeger show us how mass

---

[1] *TLS*, 213.

[2] Chapoutot, 202. The quote is from Hans Guenther's work, *Plato: The Guardian of Life* (J.F. Lehmann's, 1928), 33. Also see Simona Forti, "The Biopolitics of Souls: Racism, Nazism, and Plato," *Political Theory* 34, no. 1 (2006), 9-32, http://www.jstor.org/stable/20452432.

[3] *TLS*, 51.

murder could be justified *on purely intellectual grounds by that very tradition*. Even if Plato's realism about Forms had never been replaced by Feser's hated nominalism or conceptualism, villains such as the Nazis would still have committed the very same crimes—they would simply have to pretend that Plato believed in the same rigid racial hierarchy they did. In other words, it seems much harder for Feser to argue that abandoning the classical tradition was actually the primary "intellectual factor" leading to racial genocide. If that tradition had not been abandoned, the Nazis would have simply found a way to shoehorn it into their mad schemes.

Even so, while Feser respects Plato, he is much more a follower of Aristotle (through Aquinas). And, if he were to read the preceding passages, he might be inclined to gloat over how the Nazi philosophers I have quoted make very little mention of the Stagirite. Indeed, as Chapoutot says, "[t]he contrast between the Third Reich's avid interest in Plato and its relative neglect of Aristotle is shocking but instructive."[1] While some Nazi writers used a term, "politischer Mensch," similar to Aristotle's "political animal," direct references to Aristotle himself were usually negative. The propagandist Alfred Rosenberg dismissed Aristotle as being too cerebral compared to Plato, strong in both mind and body. Ernst Krieck had an even lower opinion of the Philosopher, accusing him of being bloodless and overly abstract, disconnected from the connections between material and spiritual things, and "responsible for the entire decline of traditional Greek education." A handful of Hitler-era writers were more positive—Ludwig Schemann approved of Aristotle's defense of slavery, and one secondary-school textbook claimed Aristotle had presaged Nazi theories on the supposed evils of race-mixing.[2] But, in general, positive references to Aristotle and Aristotelianism were rare and mostly eclipsed by a focus on Platonism.

Perhaps, then, Feser would claim his beloved classical tradition is off the hook. As much as he likes Plato, we have already seen (and will

---

[1] Chapoutot, 206.
[2] Ibid., 205-207.

see again in future chapters) that Feser thinks Aristotle was correct to a much greater extent than Plato, and thus more important to the tradition Feser believes is so important. He would therefore hold on to his claim that only "Aristotelians and Thomists" could objectively condemn the genocidal ideals of the Nazis, needing only to drop the Platonists. But even that position would be much harder to maintain if Feser realized the other high-bodycount ideology he attributes to modernity—Communism—owed as much to Aristotle as the Nazis did to Plato.

4.3: Aristotle and Communism

For Feser, as for most conservatives, Communism (rather than Nazism) is the ultimate evil, and if non-Aristotelian philosophy helped lead to it, that alone would be the ultimate condemnation of moderns like Hobbes, Hume, and their descendants. Most of the "polemics" Feser put into *The Last Superstition* are aimed at them, but he also offers more than a few unkind words to Karl Marx and his followers. According to Feser, "Dawkins, Harris, and Hitchens, with practiced dudgeon, distance themselves from Stalin, Mao, Pol Pot, and other Communist mass murderers—devout atheists all—on the grounds that people so obviously wicked and irrational surely cannot be representative of 'real' secularism." Feser goes on to condemn Hitchens for "refusing to allow even one of the 100 million corpses produced by Communism to count as evidence against the moral claims of atheism."[1] However, it is not just atheism to which Feser attributes these crimes. It is "abandoning Aristotelianism" which "is implicated in...mass-murder on a scale unparalleled in human history;" the belief that "modern science has somehow 'refuted' Aristotelian metaphysics" is a "centuries-long scam" that "led to a debasement of man the most brutal realizations of which were National Socialism and Marxism."[2] Unfortunately, Feser goes into very little detail about how, precisely, Marxist philosophy departed from Aristotelian metaphysics. This is understandable from an editorial

---

[1] *TLS*, 159-160.
[2] Ibid., 51, 222.

perspective. *The Last Superstition* is not a specifically political or economic treatise, so it would have been unwise to spend too much time on detailed analysis on what Marx wrote about Aristotle or how the governments of Lenin and Stalin provided philosophical backing for their policies. However, Feser's blog is under no such restrictions; he can write on whatever he wants at whatever length he wants over there. And as it so happens, a recent (at the time of this writing) entry addresses precisely that subject.

In a series of posts called "Adventures in the Old Atheism," Feser takes a closer look at what very famous atheists from the 19th and early 20th centuries actually believed and contrasted their (supposedly) more mature, far-sighted critiques of religion to (in Feser's view) the more jejune, callow insults contemporary atheists like Richard Dawkins supposedly provide. In the fourth entry, Feser examines the thought of Karl Marx and, despite his deep disagreements with it, deems it much more intellectually reputable than the sort of argumentation one would find from a "pimply atheist teenager mouthing off on Reddit."[1] Curiously enough, the reason Feser finds Marx so (comparatively) respectable is that unlike the Reddit teenager, *Marx was, in some respects, an Aristotelian!*

While noting that Marx, unlike Aristotle, was an atheist and a materialist, Feser admits that he did believe (as do some contemporary atheists like Thomas Nagel) in a naturalistic sort of teleology. Marx thought that "material systems reliably exhibit tendencies toward certain outcomes, and that identifying the outcome toward which a component of the system aims or for the sake of which it operates is a crucial part of explaining it." Additionally, Marx seemed to have shared Aristotle's ideas of what constituted a good life, which naturally informed his beliefs on proper social organization. Feser quotes the

---

[1] Edward Feser, "Adventures in the Old Atheism, Part IV: Marx," *Edward Feser* (blog), January 23, 2020, last accessed on July 5, 2020, http://edwardfeser.blogspot.com/2020/01/adventures-in-old-atheism-part-iv-marx.html

scholar Allen Wood, who said "the good life, for both Marx and Aristotle, consists chiefly in the actualization of one's powers." Now, as Feser immediately notes, Marx placed too much emphasis on economics in his assessment of the human Essence and its corresponding good (or actualization), and Marx's economics were quite dubious anyways.[1] But this would not make Marx some sort of anti-Aristotelian, and it is no proof he attempted to either refute or abandon Aristotelianism. It would merely prove he was mistaken about economics, history, sociology, and other matters tangential to Aristotle's metaphysical teachings.

It is worth noting here, and at some length, that Feser's assessment of Marx is well supported by other scholars. In fact, if anything, Feser has very much *understated* the case for Marx's Aristotelianism. According to scholars such as George McCarthy, Jonathan Pike, and Philip J. Kain, Aristotle's influence ran through huge amounts of Marx's work. McCarthy claims that "Marx's analysis of Ricardo's Principles of Political Economy and Taxation makes sense only within the context of Aristotle's Nicomachean Ethics." Kain, examining Marx's dissertation and several letters written over the course of his life, concludes that Marx "[saw a] normative criterion of civil law as rational and rooted in nature and, like many natural law theorists, sees a close relationship between descriptive laws of nature and laws as prescriptive social norms." And with regard to the *Grundrisse*, another monograph Marx had written further exploring the ideas of his *Communist Manifesto*, Pike finds that Marx's attitude towards universals and the process of abstraction was closer to Aristotle than Plato or any other philosopher.[2] While I obviously wouldn't claim that Feser is right about

---

[1] Ibid., Allen Wood, *Karl Marx, 2nd Edition* (Routledge, 2004), 37. According to Wood, however, there is an important way Marx departs from Aristotle—on page 128, Wood mentions that Marx was "at least as concerned" about material evils such as poverty, disease, and overwork as he was about capitalism's frustration of the human capacity for "self-actualization."

[2] George E. McCarthy, *Marx and the Ancients: Classical Ethics, Social Justice, and Nineteenth-Century Political Economy* (Rowman and Littlefield Publishers, inc., 1990), 1, 61, 112-113, Philip J. Kain, "Aristotle, Kant, and the Ethics of Young Marx,"

everything (or even most things), if so many specialists on Marx are backing him up when it comes to the Santa look-alike's Aristotelian sympathies, I think it's fair to say he's right on this point.

Why bring all this up? If Feser's assessment of Marx is so accurate, isn't that a credit to Feser? It is, but unfortunately, it is *much less* a credit to the philosophical system he so fervently defends—namely, Aristotelianism.

Remember what Feser wrote in *The Last Superstition?* The belief that Aristotelianism has been refuted is a "scam" that "has led to a debasement of man the most brutal realizations of which were National Socialism and Marxism."[1] But unless Feser's intellectual positions have changed drastically since he wrote *The Last Superstition* in 2008 (and while I may be mistaken, I don't think they have), it is much harder to see how he could make this claim today. Marx may not have believed in "the immortality of the soul" or "the existence of God," but he did believe in something similar to the natural law[2], given his acceptance of a materialist sort of Aristotelian teleology and essentialism. As far as I can tell, if Feser, Pike, McCarthy, Wood, and most other academics who have studied Marx, are right, Marx definitely did not believe that the science of his day had "refuted" Aristotle with regard to teleology. Marx apparently did not buy, at least entirely, into the "scam" Feser decries. *So then how could Feser possibly argue that such a "scam" was responsible for all the corpses Marxism ended up producing?*

Feser would and does claim that Marx's "economic reductionism, vision of human life as a struggle of antagonistic classes, [and] hostility

---

in George E. McCarthy, ed., *Marx and Aristotle: Nineteenth-Century German Social Theory and Classical Antiquity* (Rowman and Littlefield Publishers, inc., 1992), 220, Jonathan E. Pike, *From Aristotle to Marx: Aristotelianism in Marxist Social Ontology* (Ashgate Publishing, 1999), 35. Also see Karl Marx, "The German Ideology," *Karl Marx and Friedrich Engels, Collected Works,* vol. 5 (New York: International Publishers, 1976), 83.

[1] *TLS*, 222.
[2] Ibid.

to the family...are all repulsive and inhuman," and such errors contributed to if not caused the various atrocities Communist regimes were known for.[1] That may be true, but it is also irrelevant to Aristotelianism. Nothing in Aristotelian metaphysics inherently or necessarily denies class struggle, the belief that the family is useless or outrightly harmful to economic justice, or whatever. You could say that anyone who holds such positions has gravely misunderstood the Essence of Humanity and its associated *telos*, but you could not say they are outrightly denying that such things exist at all. Thus, it seems that Feser was simply wrong to ascribe Communism's death toll to any "refutation" or "abandonment" of Aristotelianism. Feser might claim that Aristotelianism is unassailable and absolutely necessary on *philosophical* grounds (and we'll see that's not the case in the upcoming chapters), but Feser absolutely cannot recommend it on *historical* grounds. He will have to find different ways of arguing for it aside from a fear of Soviet or Maoist-style atrocities occurring if it is abandoned, because as *he himself* has written, those Marxists never really abandoned it either.

Or did they? Aristotle was a theist, after all, so if the Communists were good Aristotelians, wouldn't a belief in teleology also necessitate a belief in God? Looking at the history of religion in the USSR, however, we can see that the answers to such questions are much more complex. In her magisterial examination of Soviet religious policy, Victoria Smolkin notes that Soviet opposition to religion was itself explicitly teleological; directed towards a certain specific, non-random end or goal:

> The Marxist-Leninist framework within which the Bolsheviks understood religion followed a clear telos. Since religion was considered to be the product of oppressive political structures and

---

[1] Feser, "Adventures in the Old Atheism, Part IV: Marx," last accessed on July 5, 2020.

unjust economic relations, the revolution could not be considered complete until religion was exorcised from the body politic.[1]

The persecutions that followed from this—the closing of churches (and synagogues), executions of the clergy, and so on—were therefore *not* the result of some "depersonalization of man" Feser decries in *The Last Superstition*. Precisely the opposite! The belief that there was a certain telos the course of history tended towards—the replacement of "primitive superstitions" with science and economic justice—was simply a belief in a certain final cause, or purpose, and it just so happened that religion ought to have been destroyed in the pursuit of that purpose.

Perhaps, in this case, Feser would argue that the Soviets (at least) were *bad Marxists themselves*. Interestingly, Feser credits Marx with a considerably more nuanced take on religion and God than he is often portrayed as having. According to Feser, Marx did not believe religion could simply disappear, with everyone subsequently becoming happy and enlightened. Rather, he believed that religion was intimately entwined with the capitalist stage of social development, and absolutely could not disappear without capitalism declining first. By the same token, religion is not "just" a means for corrupt priests, bishops, or whoever to oppress the masses, and cannot be extirpated simply by exposing or even destroying those elites. In Feser's view, Marx would therefore say that his Soviet followers were putting the cart before the horse in their persecutions of religion.

Alas, I don't think this tells the whole story. Soviet leaders like Vladimir Lenin might have actually agreed with Marx's view that

---

[1] Victoria Smolkin, *A Sacred Space is Never Empty: A History of Soviet Atheism* (Princeton University Press, 2018), 26, 40, 43. Feser himself has recommended this book, albeit indirectly. See Edward Feser, "Caught in the Web," *Edward Feser* (blog), October 1, 2018, last accessed on July 5, 2020, https://edwardfeser.blogspot.com/2018/10/caught-in-web.html where he links to a favorable review of Smolkin's book: Gary Saul Morson, "Among the Disbelievers," *Commentary Magazine*, September 2018, https://www.commentarymagazine.com/articles/among-the-disbelievers/

religion and the capitalist order were entwined to such an extent that you could not destroy the former without destroying the latter. However, in practical terms (namely what policies would most speedily replace capitalism with communism), Lenin would have argued that oppression of religious institutions and discouragement of religious belief was both necessary and a prerequisite for such economic development. The Orthodox Church in Russia possessed large amounts of economic resources (land holdings, money, etc.) and exercised a great degree of influence over secular aspects of social life, such as administration of land, recording marriages and births, and so on. Now, as Smolkin notes, "for Lenin, the success of the [Communist] revolution depended on the modernization of the state, and he considered the subjugation of religion to state authority to be an essential component of the modern political order." Given that, a modern state capable of undertaking the historic shift from capitalism to a communistic economy would require control of all land (explaining Lenin's nationalization of monastic and church holdings in 1916), a secular bureaucracy to keep track of births, deaths, and marriages (explaining why Lenin created such a bureau and arrogated to it many responsibilities formerly held by church officials in 1917), and a standardized education system subservient to the state rather than any other entity, religious or otherwise (explaining why Lenin cracked down on religious schools in 1918).[1] You don't have to be a genius to anticipate that this would arouse a lot of resistance from the religious, clergy and laymen alike. However, Lenin would likely have argued that such measures were simply necessary to modernize the state and thus bring about true Communism, and that any resultant oppression of the religious (mass execution of recalcitrant priests, demolition of religious buildings, and so on) would therefore not truly violate Marx's teachings with regard to the eventual diminution of religion. And since such oppression would be "directed towards the goal" of establishing

---

[1] Smolkin, 26-28.

Communism rather than anything else or nothing at all, you could say that Soviet anti-religious atrocities were Aristotelian in spirit.[1]

4.4: Thomistic Tragedies

As mentioned earlier in our discussion of Nazism, Feser is willing to admit that "other, non-intellectual factors," such as economic and social changes, were "more important" than "abandoning Aristotelianism" in explaining the terror and violence attending Nazism and Communism.[2] But while I am not blaming the classical tradition for such terrible crimes, I hope I have proven that Feser has not conceded enough to his opponents. The historical evidence implies that these material factors for totalitarianism were not just "more important" than philosophical ones, but quite decisive. If proslavery Southerners, Nazi "race scientists," and Communist theorists could use many parts of the classical tradition to support their endeavors, why should we believe Feser's argument that abandoning the classical tradition was a contributing cause to their villainy?

Because of Christ, perhaps. Feser might point out that I have primarily described how slavers, Commies, and Nazis have utilized the teachings of Aristotle and Plato. I have made little attempt to associate Aquinas and Augustine with these shady characters, and for good reason. The Communists were notoriously atheistic and the most recent scholarship on Nazism has concluded that Hitler was personally hostile to Christianity but did not admit that publicly—for instance, he was forced to publicly repudiate the murderous Aktion T4 program due to

---

[1] This, amusingly enough, can also serve as a refutation of a common and irritating right-wing talking point. More uncouth right-wingers—that is to say, neo-nazis—typically claim that Communism and its associated death toll were some sort of Jewish plot. However, so far as I am aware, Lenin never quoted the Torah and Marx never cited Maimonides, whereas Aristotelian teleological thinking seemed to permeate their ideologies. Regardless of their ethnicity, then, one could much more accurately call Communism "Greco-Bolshevism" rather than "Judeo-Bolshevism."

[2] *TLS*, 51.

protests raised by a Catholic bishop, leading him to privately swear vengeance against the Catholic Church once he won WWII.[1] Pro-slavery Southerners, on the other hand, most often considered themselves Christian and saw their defenses of slavery as defenses of true Christianity, but Northern abolitionists often (though not always) opposed slavery on Biblical grounds as well, so it is difficult to argue that theism or Christianity go hand-in-hand with human bondage.[2] That being the case, a Thomist like Feser might say that the classical tradition is not complete without theism, particularly Christian theism. Nazis and Communists might have been able to misuse Plato and Aristotle, but they could never have justified mass murder without rejecting Aquinas, since such actions cannot be justified if one believes all humans are made in God's image. In other words, Plato and Aristotle themselves do not constitute the classical tradition—rather, it is Aristotelianism wedded to Christianity that is the true classical tradition, and *that* tradition could have prevented mass murder on a Nazi or Communist scale.

Fortunately for Feser, this is a difficult argument to disprove. Unfortunately for him, it is also very difficult to prove. It is a counterfactual: Since, in reality (as Feser laments), Thomist philosophy was largely "abandoned" after the eighteenth century outside of the

---

[1] Gerhard L. Weinberg, *Visions of Victory: The Hopes of Eight World War II Leaders* (Cambridge University Press, 2005), 25-29. Aktion-T4 was a secret Nazi order to exterminate the disabled (not just Jews and Poles, but many Germans as well). The deployment of gas vans to surreptitiously kill the victims was a precursor to the notorious gas chambers used in the Holocaust, see Kershaw, *Hitler, 1936-45: Nemesis*(W.W. Norton, 1999), 427-430. Richard Carrier has argued that Hitler was Christian, but admits that Hitler certainly did not believe in the Trinity, thought Paul was a liar, and even claimed Jesus was the result of adultery between the Virgin Mary and a Roman soldier! Even the most lax, secular Christians who don't believe in the Virgin Birth think He was at least Joseph's son, so Hitler strikes me as a little too heterodox to really be called a Christian, even a Protestant one. See Carrier, "No, Hitler Wasn't a Pantheist," *Richard Carrier Blogs*, December 16, 2016, last accessed on July 5, 2020, https://www.richardcarrier.info/archives/11792
[2] Davis, *Inhuman Bondage*, 250-255.

Catholic Church, whatever historical evidence we possess can shed light only on events influenced by that factor, because it is what happened in reality rather than a possibility.[1] A world where Aquinas was *not* abandoned is merely a conceptual possibility—the historical evidence we can access only allows us to guess at what such a world *might have been like*, and only through extrapolation. And even through that process (conceptualization and extrapolation based on historical evidence rather than direct analysis of historical evidence), there is not much reason to believe the twentieth century would have been much less bloody under the reign of Thomists.

I must concede, to begin with, that in some ways Aquinas would indisputably oppose the genocidaires of the twentieth century. With respect to Jews, while he believed their religion was wrong and that they should be segregated from the rest of Christian society and their liberties strictly curtailed, he thought they could be converted and thus should not be outrightly exterminated as Hitler wanted.[2] However, he was considerably less sporting when it came to heretics. As he wrote, "if forgers of money and other evil-doers are forthwith condemned to death by the secular authority, much more reason is there for heretics, as soon as they are convicted of heresy, to be not only excommunicated but even put to death." Given his definition of "heretic" as one who "devises or follows false or new opinions," Protestants and Eastern Orthodox Christians would count as "heretics" from a Catholic perspective.[3] Thus, even if the Thomist would not condone mass murder on the basis of Nazi racial theories or Communist economic plans, he might still do so

---

[1] *TLS*, 51: "Abandoning Aristotelianism, as the founders of modern philosophy did, was the single greatest mistake in the history of Western thought." Now, you could argue that Aristotelianism hasn't actually been abandoned, but in that case one wonders why Feser is lamenting "modern philosophy's" lack of Aristotelianism if the Stagirite's ideas actually maintained as much currency as Feser wishes they did.
[2] John Y.B. Hood, *Aquinas and the Jews* (University of Pennsylvania Press, 1995), 79.
[3] Thomas Aquinas, *Summa Theologiae,* second part of the second part, question 11, article 3, *NewAdvent.org,* 2017, last accessed on July 5, 2020
http://www.newadvent.org/summa/3011.htm#article3

on the basis of purging any subversion of the Catholic faith. Given how many billions of Protestants are scattered across the world, a Thomist regime which ruled over as many people as Hitler's Germany, Mao's China, or the Soviet Union might well have racked up a death toll rivaling any of those.

Feser could argue that Aquinas, a scrupulous Aristotelian, included safeguards against those excesses in his system of thought. In the previously quoted section on heresy, Thomas maintained that heretics should only be executed by secular authorities after a trial has determined them to be incorrigible. But many genocidal regimes took pains to portray themselves as acting on justified, legal grounds in carrying out mass murder. Russian officials, for instance, concluded that internal saboteurs were responsible for the failures of farms to hit their production targets in Ukraine and thus requisitioned even more grain from them, contributing to the great famine, or Holodomor, during the 1930s. During the same period, Nazis accused German Jews of conspiring with foreign powers and weakening Germany's economy. While this campaign of slander contributed to extra-judicial pogroms such as Kristallnacht, it also provided Nazi authorities a "legal" justification to intern and deport as many Jews as possible and confiscate their supposedly ill-gotten wealth.[1] These examples from history provide little reassurance that Thomism's legal restraints would really hinder a determined mass-murderer. A Thomist dictator of an industrialized age could easily justify the industrialized collective slaughter of Protestants (or any other group of non-Catholics, for that matter) by claiming such a group was committing crimes or subverting the polity en masse, that the situation was too dire to spend time and resources on lengthy trials for each of them, and that therefore the spiritual health of the state mandated the execution of all the Baptists or Orthodox or whoever.

---

[1] Timothy Snyder, *Bloodlands* (Basic Books, 2010), 43-45, Adam Tooze, *The Wages of Destruction: The Making and Breaking of the Nazi Economy* (Viking Press, 2006), 274-278.

This is by no means an entirely hypothetical thought exercise. During the Spanish Civil War, Catholic militias casually executed Protestants in the regions of Piedralaves and El Barraco, as Protestants were just assumed to have been allied with Communist and leftist forces.[1] The Ustashe regime which controlled Croatia and allied with Nazi Germany during World War II had an explicitly Catholic society as its ultimate goal. In the pursuit of that goal, it murdered the Orthodox population under its control with such barbarity that even its Nazi allies were shocked (though, bizarrely enough, the Ustashe approved of Islam and believed its Muslim population to be allies against the Orthodox and Jews).[2] These two examples—there are many, many more throughout Western history I could list, had I space—do not exactly inspire confidence in the idea that government based on "natural law" would be much more benevolent than the more materialistic regimes of the twentieth century. If Aquinas's followers seem not to have killed as many people as the Nazis and Communists, it is only because they never attained absolute control over as much land as the Nazis and Communists did.

Now, Feser might argue that Catholic militias in Spain and the Ustashe regime in Croatia were not devoted Thomists, or that they did not even take very seriously the ethical principles held by Aristotle and the natural law tradition as a whole. The problem with this line of thought is that defenders of slavery and Communism (at least) have said the same thing—that especially brutal or destructive manifestations of their ideology were perversions of it, and such criminals supposedly representing the ideologies were not "true" Communists or benevolent slaveholders or whatever. Robert Lewis Dabney tried to argue that violence, cruelty, and sundering of families were unfortunate deviations from what slavery was supposed to be and that for the most part, true

---

[1] Michael Seidman, *Republic of Egos: A Social History of the Spanish Civil War* (University of Wisconsin Press, 2002), 34.
[2] Mark Mazower, *Hitler's Empire: How the Nazis Ruled Europe* (Penguin Books, 2008), 345-348, 351.

Christian slaveowners treated blacks with love and tenderness.[1] Karl Marx once told some French followers of his, "all I know is that I am no Marxist," and today many Communists condemn Stalin (among others) for betraying the tenets of Communism.[2] I suppose Nazis don't often try to excuse their ideology as much as just deny the Holocaust (and Generalplan Ost, and the Intelligenzaktion, and the numerous other crimes the Nazis committed against non-Jews), but in any case, my point is hopefully clear: To say that the natural law tradition could not really condone horrible crimes if it were properly understood, or that less savory Catholic regimes in recent history were "No True natural law Adherents," is an unconvincing defense.

We can certainly say the "classical tradition" has much to answer for, judging by everything we've gone through in this chapter. First, we explored the many ways in which Americans justified racial chattel slavery through Aristotle, examining how they claimed Africans had different "Essences" than whites and thus deserved their chains. We turned to an even darker path in looking at Nazism. Going by the writings of many Nazi functionaries, it seems like Aristotle wasn't very popular, but quotes from these goose-steppers showed how Plato, and by extension realism about Forms and other universals, was quite compatible with racial genocide: Nazis could use the "principle of totality" to argue for the extermination of the disabled or Jews or other "degenerates." Rounding off our jaunt through villainy, we explored how Marx was an enthusiastic student of Aristotle and how the many purges of the Communist regimes could have easily been justified under Aristotelian metaphysics, at least if one believed that the establishment

---

[1] Robert Lewis Dabney, *A Defence of Virginia: And Through Her, of the South, in Recent and Pending Contests Against the Sectional Party* (New York: E.J. Hale and Co, 1867), 260-266.
[2] Alex Callinicos, *The Revolutionary Ideas of Karl Marx* (Haymarket Books, 2012), 34. In reference to Stalin, Leon Trotsky was rather notorious for believing the dictator had betrayed authentic Communism and eventually received an icepick to the head because of it. See Leon Trotsky and Max Eastman, trans., *The Revolution Betrayed: What Is the Soviet Union and Where Is It Going?* (Pathfinder Books, 1937).

of a Communist state (rather than serving God) was the final cause, or Telos, of human activity. Even so, all this is based on history, and Feser is a philosopher. He might demand a philosophical explanation for how Aristotle's thought could have supported all the nastiness we have previously described. Or, in other words, how aspects of Aristotle's *metaphysical* theories lead to problems in *ethical* implementation. Fair enough—we turn to that question presently.

Chapter 5: Fallacious Forms

Aristotelianism, it seems, is far from perfect as a guide to morality. If slaveowners, Nazis (at least with regard to Aristotle's predecessor), *and* Communists have been able to utilize it, we can probably say that Edward Feser has *massively* oversold it. But it is not enough just to point out how unsavory characters of many different political persuasions have been able to exploit Aristotle's ideas. We must also understand *why* those ideas lend themselves so well to abuse. This is possible through a close examination of how Aristotle's ethical thought related to his metaphysics, how the latter did not, does not, and cannot entail the conclusions the former reached, and why that failure severely weakens the moral claims of not only Aristotelianism but its descendants, most notably those of Feser's favored natural law tradition.

The most obviously glaring disconnects between Aristotelian metaphysics and Aristotelian ethics can be seen in the attempted refutation of David Hume's famous fact-value distinction (as discussed in the following section). I contend that Aristotle's proposed solution is in fact entirely fallacious. The fact-value distinction only disappears if one agrees to define "good" as adhering to a Form, but there is no especially convincing, non-arbitrary reason to agree with such a definition. From this issue springs two others: It is very difficult to discern when something instantiates a defective instance of a Form as opposed to a different Form entirely; in the case of living creatures as opposed to abstract objects it is very difficult to discern what their Forms actually are. These shortcomings will allow the reader to see how the crimes of various dictatorial regimes throughout history could be coherently justified under an Aristotelian framework.

Other philosophers such as Philippa Foot have made valiant attempts to refine Aristotelianism in order to prevent such outcomes, but, as I will demonstrate, her brand of Aristotelianism entails distinctly non-Thomistic conclusions—her logic implies that religious duties are not in fact the primary purpose of human rationality. Indeed, in purely logical terms, several aspects of Thomistic moral teaching are incompatible with its metaphysics: The Thomistic solution to the Euthyphro dilemma is incoherent and its doctrine of transcendentals undermines Feser's attempts to solve the problem of evil. This chapter will conclude with a few bizarre ethical quandaries for the Thomist which spring from the previously described problems in his philosophy, which lead into the next chapter, dealing with *metaphysical* problems in the Aristotelian and particularly Thomistic framework.

5.1: Fact and Value

As usual, let's quickly recap the Aristotelian view of ethics. If we assume everything has a Form—a certain intrinsic principle that defines something and distinguishes it from everything else—then the Aristotelian concludes that we have a standard by which we can call things good and bad. The Form of a triangle is to be a closed figure with three straight sides. However, a triangle drawn carefully with a Rapidograph will have straighter sides than one drawn hastily on a bus seat. Since the former triangle more closely adheres to the standards entailed by its Form (namely having straight sides), it is a "good" triangle in comparison to the latter, which is "bad."[1] That doesn't necessarily say much in and of itself, but since "good" and "bad" can be understood in that way, if we know the Form of a human being is a "rational animal," it follows we should try to live up to the standards entailed by that Form as much as we can (which we would do by being rational rather than irrational), because everyone wants to do what is good in some way (even criminals, who seek some perceived good such as wealth or power through theft or murder). As it happens, adhering to Forms is the only real, objective good, so people ought to avoid irrational activities such as theft and murder, because those only *seem* like they lead to good. Now, Feser also believes that rationality entails being Christian (and Catholic specifically), but as described in chapter 2, the arguments for

---

[1] *AQ*, 176-77, *TLS*, 36-37.

Catholicism (in particular) do not really work. So, let's just concentrate on Feser's Aristotelian definition of Good as "adhering to a Form" generally.

The first and biggest problem with that definition: It's rather idiosyncratic, at least so it seems to me. Feser insists that "we would naturally call [a hastily drawn triangle] a *bad* triangle and a [painstakingly drawn triangle] a *good* one."[1] But after over 30 years of living in the United States, at least, I'd never once heard this usage before stumbling upon it in Feser's books. The words "good" and "bad," so far as I had always been aware, referred to either morality (Hitler was a bad man, Mister Rogers was a good one) or function (good milk is tasty, bad milk will make you sick, a good guitar plays well, a bad one needs to be replaced). Now, Feser would say that both morality and function, in the above examples, can be understood through an Aristotelian philosophical lens, with good defined as fulfilling a function and bad defined as failing to do so. Be that as it may (and we'll come back to the subject in the very next section), it seems to be a different thing than good and bad defined in relation to an abstraction like a Form.

Still, this might have been just me. Maybe I grew up in a strange area, though I doubt a typical Northern metropolis is that strange linguistically. Far more compelling than my personal experiences would be the dictionary. Let's take a look at what Merriam-Webster tells us "good" is: "Of a favorable character or tendency, agreeable, pleasant, advantageous, suitable, or satisfactory."[2] This seems like a reasonable definition to me, and even readers less perceptive than mine can notice something obvious: Nothing in that definition mentions "perfectly [instantiating] the essence of [a kind of thing an entity may be]."[3] According to the dictionary, even a triangle that wasn't entirely closed,

---

[1] *AQ,* 176. Italics are Feser's.
[2] "Good." Merriam-Webster.com. Accessed July 5, 2020. https://www.merriam-webster.com/dictionary/good.
[3] *AQ,* 176.

or had uneven, non-straight sides would still be a "good" triangle if it were agreeable, pleasant, or advantageous to someone in some way. Why, precisely, should we take an esoteric definition of "good" apparently used only by Aristotelians over the simple, common-sense one everyone can understand?

Feser might accuse me of just dismissing the Aristotelian definition in an offhanded manner, but in *Scholastic Metaphysics*, he himself offers some very good reasons to be very cautious of anyone insisting that their peculiar definition of a word is the only legitimate one. While discussing the definition of the word "existence" (which we'll come to in chapter 6 of this book), Feser summarizes an analogy from yet another of his Thomist friends, Gyula Klima:

> [C]onsider the word 'bat,' which in English can mean either 'mouse-like flying mammal' or 'wooden implement used in baseball or cricket'... or 'to blink.' Now consider C, a person whose grasp of English is tenuous and who is only familiar with the first of these meanings, who overhears someone uttering the sentence 'She didn't bat an eye when he confronted her.' C supposes that what the speaker is saying is 'She didn't mouse-like flying mammal an eye when he confronted her,' and concludes, quite confidently but also quite wrongly, that the speaker is uttering gibberish.[1]

All well and good (heh), but note here that Feser (and, I assume, Dr. Klima) is not denying the validity of any of the three definitions of "bat." The very strength of his example lies in the fact that the latter two definitions are every bit as true and legitimate as the first—it's simply a matter of discerning which definition is appropriate. But when we apply this line of thought to the multiple definitions of the word "good," things get rather dicey for the Aristotelian. As a prelude, allow me to introduce a pair of characters—a rather dashing young scamp whose initials happen to be G.L., and a rather less sensible space cadet whose initials happen to be E.F. These two are, of course, entirely the figments of my

---

[1] *SM*, 254.

imagination and bear no relation whatsoever to anyone any of us might actually know. Let's imagine they have a conversation that goes a little like this:

GL: I think bats are kinda cute.

EF: What? You think wooden implements used in baseball and cricket are cute? That's weird.

GL: Huh? No, no, I mean "bat" as in the small, mouse-like flying mammals. They're cute.

EF: What are you talking about? The word "bat" can only refer to wooden sports equipment. That's just the perfectly objective definition of the word!

GL: What the hell? Just look it up in the dictionary. The word "bat" can refer to what you describe, yes, but it can also mean a small flying mammal, or to blink, as well. My usage of the term is no less "objectively legitimate" than yours. Why should I only adhere to a single definition of the word you happen to prefer when the other one is also perfectly acceptable?

EF: I can't believe I'm hearing this! How can the modern world possibly get any more degenerate? William of Ockham, this is all your fault!

GL: Yeah, OK, I think we're done here.

It hardly seems like a stretch to assume most people would assume Ed—er, I mean, EF, is being silly and unreasonable in this scenario. But let's see what happens when we add the word "good" to the mix. Let's say our friends are now sitting in a bus and trying to pass the time:

GL: My, what a good triangle I've drawn on the back of this bus seat.

EF: What? Impossible! This triangle's sides aren't perfectly straight, and this corner right here isn't even fully closed! This isn't a good triangle at all, it's bad!

GL: Wait, why isn't it good? I drew it to entertain myself and because I wanted to look at something. As far as I'm concerned, it's pleasant and agreeable. That's what the word "good" means.

EF: Well, you're wrong. It isn't a matter of "opinion" that your triangle is bad. Triangles objectively have straight sides as part of their Form, therefore your squiggly, scratchy triangle cannot be good!

GL: What do Forms have to do with anything? Yes, you're correct about my triangle not adhering to the Formal characteristics of Triangularity very well, but why does that make it a "bad" triangle rather than just an irregular or non-standard one? Looking it up on Merriam-Webster, the definition of the word "good" doesn't even mention anything about conforming to any given Form or anything like that. Why should I only acknowledge your particular definition of the word? What makes "adhering to Forms" any more accurate a definition of goodness, especially when that definition seems to be much more obscure than the far more general one given by the dictionary?

It's rather unclear what sort of sensible response EF could give me—er, I mean, that other guy named G.L. And E.F.'s failure here would also be a failure of Aristotelianism in general. Given the multiple competing definitions of good, what's the point of using the Aristotelian one? Perhaps it may—*may*—be useful under certain circumstances. But Aristotelian ethics, and by extension those of its descendant traditions such as Thomism, require that single, very peculiar definition be the only one anyone uses, or else their ethical theory loses its claim to universal validity.

Perhaps the Aristotelian might say the dictionary is only a list of certain terms and offers only linguistic value—for instance, flying mammals and sports equipment are different *things*, and happen to have the same word, or **nominal definition** listed for them in the dictionary due to a quirk of the English language, so it remains to the (Aristotelian) philosopher to discern their true Essences, or **real definition**.[1] But the dictionary does offer a serviceable description of both the Essence/real definition of a sports bat *and* the Essence/real definition of the living creature under its heading of "bat."[2] So it seems that the dictionary definitions of things correlate reasonably well with the true Essences of what they describe. Why should we not assume the same also applies to the concept of goodness? Why should we not assume that the Aristotelians are wrong, and what they identify as the "Form or Essence of Goodness" is actually something other than "adhering perfectly to some particular, individual Form or Essence?"

Why is all this important? Well, the eighteenth-century philosopher David Hume—another one of Feser's bête noirs—came up with something called the "fact-value" distinction, commonly known through the aphorism "one cannot derive an ought from an is." Feser thinks that Aristotle provided a solution to this conundrum: If you know what something is, you can also know what or how it ought to be. As Feser says,

> …there is no such thing as a purely "factual" description of reality utterly divorced from "value," for "value" is built into the structure of the "facts" from the get-go… it is of the essence of a triangle to be a closed plane figure with three straight sides… These are straightforward objective facts, and remain so even though there are triangles which fail perfectly to match this description…

with the aforementioned implication that triangles that better match that description are "good," and ones which don't are "bad." As Feser concludes,

> …it would be silly to suggest that we have somehow committed a fallacy in making a "value" judgement about the badness of the triangle drawn on the bus seat on the basis of the "facts" about the essence of

---

[1] *SM*, 231.
[2] "Bat." Merriam-Webster.com, last accessed July 5, 2020. https://www.merriam-webster.com/dictionary/bat.

triangularity. Given that essence, the 'value judgement' in question obviously follows *necessarily*.[1]

Actually, Feser's conclusions aren't true. Since the definition of "good," as I have demonstrated above, has nothing necessarily to do with adhering to Essences or Forms, it wouldn't be silly at all to say Feser is committing a fallacy by making a value judgement concerning any sort of triangle, and any value judgements he makes are not at all logically necessary. And we do not have to "deny the reality of essences," falling into the supposed traps of nominalism and conceptualism, to arrive at this conclusion. We can agree entirely with the Aristotelian that things such as triangles have Forms, but there is no reason whatsoever to use words like "good" or "bad" to describe them.

A moment's thought combined with a reasonably large vocabulary can drive this point even further home. Let us assume that Essences do exist, and let us assume it really is true that triangles have a certain Essence, namely to have three closed straight sides. But why, precisely, are we absolutely obligated to use value-laden language like "good" or "bad" to describe conforming or deviating from a certain Form? If we see a triangle drawn with a ruler that has perfectly straight sides, why should we not use the words "regular," or "standard" or "conforming" to describe it? All of those words accurately and objectively describe the triangle (it adheres or conforms to the standard entailed by its Form) while being entirely value-neutral, as there's nothing necessarily desirable about being standard or conformist (obviously demonstrated by the fact that we deride things like "the regular routine" or a "conformist" person). By the same token, when we see a hastily drawn triangle on the back of a bus seat, why can we not call it "irregular," "non-standard," or "non-conforming?" Again, all those words objectively and accurately describe the bus triangle's relationship with its Form without the negative connotations of the word "bad" (since terms like "unconventional" and "nonconformist" can be positive).

---

[1] *TLS,* 139, *AQ,* 175-76.

There seems to be no convincing reason for Feser to use the value-laden language over the neutral verbiage. And without such a reason, Hume's old fact-value distinction remains an insurmountable problem. Even if Hume were to come back to life and accept the reality of Forms, Feser would not be able to convince him that the "objective facts" about Forms entail any obligations (ethical or otherwise) on things that may instantiate those Forms. It may be an "objective fact" that some triangles more closely adhere to the definition of triangularity than others, but that doesn't make them "better," it merely makes them "more regular/standard/conforming." There is, therefore, no particular reason a bus triangle should care about or want to (so to speak) adhere to its Form as much as a ruler-drawn triangle. What's wrong with being non-conformist?

This point can be driven even further home by the understanding that virtually no-one understands "good" to mean "adherence to the standards entailed by a certain Essence," or even having any necessary relationship to anything's Form in particular, and that in certain circumstances deviating from a certain Form or Essence can actually be *good*. You'll understand why if you just think through a couple of these thought experiments.

First, imagine some small plastic toy triangles, squares, and pentagons intended as part of a children's playset, perhaps to help teach them geometry. To prevent children from hurting themselves on the edges of the toys, their corners are rounded. However, this would be a violation of the Essence of triangles, squares, and pentagons, since they are defined as having *straight* sides, and rounded angles mean their sides have to bend at the edges. Would Feser say these are "bad" geometric shapes? If he would prefer them to have proper angles and thus distinctly sharp edges, that would mean they run the risk of accidentally hurting children, which would contravene their function of providing amusement and edification. In this context, why should anyone—the toymaker, the parents buying the playset for their children, whoever—care about some abstract definition of good based on "perfectly instantiating the Form of Triangles/Squares/Pentagons?" Most reasonable people would find such a concern to be very silly. Far more important that the toys bring pleasure and edification to children than anything else.[1]

Second, and somewhat more distastefully, let us return to the Nazis we discussed in the previous chapter. An off-the-cuff definition of a Nazi, the "Form of a Nazi," if you will (for the purposes of armchair philosophy, not professional history) could be fairly summarized like this: Nazis are cruel, anti-Semitic, and fanatically loyal to Hitler. So, in this sense, Reinhard Heydrich, who was viciously cruel, extremely anti-Semitic, and by all accounts very loyal to the Fuehrer, would have been a "good" Nazi, in the sense of perfectly instantiating the Form of Nazism. On the other hand, Oskar Schindler, a registered member of the Nazi party, was compassionate towards Jews and not loyal to Hitler at all, since he betrayed the Fuehrer by helping innocent Jews escape Nazi tyranny. Thus, again looking at the Form of Nazism, Schindler was a "bad" Nazi. Yet any sensible person would say that Schindler was a good man and Heydrich was a bad one. In fact, Schindler was a good man *precisely because* he was a bad Nazi, and Heydrich was a bad man *precisely because* he "perfectly instantiated the Form of Nazism." But how could this be if goodness and badness are merely and exclusively adhering more or less to the standards of a given Form?[2]

Perhaps in both of the above examples, there are separate Forms the entities involved "ought to" instantiate. For instance, in the case of a children's toy, the "Form of Toyness," so to speak, takes precedence over the Form of any given geometric shape. A plastic triangle being "bad" in the sense of not having perfectly straight sides is acceptable, because

---

[1] The Aristotelian might say it is more important for the toy to fulfill its Function than adhere to its Form—we will return to this question in section 5.7.

[2] More extreme right-wingers who feel personally attacked by the use of Nazis in this example (or who simply deny that the Nazis did anything wrong at all) can just replace anti-Semitism with anti-capitalism, Hitler with Stalin, Heydrich with some famous Soviet murderer, and Schindler with some famous defector from the USSR.

that would allow it to more perfectly instantiate the attributes of toy-ness, such as being safe for kids. In the case of Heydrich and Schindler, Feser would say that adherence to the Form of Man (in other words, being rational), is more important than adhering to the Form of Nazism, and since Nazism is inherently irrational, being a "bad" Nazi is commendable since that (usually) means you are a good human. This is at least somewhat less absurd, but it still weakens the foundations of Aristotelianism. In both *The Last Superstition* and *Aquinas,* Feser tells us that "good" is simply instantiating Forms. But now he would assumedly admit that perfectly instantiating certain Forms in certain contexts can be bad, at least if it prevents us from instantiating more important Forms. So how do we decide which Forms are more important? What tools does the Aristotelian-Thomistic tradition provide to discern this?

The first candidate that comes to mind would be a variant of the "Principle of Totality" we discussed earlier in Chapter 3. The variation would say that objects have a primary Form they instantiate first and foremost, with any other Forms they might exemplify being subordinate to that one. The only reason a plastic triangle would exist at all is to provide amusement to children, so its secondary purpose of maintaining a certain geometric shape would be subordinate to that. One cannot be a Nazi without being a human being, so being a good human being is more important than being a good Nazi, meaning it is acceptable to badly instantiate the Form of Nazism in order to properly instantiate the primary Form of a human.

This may be a somewhat coherent solution, but it strikes me as a rather parlous one. Doesn't this line of thought veer too close to consequentialism? One of the knocks against consequentialism, in Feser's view, is that it exhorts us to do evil in the service of some greater good. The consequentialist might say it is acceptable, even obligatory, to kill an innocent child in cold blood to save the lives of two innocent people. Feser (and his friends like David Oderberg) would say that is monstrous.[1] But then they tell us (so I assume), according to the Principle of Totality, it is acceptable to do bad (poorly instantiate a certain Form) in order to do good (properly instantiate a more important Form). That doesn't seem to be much better than the consequentialist's supposed ruthlessness, just with a different definition of good.

Secondly, the example of good and bad Nazis should highlight another curious problem with the Aristotelian idea that "failure to instantiate a form perfectly does not mean one does not instantiate that Form at all." According to Feser, being a good Nazi (or a good Communist, Jihadi, or whatever) is incompatible with being a good human being—a human is bad or defective to the extent that he is a good or perfect Nazi. Yet we do not speak of anything else this way. For instance, it would be absurd to look at a four-sided figure and say, "this triangle is bad to the extent it perfectly instantiates the Form of a Square." We would simply say that we are looking at a square. But in the case of humans, we speak of a man being bad to the extent he perfectly instantiates the Form of something else (Nazism). There must therefore be something in the Form of Nazism that contravenes the standards entailed by the Form of Man (rational animality), in the same sense that something in the Form of Squareness contravenes the standards entailed by the Form of Triangularity. But then how is it possible to be a bad man by virtue of being a good Nazi? If these two Forms (rational animality and Nazism) truly did contradict each other, it would be *impossible* to be both at the same time, much less a good instantiation of one or another, just like it is *impossible* to be both a four-sided figure and a triangle.

Is it the case that a Nazi is simply a "damaged" human, in the same sense a poorly-drawn triangle is a damaged triangle, but still a triangle? It is hard to see how. No-one would say a four-sided figure was a

---

[1] Edward Feser, "Happy Consequentialism Day!" *Edward Feser* (blog), August 9, 2010, last accessed on July 5, 2020,
http://edwardfeser.blogspot.com/2010/08/happy-consequentialism-day.html

"damaged" triangle rather than a square, or in other words, perfectly instantiating one Form should not equate to being a "damaged" specimen of another Form. Either there is nothing entailed in the Form of Man that prevents one from also adhering to the Form of Nazism, or that "good" Nazis simply are not human, in the same way good squares simply are not triangles.

The second solution to the dilemma is, I think, untenable. However much we might hate those guys, Nazis are still technically human, even if evil, vicious humans. So, we are left with the first solution, that there's nothing in the Form of Nazism that contravenes the Form of Man. But under an Aristotelian moral framework where the most important gauge of goodness is adhering to Forms, there would then be nothing wrong with adhering to the Form of Nazism. Considering how unpalatable such a proposition obviously is, we must conclude that the Aristotelian moral framework might not be much to write home about after all.

5.2: Whose Form Is It Anyways?

But let us disregard all that. Let us assume that "adhering to a certain Form" really is the only legitimate, objective definition of "good." Even in that generous case, Aristotelian ethics fails on epistemological grounds—it is quite difficult to discern which specific Form something should adhere to, and whether or not any given entity is a defective instance of a Form or something else altogether. Such an ethical system is also very vulnerable to exploitation from dishonest or even simply self-interested actors, further reducing its utility.

It is pretty safe to assume that Aristotelian realists about Essences or Forms believe just about everything has a Form, given the extent to which luminaries such as Edward Feser and David Oderberg have defended this belief. But even a staunch realist like Oderberg can admit that it is not always, or even often, easy to discern what entities instantiate which Forms. He states that it is not "part of essentialist doctrine that ultimate explanations are easy to come by...essentialism is perfectly compatible with, and indeed requires, a level of modesty and humility in our investigative practices." The example he provides is of whales: For centuries, people thought they were a type of fish, or "instantiated the Form of fish," as the Aristotelian might put it. Only after painstaking research and observation did we find the truth, that whales actually instantiate the Form of mammals.[1] Oderberg argues that these kinds of mistakes do *not* mean that Forms do not exist, only that we have to be very careful when trying to assign things Forms. But however true this may be, it seems to raise some rather troublesome epistemological problems that further undermine the power of Aristotelian ethical theory. To see why, let's return to our friends G.L. and E.F. on the bus, where G.L. is happily scribbling away on the back of the seat in front of him.

EF: What's that, are you trying to draw another triangle? Look how bad it is! Its sides aren't straight and it's not even fully closed!

GL: It's not bad at all.

EF: What do you mean? The Form of a triangle is to have three straight sides and also to be a closed plane figure!

GL: That may be so, but what I'm drawing is not a triangle.

EF: Well, it clearly looks like it has 3 sides. What else could it be but a triangle?

GL: Haven't you read your David Oderberg? It's not always easy to tell what Form or Essence something instantiates, and a good essentialist will be modest and humble in his observations. In this case, my little figure is not a triangle and therefore doesn't have to worry (so to speak) about instantiating the Form of one. It is, rather, just a scribble, and instantiates

---

[1] Oderberg, *Real Essentialism,* 32-33.

the Form of a Scribble, which is: "A careless, hasty drawing made simply for the purposes of amusement that does not have to conform to any particular geometric shape." This particular Scribble may seem like a triangle, but it's really not and therefore can't be judged by a triangle's standards. It does, however, fit the definition of a Scribble quite well and fulfilled its purpose of amusing me, which therefore makes it a good Scribble.

As amusing as this little exchange might be, it has dire implications for Aristotelian theory beyond scribbles and shapes. Why wouldn't G.L.'s argument apply equally well to everything else? Let us say we run into a Nazi, a Communist, or an ISIS terrorist and tell them that they are "objectively wicked" because their behavior contradicts the Form of a human being (as always, rational animality).[1] But any of these villains could snidely respond, "well, maybe you ought to display a little more humility and modesty in your judgements, Mr. Aristotelian. If you actually knew as much about the Forms as I did, you'd see I was perfectly rational." The goose-stepper could claim that Jews only *appeared* human but, in fact, possessed the Forms of destructive parasites, and that exterminating them would therefore not be a crime—Hitler himself said exactly this in *Mein Kampf*, repeatedly calling them by that word, and insisting that anyone who didn't believe him had been fooled.[2] The Commie could claim that since the establishment of Communism was the *telos* of human history, any group that opposed it (such as the kulaks) was therefore irrational (in the Thomistic sense) and deserved prompt extermination for their "crimes."[3] And the Islamic terrorist wouldn't even have to go that far: As described in chapter 2,

---

[1] *TLS*, 213.
[2] Adolf Hitler and Ralph Manheim, trans., *Mein Kampf* (Houghton-Mifflin, 1943), 150-153, 560, 562.
[3] Another blogger has made precisely the point. See the section titled "The Problem of Morality" at One Brow, "Review of TLS – Problems, problems, problems," *Life, The Universe, and One Brow*, December 24, 2009, last accessed on July 5, 2020, http://lifetheuniverseandonebrow.blogspot.com/2009/12/review-of-tls-problems-problems.html

Aristotelianism implies that Islam is more likely true than Christianity, meaning that the ISIS goon is actually conforming to the Form of a Rational Animal if Allah, the Purely Actual Unmoved Mover, has told him to fly a plane into a building.

This is, ironically enough, a critique similar to one Feser made of Locke. Locke was a conceptualist—that is to say, he believed Forms were matters of human convention rather than having any sort of objective reality. According to Feser, this demolished Locke's argument for natural human rights, because "if you say that every human being has natural rights...but then go on to say that what *counts* as a human being in the first place is ultimately a matter of human convention," you leave the door open for Nazis, Communists, or whoever to just define who is human and who is not however they like, which means they get to say Jews, blacks, kulaks, or whoever aren't human and therefore fair game for oppression or genocide.[1] But if Locke's argument failed on logical grounds, Feser's fails on epistemological ones. Unless he can prove that God or some other infallible font of knowledge is talking to him right now, there is always the chance he could be wrong about what the Form of humanity is or who instantiates it. Thus, *even if we assume Forms are objectively real and mind-independent,* the door remains open for Nazis, Communists, or whoever to say that they, not Feser, truly grasp the Form of humanity, and by extension arrived at the genuine truth that Jews, blacks, kulaks, or whoever are not actually human. Not exactly a ringing endorsement for Aristotelianism, I'd say.

Feser, and assumedly Oderberg, might say that all those people are wrong, and that the true natures of all Forms important to human life are not at all what the Nazi or Communist might claim they are. But why should we believe Feser, or Oderberg, or any other Aristotelian? How can we be certain the Aristotelian is any more moral or any less of a bad actor than the totalitarians? Aristotelianism itself seems to provide very little help in that regard, a point made by a very perceptive Amazon

---

[1] *TLS* 211.

review of the Kindle version of *The Last Superstition*. One reader, Dan Lawler, put it as well as I could ever hope to, saying

> Even assuming the existence of Forms, who defines them and determines which particular things belong to what Form? That is an insurmountable problem for Aristotelianism. Take Ed Feser (please!) who considers himself an authority on the identification of Forms and their corresponding particulars. He writes, "Paying your phone bill, staying faithful to your wife, and voting to strike down Roe v. Wade are just actions because they participate in the Form of Justice." (796.) Sez who? Ed? Even if you agree with his assessments here, what about the countless other Forms and particulars out there. Do you have to check in with Ed on those too? Whomever you let define the Forms and allocate the particulars becomes the god of your life; your creator of reality, truth and meaning. Who possesses this god-like authority, and what check is there against its abuse? Aristotelianism has no answer.[1]

The strength of "traditional" Aristotelian ethics as drawn from realism about Forms and Essences is that they supposedly provide a completely objective basis of morality (and religion, for the Thomist) which binds all of humanity. But as even Amazon reviewers have noted, its own apostles, such as Edward Feser, have cut its legs out from under it. Any ethical theory based on adherence to Forms relies on those Forms being easy to discern and uncontroversial in their definitions. If they are not, a proposition for which David Oderberg has successfully argued, then there is no effective way of telling what Form anyone actually instantiates, leading to the sort of moral anarchy Aristotelianism is supposed to prevent. Anyone can plausibly claim to instantiate a different Form than what the Aristotelian says they do or should, robbing the Aristotelian of any ability to tell them to behave in any given manner. And the Aristotelian himself has no particular right to even make the attempt unless he wishes to give himself the "god-like"

---

[1] Dan Lawler, "Medieval Times (are here again!)," *Amazon.com review of the Kindle edition of The Last Superstition*, October 19, 2014, last accessed on July 5, 2020, https://www.amazon.com/gp/customer-reviews/R2RETCY4TFAQ5D/ref=cm_cr_getr_d_rvw_ttl?ie=UTF8&ASIN=1587314525

authority of defining truth, reality, and meaning for other people—a rather difficult task, unless he is willing to dismiss Oderberg's advice about modesty and humility.

5.3: Live and Die by the Forms

These problems grow even more crippling when we give further thought to Forms in relation to living creatures like human beings *considered* as living creatures rather than instantiations of certain abstractions. It's one thing to say that geometric axioms, universal concepts like colors, and scientific truths (like water having the chemical composition of H_2O and freezing and boiling at specific temperature/pressure combinations) have objective reality. It's quite another to say, as Aristotle, Aquinas, Oderberg, and Feser all did and do, that pretty much everything has an Essence—human beings, squirrels, and even abstract concepts like justice, virtue, and love. As we saw above, Oderberg would allow that it is *difficult* to figure out the Essences of living creatures like whales, but if we compare the whales of his example to the shapes and scribbles of mine, Aristotelian realism itself becomes strange and puzzling rather than clear and useful.

    It's easy to see how we come to grasp mathematical truths, and as a result, easy to see why mathematical Forms (such as the properties of triangles and squares) are more or less indisputable. We can prove, through logic, and without any doubt, that the Essence of a right triangle is to have 3 straight sides, one 90-degree angle, and that the square of its longest side equals the sum of the squares of its other sides (the Pythagorean Theorem). That is, in Feser's words, what makes a right-angled triangle a right-angled triangle, what defines it and differentiates it from, say, squares or isosceles triangles. But how, precisely, can we discern the "Essence" of whales, squirrels, humans, or other living things? There is no mathematic or logical equation that objectively states a squirrel or dog is specifically something or another. We must rely on empirical observation to ascertain what the Essence of such creatures may be, and such observation is inductive rather than deductive, and thus unreliable.

It's equally difficult to separate "Essential" or "substantial" qualities from "accidental" ones, which is an important distinction Feser makes in *The Last Superstition*. In reference to things with substantial Forms (different from artifacts, as we discussed in chapter 3), essential attributes are those mentioned in its Form, such as a triangle having three sides. If you change those, you change the thing's Form (such as turning a triangle into a square). Merely accidental qualities are those other properties it may have that don't determine what it is—for instance, a triangle can be blue or green or of some size or another, but it would still be a triangle because color and size are not a part of the Form of Triangularity.

But even in reference to physical objects, this line of thought breaks down. Look at the example Feser provides:

> For a ball merely to change its color is for its matter to lose one accidental form and take out another, while retaining the substantial form of a ball and those remaining the same substance, namely a ball. For a ball to be melted into goo as for its matter to lose one substantial form and take on another, just becoming a different kind of substance altogether, mainly a puddle of goo.[1]

The perceptive reader will wonder how to determine what a sort of substance a thing might be. Don't a thing's "substantial" qualities depend on your frame of reference? For instance, if you think of a red ball as a spherical red object instead, its shape would be its accidental property, not its color—melting it would turn it into a gooey red object rather than a spherical one. But if you painted it blue, it would be a substantial change from a red thing to a differently colored thing.

---

[1] *AQ*, 13-14.

This is even more confusing when you think of animals. Let's return to Feser's squirrel in *The Last Superstition*. He tells us "a squirrel who likes to scamper up trees and gather nuts for the winter" is a more perfect instantiation of the Form of Squirrel than one who doesn't.[1] So it seems he considers the Form to refer to both physical attributes (two eyes, grey fur, bushy tail, mammal) and behavioral attributes (living in trees, eating nuts, burying acorns).

But how does he know this? Why should this be the case?

Feser would almost certainly admit that it's possible to be wrong about what the Form of something is. If I were to say, "No, Dr. Feser, the Form of the Squirrel is to eat toothpaste or live on freeways, and a squirrel that does is a Good Squirrel!" or "Triangles *must* be black, any that aren't are Bad Triangles!" he would obviously tell me I was incorrect. But on what basis? It's never made particularly clear in any of his books, and his friends like Dr. Oderberg, who believe it is not always easy to discern the truth of anything's Form, are not very much help. It's easy enough to say such a strange definition of triangularity would be incorrect, as nothing in their axiomatic definition says anything about color. But squirrels? It may be easy enough to determine their essential physical attributes by looking at them, but how would Feser figure out their essential behavioral attributes? And how did he decide those attributes were essential rather than accidental?

Feser might say these are silly questions, but not so fast—we need to consider these epistemological issues because they seem to highlight some conceptual problems with Aristotelian morality. Plato and Aristotle told us that a thing's Form or Essence "defines it and distinguishes it" from everything else. They "are the standards by reference to which particular things in the world of our experience count as being the kinds of things they are." But if these "standards" define a creature, who "defines" these standards?[2] Why should we listen to Feser

---

[1] *TLS*, 36-37.
[2] Ibid.

when he tells us eating nuts is part of what defines a squirrel (i.e., its Form/Essence)? Merriam-Webster says a squirrel is a small rodent that lives in trees and has a bushy tail and strong hind legs. You'll notice it says nothing about diet (or even number of legs, etc. but let's leave that for now). Going by that definition—those "objective standards," which supposedly thus determine the "Form of Squirrel" and therefore what is "Objectively Good or Bad" for it—its diet is an accidental, not essential characteristic. A squirrel that ate toothpaste would Instantiate the Form of Squirrel just as well as one that ate nuts as long as it had a long bushy tail, fur, and lived in trees, for the same reason a green triangle instantiates the Form of Triangle as well as a black one.

Again, Professor Feser might say I'm still being silly. "Of course we know that eating nuts rather than toothpaste is an Essential Characteristic, not an accidental one!" And once again, I would ask how. I have support from the dictionary, and where else are we supposed to go for definitions but a dictionary? Is it a question of logic? I would be very interested to see him axiomatically demonstrate through pure logic and/or mathematics that eating nuts is an essential, defining characteristic of a squirrel, in the same way that the Pythagorean Theorem can be demonstrated through a logical syllogism or geometric proof.[1]

All this would merely be an amusing digression for a biologist (or a fan of rodents). For the Aristotelian, however, it represents a rather dark cloud on the moral horizon. Their entire ethical theory rests upon the Form of Man being a rational animal. But why should we believe rationality has anything to do with the Essence or Form of human beings, at least considered as an essential rather than accidental part of that definition? The ever-trusty Merriam-Webster informs us that

---

[1] This, by the way, should be casting a few more aspersions on Aristotelianism right now—it seems to rely on taking a methodology useful in some fields (formal logic, geometry, mathematics) and inserting them in very different ones (biology, human affairs); a sort of category error, if you will.

humans are merely bipedal primate mammals.¹ There are obviously many accidental characteristics we possess, such as height, skin color, and so on, but those are all irrelevant to what makes us human, according to the dictionary—as long as we are bipedal primate mammals, we adhere to our essential Form. But, as you've noticed by now, dear reader, that Form doesn't say anything about rationality one way or the other. If morality is a matter of adhering to one's Form, that means there is no basis for calling rational or virtuous behavior "objectively" good and the opposite bad. Nazis and Communists and jihadis may be violently irrational, but they are still mammalian primate bipeds, so they still conform to the Form of Man and are therefore not objectively bad (their irrationality merely being an accidental characteristic of no necessary relation to their Form/Essence). The same applies to any other kind of irrational or evil behavior—we cannot actually call any of it objectively evil unless it makes the actor less bipedal or less mammalian (however that could possibly work) in some way. And none of this ethical absurdity stems from "denying that there are Forms in the Aristotelian sense."²

In order to escape from this quandary, Aristotelians like Feser have three choices that I can think of. First, they could call actions good or evil without reference to merely conforming or adhering to a Form. This is certainly reasonable to me, but I doubt Feser or Oderberg would care much for that approach. What sort of alternative would they propose? Divine Command theory? Given the issues raised in Chapter 2 regarding the knowability of any religious claim, that seems

---

[1] "Human." Merriam-Webster.com, accessed July 5, 2020. https://www.merriam-webster.com/dictionary/human.

[2] *TLS,* 139. There's a story about another philosopher, Diogenes the Cynic, who mocked Plato's definition of man as a featherless biped by plucking a chicken and calling it a man. But, of course, the joke doesn't work quite as well if man is a specifically *primate* biped.

unsatisfactory. How about consequentialism or Kant's Categorical Imperative? Feser at least does not care much for those at all.[1]

The second solution would be to demonstrate that the dictionary is incorrect, or that the morally-obligatory Form of Man is different from what simple definition one can find in the dictionary. Aristotelians like Feser would obviously prefer that second solution, but it runs into the epistemological problems with Forms touched on above. Since, as Oderberg mentions in *Real Essentialism*, Forms are often difficult to discern and we ought to be "modest and humble" in our judgments, Feser will have to provide some very, very good reasons to trust the assessment of armchair philosophers over the dictionary (and professional biologists, by the by—they don't go by the "rational animal" definition either).

The third solution would be to simply assert that humans are "empirically" necessarily rational animals, and that is that.[2] But the problem with empirical investigation is that empirical investigations can fail, providing incomplete or inaccurate data. For instance, imagine someone saying "I have conducted an exhaustive empirical investigation of the squirrels living in Edward Feser's neighborhood, and since they are all grey, it follows that the Essence of squirrels necessarily entails they can be no other color." This would obviously be false—red squirrels are common in Europe, for instance, or in other words, the color of a squirrel is an accidental rather than a necessary or "essential" trait. There seems to be no way of ensuring any "empirical" truth about any given thing's Essence is *actually* necessary instead of merely apparently so due to our lack of knowledge or investigative ability. Thus, if Feser wishes to claim that human nature is exactly what he says it is according to empirical investigation, we can say that his empirical investigations

---

[1] Ibid., 216.
[2] Edward Feser, "The Problem of Hume's Problem of Induction," April 9, 2017, last accessed on July 7, 2019, https://edwardfeser.blogspot.com/2017/04/the-problem-of-humes-problem-of.html#more

were flawed and do not present an accurate picture of what our Essence truly is.

Feser might respond by pulling out the **method of retorsion**. As you know if you remember the definition of 'retorsion' from chapter 1, this method is used to critique an argument someone else has made: The critic points out how the argument is self-contradictory or otherwise proves itself false.[1] In this case, Feser might use the method to say a human being who denies his Essence entailed rationality would make a mockery of his own argument, because an irrational animal wouldn't argue for *anything*.[2] You don't see many spiders or pigs doing philosophy outside of *Charlotte's Web*, after all. But on closer thought, this argument falls apart. It might be necessary to assume we are rational creatures, but why should we assume we are *essentially* rational creatures as opposed to *accidentally* rational creatures? Accidental characteristics are perfectly capable of exerting a real influence on the world, aren't they? For instance, size is an accidental characteristic of Feser's squirrels—they can be small or large, but that's irrelevant to whether they're good or bad in relation to their physical health (having all four limbs and a bushy tail) or behavior (scampering up trees instead of eating toothpaste). Yet their size is a factor in how they interact with the world, and not necessarily good or bad—a fat squirrel is less likely to starve when winter comes, while a thin squirrel could better evade predators. By the same token, rationality as an accidental characteristic could easily do the work Feser and Oderberg think is necessary to avoid the charge of retorsion while being morally neutral, neither good nor bad. An essentially bipedal hominid who just happens to be rational will comprehend Forms to understand the world around him (and therefore make arguments like this), meaning if he were to encounter an irrational human, he would realize that his own Form necessarily entails only being mammalian and bipedal, with his own particular rationality being

---

[1] *TLS*, 35.
[2] This is a very condensed and slightly modified version of David Oderberg's summary of Crawford Elder's argument for essentialism based on the foundational nature of the human mind. See *Real Essentialism*, 43-45.

merely accidental. He would therefore conclude that his irrational friend is merely different, not necessarily better or worse (in the same way a red triangle is different from a black one, but not better or worse, since color is irrelevant to conforming or deviating from the Form of a triangle).

Indeed, it makes even more sense to consider rationality an accidental rather than essential characteristic when we consider the Thomistic distinction between substances and artifacts mentioned in Chapter 2. According to Feser in *Scholastic Metaphysics*, a liana vine would be a substance, or possess a Substantial Form, because its particular behaviors stem from something intrinsic to it. On the other hand, a hammock made of liana vines would be an artifact, because liana vines have no inherent tendency to come together in the ways a hammock does—such an arrangement must come about through human action.[1] If that applies to liana vines (or marriage, as I implied earlier), is it not possible that human beings have rationality grafted on to us, and that it does not flow from any intrinsic principle (i.e., our Form or Essence) we possess?

Take a closer look at Feser's example of the liana vines. An unstated implication of the substance/artifact distinction seems to be this: Substances display the characteristics or behaviors they do "on their own," without any external actor putting any effort into making them so. A liana vine, for instance, will photosynthesize and draw nutrients out of the soil entirely by itself. No-one or nothing else has to help it along in that effort as long as there's sunlight and soil around. An artifact, on the other hand, requires someone or something to set them up in such a way as to produce the desired behavior or effect; in other words, an active effort from an external actor. Since liana vines do not naturally grow into hammocks, a human craftsman, not the liana vines themselves, will have to put in the time and work required to fashion a hammock out of them.

---

[1] *SM*, 164-165.

Doesn't the same apply to humans considered as rational animals? Feser himself would be the first to admit that it takes a lot of work to turn a human into a rational creature. As he mentioned in *The Last Superstition,* children "need education in both what is useful and right, and correction of error...procreation...is not just a matter of producing new organisms, but also of forming them into persons capable of fulfilling their nature as distinctly *rational* animals."[1] But in light of what Feser wrote in *Scholastic Metaphysics,* this does not make much sense. If human beings really had the Substantial Nature/Essence/Form of a Rational Animal, they would not need so much help to "fulfill" it. It would be silly to say that liana vines actually had a Substantial Form or tendency to become hammocks, and merely needed the help of human tailors to fulfill that purpose. Liana vines may have a capacity to become hammocks, in the sense they make better materials for such artifacts than many other things, but since they require external aid to that end, we cannot say "hammock-ness" is some sort of internal principle of liana vines. By the same token, while humans may be the only creatures on Earth with any capacity for rationality, the fact that we need so much help to achieve it indicates that our rationality does not stem from any principle inherent or intrinsic to us—it must be imposed on us, so to speak, by our parents or caretakers. We can easily understand this by thinking of a human baby somehow born in the depths of space or an endless void of nothingness. The baby would die of starvation, obviously, but even if it didn't it would never develop language or have any grasp of ideas, logic, or anything else. It would just be hairless and two-legged, not rational in any sense. Therefore, the only substantial characteristics that seem to flow inherently from the Form of a Human are what the dictionary tells us—being a two-legged hairless primate.

Feser might argue that human beings are almost always raised by parents who allow them to reason to some extent (though of course, some parents are better than others). But this would not prove humans were *substantially* rational animals. Imagine if every single liana vine on

---

[1] *TLS,* 143.

Earth grew in a greenhouse, where it would be harvested to produce hammocks. Would that mean the liana vines had the substantial Form of being hammocks, or more accurately the final cause of becoming hammocks? No, because even if human beings (or sentient aliens or whatever) always and inevitably turned the vines into hammocks, the vines themselves would have no internal principle dictating they develop into hammocks. An externally imposed goal or state is still externally imposed, even if it is imposed one-hundred percent of the time. By the same token, even if human babies are molded into rational creatures by their parents or guardians nearly one-hundred percent of the time, the fact that they need to be *molded* is proof they are *artificially* rather than *substantially* rational.[1]

Regardless of its origins, might the exercise of rationality itself make human beings a substance? Feser quotes the philosopher Eleanor Stump, who postulates that water and Styrofoam constitute substances even when created by humans, because they have "properties irreducible to their constituent parts," for instance water is wet despite oxygen and hydrogen not being so, and Styrofoam acts very differently from its constituent chemicals.[2] In Feser's view, this would apply to human beings, since (as we touched upon in Chapter 1 and will return to later) Thomists believe rational activity is immaterial rather than the product of any physical process in the brain.

But it seems to me that Stump's choice of example somewhat harms its utility for Feser's purposes. Even if Styrofoam is a substance, with a certain set of behaviors its constituent chemicals do not display, it is an *artificial* substance. It does not appear in nature and would not exist without humans, which means that the final cause of whatever Substantial characteristics it may have is to serve human needs. Would Feser say that there is some intrinsic principle that a piece of Styrofoam must fulfill in order to be good Styrofoam? Only to the extent that

---

[1] This analogy draws upon the extended discussion Feser offers in his essay, "Between Aristotle and William Paley: Aquinas's Fifth Way" in *NSE,* 151-152.
[2] Ibid.

fulfilling that principle serves human needs—for instance, good Styrofoam would protect a package well, while bad Styrofoam would fail to do so. If that is so, why would we not expect the same to apply to human rationality? Even if humans were substantially rational creatures in that sense, we would be "artificial substances" because we need external actors to turn us into rational beings. That would suggest, from Stump's example, that the final cause of our rationality would be to serve *those external actors*, like Styrofoam should serve its creators. A Rational Animal would be "good" not to the extent he or she acted rationally, *but to the extent that rational activity served his or her parents or guardians.*

Feser might not see much in this assessment to disagree with at first glance, but further thought reveals it is incompatible with his brand of Aristotelian ethics. The Good for human beings consists in serving one's parents rather than seeking truth or wisdom or God. And if one's parents happen to be Nazis or Communists or jihadists, the proper use of one's rational faculty would involve furthering Nazism or Communism or the Islamic State. Whoops!

As a very last resort, the Thomist might concede that human rationality is an artificial substance, but still maintain it is one created by God rather than the individual's parents or the society to which he or she belongs. Since Thomists hold that rational activity is necessarily immaterial, they might claim the principle of proportionate causality (discussed at greater length in the next chapter) implies that only God, the most immaterial Being that exists, could confer rationality to anyone (or anything), regardless of whether or not our parents or caretakers assist in that undertaking. Thus, we would be (in a sense) artifacts created by God like Styrofoam is an artifact created by us, and our purpose would still be to serve God (which we cannot do by being Nazis or Commies).

Unfortunately, this still cannot provide a solid grounding for ethics, because rationality cannot tell us how to serve God. Flip back to section 2.4 of this book, wherein we established that the proof for any given "revelation"—Christian or otherwise—is a posteriori and contingent historical evidence upon which we can only reason inductively, not deductively. Thus, there is always the chance that any sort of revelation, ranging from the Bible to the Qu'ran any other holy text, was incorrect or outrightly falsified. We would require yet another divine revelation to assure the verity of the original one, and *that* revelation would require another revelation to assure *its* verity, and so on, ad infinitum. So, we can conclude that there is actually no way to discern what God wants us to do in terms of religion (or anything else, really), and therefore no way to ground our ethics in God's will.

With this understanding, then, the Aristotelian ethical system falls apart. As Feser would say, we are only ethically obligated to adhere to our Primary Substantial Form. *If* that Primary Substantial Form *actually were* "Rational Animal," then we might be able to agree with Aristotelian morality, that it is good to be rational and bad to be irrational (where, for Thomists, rational equates to being Catholic, and irrational equates to being a Nazi or Commie or whatever). But it is quite possible that the Primary Substantial Form of a human being is not a "rational animal," but merely a bipedal hairless primate. Our rationality is merely an accidental characteristic or a non-substantial one rather than an essential one. Even being as generous as possible to Feser, the most we could say is that humans considered as rational animals are artificial substances, not natural ones. And even if we say God Himself gives us the gift of rationality, there is no way to discern which religion He wants us to join. Therefore, there is no reason being a Catholic, or being rational in any other sense, would necessarily be "good" in any objective way.

5.4: Putting the Foot Down

Still, most people would say that human beings ought to be rational. After all, in terms of the dictionary definition of good, rational people are generally if not necessarily more agreeable, pleasant, and profitable (to themselves and others) than irrational people, especially Nazis. So perhaps Feser could argue that human beings should strive for rationality as a kind of general ideal, even if we might not specifically have the Primary Substantial Form of a Rational Animal. This approach might be supported by the famous philosopher Philippa Foot, whom Feser summarizes as such:

> Philippa Foot, following Michael Thompson, has noted how living things can only adequately be described in terms of what Thompson calls "Aristotelian categoricals" of a form such as S's are F, where S refers to a species and F to something predicated of the species... "Cats are four legged," and "Human beings have thirty-two teeth" would be instances of this general form. Note that such propositions cannot be adequately represented as either existential or universal propositions... "Cats are four legged," for instance, is not saying "There is at least one cat that is four legged"; it is obviously meant instead as a statement about cats in general. But neither is it saying "For everything that is a cat, it is four legged," since the occasional cat may be missing a leg due to injury or genetic defect. Aristotelian categoricals convey a norm.... If a particular S happens not to be F – if for example a certain cat is missing a leg – that does not show that S's are not F after all, but rather that this particular S is a defective instance of an S. In living things the sort of norm in question is, as Foot also notes, inextricably tied to the notion of teleology.... There are certain ends that any organism must realize in order to flourish as the kind of organism it is, ends concerning activities like self-maintenance, development, reproduction, the rearing of young, and so forth; and these ends entail a standard of goodness. Hence an oak that develops long and deep roots is to that extent a good oak and one that develops weak roots is to that extent bad and defective; a lioness which nurtures her young is to that extent a good lioness and one that fails to do so is to that extent bad and defective; and so on.[1]

Feser, as you can probably tell, calls upon Foot in defense of a very Aristotelian account of good and bad. But considered on purely Aristotelian terms, the argument falls prey to the problems I discussed in the previous section. If we want to say a Nazi is a "sickly or defective instance" of a human being, we will have to explain how he can be a

---

[1] *AQ,* 177-179.

flourishing instance of a Nazi since he conforms to the Form of Nazism. Given the difficulty of that task, we would have to admit that rational activity is not a necessary characteristic of human Nature, meaning that "the ends set for the human organism by its Nature" are merely (being very generous to Feser) shared with other mammals like lions, namely preserving one's physical health and successfully reproducing. If that was true, then a physically strong Nazi soldier with a litter of Hitler Youth children, a hearty Communist commissar with a brood of little New Soviet Men, or a jihadi living in the mountains with 20 kids by 4 wives would exhibit more "natural goodness" than a celibate Catholic monk who goes hungry so as to feed the poor.

A stronger approach—a steelmanned version of the argument, you could say—would revolve around the more general "norms" Foot described (Feser is quoting from her book *Natural Goodness*). Humans might not be "substantially rational," but it does seem to be the case we generally do better when we are rational. Nazis have a bad habit of invading Russia during the winter, Communists have a bad habit of starving themselves, and ISIS goons have a bad habit of blowing themselves up, which obviates their ability to keep themselves alive and reproduce, even if any individual Nazi or Commie or jihadi meets with more success. Thus, we could say human beings are normatively rational, in the sense that the characteristic helps us survive as living creatures, which is good enough to make it something we should all seek. This would provide a basis for calling Nazism and other forms of murderous fanaticism "bad" and lauding virtuous, reasonable behavior as "good," so Foot's brand of Aristotelianism has a certain appeal. However, even if Foot might have possibly salvaged Aristotelian ethics, her logic has several implications which are considerably less salutary for Thomists in particular.

In trying to figure out which characteristics truly contribute towards an organism's flourishing and which are merely tangential to it, Dr. Foot compared a blue tit with a somewhat drab head and a peacock with a drab tail. The color of a blue tit (assumedly) "played no part" in the role of the tit's life, but the peacock relies on his flashy tail to attract a mate. Thus, a drab-headed blue tit wouldn't really fail to live up to the "norm" of his species because being drab would not prevent him from carrying out any of his natural ends, making it a harmless characteristic. On the other hand, a drab-tailed peacock would be less able to reproduce, and since reproduction is the proper end of a living thing, the status of his tail is salient to whether or not Mr. Peacock is flourishing.[1] In this case, then, our rationality might be like a peacock's tail: It's much easier for us to reproduce and raise healthy children if we understand what is true and what is false, and much harder for us to do so if we pick fights with both the United States and the Soviet Union at the same time, or commit other similarly silly pratfalls.

    The perceptive reader will note that none of this description has anything to do with religion. Under a strictly Thomistic view, the Form of Man entails being a Rational Animal, which would entail we are obligated to use our rationality to "know God." However, Foot's more flexible brand of Aristotelian "general norm" ethics implies that our ends are to survive and reproduce, with rationality merely being generally necessary to do so. In this light, religion is completely irrelevant. An atheist, pagan, Jew, or Muslim who earns the goodwill of his community through virtuous living and rears a brood of healthy, virtuous children is more "rational," in Foot's sense, than an overwhelmingly devout Catholic who dies alone and childless in the desert because he wanted to become a pious hermit. The former has achieved the ends common to humans and indeed animals in general while the latter has abdicated them. The "duties to pursue knowledge of God" which Feser says are our highest responsibility[2] are, in reality, as irrelevant to our flourishing as the color on a blue tit's head, to use Foot's example. Given the problems with claiming Christianity is true (as described in Chapter 2), it seems that if Mr. Pure Act really does exist, He does not care if you're Catholic or Muslim or Jewish or pagan or whatever. Going simply by the general

---

[1] Philippa Foot, *Natural Goodness* (Clarendon Press, 2003), 30-35.
[2] *TLS,* 153.

norms of our species He has set and Foot has discerned, as long as you use your rationality to live a good life, be a good citizen, and raise a good family, you are in all important respects a good man or woman.

Even more troubling for Feser, sexual morality becomes much less ethically salient under Foot's theory. Actions such as rape would be irrational and forbidden, of course, because they make one a danger to the community as a whole, and it's hard (in general) to survive and rear children when you're being hunted down by angry vigilantes. But there would be nothing "irrational" about masturbating a lot or even having homosexual relations, because any *individual* or *particular* non-procreative sexual act does not necessarily prevent one from fulfilling the procreative function *generally,* or within its proper *social context.* A man who masturbates occasionally can still impregnate a woman and raise children with her later on in life, after he's put down the Playboy. Gays and lesbians can successfully reproduce via sperm donation, and there is not exactly much evidence proving they are much worse at raising children.[1] In other words, even if we were to grant that homosexuals are violating the immediate, "ground level" procreative teleology of their sexual faculties, they are still perfectly capable of fulfilling what Foot would call their more important "big picture" general teleology: Rearing healthy children who will grow up to become contributing members of society.[2] This may be a very displeasing prospect for Feser, but given that Philippa Foot apparently described

---

[1] Jimi Adams and Ryan Light, "Scientific Consensus, the law, and same sex parenting outcomes," *Social Science Research*, vol. 53, September 2015, 300-310, https://www.sciencedirect.com/science/article/pii/S0049089X15001209

[2] It is prudent to note here that Foot seems to have *explicitly repudiated* Feser's preferred brand of sexual morality in the book on which he relies. On page 109 of *Natural Goodness*, she states, "in our own lifetime extant moral beliefs about various sexual practices have come to many of us to seem mistaken; we have re-evaluated old beliefs about the baneful influence of, for instance, masturbation or homosexuality, and so revised former evaluations."

herself as a "card-carrying atheist,"[1] I suspect she would be less perturbed by such a distinctly un-Thomistic conclusion.

5.5: The Rewards of Rationality

Feser would probably respond by saying "mere survival" alone could not be the ultimate goal of our rational faculties. He might tell us to think about final causes rather than Forms. As we all know by now, a Form is what defines and distinguishes a thing, but Feser also believes everything (or at least almost everything) has a final cause. The final cause of something is its function or purpose, the sake for which it exists. This is supposed to provide yet another "objective" standard of goodness, since something that fails in its function would be considered objectively bad, and one which fulfills it objectively good.

So, what is the final cause of human rationality? As mentioned earlier (again, we will revisit this subject in the next chapter), Feser takes rationality to be an immaterial operation—since, according to him, rational activity is grasping and understanding Forms, a rational mind must be immaterial or otherwise it would just become whatever Form it was currently thinking about. Now, to understand a Form is to understand a true fact about reality—if you understand the Form of Triangularity, you have an accurate grasp of that part of mathematics, and if you understand the Form of Cats or Squirrels or any other creature, you understand what those animals are really like and how they really operate in the world around you. So, Feser and Aquinas said that "the natural end or final cause of the intellect, with its capacity to

---

[1] Rosalind Hursthouse, "Philippa Ruth Foot, 1920-2010", *Biographical Memoirs of Fellows of the British Academy*, XI (2012), 183,
https://britac.ac.uk/sites/default/files/11_07-Philippa_Foot.pdf . To be fair, Dr. Foot did allow for the moral rectitude of celibacy; as she said on page 42 of *Natural Goodness*, for human beings that live in a diverse society, on some occasions, "the demands of work to be done may give a man or woman reason to renounce family life." But the choice of words there, "work to be done," would not necessarily let a Catholic religious man or woman off the hook if he or she merely prayed a lot instead of performing important work among fellow human beings.

grasp abstract concepts and to reason on the basis of them, is to attain truth (In Meta I.1.2–3)...the intellect's capacity to know the truth is more fully realized the deeper is its understanding of the nature of the world and the causes underlying it; and in Aquinas's view the deepest truth about the world is...that it is caused and sustained in being by God. Hence the highest fulfillment of the human intellect is to know God (ST I-II.1.8)."[1]

It seems to me that there are several reaches here. Let us be charitable and ignore the considerations brought up in the previous sections. For the purposes of argument, let us accept that the Function or final cause of the human mind would be to know the truth about various things. But that does not entail that its function is to know the truth about *all* things, or the most "fundamental" things. Take, for instance, a nerd who has dedicated his life to cataloging the most obscure, finely-grained details about trains or classic films or some other esoteric, eccentric field. He could tell you to the right millisecond the date a certain model of train was first operated, or the exact length in inches of the reel of film on which *Citizen Kane* was first shot. All of these facts would be true—they may be interesting pieces of trivia. But if our nerd spent most of his time studying them rather than learning about more practical pursuits and areas of knowledge, we probably would not say his mind, his Rational Faculty, was successfully fulfilling its function. We would instead chide him for wasting his life, even if every fact he pored over was true. How could this be if the only purpose of our intellect is to know truth? We can, therefore, conclude that Aquinas and Feser's assessment of the mind's purpose is, if not incorrect, at least incomplete. The final cause of the human intellect may be to understand certain truths, *but only so far as those truths can be put to some practical use.*

Now, of course, Feser might agree with me that trivial knowledge, even if true, is at best an amusing distraction and at worst a waste of

---

[1] *AQ*, 142-143.

time, nothing more. On the other hand, he would undoubtedly say that knowledge of God is far more important. After all, given the classical theist worldview, God is ultimately responsible for *absolutely everything*—change, the laws of physics (or the powers of things, as Feser might prefer), and so on, and so forth.

However, that does not mean knowledge of Him can be put to any practical use. Yes, God might be the "ultimate reason" that, say, water turns to ice or steam (its potentials are actualized) or that the attraction between electrons and protons is what it is. But even if we know that, what are we supposed to do with it? Pray that these things can be changed? It is unlikely God would answer that in the affirmative. So, at the very most, we can say that the final cause of human rationality is to understand the truth that some Purely Actual thing exists, but pay no more attention to the matter than that. We are rather "meant" to spend our time and effort on understanding the lower truths, since knowing how to boil or freeze water, or how electricity works, can be put to immediate practical use, unlike "knowledge of God." Now, if it were the case that Mr. Pure Act demanded some religious duty, then rationality would dictate we carry it out. But, as I demonstrated in Chapter 2, there is no way of knowing with deductive certainty if any religion is true. We might be able to argue for one or the other being more likely true, but cannot be absolutely sure if being Catholic (or Jewish, or Muslim, or Pagan, or whatever) and carrying out that religion's particular duties is the actual final cause of our intellects.

Feser might now fall back to the traditional Aristotelian belief that "contemplative reason," and "pondering first principles" is that final cause of final causes. In this traditional view, "the prediction and control of nature" has its place, but the primary purpose of rationality is "wisdom and understanding." Apparently, we moderns have been entranced by the material promises of science, following Protestants like John Calvin in forgetting "the dangers of wealth and the benefits of poverty" and embracing "industry, thrift, and acquisition" on very parlous philosophical grounds.¹ But as I have just described, we cannot be sure of that either. Human beings generally prioritize truth that can be put to practical use over any old kind of truth generally, which seems to indicate that the real final cause of our truth-seeking faculties is to use truth productively rather than seek truth for its own sake. And despite what Feser might have us believe, we do not arrive at this conclusion by abandoning Aristotelian realism about Forms and final causes. Quite to the contrary, a nuanced grasp of such final causes (aided by the dearly departed Philippa Foot) *proves* that the only reason we seek "wisdom and understanding" is to aid in our "prediction and control of nature," so that we may more successfully survive and reproduce. More good news for the Aristotelian, I suppose—maybe we don't have to jettison Greek philosophy entirely—but not so good for the Thomist.

This line of reasoning is considerably bolstered by evolutionary theory. Feser would agree, I'm sure, that the body parts of animals in general have specific "final causes" in the sense of having specific functions or doing certain things, but that their true purpose is to ensure the overall health of the organism. A spider's fangs have the specific function of piercing prey and injecting venom, but that serves the overall higher final cause of feeding the spider and ensuring its survival, not because piercing and poisoning are good on their own. A squirrel buries nuts in order to store food for the winter, not because storing nuts is any sort of final goal in and of itself.

This is all basic evolutionary biology, and given that Feser has criticized "intelligent design" proponents in both *The Last Superstition*

---

[1] *TLS*, 176-179. As an aside, the aforementioned Dan Lawler's Amazon review of the book makes a very wry point about Feser's apparent inability to live up to his own admonitions. As Lawler asks, "why did I have to pay for this book? Why doesn't Feser freely distribute it to promote Scholastic values and the love of wisdom? Looks like he's not such a big believer in poverty-is-virtue after all and has become a hard-core, pipe-hittin' Calvinist when it comes to book sales. ;-)" Refer back to "Medieval Times (Are Here Again!)," https://www.amazon.com/gp/customer-reviews/R2RETCY4TFAQ5D/ref=cm_cr_getr_d_rvw_ttl?ie=UTF8&ASIN=1587314525

and *Aquinas*, I doubt he'd contest it. However, when we apply this line of thought to people, things get a little interesting. Human beings, as it turns out, are queer creatures. We must hunt and gather to eat, but we have no in-built weapons like spiders do, and we can't just bury nuts and then eat them raw like squirrels can. So how did we survive before the advent of civilization? As it so happens, our intellects were our best weapons. Our ability to grasp concepts like triangles helped us craft stone and flint weapons to kill dangerous foes far larger than even the nastiest spider (triangular arrowheads are better than, say, circular ones), and our ability to comprehend patterns of regular behavior and cause-effect relationships allowed us to invent agriculture and gain our food that way.

Good for us—but you'll notice I haven't mentioned God once. It seems, taking an evolutionary view of our "Nature" as "rational animals," that rationality itself is, first and foremost, a tool we used to survive. Perhaps it's a good thing that we can comprehend God exists, but if so, that would be merely an "accidental characteristic"—the actual end, or "final cause" of our rationality is to help us survive, reproduce, and keep our children fed. And we arrive at this distinctly un-Feserian conclusion by relying entirely on his *own metaphysical methodology*. Again, a spider's fangs have the function of killing prey—that is its immediate final cause. But its true final cause, the sake for which it exists at all, is to kill prey so it can be digested and help the spider survive and reproduce. A squirrel buries nuts—that is the immediate final cause of its instincts. But the true final cause of its behavior is to store food so it can survive winter. And human beings are the same way. Our minds are capable of grasping truth because we lack fangs or claws and needed something else to help us survive, and an intellect that could grasp, say, triangularity or predictable animal behavior would allow us to create pointy arrows and spears and hunt dangerous animals better. From this perspective, then, the final cause of our intellect is not necessarily to know God, but to know just enough to ensure our survival and propagation.

Now, this might fall into the trap of the "Evolutionary Argument Against Naturalism (or EAAN)." The argument, made by the philosopher Alvin Plantinga and repeated by Feser on his blog, goes like this: Evolution favors beliefs that are amenable to survival, not necessarily true—for instance, a proto-human who believed that running away from tigers led to food would pass on such an obviously false belief just as well as a proto-human who correctly recognized the tiger as a predator, since both hominids would avoid being eaten. Thus, a purely evolutionary account of rationality implies that *nothing* we believe is necessarily true as opposed to merely adaptive. The only way to get around this, in Feser's view, is to hold that God "ensures that the neurological processes generated by natural selection are generally correlated with true beliefs."[1]

But *even if* we assume the EAAN works, it wouldn't necessarily entail that the final cause of our rational faculties is to "seek truth" alone. As described above, there are many "truths" which are quite reasonably held to be useless bits of trivia, and this would remain the case even if God were actually helping our limited, material monkey brains perceive them correctly. Thus, it seems reasonable to conclude that if the EAAN holds and God is ultimately responsible for ensuring our beliefs and thought processes are generally correlated with the truth, God does so merely to facilitate our putting those beliefs to practical use so that we can survive and reproduce. Or, in other words, even if the EAAN is true, it is still the case that the final cause of our rational faculties is to aid in our survival and reproduction—it just so happens that God is giving us some assistance towards that end, and does not really care whether we worship Him or not.

This would, of course, concede too much to Feser anyways. To say that the EAAN is controversial would be an understatement—very many

---

[1] Edward Feser, "Schliesser on the Evolutionary Argument Against Naturalism," *Edward Feser,* January 21, 2013, last accessed on July 5, 2020, http://edwardfeser.blogspot.com/2013/01/schliesser-on-evolutionary-argument.html

scientists and philosophers alike have pointed out its flaws. John Wilkins, for instance, has noted that for any belief about the environment to be adaptive, it must be true in at least some sense, while beliefs about abstractions might perhaps be less reliable. So while we ought to be suspicious of our beliefs about God or metaphysics, we could probably be pretty certain running away from tigers wouldn't necessarily lead to food even if God didn't exist. Massimo Pigliucci goes even further and states that creatures that have consistently false beliefs about the natural world would quickly go extinct—the Dodo, for instance, held false beliefs about the benevolence of human visitors and quickly died out because of it. Thus, the fact that we still exist as a species is proof our basic intuitions about the world around us are reasonably reliable.[1] If one holds that the pursuit of truth is generally a good thing, it is not an absolute necessity to hold that God assists us in that endeavor.

This assertion is further buttressed by the fact our very nature as material beings—our *Form* or *Essence* as rational *animals*—necessarily prevents us from knowing and understanding God perfectly or even to any great extent. In "Trinity and Mystery," Feser tells us,

> Consider first that, at least on the conception of God enshrined in Classical Theism (especially, I would say, as interpreted within Thomism) it is quite obviously far more plausible to suppose that God should be incomprehensible to us than that the relationship between matter and consciousness should be. If God exists, then He is Pure Actuality… and thus beyond the classifications by means of which we understand the things we can understand. He is not one object among others within the world but that which sustains all objects in being, from outside any possible world. What we say of Him is true not univocally but analogically. Etc. Neither matter nor consciousness is anything remotely like this. Instead, they are both conceptually and

---

[1] John Wilkins, "Plantinga's EAAN," *Evolving Thoughts*, January 31, 2012, https://evolvingthoughts.net/2012/01/31/plantingas-eaan/ , Massimo Pigliucci, "Plantinga's Evolutionary Argument Against Naturalism," *Rationally Speaking*, July 15, 2013, http://rationallyspeaking.blogspot.com/2013/07/plantingas-evolutionary-argument.html (both last accessed on July 5, 2020).

epistemically far closer than God is to the things we suppose we can understand. Hence there is prima facie a much stronger case for supposing that God's nature should be incomprehensible to us than there is for saying that the relationship between matter and consciousness should be. God is precisely the sort of thing we should expect to be unable fully to understand, while matter and consciousness are not (even if it turns out that we cannot fully understand them either).[1]

Very nice, and I will admit this makes sense, given everything else Feser has written. If God truly were the Ground of All Being, it would follow that if He is the most immaterial thing in existence, then it seems plausible He would be very difficult for humans to grasp, as our minds are (partially) material[2] and limited. We haven't even figured out fusion yet, it'll be quite a while before we unlock the secrets of the creation of the universe, right?

But...that should tell us that perhaps understanding God isn't our final cause, from an Aristotelian standpoint.

Remember, Feser is big on the idea the Form follows function. We will critique that idea later on, but let's pretend to accept it at the moment. *Even if we do*, it's obvious that the Form of Humanity is very poorly suited for the "final cause" of knowing God. We may perhaps be better at it than dumb animals, but that's not saying much. If God had really wanted us to know Him, He could have made us much smarter and/or less material than we actually are. The fact that we're not, however, seems to be proof that we weren't really intended to know Him. Or, to put it another way, if you encountered a blunt object with a minimal (if any) edge, would you conclude it was a knife with the "final cause" of cutting? Of course not, or at most, you would conclude it was

---

[1] Edward Feser, "Trinity and Mystery," *Edward Feser*, February 10, 2010, last accessed on July 5, 2020, http://edwardfeser.blogspot.com/2010/02/trinity-and-mystery.html

[2] In Feser's words, our minds, despite operating immaterially, are "embodied" in contrast to those of angels and God, which are *entirely* incorporeal. AQ, 123.

a very blunt knife, so poorly suited to its purpose that it ought to be thrown away. So, if you look at human beings, with our minimal capacity, at best, to know God, would you conclude that knowing God was our final cause? Probably not.

Indeed, when you really start to ponder the relationship God has to morality, the problems attending Aristotelianism in general and Thomism in particular grow more, not less, severe. As this section has hopefully demonstrated, even if one is a realist with regard to Forms, that offers little helpful guidance in determining what is good or bad. As also demonstrated in the above paragraphs, even if we assume God exists, it's similarly unclear which Forms or Functions He wishes us to instantiate or fulfill. But the very *question* of God's existence deepens these quandaries. How *would* Mr. Pure Act determine what is morally good or bad? How could a morally good God permit evil of *any* sort? Philosophers have been debating these questions since at least the time of the ancient Greeks, and Feser would like to think that Aristotle and Aquinas have decisively answered them. Unhappily, as we will see, their solutions to these evergreen issues are as profoundly unsatisfying as their solutions for the is-ought dilemma.

5.6: Euthyphro's Revenge

The Euthyphro Dilemma is one of the most famous and intractable problems in the history of philosophy. It can be dated to ancient Greece, found specifically in Plato's writings. Plato recounted a debate between Euthyphro and Socrates, in which the former asked, "Is the holy holy because it is loved by the gods, or do they love it because it is holy?"[1] Edward Feser offers a more detailed breakdown of the challenge this poses to theists in *Aquinas*. Essentially, Euthyphro's questions offer two horns of a dilemma. When he asked, "is the holy holy because it is loved by the gods," the implicit assertion there is "that something counts as

---

[1] John Hare,"Religion and Morality", *The Stanford Encyclopedia of Philosophy* (Winter 2014 Edition), Edward N. Zalta (ed.), last accessed July 5, 2020, https://plato.stanford.edu/archives/win2014/entries/religion-morality/

good or bad because of God's will." Euthyphro's second question, that the gods love good things because they are holy, implicitly asserts that things can be good or bad "by reference to some standard external [to God]." As Feser admits, neither of these positions is very theologically satisfying, since "the first seems to make morality entirely arbitrary, insofar as it appears to entail for example that torturing infants for fun would have been good if God had willed this. The second seems to entail that morality is ultimately independent of God, which seems incompatible with the idea that everything that exists other than God ultimately derives from him."[1]

How do Thomists like Feser escape from this conundrum? According to him, Aquinas proved the dilemma was "false" way back in the Middle Ages. It all comes back to the Forms I'm sure you're sick of by now. Everything has a Form, and thus some objective standard of good and bad, *even without reference to God*. Good triangles have three straight sides, bad ones don't, good humans are rational, bad ones aren't, yadda yadda yadda. But check back to chapter 1—Forms, as abstract objects, can only really exist in God's mind, because otherwise they couldn't be universal (that is to say, applicable across many individual physical objects, or existent even in the absence of physical objects). So even though good and bad can be understood in a "secular" manner, by referring to Forms rather than God, good and bad are still *ultimately* dependent on God because God is the one who came up with everything's Form in the first place. This also means that God's moral commandments are ultimately not "arbitrary" even if He is their ultimate source. Yes, God determines what Forms there are, but He only determines them "in accordance to reason," and since He is pure good, He would never order us to do anything that contradicts those Forms (which would be bad). So, for instance, God ultimately determines that the Form of Triangularity would involve having three sides, but He would never dictate that triangles have four sides, since that would contradict their Form and He only ever wills "in accordance to" His

---

[1] *AQ*, 128-129.

intellect. By the same token, God ultimately determines that the Form of Man is a rational animal, and could therefore never tell us that torturing babies is good, because such an act would contradict our Form. This is, according to Feser, a "third option" that avoids the pitfalls of either horn of the Euthyphro dilemma.[1]

Now, I find the "divine mind" solution to the problem of universals to be unsatisfactory, but we can leave that for the next chapter and concentrate purely on morality. If you have been paying close attention to the issues raised in the preceding pages here, you will probably not agree with Feser even with regard to that subject alone. Even if we accept the reality of Essences, they provide astonishingly little help in discerning what is good and what is bad. How can we be sure the true Form of a human being is a "rational animal" rather than just a hairless biped? How can we be sure that various kinds of historical villains ranging from Nazis to Communists to jihadis don't instantiate their own Forms? If we can't even be certain of which Forms to instantiate and how to do so, it is completely useless to say that God's commands are not arbitrary if they accord with our Forms, because many hideous, arbitrary commands accorded with certain Forms. Could God have ordered Mengele to torture and murder Jewish or Romani children because he was a Nazi and such actions would have been good for him according to the Form of Nazism? How could the Aristotelian Thomist deny this?

Even more problems arise when we consider how vague the traditional Aristotelian and Thomistic definition of the human Form as a "rational animal" happens to be. Feser tells us "our nature or essence is to be rational animals, and reason...has as its final cause the attainment of truth."[2] So, it seems that the Thomistic position is that attaining truth is the mark of a good Rational Animal (much like having three straight sides is the mark of a good triangle). But many abhorrent behaviors are perfectly compatible with that Form, at least given the

---

[1] Ibid., 128-129, 181-183.
[2] *TLS*, 139.

minimal details Feser has provided. For instance, how would torturing babies contradict the Form of a Rational Animal? Such an evil pursuit would involve the attainment of truth: The torturers would have to figure out which methods caused the most pain, how to build devices capable of inflicting the most pain, how to measure pain reliably and objectively, and so on. All of these lines of inquiry, however disgusting they may be, involve the cataloging of true facts and subsequently reasoning upon them. Therefore, God could certainly order us to torture babies (for fun or any other reason), because we would still adhere to our Forms as rational animals by attaining and reasoning upon truth with regard to the sensation of pain.

The reasoning is certainly ugly, but it is at least somewhat consistent: God still couldn't order us to do "anything at all," because some actions *would* seem to violate even the thin definition of "Rational Animal" provided; for instance learning and acting on false information would be the opposite of a Form that demands we seek truth. Even so, this attempted solution to Euthryphro's dilemma *still* makes God mostly arbitrary, since there are so very many actions (including obviously evil ones) that are still consistent with our Form. For all Feser knows, God may well order us to "seek the truth" about torture or infanticide or rape, or whatever, the day after tomorrow. It is little comfort indeed to worship a mostly whimsical, capricious God as opposed to an entirely capricious one.

But it gets even worse for the Thomist. As touched upon in the last chapter, while Thomists hold that the final cause of our rational faculties is the attainment of truth, the ultimate truth is God. This means, according to Aquinas and Feser, that "God alone" is "the *highest* or *ultimate* good for us, that to which every other good is subordinated."[1] In other words, *given our Form, Nature or final cause*, serving God is the highest good for us. But this completely vitiates Feser's argument that God could not do absolutely anything to us or order us to do something

---

[1] *AQ*, 181. The italics are Feser's.

psychotically evil like torture babies. Yes, God only wills us to do things in accordance with our Forms or final causes, but the human Form as a rational animal is, in the ultimate analysis, *merely a God-serving creature*, so to speak. God really *could* order us to do just about anything at all, because *any* action God told us to do would not contradict our Form or Nature, since our Form entails we must serve God *above all else*. If God ordered us to kill or torture babies, doing so would in fact *fulfill* our Nature, because according to Aquinas, our Form entails that we are to do whatever God says above anything else. Torturing babies would thus *become* good for us, or in accordance with our Form, simply by dint of God having ordered it.[1]

It seems to me that the Thomist's failure lies in how he understands the term "Rational Animal" and what that entails. It simply is not enough to say that we ought to seek truth and serve God, since as I have just described, even evil activity could involve truth-seeking or serving God. To be fair, it seems that Aquinas was at least vaguely aware of this necessity; Feser notes that the plump Doctor also set out other traits a good Rational Animal should have, such as "[living] in society" and "[not] offending those among whom one has to live."[2] But even this definition of Rational Animality still leaves God too much leeway for comfort: He could still order us to do things like torture babies if such a practice were accepted by a society and considered inoffensive by its people (as was the case for, say, idolators who supposedly sacrificed children to Moloch, according to the Old Testament[3]). And in any case, Aquinas still held that the ultimate good for Rational Animals was obeying God. Thus, according to the Principle of Totality described

---

[1] Another blogger has made a slightly different critique of Feser's argument. Interested readers are directed to Alex SL, "Euthyphro," *Phylobotanist*, March 12, 2015, last accessed on July 5, 2020,
http://phylobotanist.blogspot.com/2015/03/euthyphro.html
[2] *AQ*, 180.
[3] Gigot, Francis. "Moloch." *The Catholic Encyclopedia.* Vol. 10. New York: Robert Appleton Company, 1911. 20 Dec. 2019,
http://www.newadvent.org/cathen/10443b.htm

previously, God could still order us to torture babies even if doing so would offend our neighbors or prevent us from living in society, because those goods are subordinate to our ultimate good (doing whatever God tells us to).

I would say the Dilemma can only really be solved through (what Feser would consider) a radical reassessment of what "good" is for Rational Animals. Rather than holding that a good Rational Animal merely "seeks truth in order to ultimately serve God," a more satisfactory description of our Essence would go like this:

"The Form of a Rational Animal is such that we should generally seek truth and avoid error *so that* we may live in society and avoid offending our neighbors, allowing us to successfully raise our children and enjoy peace and prosperity. God may be ultimately responsible for our Form or Nature being this way, but this does *not* mean that serving Him is our ultimate end; our Form dictates that we should obey His commands *if and only if* they do not prevent us from living inoffensively in a peaceful, prosperous society."

I think these are very generous terms for Dr. Feser. Under this understanding of the human Form, God would never command us to torture babies, because such an action would harm the peace and prosperity of society as a whole (this also applies to other crimes, such as rape and murder). It also does not deny that God is the ultimate arbiter of good and evil, since He is still the Guy who defined the Form of Rational Animality as living in a peaceful and prosperous society. However, this understanding (the Lairdian definition of Rational Animal, let's say) does not require any specifically religious duties at all. In fact, it explicitly subordinates serving God to the ultimate end of living in a prosperous society, and Aquinas thought things were the opposite way around (i.e., that living in society, while nice, is ultimately subordinate to serving God). Thus, I suspect that the Thomists, holding as they do a particularly religious devotion to the Catholic God above all things, would be less than entirely happy with my proposed solution to the Euthyphro Dilemma.[1] Oh, well.

5.7: The Trouble with Transcendentals

The sympathetic reader will note that I have so far been discussing the idea of good and evil, along with God's relationship to them, very much on Feser's terms. Despite outlining the problems with it in the first two sections, ever since, I have been perfectly content to go along with his definition of "good" as "conforming to a certain Form or fulfilling a certain Function," and his definition of "bad" or "evil" as the opposite. Now is a good time to set aside that bit of sportsmanship, because a closer look at how Thomists like Feser use those terms can expose even more flaws in their attempt to build ethics (religious or not) out of their

---

[1] Thomists like Feser would say that all of our faculties are subservient to the cause of "knowing God" because they believe that is the way things are ordered for all living creatures. As Feser says in page 181 of *Aquinas*, "the lower goods [vegetative, which plants have, and sensory, which animals have] are subordinate to the higher ones [rationality for us] in the sense they exist for the sake of the higher ones. The point of fulfilling the vegetative and sensory aspects of our nature is, ultimately, to allow us to fulfill the defining rational aspect of our nature." But this strikes me as precisely backwards—Feser himself admits on the same page that the so-called higher goods "presuppose" the existence of the lower ones. If the higher goods are dependent on the lower ones, why wouldn't they be subordinate to the lower ones, particularly in relation to the Function or final cause of the whole organism? A comparison between plants and animals is apt. Animals are higher in the hierarchy since they possess a sensory soul (imbibing and acting upon sensory data) *in addition* to a purely vegetative soul (simply growing and taking in nutrients). But the final cause of a plant and animal are *exactly the same*. Both the plant and the animal exist for the purpose of reproducing themselves. It's just that an animal requires sensory abilities in order to secure food, shelter, and ultimately lay eggs or give birth, while a plant has no need of sense or movement because it can photosynthesize and produce seeds by just sitting there. By the same token, human beings have the exact same final cause as animals and plants—to survive and reproduce. It just so happens that we need to use reason to do so, since we cannot photosynthesize and possess no natural weapons besides our minds. It is therefore clearly the case that reason exists for us to fulfill our "vegetative nature," not the other way around.

metaphysics. To understand why, we must take a brief look at the idea of transcendentals, first postulated by Aquinas himself.

As touched upon in chapter 1, Aquinas believed the "transcendentals" are a group of positive traits that are actually the same thing—that is to say, they are **convertible.** These transcendentals are "*thing, one, something, true,* and *good,* and each is convertible with [the word] *being* in the sense that each designates one and the same thing— namely being—under a different aspect."[1] We can leave aside the first four words and concentrate on "good" alone. The problem this doctrine of transcendentals poses for Thomism is that the different uses of "good" in reference to Form on the one hand and function on the other, are *not actually the same thing.* This would mean that "good" is not even convertible (designating the very same thing) as *itself,* which seems to be quite a logical inconsistency in Thomistic metaphysics that also makes Thomistic ethics quite confusing, to say the least.

How can it be that goodness in the sense of adhering to a Form and goodness in the sense of fulfilling a function are different things? Let's go all the way back to *The Last Superstition,* where Feser explains the difference between Formal and final causes:[2]

> The first [cause] is what is traditionally called the material cause or underlying stuff that a thing is made out of, in this case rubber. Then we have the formal cause, which is the form, structure, or pattern that the matter exhibits, which in this case comprises such features as sphericity, solidity, and bounciness. As you can see, the material and formal causes of a thing are just its matter and form, considered as components of a complete explanation of it. Next we have the efficient cause, which is what brings a thing into being...in that case, it would be the actions of the workers and/or machines in the factory.... Finally, we

---

[1] *AQ,* 30-35, "Being, the Good, and the Guise of the Good" in *NSE,* 300-305
[2] I am indebted to Reddit users /u/classicalecon and /u/reubencogburn for the discussions in which I sharpened and refined these points.

have the final cause, which is the end, goal, or purpose of a thing, in this case providing amusement to a child.[1]

Here, it seems like Feser (and Aristotle, and Aquinas, assuming his summary is accurate) holds that the *Form* of a ball is to be solid, round, and bouncy. Any ball that has those characteristics is to that extent a good ball, and any that doesn't is a bad one. Then, he tells us that the final cause of the ball is to provide amusement to a child. So, in reference to the ball's *Function*, a good one brings amusement to a child, and a bad one fails to do so.

Both adhering to a Form and fulfilling a Function are "objective" definitions of the word good, as Feser never tires of telling us. If that is the case, one would expect both references of goodness to correlate perfectly, or at least very closely, to each other. After all, if the word "good" is convertible with things like "true" or "being," one would certainly expect "good-in-reference-to-Form" and "good-in-reference-to-function" to be convertible with each other. The problem is that instantiating a certain Form and fulfilling a certain function do *not* have any necessary relationship to each other, as a thought experiment involving Feser's ball will demonstrate.

Imagine a rubber ball that's not spherical—one that has many pits or an oblong, imperfect shape. Perhaps the ball has also been slightly melted, so it is no longer solid or bouncy. Despite its failure to perfectly instantiate its Form in any respect, one can easily imagine the ball perfectly fulfilling its Function. A young child might have a great deal of fun squishing the "ball" or throwing it into the air and catching it, much more than he would have had bouncing it around. Now, imagine an absolutely perfect rubber sphere with no blemishes at all, not even microscopic ones, and that is also perfectly solid and perfectly bouncy. Such a thing is impossible in real life, of course, but imagine one for the purposes of thought. Given the perfect instantiation of its Form, one would expect it to perfectly fulfill its Function. But it is easy, and most

---

[1] *TLS*, 62.

importantly coherent, to imagine this not happening. A child being given this perfect rubber ball might say, "No! Bouncy balls are boring! I'm not having fun at all!" Frustrated by the child's intransigence, you might be tempted to throw the ball at him, in which case its perfect sphericity and perfect solidity crack his skull, and its perfect bounciness makes it careen off his head, into the wall, and back into his head again, knocking him out cold. He is, naturally, not amused at all—quite the opposite. The very perfection of the ball's Form has led to it actually contravening its function—or, in other words, its very goodness in one respect has led to it being very bad in another respect.

Thus, it seems to me that goodness in terms of Form and goodness in terms of Function are *not* "merely the same thing considered in different respects," or in other words, *not* actually convertible. Indeed, they seem to share no necessary relation at all! Given this, any non-Thomist would apparently be handily justified in asking why she, or anyone else, ought to pay much attention to the supposedly "objective" Thomist (and Aristotelian) definition of goodness. It doesn't seem to be very useful if it can and occasionally does conflict with itself. There doesn't seem to be a very strong reason as to why the more commonplace definition of good as profitable or pleasurable captures less of its Essence than the incoherent Aristotelian definition.

One way Feser might try to escape this conundrum would be to simply jettison Form as any barometer of any sort of goodness. He might concede to the suggestion I raised earlier—to simply use neutral, non-value-laden words like "regular" or "irregular" to describe adherence or deviation from certain Forms, and reserve the word "good" to refer to function only. In this view, a rubber ball's physical attributes, such as bounciness or solidity, would be irrelevant to its goodness, which would refer only to whether or not it successfully provided amusement to a child.

The problem is, building an objective theory of goodness and badness on "Function" alone isn't much easier than building one around both Form and Function. It's very difficult to say that anything "objectively" fulfills a function because a function is necessarily relative. Again, take the rubber ball—from the perspective of a child, its function may be to provide amusement, but from the perspective of, say, the CEO of Acme Ball Corp., its function is simply to make him money. In that sense, a ball which somehow failed to amuse a child (for whatever reason) would still fulfill its function, and thus be a "good" ball, if whoever bought it paid for it. Goodness and badness, then, become a mere matter of perspective rather than objective truth, *even if we continue to define "good" in both Aristotelian and Thomistic terms.* Neither the originator of the tradition nor his most apt medieval pupil offer much help here.

Perhaps Feser would say that artifacts might have only subjective, relative functions, but natural substances (remember, we discussed this distinction in chapter 3) have objective ones. His favorite example of the existence of function "even without conscious intent" is bodily organs. Ears have the function of hearing, hearts have the function of pumping blood, and whatever evolutionary biologists might say, it is impossible to understand any of these things without assuming they have such functions, even if they arose through natural selection rather than conscious design.[1] But even assuming this is true, such organs only have functions *considered as a part of a larger organism*. Only from the perspective of the creature with a heart does the heart have the function of pumping blood—from the perspective of, say, the creature's predator, the heart has the "function" of providing a tasty meal. From the perspective of the ecosystem, the heart has no apparent function, or none other than eventually providing fertilizer when the organism dies.

Now, according to Feser, this is the difference between **transeunt** and **immanent** causation we mentioned briefly in Chapter 1. As he said in *Aquinas*, "Immanent causation begins and remains within the agent...and...involves the fulfillment or perfection of the cause [in this case, for instance, some creature like a rabbit or mouse sustaining itself].

---

[1] *TLS*, 62, 70-71.

Transeunt causation, by contrast, is directed entirely outwardly [in this case, a rabbit or mouse being eaten by a snake; their deaths obviously do not serve themselves but an external actor, namely the predator]."[1] However, this distinction does not detract from my argument here—quite the opposite, in fact! We can judge that a certain organ is performing its function well or poorly *only in reference to the immanent causality of the animal to which it belongs*. A rabbit's heart or stomach or whatever is good *to the extent* it contributes to the rabbit's flourishing, fulfillment, or perfection. In other words, saying something is good is *unintelligible outside of its relation to a larger whole* (an organism, in this case) Thus, function is still relative, *even when speaking of some natural substance*.

Feser might be willing to admit this—as he said in *Aquinas,*

> ...[a]ll functions are instances of final causality, but not all final causality involves the having of a function.... A match, for example, reliably generates flame and heat when struck, and never (say) frost... or the smell of lilacs.... [I]t inherently 'points to'... *this* range of effects specifically, and in that way manifests just the sort of end- or goal-directedness characteristic of final causality, even though the match does not (unlike a heart or a carburetor) function as an organic part of a larger system.... When Aristotelians say that final causality pervades the natural order, they are not making the implausible claim that everything has a function of the sort biological organs have, including piles of dirt, iron fillings, and balls of lint. Rather, they are saying that goal-directedness exists wherever regular cause and effect patterns do.[2]

Such a more-nuanced analysis might be good for Aristotelian metaphysics, but unfortunately makes a hash of Aristotelian ethics. The problem is that words like "good" and "bad" make sense when used in reference to a function, but *not* in reference to mere regularity. Say we strike a match and it fails to light. We might call it a "bad" match because

---

[1] *AQ*, 135. Brackets are mine for clarification.
[2] Ibid., 17-18.

it has failed in *our* purpose for it. If we needed to start a fire or get a little extra light, the match's failure to do so would be an inconvenience for us. But when we consider the match itself, its failure to light could only be explained by another physical regularity, and thus such a failure would *itself* be an example of final causality. For instance, perhaps the match had gotten wet. It is simply a causal regularity that wet matches do not light, rather than produce flame (or lilacs or anything else). And since, as Feser just told us, *any sort of cause-and-effect pattern* is an instance of final causality, there is no Aristotelian reason we can say a wet match is defective while a lit one is "working," because the "final cause" of a wet match is to *not* light to the same extent and for the same reasons the final cause of a dry match is to catch fire.

Thus, in order to distinguish between goodness and badness (and eventually moral virtue and vice), the Aristotelian must find some way of distinguishing between "good" instantiations of final causality and "bad" ones. However, the only way to do so is in reference to a function, and only components of a larger system or tools used by another have functions in that sense. In the case of human beings, even assuming our final cause is to "know truth," in the sense of rational activity being what we regularly do and what contributes to our flourishing, why would God reward or punish us for doing or not doing that? Success would not benefit Him in any way, nor would failure hinder Him in any way, the same way a good or bad match (in the Aristotelian sense) might do for humans.

The only other thing human beings seem to be parts of or related to, at least in a relevantly analogous way to bodily organs or tools, is society. One could argue that humans should seek truth and avoid error in order to ensure the society in which they live remains stable and prosperous. That seems reasonable enough to me, but once again, it makes God and religion irrelevant to the idea of good. It also makes seeking truth merely instrumental in the service of a greater good (societal prosperity and harmony) rather than a good in and of itself, much the same way the proper functioning of a bodily organ or a match is merely instrumental to the benefit of the whole organism or the person using the tool. Thus, I doubt the highly-Catholic Thomist or even the somewhat more secular Aristotelian would be very fond of that solution.

5.8: The Problem of Evil

The more one thinks about God, the more puzzling the idea of goodness becomes—either in the Aristotelian definition of adhering to a Form, or even the considerably more common-sense definition of pleasant and agreeable, as opposed to painful or repulsive. Remember, theists traditionally believe that God is entirely omnibenevolent, with not a trace of evil or badness in Him. Classical theists like Thomists go even further and say that God is Goodness itself—pure, subsistent goodness (and that God's goodness is the same as His power, His intellect, and so on). So then how do we explain the existence of any sort of badness or evil? According to Feser, Nazis, Communists, and jihadis are "objectively wicked;" they and their actions grossly deviated from the proper Form of Man and thus exemplified terrible badness. How could a God that is both all-good and all-powerful—Goodness Itself and Power Itself—allow atrocities such as the Holocaust or the Holodomor or 9/11 to occur? Couldn't an all-powerful God somehow rescue all the people who died in those horrors, smite the evildoers before they could carry them out (perhaps by turning Hitler, Stalin, and Mohammed Atta into pillars of salt, say), or manipulate events in such a way that the villains would never be twisted into such cruel and spiteful creatures in the first place?

God *could*, but according to Feser, He does not because doing so would actually prevent greater goods from arising, ones which considerably outweigh even the terrible miseries wrought by war, genocide, and terrorism. As Feser says,

> Suppose your child is trying to learn how to play the violin. This will require much practice, and thus a sacrifice of time that could be spent playing. It will also require hours of frustration and boredom, some pain and discomfort as he gets used to keeping his arms and head in an

awkward position for prolonged periods of time and builds up calluses on his fingers... On bad days he might almost hate you for what you're putting him through. But eventually he becomes very good indeed, and the frustration he once felt disappears entirely... if anything, his accomplishment will have the value for him that it does precisely because he had to suffer for it. In hindsight, he might well say that he wouldn't have had it any other way. Such examples could be multiplied indefinitely. Of course, I am not claiming that the relatively minor suffering in question is comparable to the death of a child, or bone cancer, or Auschwitz. But then, neither could the relatively minor joy of being a great violinist compare to the beatific vision. Indeed, even the greatest horror we can imagine in this life pales in significance before the beatific vision.[1]

It is certainly hard to imagine that any sort of good could exceed the evil that was committed at Auschwitz or many other places, and Feser freely admits it. However, in this example, he also asks us to consider that God, in His infinite power, might be able to bring good out of the greatest evil, in ways we cannot imagine simply because our perspective is too limited, much like a child who cannot understand that his parents force him to play the violin for some greater good. While Feser would assumedly offer many examples of great goods arising from great evils, the one he chose here, the "beatific vision" refers to the Christian heaven. Since, as described in chapter 1, the human soul is supposedly immortal, all the innocent people who died at Auschwitz (and in Stalin's Ukraine, and during 9/11, and so on) have ascended to Paradise, where their souls will enjoy God's presence for *eternity*. Since the Holocaust, Holodomor, and other such terrors were obviously limited and finite instead of eternal and infinite, they are still far outweighed by the good God gives to their innocent victims in heaven. Thus, both God's omnipotence *and* his omnibenevolence are preserved: God chose not to intervene in the Holocaust or any other multitude of earthly evils, not because He was either unwilling or unable, but because

---

[1] *TLS,* 161-162.

the limited evil of those things gave Him an opportunity to create unlimited good.

All that is certainly very inspiring and uplifting, but unfortunately, it is also rather muddle-headed. This argument must be read in light of Feser's belief in the existence of hell.[1] Thus, when he tells us that the beatific vision outweighs the most horrible sufferings imaginable in this life, we must also take into account that an eternity in hell outweighs the most glorious joys as well. Considering how Feser would likely say most if not all of the gays, Romani, and Jews who were sent to the death camps, and most if not all of the non-Catholics who died in Communist and Islamic persecutions, are roasting forever in hell, even the prospect of the beatific vision might not be enough to convince a skeptic that God really is bringing infinite good out of finite evil. At the very least, He seems to be producing infinite amounts of evil as well—unless, of course, all of us go to heaven eventually. But if Feser is any indication, that is certainly not a Thomist doctrine.

Even more importantly from a metaphysical perspective, the examples Feser has chosen do not really reconcile God's omnipotence with His omnibenevolence, and a philosopher by the name of Aaron Boyden summarized the problems with them very well:

> God might have good reasons for evil which are very much like the good reasons a person might have for causing or enduring some unpleasantness, totally ignoring that for a person causing or tolerating something bad often seems like the best choice precisely because our options are limited, because we're not omnipotent. But Feser hasn't forgotten God's omnipotence; it gives God endless capacity to bring unlimited good out of any evil. And yet Feser's imagination suddenly stops again before the obvious next step, or perhaps God's omnipotence disappears and we're back to non-analogical human-like powerful God, as Feser doesn't even consider that God's omnipotence

---

[1] Edward Feser, "How to Go to Hell," *Edward Feser* (blog), October 29, 2016, last accessed on July 5, 2020, http://edwardfeser.blogspot.com/2016/10/how-to-go-to-hell_29.html

should surely extend to the endless capacity to bring all the same unlimited good out of no evil.[1]

The trouble with Feser's analogy of teaching a child how to play the violin, as Boyden notes, is that human beings are distinctly *not* omnipotent. We often *must* endure struggle or other "bad" things in order to achieve a goal simply because we are not powerful enough to reach our ends easily. Given the limitations of the human intellect, we must endure a lot of exhausting, time-wasting repetition to inscribe a given skill or knowledge into our memories, or spend a lot of energy and effort on some good work, such as building a church or teaching students or whatever. We cannot simply snap our fingers and have a building pop out of thin air, or insert knowledge directly into our brains (as machines could do in *The Matrix*, for instance). But God has none of these limitations. He could very well simply snap His fingers (metaphorically) and simply bring whatever good He wanted into existence on its own. So what reason could He have to tolerate even minimal evil in His creation?

Might it be the case that goodness requires evil as a matter of logical necessity? Feser makes this point in *Five Proofs*. He tells us that

> [I]f it turns out that there are some goods which logically cannot be had without tolerating certain evils, then even God could not create those goods without tolerating the evils in question, any more than he could make a round square... there are still certain kinds of exercise of free will that presuppose the existence of people who choose evil. For example, acts of forgiveness and mercy are not possible unless there are people who actually do evil things for which they can be forgiven.... Then there are moral virtues which do not presuppose that some people choose to carry out evil actions, but which still presuppose that there exists evil of other sorts. For example... you cannot show

---

[1] Aaron Boyden, "Feser Chapter 5," *Neurath's Boat*, October 21, 2011, last accessed on July 5, 2020, http://protagoras.typepad.com/adrift_on_neuraths_boat/2011/10/feser-chapter-5.html , archived at https://archive.is/4nOr6

compassion unless there are people who have suffered misfortunes of some sort (whether it be illness, the death of a loved one, unemployment, or whatever) and toward whom you can act compassionately. You cannot choose to sacrifice something for the sake of either your own moral improvement or the good of another person without thereby losing the good thing that you are sacrificing. And so forth.[1]

This is certainly an inventive argument, but it should still be an unsatisfying one given what we have discussed about A-T metaphysics. For Feser's argument to work, he would have to demonstrate that those goods which necessitate badness of some sort, such as mercy, compassion, and self-sacrifice, are on par with the very highest good, which for Thomists would be religious (knowing God). I suspect he would be at the very least unwilling to do so. Then the problem would remain: Why would God have created a universe filled with evil if He could have created one filled with nothing but immaterial beings (angels or souls or whatever) praising Him for all eternity? If worshipping God is the highest good, He would have no need to create a world containing any sort of pain, suffering, or any other kind of evil. Even if that evil was necessary to produce goods like mercy and compassion, mercy and compassion are themselves inferior goods compared to piety. So why would an omnibenevolent God even bother with them at all?

Making Feser's argument even stranger is its apparent incompatibility with another part of Thomist doctrine—the idea of Transcendentals, which imply that evil is actually nothing at all but a sort of privation. In speaking of transcendentals, he says:

> The claim that being is convertible with goodness might nevertheless seem to be falsified by the existence of evil. For if evil exists, then (so it might be thought) it must have being; and since evil is the opposite of good, it would seem to follow that there is something having being that is nevertheless not good. But Aquinas would deny the first premise of this argument. He writes that "it cannot be that evil signifies being, or

---

[1] *FP*, 295-297.

any form or nature. Therefore it must be that by the name of evil is signified the absence of good. And this is what is meant by saying that evil is neither a being nor a good. For since being, as such, is good, the absence of one implies the absence of the other" (ST I.48.1). Precisely because good is convertible with being, evil, which is the opposite of good, cannot itself be a kind of being but rather the absence of being. In particular, it is what the Scholastic philosophers called a privation, the absence of some perfection which should be present in a thing given its nature. Hence blindness (for example) is not a kind of being or positive reality, but rather simply the absence of sight in some creature which by its nature should have it. Its existence, and that of other evils, thus does not conflict with the claim that being is convertible with good."[1]

Hey, wait a second. In T*he Last Superstition*, Feser told us God can bring infinite good out of evil—just like one can bring being a master violinist out of the annoyance of learning to play, God can bring the "beatific vision" out of Auschwitz. But Feser also told us that the principle of **proportionate causality** states that nothing can give to something else what it does not have to give. According to Aquinas and Feser, evil is nothing at all, simply the absence of being, or good. But God allows evil so that good may come of it. Yet that would seem to imply that evil has something of good inside it, whether an "eminent power to generate good" or something else, which both is absurd and in contradiction to Aquinas, who claimed that evil was nothing at all. But if evil was truly just nothing, nonexistence, or nonbeing, how could it give rise to good, which is something, existence, and being? To say that any sort of good—compassion or forgiveness, for instance—must logically depend on some kind of evil like misfortune or sin is to say that some sort of existence logically depends on a corresponding non-existence, which is pretty hard to swallow, to put it mildly.

There is also the matter of evil that apparently serves no good whatsoever. The philosopher William Rowe has raised the example of a

---

[1] *AQ*, 34-35.

forest fire causing many animals to suffer and die horribly, which represents a grave evil (pointless suffering) with no associated opportunity to display mercy or courage or any other "good." Feser acknowledges he must wrestle with this fact to solve the problem of evil. His response is to appeal to our limited knowledge. If some evil *seems* pointless to human beings, does that mean it is *actually* so? Not necessarily—since we know for a fact that the existence of change necessitates the existence of a being of Pure Act which is also by necessity pure good, we "have independent reason to think that there is in fact such a greater good" to be drawn out of apparently needless suffering. It's just that our limited human minds are incapable of grasping it, and only God knows for sure.[1] A nice, tidy solution to that dilemma...except it also demolishes Feser's solution to the Euthyphro dilemma.

If God knows so much and we know so little, one would naturally wonder what other kinds of things we don't know, or might in fact be *incapable* of knowing. For instance, if we only know for sure that there is a purely good God, and if we are incapable of knowing what specific sorts of good He might bring out of evil, perhaps we are incapable of knowing exactly what sorts of Forms things possess—only that they do have Forms. And if we were to believe that, then it would be impossible to forge any sort of coherent ethics out of even "indisputable" A-T metaphysics.

Recall Feser informing us that God could never tell us to torture babies for fun because such an activity would contradict our Form as "rational animals." But perhaps it is the case that torturing babies actually is a "rational" activity, and we simply do not understand how given the current state of our knowledge and/or inherent mental limitations. Thus, if were to have dreams or visions in which God ordered us to torture babies, or even just kill our own children (as

---

[1] *FP*, 297-299.

Deanna Laney of Texas told the court she had[1]), Feser's logic would obligate us to carry out such heinous commands. If we know beyond any doubt that God exists and is all-good, we must conclude there is some greater good He is drawing from the deaths of our children, and that therefore killing them is actually in keeping with our Form, even if we cannot see how.[2] Feser, it seems, has unexpectedly revived the nominalism, or at least conceptualism, of William of Ockham. God really *could* dictate that just about anything was actually good for us—rape, murder, torturing children, or hating Him. After all, if we only have incomplete knowledge of Forms, and only God has full, complete knowledge of them, we would be obligated to accept that any action God ordered would accord with our Forms due to His perfect knowledge. Faith and reason, working hand-in-hand. Isn't that wonderful?

That, I suppose, may be a rather horrifying idea. But even if we tone it down a bit, Feser's solution to the problem of evil can still entail a sort of moral paralysis. His examples of good being drawn out of evil all seem to rely on somehow alleviating or stopping some evil. Courage is what you display when you bravely struggle to stop a threat or natural disaster, like a fireman putting his life on the line to douse a fire. Mercy or compassion occur when you alleviate someone else's suffering, such as a doctor treating a patient free of charge. But if God brings good out of evil, wouldn't any attempt to undo an evil also prevent God from bringing some "greater good" out of it? Take, for instance, Feser's example of the Holocaust. Let us assume that God permitted it to happen so that the rest of us could display courage, compassion, and heroism in rescuing Jews. But wait, how can we be sure which "greater goods" God wants to enact through that tragedy? Say we have an opportunity to save a Jewish family from the gas chambers. Ostensibly,

---

[1] CNN.com Law Center, "Attorney: Woman Thought God Told Her to Kill Sons," *CNN.com,* March 30, 2004, last accessed on July 5, 2020, http://www.cnn.com/2004/LAW/03/29/children.slain/index.html

[2] For an extended examination of the problems God permitting evil raises for the theist, see Stephen Maitzen, "Ordinary Morality Presupposes Atheism," *European Journal for Philosophy of Religion 2* (2009), 107-126.

the reason God put them in such a predicament is to give us an opportunity to save them. Declining to do so would quite naturally be evil. But could it be that God intends that evil as well? Perhaps if we saved that little Jewish boy, he would grow up to be an intelligent and able apologist for Judaism, winning many converts and leading people away from Christianity. By committing the minor evil of leaving him to the Gestapo, our dedicated Thomist has prevented an even greater evil of countless Catholics being converted to Judaism. In the process, he would be demonstrating the Aristotelian "virtues" of rational thinking and foresight, since his devotion to the Catholic religion overruled his basic emotional response of compassion. And before my more conservative readers get too excited about Nazism, the same defense applies to Communists and Islamists—perhaps the predations of the NKVD or ISIS gutted the Orthodox Church or non-Catholic denominations of the Middle East and made more space for Catholicism, implying that good Catholics should have, if not supported, done nothing to oppose Communist or Islamist persecutions. The "greater good" solution to the problem of evil, then, seems to pose yet another ethical problem of its own.

"More problems than solutions" seems to be a good summary of Feser's ethical arguments. As we saw in the opening of this chapter, the force of natural law rests on a very specific definition of "good," and as it turns out, there's no way for Thomists to claim that particular definition is the only one we should use. Even worse, we reviewed several examples of how difficult it is to decide on what particular Form something instantiates, making natural law ethical theory supremely unhelpful even if we accept the Thomist's preferred definitions. We then looked at a modern-day Aristotelian, Philippa Foot, whose theory of "natural goodness" solved some of these issues, at least with regard to living things. In doing so, however, we also found her ethical theory to be quite liberal with regard to both religion and sexuality, and thus anti-Thomistic. We then detoured to some common arguments used by theists (not just Thomists) pertaining to human rationality (such as the Evolutionary Argument Against Naturalism), concluding that they do not prove worship of God to be an important part of human life. Then we returned to the main course to dig into the Euthyphro Dilemma, figuring out how the Aristotelian "principle of totality" undermines Thomist solutions to the dilemma, and how the Thomist concept of good being a "transcendental" makes its definition of "good" incoherent on its own. We ended with the evergreen problem of evil, coming to the unhappy conclusion that Aquinas never really solved it: To say that God brings good out of evil makes a hash of Thomist metaphysics, and the unfortunate limitations of the human intellect mean it will always be possible for God to bring good out of evil we might otherwise think to prevent—or even that God might order what reasonable people would think to be evil!

Yes indeed, there seems to be less and less to recommend in Aristotelian-Thomist philosophy. It provides no good answers in the realm of religion and rather lacking ones in the realms of both sexual and general ethics. But are we not stuck with it in purely metaphysical terms? Even if it cannot answer questions of religion and morality, doesn't the A-T conception of God provide the only satisfactory solutions to the Problem of Universals? Don't we need A-T philosophy to understand the distinction between "essence and existence" among contingent things? Upon close examination, I think you'll find that's actually not the case.

Chapter 6: Exasperating Existence

For all the flaws Aristotelian-Thomism may have as a guide to morality, Feser would likely remain unwilling to give it up. At the most basic levels of reality, Feser would cry that we cannot avoid it. The "Aristotelian" part of it is necessary to make sense of how abstract objects can affect the world and how change can occur, and the Thomist part of it is necessary to understand how anything can exist at all. Even if we dismiss A-T ethics and A-T essentialism, wouldn't we still have to keep A-T metaphysics, which inevitably lead us to God? I don't think that's true either. Although the study of metaphysics is often even more abstruse than the study of ethics, with a little work I think most readers, even those with no background in philosophy, will be able to detect the same inconsistencies in argumentation that we have seen bedeviling the Thomist throughout this book.

This chapter will address various metaphysical odds and ends, its general approach being to examine many metaphysical problems Feser claims only Thomism can solve, and exploring how the Thomistic solution raises problems of its own. We'll start with universals, possible worlds, propositions, and other abstract objects, where it seems as if placing such things in the mind of God makes their objectivity and universal nature unintelligible. Then we'll address the Aristotelian-Thomist idea of final causality, and how God would not have to be intelligent in order for Him to uphold certain forms of regularity across the universe. Then we'll examine the supposed distinction between Essence and existence and how it's much less consequential than Thomists hold, and end things with a penetrating dismissal of the A-T definition of change as having anything to do with "act" and "potency."

6.1: Abstract Objects

Let's return to the topic of abstract objects, which we briefly discussed in chapter 1, and examine it in more depth. The Forms—the "intrinsic elements" which define and distinguish the things of our experience and also determine what is good and bad for them—are examples of universals. Again, to take Feser's favorite example, the Form of a squirrel is to be a furry grey rodent with a bushy tail. But this Form is not reducible to any one squirrel, since there are obviously many. It isn't even reducible to all of the squirrels in the material world, since you can grasp the idea of a furry, bushy-tailed grey rodent in your mind without any part of your brain actually turning into such a thing. The same applies to pretty much everything else in existence. The Form of a triangle is a three-sided closed figure, which would be the case if there were only one triangle materially existing, very many, or even none at all, the concept existing only in our minds.[1]

A blogger whose *nom de plume* was Arithmoquine has quite wryly demonstrated several severe problems with the Augustinian (and therefore, by extension, Feser's A-T) solution to the Problem of Universals. First, it would seem to raise a parallel to the famous Euthyphro Dilemma. As discussed in the last chapter, Euthyphro famously asked, "Are holy things holy because they are loved by the gods, or do the gods love them because they are holy?" If one agrees with Augustine that Universals or Forms (and other abstract objects) exist eternally in the mind of God, one is promptly led to wonder why He conceives of them the way He does:

> Do objects instantiate the universals they do because God conceives of them as doing so? Does God impose universals on the world by his choice? If so, then God can have no reason for ordering the universals as he/she does. (If Fido was a dog this morning could God make Fido a cat this afternoon if God only changed the way he conceived of Fido?) Or does God conceive things as he/she does because they are objectively like that? It's obvious that if we are to take God's conceptions as objective, they must be based on an independently existing reality, on independently existing universals. If not, then the

---

[1] *FP*, 88-90.

distribution of universals to objects must be completely arbitrary and God must have no reason for conceiving of objects as he/she does.[1]

The same issue appears in the Thomistic attempt to explain how Forms allow us to understand how different objects can be similar in varying respects:

> Do objects resemble each other because God conceives them as similar, or does God conceive them as similar because they bear an objective resemblance to each other? If we take the former answer, God's categorizations must be brute unexplainable facts (which is the same answer the nominalist gives, so there is no advantage for the Augustinian here). The answer must again be, for reasons given above, that God must recognize objective resemblances rather than create resemblances. Hence, we must have some other view of the similarity objects appear to have to each other.[2]

It seems to me that Feser would have quite a bit of difficulty in wriggling out of these new dilemmas. I would wager he would try the same tack he did in *Aquinas: A Beginner's Guide*. He might say, "things resemble each other because they share the same Forms, which even the omnipotent God could not change, because omnipotence does not encompass the logically impossible. But that doesn't make their similarities independent of God in any way, because the Forms they share are ideas in the Divine Mind."[3]

Yet this does not really solve anything. The Forms of certain things such as mathematically-defined shapes (triangles, squares, and so on) may be matters of necessity, but there is nothing logically necessary

---

[1] Arithmoquine, "Universals and an Argument for the Existence of God: More on Edward Feser's The Last Superstition an Unpublishable Review, part 2," *The Unpublishable Philosopher*, July 27, 2012, last accessed on July 5, 2020, http://currentlogic.blogspot.com/2012/07/universals-and-argument-for-existence.html

[2] Ibid.

[3] This is paraphrased from *AQ*, 183, and the discussion of the paradox of omnipotence in *FP*, 208.

about the Forms of, say, colors, sensations, or living things. If the Form of a Squirrel is to be a grey, furry animal with a bushy tail, why could God not simply decree that starting tomorrow, their Form would instead entail yellowness and stubby-tailedness? There are plenty of rodents with yellow fur and stubby tails (such as hamsters), and squirrels might have evolved such features if their evolutionary development had been different. So why is it that God regards squirrels—to use Feser's terminology, understands their Form—in such a particular way, and how do we know He will not change it in the future? If Feser cannot provide a satisfactory answer, it seems that an attempt to solve the problem of universals through God is not successful, which provides one less reason to believe in Him at all.

Indeed, thinking about what it means to be "logically possible" makes God's relationship to Forms and abstract objects even more mysterious. Again, according to Feser, omnipotence presents no paradox because a "power" to do something self-contradictory is not actually any kind of power at all. Thus, God could not make a round square, or decree that two plus two equals five.[1] But *why is it the case* that round squares, or two plus two equaling five, are self-contradictory? After all, God *could* create purple squares, or squares whose sides equal exactly four inches. So, what makes "round" and "square" incompatible with each other while "purple" or "equilateral" are compatible with square things?

The answer would have to be, "The Forms for roundness and squareness are held within God's eternal mind, and God conceives of them in such a way that they are incompatible with each other, but are compatible with the Forms of color or numbers in relation to size or whatever. By the same token, for abstract objects such as the numbers two and five, God conceives of them in such a way that two and two can never equal five." But that does not really answer our question, it simply leads to another one: *Why* does God conceive of these abstract objects

---

[1] *FP*, 207-208.

in the way He does? Or, in other words, God cannot do what is self-contradictory, but God *determines* what is self-contradictory. If He is the ultimate source of all Forms in the universe, He should be able to define them as He wishes. Is He obligated to conceive of squares and circles in such a way that they are incompatible with each other, while being compatible with different colors, sizes, and so on? What could possibly obligate the omnipotent Ground of All Being to do anything, especially with regard to the Forms existing in His mind? But without some external set of standards telling Him how to properly conceive of Forms, there seems to be no reason why He should conceive of roundness and squareness contradicting each other as opposed to anything else.

Feser might say that "will follows upon intellect, so that God always acts in accordance with reason."[1] Again, this does nothing to solve the problem. Why is it the case that God might be able to will a purple square into existence, but not a circular square? Because God's intellect conceives of some forms as contradicting each other while others do not. But why does God's intellect operate in such a manner? What makes it the case that certain combinations of Forms "accord with reason," and others do not? Is it *possible* for God to conceive of circularity and squareness as not contradicting each other? If so, why does He not do so? If not, what is keeping His intellect from doing so? The traditional paradox of omnipotence, therefore, remains unsolved.

It seems to me the problem lies with how Thomists like Feser conceive of intellect. It may be true that the intellect is what grasps Forms and other universals, and must be immaterial, and so on. However, God's Intellect seems to be constrained in a way that limited human intellects are *not*, which is very strange to say of any kind of deity, much less Existence Itself. It is easy enough to understand why human beings cannot simply decree that squares are now round and two

---

[1] Edward Feser, "God, Obligation, and the Euthyphro Dilemma," *Edward Feser* (blog), October 26, 2010, last accessed July 5, 2020,
http://edwardfeser.blogspot.com/2010/10/god-obligation-and-euthyphro-dilemma.html

and two make five. The Forms of circles and squares, and the laws of mathematics, are things we *discover* rather than invent, as Feser would tell us. They exist outside of us, preceded us, and will outlast us, so we can't simply define them however we would like.

For Forms we *do* invent, however, the opposite holds. We can define the Forms of things we invent (such as fictional creatures, the rules of sports and games, or artifacts) however we wish. The Form of the Orcs from Tolkien's famous novels entails being ugly and warlike, but he could have made them peaceful friends of the Elves if he wanted. The Form of soccer decrees that no-one but the goalie can use her hands, but we could easily change that rule if we wanted. Why would this not apply to God? Since He is the ultimate source of all Forms—squareness, roundness, color, numbers, etc.—He should be able to define them as He wishes, just as humans can say that the characteristics of Orcs or the rules of soccer are whatever we want. But there is evidently something constraining Him, something saying, "Sorry, God, but even You cannot conceive of roundness and squareness as being compatible with each other, *despite the fact that You came up with these concepts in the first place.*" And if God can be constrained by something, how is He omnipotent?[1]

---

[1] As my editor has noted, the Thomist idea of Forms existing "objectively" in a mind, even if that Mind is said to be divine, eternal, unchanging, etc. gives rise to a host of problems in *both* metaphysics and ethics (though there is not enough space to devote more time to the latter subject). See Jonathan MS Pearce, "God's Morality or Meaning Is Merely Subjective," *A Tippling Philosopher*, December 6, 2019, last accessed on July 5, 2020, https://www.patheos.com/blogs/tippling/2019/12/06/gods-morality-or-meaning-is-merely-subjective/ . The problem boils down to this: "Objectivity," as we understand it, means conforming to reality outside of any individual mind. But if the Forms are dependent on God's Mind, they are obviously *not* mind-independent, which means they are not objective. The Thomist might argue that since God is eternal and unchanging, the Forms in His Mind have objectivity in that (peculiar) sense, but that runs into the problem I just described: How can an omnipotent God have less power over the Forms in His Mind than mere humans do over Forms we ourselves make up?

It is equally puzzling as to how God can truly be unchangeable and immutable, which as we will recall from chapter 1, Feser holds to be necessary characteristics of the omnipotent and omniscient Purely Actual Being. When the philosopher Parmenides claimed that change was impossible, Feser replied that the mere act of making the argument refuted it: "Suppose you try to convince someone, even if only yourself, that change is an illusion—whether via Parmenides' argument or some other argument. Your mind entertaining one premise after the other and finally reaching the conclusion is itself an instance of the change the argument denies. The very act of casting doubt on whether change occurs presupposes that it occurs."[1]

However, despite Feser's reply according with our everyday experience and common sense, it raises a few logical questions. *In what way* is the mind changing? Why is entertaining a succession of premises and then reaching a conclusion an example of change? The most common-sense answer I can think of is that mental activity is a sort of change. The mind starts off in one state, progresses through others, and ends up in a final state. Reasonable enough, but this has profoundly dire implications for the Augustinian solution to the Problem of Universals.

All the Forms we see in the universe are held in the Divine Mind. Okay. But as is obvious from looking at the world around us, things are acquiring and shedding Forms all the time. Caterpillars shed the Forms of Green-ness, worm-ness, and so on and acquire the Form of a Butterfly, for instance. But if all these Forms ultimately exist in God's Mind, they would seem to be perpetually changing and shifting as different beings take them up and cast them away—even if they remain eternally the same in terms of what defines them, the number of things instantiating them are constantly changing, and if God maintains all those things in existence, He must be responsible for those changes. So then something in God's Mind would be changing—as established above, that is the simple definition of mental activity. But if God is completely immutable

---

[1] *FP*, 18.

and unchangeable, how is it possible for any activity to occur inside of His Mind?

Now, Feser might say that this sort of change has to do only with **"Cambridge properties,"** defined as properties any given object has only *in relation* to other objects, *not* intrinsic to the object itself. The stock example Feser gives is this: If Socrates grows from (let's say) five feet, five inches as a child to six feet as an adult, one of *his own* characteristics (height) is now different, meaning he has truly undergone a change. Now, if his friend Plato has grown faster, from five feet as a child to six-and-a-half as an adult, one of Socrates's characteristics seems to have changed—he has gone from being taller than Plato to being shorter. However, "taller than" and "shorter than" (emphasis on the 'than') are Cambridge properties because they don't reflect a real change in Socrates himself, only his *relation* to Plato.[1]

So Feser might say the changes I've described above are mere "Cambridge" changes. The *number* of creatures instantiating any given Form might change, but the *Forms themselves* never do—even if Mr. Caterpillar turns into a butterfly, the Forms of Caterpillar-ness and Butterfly-ness, respectively, have changed *only* in respect to their *relation* to the world (one more being instantiates Butterfly-ness and one less Caterpillar-ness).

The problem here is that *all* change cannot just be Cambridge changes, or else Parmenides was right and there isn't really any change at all. Socrates ending up shorter than Plato isn't a change for Socrates, but it is a change for Plato, who must have grown taller himself. And if that sort of change is occurring inside God's Mind, then something in that Mind must be changing, which ought to be impossible for an entirely unchangeable Purely Actual Being.

I believe Feser would say that while the Forms undergo only Cambridge changes, the bits and pieces of matter that compose all the

---

[1] Ibid., 195-196.

individual things of our experience really do experience true, substantial change. In the above example, the parcel of matter that constitutes Mr. Caterpillar is what undergoes substantial change from caterpillar to butterfly, which is why we say that our friend has transformed (i.e., that there's some underlying thing subsisting throughout the transformation) rather than a caterpillar disappearing and a butterfly appearing.[1] But where does this matter exist? If it exists in God's Mind, perhaps as an object in a "story" He thinks of (we will return to this example in section 6.5), then something in God's Mind has experienced true change, and God's Mind is supposed to be changeless. On the other hand, it doesn't seem possible for the opposite (that matter exists outside of God's Mind, or outside the 'story' He thinks of) to be true in the A-T scheme. Where could anything even exist outside of God's infinite Mind?

It seems that the natural law thinkers have written themselves into a bit of a corner. On the one hand, they claim that the mental activity involved in even agreeing with Parmenides's argument is a sort of change. But on the other hand, they say that the Forms of everything in the universe, which are constantly changing (in terms of which objects belong to them), exist in God's unchanging Mind. They can't have it both ways: if Feser would like to say that various things instantiating and giving up Forms held in the Divine Mind does not actually constitute any sort of change within that Mind, why can't a modern-day Parmenides say that any apparent change involved in evaluating his argument is illusory as well?

6.2: Possible Worlds

Let's look at Feser's next example of an abstract object—possible worlds. This is another case where he finds the existence of a Divine Mind to be

---

[1] *Aristotle's Revenge*, 29-30. I should note here that the matter in question isn't actually atoms or quarks or any similar sort of tiny particle, but rather a kind of "pure potentiality" called prime matter. However, the concept is very complex and to fully explain it is a task better suited to a separate monograph.

necessary, and here's why: We can imagine worlds very different from the one we live in. For instance, there might have been a world in which the speed of light was 800 million miles per hour rather than 671, or 200 million, or whatever. Maybe the force of gravity could have been stronger or weaker. The same applies to history—perhaps there is an alternate world in which Hitler was victorious, as in the famous novel *The Man in the High Castle*.[1] Or a world in which humans evolved from reptiles rather than apes. These worlds *could* exist, as nothing about them entails any logical impossibility—one can imagine a universe where Hitler won, but one cannot imagine a universe containing round squares. But they do not exist materially, since as we know from looking around us, the material evidence overwhelmingly points to the speed of light being what we know it to be and Hitler having blown his brains out in 1945. So what grounds the possibility of these worlds which might have existed but do not? It cannot be human minds, or any other sort of limited, contingent mind, because one can imagine a possible world in which no sentient life at all ever existed. Such a ground of possibility for alternate universes must therefore be a necessarily existing Divine Mind.[2]

In that case, one might begin to wonder: How can we be certain all these "possible worlds" are merely possible as opposed to existing somewhere else? The Divine Mind is omnipotent as well as omniscient, after all. If He could create one universe, He could surely create many, or an infinity, in fact. Might it be the case that we live in a multiverse rather than a single universe? This idea has been brought up by atheistic writers such as Alex Rosenberg, usually to deny that God needed to create our own universe (since it could have just branched off from another one). Feser does not think this poses much of a challenge for theism, because a whole multiverse would still require God to sustain

---

[1] *Aristotle's Revenge*, 320.
[2] *FP*, 92-96.

the whole thing.[1] That may be true, but I think it poses quite a challenge to the objectivity and reliability of religious claims that Thomists in particular hold so dearly.

As we have just discussed, possible worlds are those in which the facts of physics, history, and other such things are different from our own. But the claims of any given religion, including Catholicism, are based on historical evidence (even if the existence of God can be proven through metaphysics). That implies *there may be possible worlds in which monotheistic religions other than Christianity are true*. Again, to take the example I just used, one can imagine a possible world in which Hitler won World War II or the speed of light was different. Given God's omnipotence, it is also possible that such worlds exist—we might not be living in them, but others might be, and God has simply not allowed us to interact with each other. In that case, surely it is possible that there are worlds where Christ was not born, or where He did not establish any sort of Church, or perhaps where the Jewish people never even existed at all? There is no logically necessary reason for any of these events, people, or groups to have occurred or come into being—if we can imagine a possible world where gravity is only half as strong or light twice as fast, we can imagine a world where Christ became a hermit instead of dying at the hands of the Romans, or a world where He was born to, say, indigenous Australians rather than Jews.

Given what we know of Middle Eastern history, we are not living in such a world. But let us imagine two alternate universes, A and B. In universe A, Christ died and rose from the dead, and His disciples gave an entirely accurate account of the event. In universe B, Christ did not die but immediately ascended to heaven, and His disciples mistakenly reported that He had perished and been resurrected. It was left to a corrupt Arab warlord to correct those mistakes several hundred years later. The perceptive reader will note (especially if she reviews chapter 2

---

[1] Edward Feser, "Reading Rosenberg Part III," *Edward Feser*, November 10, 2011, last accessed on July 5, 2020, http://edwardfeser.blogspot.com/2011/11/reading-rosenberg-part-iii.html

of this book) that Christianity is true in universe A, while it is false in Universe B (Islam being true). Given God's infinite power, He could have created both universes, along with a multitude of others inside of a majestic multiverse.

So, then, how would we be able to tell whether we are living in universe A or universe B?

This is not an attempt to disprove God's existence by raising questions about what His characteristics might be in various possible worlds—David Schrader made the attempt and Feser found it unconvincing.[1] For the purposes of this argument, we can assume that God's characteristics are unchangeable and are actually the same in every universe (though they might appear different only from the perspective of the residents of every world). I am instead pointing out that saying God is necessary to ground possible worlds makes it much more difficult to argue that any historically-contingent religion correctly worships Him. *If* one believes that alternative worlds are possible (as Feser seems to do), *then* one must be able to prove we are not actually living in one such alternative universe. This is pretty easy to do in the case of possible worlds with different laws of physics (toss a ball into the air to see that we do not live in a world without gravity) or obviously different recent histories (look at a history book to see who won World War II). It is much harder to do with regard to ancient history, at a time when photographs or video did not exist.

There may be one universe in which a strange event that occurred two thousand years ago genuinely happened, and there may be another in which that event was a trick or scheme. There seems to be no foolproof metaphysical way to distinguish the two universes, or even tell which one we're living in. That means there's no foolproof way to be sure if Christianity is true, or if Islam is true, or if Mormonism or Hinduism or any other monotheistic religion might be true, since there could be alternate universes where God Incarnated in the Americas or the Indian

---

[1] *FP*, 203-205.

subcontinent. To prove Christianity beyond any shadow of a doubt, Feser must complete at least one of these quests: He must demonstrate that there is only one world that exists, and that God would be unable to create a multitude, despite His infinite power. If Feser cannot do that, he will have to explain how his specific religion would necessarily have to be true in every single world that God might have chosen to create—in other words, he would have to demonstrate that an alternative world in which Christ had not risen in Judea would be an impossibility in the same sense an alternative world that contained square circles would be. I daresay this is easier said than done.

6.3: Propositions

Feser's treatment of propositions opens him up to similar objections, though these cut at the foundations of theism itself rather than any specific religion. In his view, the Divine Mind must exist as a ground for certain kinds of propositional statements for the same reason it must exist as a ground for universals. He asks us to consider this:

> ... the proposition that there is no material world nor any human mind in existence would be true if the material world and human minds all went out of existence tomorrow.

Feser notes that this proposition cannot exist inside human minds, since it would be true if they did *not* exist. The only alternative, he claims, is for these propositions to exist inside the mind of God, which *must* exist, in the sense of being incapable of failing to exist.[1]

But there are certain statements one can make about God that would be true if He did not exist, and with which even Feser would seem to agree. For instance, he believes that God is necessary to explain any sort of regularity in the universe—as he said in *The Last Superstition*, "if the Supreme Intelligence were to cease his directing activity, final causality would immediately disappear." The same applies to morality—"given a modern mechanistic-cum-materialistic view of the world,

---

[1] *FP*, 102.

[moral behavior] would inevitably be *nothing more* than a pretense, with morality itself being an illusion."[1] The second quote is most telling—a "mechanistic-cum-materialistic view of the world" implies that God does not exist. So, one can rephrase these statements as propositions:

The proposition that final causality does not exist would be true if God did not exist.

The proposition that morality is an illusion would be true if God did not exist.

These propositions seem to pose a problem for Feser's position. If we require a Divine Mind as a "truth-maker" for propositions involving the complete nonexistence of any kind of lower mind or the entire material universe, what serves as a "truth-maker" for propositions involving the nonexistence of God? Feser might say that God is necessary, as mentioned above, and that He is simply not the sort of thing which could conceivably fail to exist. In other words, any proposition that questions His existence is simply gibberish. But if that were so, how is it possible to cogently speak of any state of affairs in which God does not exist? The statement "If God did not exist, morality would be an illusion" is perfectly comprehensible, and Feser would probably consider it defensible, if not agree with it entirely.[2] He has

---

[1] *TLS*, 117, 213.

[2] Recommended further reading is "Does Morality Depend on God? (Updated)," *Edward Feser,* July 19, 2011, http://edwardfeser.blogspot.com/2011/07/does-morality-depend-on-god.html, last accessed on July 5, 2020. A Thomist might claim morality and final causality exist in the absence of God in a *certain* sense— according to Feser, "proximately ethics can be done at least to a large extent without reference to God, just as natural science can. In that sense, many moral truths would still be true even if, per impossibile, there were no God — just as the periodic table of the elements would be what it is even if, per impossibile, there were no God." But as Feser says in the previous paragraph, such things could not have any causal power "if God as first cause were not imparting that causal power to them at every moment." So a more formal statement would be:

certainly written very many words on the subject, which is quite a lot of effort expended on a proposition that should be merely unintelligible gibberish. Thus, wouldn't we need another "truth-maker," one independent of God's Divine Mind, to ground propositions involving Him? But that truth-maker would therefore be God. Then the same problem would arise, and we would be led into a hopeless, never-ending regress. The existence of abstract objects in general and propositions in particular seems to be an insurmountable problem, and there's no way your humble narrator would be able to solve it—but I don't think the "God of the philosophers" solves it either.

6.4: The Birds and the Bees

The question of God's relationship to final causality is a fraught one, and leads to even more pitfalls for a philosopher of Feser's bent. Ironic, since the idea of it is one of the A-T tradition's stronger arguments for the existence of God. As usual, we touched upon this concept in chapter 1, returned to it in chapter 5, and now we shall examine it in greater depth to find yet more reasons Feser's particular God might not exist, and more reasons for considering deism or pantheism serious alternatives.

Although he spends many words on the subject in *The Last Superstition* and *Aquinas*, Feser's most sustained treatment of final causality can be found in his essay, "Between Aristotle and William Paley: Aquinas's Fifth Way." Recall the examples we went over back in chapter 1: The world around us is full of regularities. A struck match regularly produces flame rather than lilacs or ice cubes, an ice cube

---

The proposition that final causality and morality are unintelligible would be true if God did not exist.

Now, Feser would agree with this statement, and it's no good to simply add a "per impossibile" in there. The above statement is coherent and indeed can be used by Thomists to refute atheists who take regular cause-effect relationships or objective morality as a given. But how could this be if it really were impossible for God to have failed to exist? So there must be a truthmaker for statements concerning His non-existence, which leads us again into paradox.

dropped into water will reliably cool it down instead of heating it up or making it explode, and so on, and so forth. You could say that matches are "directed towards" or "have their goal as" the production of fire, since they produce that rather than anything else, and ice cubes are "directed towards" cooling things down. However, fire, ice cubes, and everything down to atoms themselves are inanimate, mindless objects. How could they "direct" themselves to any sort of goal? Directedness and goal-seeking behavior are the hallmarks of intelligence. Thus, Aquinas concluded (and Edward Feser concurs) that every inanimate object in the universe must "be directed by some being endowed with knowledge and intelligence; as the arrow is shot to its mark by the archer. Therefore some intelligent being exists by whom all natural things are directed to their end; and this being we call God."[1]

The interesting thing here is that this argument (the fifth of Aquinas's famous *Five Ways*) is one of the few instances where the Thomistic tradition breaks from Aristotle. Feser notes that while Aristotle believed in God, he did not believe God directed all of the inanimate objects in the universe to their ends. Rather, the Forms (or Natures, or Essences) of those individual things deserved the credit. In Aristotle's view, matches produce flame simply because the Form of a Match entails they do, and ice cools water simply because the Form of Ice entails it produces a cooling effect rather than light or explosions or whatever.[2] Feser would say the Aristotelian view raises several problems that only a Divine Mind can solve, as he did with the Problem of Universals.

First, as mentioned in both *Neo-Scholastic Essays* and *The Last Superstition,* "one of the raps against final causation is that it seems clearly to entail that a thing can produce an effect even before that thing

---

[1] *NSE*, 155, 147. Feser is quoting directly from Book I.2.3, Saint Aquinas in the *Summa Theologica,* trans. Fathers of the English Dominican Province (New York: Benziger Brothers, 1948). This is apparently the same translation they use at http://www.newadvent.org/summa/1002.htm.

[2] *NSE*, 157-158, 165-170.

exists." If we say that a match is directed towards producing fire, that sounds as if the fire is "telling" the match to do something, even if the match is just sitting in its box, unlit—that is to say, even before it has produced a fire, or even before the fire exists. How, then, can final causality operate? Feser asks us to consider the example of a carpenter building a house: Even though the house does not exist yet, the workman holds its Form within his mind, which allows it to exert an effect in reality (him actually constructing it). By the same token, if we assume all Forms exist in God's mind, then we can understand how a non-existent flame can have an effect on an inert match: God brings the Form of a flame into reality just like a carpenter turns the Form of a house he has in his head into an actual house.[1]

The second problem with Aristotle's original conception of final causality is that it provides no account of how the very many ends and final causes of all the things in the universe coordinate with each other in such a way as not to result in chaos. Only a single Divine Mind is capable of coordinating them all in an orderly fashion. Aquinas noted that heat and fire tend to burn and destroy things, but they do not do so infinitely—if you light a match, it will burn out on its own eventually, and even if you start a wildfire that consumes a whole forest, it will eventually burn itself out, or be doused by rain. Modern-day students can observe a similar principle in even the mightiest natural-phenomena—a great star can produce unimaginable amounts of heat for billions of years, but it will not incinerate the entire universe, and once it collapses into a black hole, it will not suck the entire universe into itself either. We can therefore conclude that a stable system of final causes exists, which means "something must ensure that their divergent outcomes are balanced against one another. This can only be something capable of grasping their respective natures in the abstract and determining how they be related in such a way that harmony is possible." As we went over in chapter 1, the only thing capable of grasping Forms or Natures is an immaterial intellect. If such an intellect

---

[1] *TLS*, 115, *NSE*, 175-76.

is grasping every Form in the entire universe, it would be omniscient, which would naturally make it God—which means that Aristotle was wrong to say that God just kind of hangs around while everything else in the universe acts according to its own Form. It is absolutely necessary, according to the Angelic Doctor, that God plays an active role in setting and coordinating those Forms.[1]

These considerations may be important, but they do not necessitate a divine being, at least not any sort of being with a mind or intelligence (i.e God). First, they are somewhat strange coming from Feser, who ought to remember Aristotle's response to Parmenides. Aristotle would likely *not* say that non-existent fire is "directing" the match towards it. For him, it would be the other way around—the actual Nature/Form/Essence of the match directs itself towards flame, because flame is one of its potentialities. The whole point of the distinction between act and potency was that potential things really do exist—they are not entirely non-existent as Parmenides would have it. Thus, if a match is "directed towards" a flame, it is not as if the flame is doing anything "before" it exists. The flame *really does* exist right now, but as a potential entailed by the Form of the (actual) match.

Secondly, let's return to Feser's example of the Form of a house being held inside the mind of its builder. His example is of a structure that does not yet exist being constructed out of various inanimate parts (blocks of stone, lengths of wood, etc.) that themselves have no inherent tendency to become a house or any other kind of building. The implication is that for any sort of unintelligent, inanimate object to be organized into a structure, or any sort of self-sustaining pattern, an intelligent mind is necessary for their direction, or final causality.

But that premise does not seem to be true, and we can see this very easily in the natural world. Many kinds of animals constantly build artificial "structures" in a way that seems no different than how human builders construct our houses. Sticks and twigs have no inherent

---

[1] *NSE*, 177.

tendency to form nests, but many types of birds construct homes for their eggs in specific, non-random ways by adherence to patterns that must, in Feser's view, be held in something's mind before coming into existence. Wax has no inherent tendency to form itself into hexagons, but the humble bees direct it specifically and non-randomly towards instantiating the Form of Hexagonality as they build their hives. Now, these creatures are "mindless" in the Aristotelian and Thomist senses. Briefly skip back to chapter 1 if you need to, but here's a brief refresher: Properties, which are also Forms, such as shape or color (to take two examples) are universals because they can apply to many physical objects and can also be abstracted away and considered apart from any given object that instantiates them (thus why universals are also considered abstract objects). Since they are independent of material things, Aristotle and his successors thought that abstract objects must be immaterial; accordingly, anything capable of understanding and reasoning based on Forms and other universals must be immaterial as well. So while animals like dogs or parrots can recognize particular material instances of Forms (which balls are red, which toys are triangular, etc) they cannot reason or even abstract Forms from whatever material things they see. Aristotelians and Thomists therefore conclude that animal minds are entirely material while human minds, capable of genuine reasoning and abstraction, are genuinely rational and therefore immaterial. This also means that humans are the only animals capable of holding the Forms of things inside our minds before they exist in reality, or imposing meaning and purpose (i.e, final causality) onto otherwise purposeless and un-ordered material things.

But whether or not birds and bees are intelligent in the A-T sense, it seems like they *can* impose certain types of order (the Forms of nests and hives) onto materials which do not inherently possess such things (twigs and wax). How, then, can we be sure that God must necessarily be intelligent in even an analogous way to human beings? Just from looking at the natural world, it seems fair to say that Aquinas was simply wrong: it is not only the metaphorical archer who can direct things like arrows to their marks. Birds, bees, and any kind of seemingly mindless creature that creates "artificial" structures can do the same. And perhaps it might be the case that God is a non-rational creator as well.

Wouldn't an intelligent God still be necessary to "coordinate" all the final causes of the world in an orderly way, such as preventing heat from consuming the entire universe? A moment's thought on the examples above proves that to be unnecessary. Birds, bees, and other animals are capable of "coordinating" their activities in measured and sensible ways. A bird that builds a nest, for instance, will not attempt to pick up every twig in a forest and construct an unreasonably massive home. Bees will not build either massive hexagons or infinitely many, but only as many as they need to comfortably store all their honey and larvae. Despite assumedly having no conception of the Forms of forests or whatever environment they build their houses in, they construct their dwellings in a way that suits their environment. Thus, it seems reasonable to assume that intelligence is not required for certain kinds of actors to limit their activities in balance with the ends of other things, which means that it might not be necessary for God Himself to be intelligent in order to limit and coordinate the various Essences and final causes we find in the universe (heat, gravity, and so on).

Perhaps Feser would say that bees themselves are directed by God, in the same way atoms and the moon and matches are directed by God. In that case, I would ask, how intelligent does this Supreme Director have to be? Looking at human beings alone, it is obvious that dull ones are as capable of purposeful and non-random direction as smart ones. Imagine, for a moment, a genius like Albert Einstein taking a trip to the beach with a dullard like Peter Griffin from *Family Guy*. Both, of course, would also be capable of directing unintelligent things towards an end— it's easy to imagine both Einstein and Peter using an unintelligent stick to push an unintelligent ball, though Einstein would likely do it to teach a class something about physics and Peter would do it just to have fun. But if we can accept that even relatively unintelligent beings can act towards ends so long as they have even a vague spark of intellect, we come to the possibility that God just might be such a dim-witted being, albeit an immensely powerful one. Perhaps God directs moons in their orbit, bees in their work, and the laws of physics in their constancy without necessarily understanding how or why, just like the, er, less-than-bright Peter would push a stick and ball around for the fun of it, without performing any higher thought.[1]

Indeed, the example of animals further undermines Aquinas's theistic account of final causality, a point ably made by the philosopher Anthony Kenny. According to the Angelic Doctor in his commentary on Aristotle's *Physics*, birds and spiders could not be intelligent because they make their nests and webs in the same way all the time, while human builders construct homes differently every time. Kenny wryly noted that Aquinas has "sawn off the branch he was sitting on" with regard to his arguments for an intelligent source of final causality.[2] Remember, Aquinas also said that regularity is impossible without a guiding intelligence—there is no way that, say, a match can produce fire every single time it is struck without exception unless an intelligent actor directs it to that end. But when birds and spiders produce the same effects (nests and webs) in the same ways without exception, that...is proof they are not intelligent! One does not have to be a genius to see the inconsistency here.

6.5: Deistic Existence

The "argument from existence" or "existential proof" is one of the stronger ones in God's favor. It relies heavily on the arguments for Forms that I have been critiquing for the last several chapters, but it still retains a hefty bit of force even if you agree with most of my critiques. The only thing the argument from existence requires is accepting realism—preferably Thomistic realism, but any kind will do—with regard to Forms. Start from there, and you will inevitably be led to the existence

---

[1] Originally posted in a slightly modified form on my personal blog.
[2] Anthony Kenny, *The Five Ways: St. Thomas Aquinas' Proofs of God's Existence* (University of Notre Dame Press, 1980), 118-119.

of God in particular, and an active, involved God, not just a distant, deistic one.

Feser provides a brief overview of the argument in *Aquinas*. Recall that a Form is what defines something and distinguishes it from everything else—the Form of a Squirrel entails having bushy tails and burying nuts, which distinguishes squirrels from chipmunks or spiders or whatever. But note how that definition says nothing about whether or not squirrels actually *exist* in reality. Sure, you and I know they're real. But imagine asking someone in an isolated, squirrel-free area—a Bedouin tribesman in the middle of a desert or an Inuit hunter working in the tree-free far north—if squirrels were a real animal. They might listen to an accurate description of the creatures and conclude that the little rodents were mythological or came from a fairy tale. On the other hand, take an entirely fictional being, such as the phoenix. The Form of that beast is to be a giant red bird that generates flame and eventually revives after burning itself to ash. From that description alone, a naïve and uninformed person would not be able to tell that phoenixes do not actually exist and were entirely made up. Thus, it seems that "if it is possible to understand the Essence of a thing without knowing whether it exists, its act of existence (if it has one) must be distinct from its Essence, as a metaphysically separate component of the thing."[1]

According to the Angelic Doctor, and by extension Edward Feser, since any given thing—anything at all in the entire universe, squirrels, water, people, whatever—has an Essence, or Form, distinct from its existence, there must be something conjoining all those Forms to existence constantly and unceasingly, every second of every day, everywhere in the entire universe. But what could carry out such a monumental task? It could not be anything material, because any given parcel of matter could conceivably fail to exist, which means the existence of anything material would be separate from its Form and thus require something to conjoin them. The only solution to this problem is

---

[1] *AQ*, 29-30.

a being whose Form and existence are *one and the same thing*. This being, or more accurately Being Itself, could be nothing other than God.[1] This idea, called the **Doctrine of Divine Conservation,** is compatible with Christianity, Judaism, and Islam, which all claim that God not only created the universe but actively oversees it and keeps it going. However, it rules out **deism**, which holds that God created the universe, but then retreated from it, allowing it to persist and go on its way (so to speak) without any perpetual, active involvement on His part.[2]

It seems to me that the "existential proof" is not actually as fatal to deism as Feser maintains. Simply thinking about the wording of Feser's argument can reveal its weaknesses as a proof of classical theism, or any sort of theism in which God actively participates in the world. For now, let us agree with Feser that there is a "real distinction" between Essence, or Form, and existence. Let us also agree that God is necessary to conjoin the two, since He is the only thing in the universe Whose Essence "just is" His existence. But what does it mean to "conjoin" an Essence, or Form, to existence? Feser doesn't really provide many specifics. In *Five Proofs*, he tells us God "adds existence" to the Essence of everything else, and does so "here and now," because the Form of a thing is *always* distinct from its existence, at every moment it exists.[3] But even if that were true, does that necessitate God's constant presence and activity? I think not.

To understand why, let's look at some examples of other things in our experience which have distinct elements added to their Forms. Imagine a lump of clay. This bit of matter instantiates the Form of Clay, which entails it has certain attributes, such as color, malleability, weight, and so on. Note, though, that its Form entails no particular shape. Our lump may be circular, squarish, flat, or whatever; nothing about what it *is* entails what it looks like. An external actor is required to give the clay a more specific shape—as Feser might put it, "conjoin" the material to a

---

[1] Ibid., 30, 96-97.
[2] *FP*, 236.
[3] *FP*, 124-125.

certain appearance, "add" or "impart" a certain aesthetic pattern to the material. For instance, the conscious activity of a potter is necessary to explain why a lump of clay now appears as a vase or pot, the conscious activity of a sculptor is necessary to explain why another lump of clay now looks like the Venus de Milo, and so on, and so forth.

The perceptive reader will note that this is a rough analogy to the relationship between God, the Forms, and existence. Since a lump of clay will not look like a pot or sculpture on its own, a potter or sculptor is necessary to impart those things to it. By the same token, since any given Form (of a squirrel, phoenix, or whatever) does not exist on its own, God is necessary to impart existence to them. However, observant readers will also note that sculptors or potters do not have to *remain* with their creations to maintain their shapes. Once a potter has taken his lump of clay off the wheel, it will remain in the shape of a pot even after the potter has gone off to do something else, and even if the potter should suddenly die or otherwise disappear forever.

How, then, can we be certain the same does not apply to God? Just as a lump of clay has no tendency to be shaped like a pot, but will remain in that shape after a potter has imparted that shape to it, perhaps the various Forms of things we see around us have no tendency to exist in and of themselves, but will remain in existence after a being whose existence is the same thing as his Form (God) has imparted existence to them, allowing God to step back from His creation, as a potter can step away from his work after its completion, rather than actively conserving it every single moment after the act of creation. This is called the **Doctrine of Existential Inertia**, which states that objects simply have a tendency to remain in existence unless something else destroys them, obviating the need for God as a sort of conserver or sustainer.[1]

---

[1] Feser, "Existential Inertia and the Five Ways," *NSE* 84-85.

Feser has given several reasons he disagrees with this doctrine, holding as he does to its opposite, but I am unsure, to say the least, that his criticisms really work. In *Aquinas: A Beginner's Guide*, he says

> ...a thing's essence and act of existing are distinct not just before it exists, but always, even after they are conjoined so as to make the thing real (To put a handle on to a brush so as to make a broom doesn't make the handle identical to the brush; neither does conjoining an essence and... existence make *them* identical). Hence it is not enough for a thing to be real that its essence and act of existing be conjoined merely at some point in the past; the essence and act of existing must be *kept* together at every point at which the thing exists. Accordingly, a thing must be caused to exist not once and for all, but *continuously,* here and now as well as at the time it first came into being... it must be *conserved* in existence from moment to moment.[1]

But it is unclear as to why such a distinction entails the things must be *kept* together as opposed to merely remaining so after having been conjoined. To return to our pottery example, the shape, or Form, of a pot is distinct from the Form of Clay, since nothing in the Form of Clay entails it be shaped like a pot or anything else. But after imparting such a shape to his clay, the potter is not necessary to ensure the clay remains in that shape, or in Feser's terms, remains "conjoined" to the shape of a pot, despite the fact that "pot-ness" and "clay-ness" are distinct and non-identical at every single instant the clay pot exists. Even Feser's *own example* undermines his point. Yes, it is true that a brush and a handle are distinct objects, and remain distinct even after a broom-maker has glued them together in order to make a broom. But after the brush and handle have been attached, the broom-maker is not necessary to ensure they remain attached. He could make another broom, change careers, or even drop dead, and the brush and handle will still stay together. Given this curious choice of example, why can the same not be said of God? Why is God necessary to "keep" Form and existence together when the distinct, non-identical things of our

---

[1] *AQ*, 85. The italics are Feser's.

existence (such as pots and clay, or brushes and handles) can be attached once and remain so forever after without any further activity?

In *Five Proofs*, Feser asks *why it is* those things stick together. Since a brush and a handle are distinct, not identical, even after being joined as parts of a broom, it is reasonable to ask why the broom *doesn't* simply go to pieces. Surely there is some reason for it. After all, the difference between a good broom-maker and a bad one would be that the former's brooms are sturdy while the latter's fall apart almost immediately. There must be some reason behind the skilled broom-maker's success, which the poor one would like to learn. Of course, we can think of some fairly obvious examples—the skilled craftsman uses Superglue to keep the brush and handle attached, or screws or nails the pieces together, and so on. Feser would say that external element (glue, screw, or nail) is responsible for the brush and handle remaining together even in the broom-maker's absence. By the same token, he would say that something similar is necessary to keep Forms and Existence conjoined. No divine Craftsman could simply attach a Form to an act of existence and expect them to stay together, they would fall apart on their own. Thus, in this view, God is to Form and existence as glue might be to a brush and a handle. If the glue of a broom disappears, even for an instant, the handle and brush will fall away from each other and return to being separate things. If God ceases His conjoining activity, Forms and acts of existence would fall apart the same way.[1]

But once again, this possible example does not prove that Feser's God must *necessarily* be such a conjoiner. The glue is a separate thing from the craftsman as well. After he applies it, a handle and a brush will remain stuck together as a broom so long as the glue remains potent. In this case, the broom-maker could *still* die or disappear and his broom would remain good if the glue did. If this is so, how can we be sure the "glue" attaching Forms and existence is necessarily the same thing as God? Perhaps there is some other way He conjoins the two that does not

---

[1] *FP*, 69-74.

require Him to be ever-present, even if it is necessary that He ordered the initial conjoining. For instance, maybe God created a sort of "universal angel" to hold Forms and their acts of existence together in an orderly fashion. As we have seen in chapter 2, Feser believes it is possible angels might be responsible for physical phenomena (such as inertial motion), so it is not inconceivable that such a being could also conjoin existence and Form.[1]

Feser might reply that such an angel would need something "conjoining" its particular Form and its act of existence itself. Alas, I do not believe that is necessarily true. If God determines the Forms of things, it stands to reason He determines the Forms of the angels He creates as well. Thus, it might be the case that the Form of the Universal Angel is this:

A: To come into existence at the beginning of time

B: To persistently exist until the heat death of the universe

C: To conjoin the Forms of everything else to existence

In this case, God, as "Pure Existence" would be necessary to determine the Form of this Universal Angel and create it in the first place, but He would not be necessary to conserve it in existence, as He determined its Form to entail existence all on its own, following its moment of creation. And that Universal Angel would serve as the "glue" which binds everything together even in the absence of the craftsman who initially applied it.

Now, Feser also has problems with the idea that a thing's Form can entail its existence in any way. A brief summary of his argument in one of his essays can go like this: Something has existential inertia if and only if it has a tendency to remain in existence after coming into

---

[1] Edward Feser, "Oerter on Inertial Motion and Angels" on *Edward Feser* (blog), January 7, 2013, last accessed on July 5, 2020, http://edwardfeser.blogspot.com/2013/01/oerter-on-inertial-motion-and-angels.html

existence. But no material object could have such a tendency. No Form of a material object (such as the Form a squirrel instantiates) could be responsible for it existing, because a Form is just an abstraction and can do nothing on its own. And matter—the raw stuff which instantiates various Forms, for instance a parcel of matter adhering to the Form of a squirrel—cannot have a tendency to exist on its own either, because every piece of matter in the universe must instantiate a Form of some sort, even if only the Forms associated with fundamental particles like protons and electrons which make up more complex things like squirrels. Therefore, God is necessary to conjoin the Forms of all things with the bits of matter out of which they are made, or in other words, conjoin their Forms to their acts of existence.[1]

As usual, my discerning readers will note that this argument applies only to *material* things. But we will also recall that Feser believes angels are entirely immaterial, simply being "Forms conjoined to an act of existence." For such immaterial beings, why would God necessarily have to conjoin their Forms to existence constantly, rather than just creating them and having their Forms entail they would continue to exist until a certain point in time, or until God decided to destroy them? For Feser's Divine Conservation argument to work, he must establish that angels cannot have Forms which allow them to exist independently. How could he do that? The only reason he believes the material universe requires a divine conserver is because material things are always "composites" of Form along with a certain bit of matter. But angels are not attached to any kind or amount of matter anywhere at all, they are simply Forms that exist without matter. Thus, the form/matter distinction seems not to apply to them.

According to Feser, Aquinas believed that a distinction between Form and existence was still necessary for angels to be distinguished

---

[1] Feser, "Existential Inertia and the Five Ways," *NSE* 107-108. The semi-formal syllogism he provides mentions "prime matter," but again, that concept is somewhat complex and would take a great deal of time to explain, which is not necessary for my critique of his argument.

from each other. If angels cannot be attached to any particular bit of matter, how would we be able to tell the difference between Michael, Gabriel, Sachiel, Zeruel, and all the other angels in the Catholic tradition (and/or Neon Genesis Evangelion)? Only by the fact that they have separate "acts of existence" can they be differentiated.[1] But the point I was making still stands: There seems to be no reason any particular act of existence, at least for an angel, must be something constantly maintained by God as opposed to simply something He brings about once and which then maintains itself according to His command. For instance, God could decree that the Form of the archangel Michael would be:

A: To come into existence at the beginning of time

B: To persistently exist until the heat death of the universe

C: To be differentiated from Gabriel in some way—perhaps Michael's responsibility is to hunt down demons and Gabriel's is to watch over expectant mothers, or something like that.

By reference to an angel's "responsibilities" (so to speak) entailed by its Form, we can distinguish them without necessitating that their individual acts of existence are maintained by God. This means it is possible for an angel to have some tendency to exist in and of itself, even if God must have created it in the first place, which means that God might have created at least one such "self-sufficient" angel and directed it to conserve the material world in His absence.

Indeed, we can go even further and say that God could simply decree that material things remain in existence until they have been destroyed, which would again allow Him to stand away from His creation—such a state of affairs would not require even the "universal angel" of the above examples. Again, for the purposes of argument, let us agree with Feser that no "composite of Form and matter" can possess a tendency to exist by itself, and such a tendency must be "imparted" to

---

[1] *SM*, 248. The Eva joke is mine, not Feser's.

it by God. But precisely *how* does God "impart" such a tendency? One way would be as a direct divine conserver, yes, but there are unlimited other ways an omnipotent, omniscient Being could do so. He could simply say (so to speak), "I have created this universe, I have created the Forms that everything inside of it instantiates, and I deem it a universal law that all the material things within it shall exist unless and until other things destroy them. Now I'm going to sit back on my recliner, relax, and see how the whole thing plays out."

Granted, God would probably not have said that last part, but the rest of it seems like something well within His capabilities. Why is it necessary to have a Divine Conserver as opposed to a Divine Lawgiver? Feser has critiqued the idea of "universal laws" or "laws of nature" in *Scholastic Metaphysics*, saying they are incapable of providing an atheistic framework for natural science—"it is certainly difficult to see how laws of nature, understood non-theologically, can plausibly *replace* causal powers. For what is a law of nature if it is not a divine decree?"[1] But this riposte has no force against my idea, which we might call the "**Doctrine of Deistically-Decreed Existential Inertia**,"[2] because it does not support atheism. It rather advances a kind of theology—merely a Deistic one. I am not denying the necessity of a simple Being whose "essence just is His existence." I am not even denying such a Being must be omniscient and omnipotent (though I have done so previously). I simply claim that such a Being could be responsible for the existence of everything else via decree rather than active conserving ability. It may certainly be true that my examples are imperfect, and leave quite a bit to be desired—professional philosophers would be able to produce other, better ones. But mine should suffice to explain how Feser's preferred A-T metaphysics do not necessitate an active conserver, even if we concede most of his starting positions. A Deistic God that left His

---

[1] *SM*, 69.
[2] I'm somewhat proud of having made up this term entirely on my own, but at the time of this writing I am unsure if someone else has also came up with the idea.

universe to either someone else (an angel) or to its own devices is still a possibility.

Now, if one considers a divine decree to be equivalent or even similar to a universal law, Feser might reply, "God cannot make just any old thing a law of nature...even God could not establish a law of nature according to which squares are round. What laws are possible is constrained by what is possible for the things governed by the law, given their natures."[1] This runs into the issue I described in section 6.1, that God ought to be able to define the natures of things as He pleases, but even disregarding that, Feser's possible riposte cannot foil the DDDEI. There is obviously a logical contradiction entailed by a round square, but there is no contradiction involved in a law or decree stating that at least some things will continue to exist until they are destroyed. Remember, Essences are existentially *neutral*. Nothing in the Nature or Form of Man or squirrels or dinosaurs or whatever entails they exist (according to the Thomists), but nothing in those Forms entails they could *not* exist either. Thus, the Deist's solution to the problem of the Essence/existence distinction seems as good as the Thomist's.

There are some legitimate reasons to think a deistic God makes more metaphysical sense than a perpetually conserving one. One of Feser's arguments for the necessity of a divine conserver is that things pass in and out of existence constantly. That means such material things are *contingent,* and could therefore only receive their existence from a *non-contingent* thing. Any such non-contingent thing would be eternally existing, which would, of course, be God.[2] This implies that God would be severing the act of existing of individual things from their Forms on a regular basis. For example, imagine a rubber ball falling into a furnace and being completely vaporized into its constituent atoms, not just gooeyified. It no longer exists, but its Form would still be out there—perhaps not its individual Form (that would be a soul, which only humans have)—but the Form of rubber balls, which exists generally. So

---

[1] *Aristotle's Revenge*, 200.
[2] AQ, 90-98.

God must have severed the ball's existence from its Form the moment it was vaporized. He was "conserving" it for every second of every day since it had been made in the factory, but He assumedly stopped when it was destroyed in the furnace.

So far, so good. But what if someone intentionally threw the rubber ball into a furnace? That is to say, destroyed it of his own volition, an action freely chosen to demonstrate his free will. God would have to separate the ball's existence from its Essence. But notice the "have" to. God doesn't "have" to do anything; He is completely independent of any of His puny creations, including humans. Yet it seems human beings can "force" Him to do things when we destroy other material objects in the exercise of our free wills, since God, if He conserves everything, would have to react to our destructive actions. The same applies to creative ones—the moment a sculptor or potter creates a pot or statue, God must maintain that object in existence.

In other words, God is reacting to human activity in a certain sense. But how could this possibly be so? Why would Mr. Pure Act, being as mighty and all-powerful as He is, accede to the whims of His creation, or be influenced by them in even the most minimal way? Since God is ultimately responsible for conserving every single thing in the universe, He is ultimately responsible for anything coming into or passing out of existence. Is it the case that He just happens to decide things exist and cease to exist whenever human beings decide to create or destroy them? That seems to be a little too convenient. Is it the case that human decisions pertaining to creation and destruction somehow convince or coerce God into conjoining or severing various Forms from their acts of existence? Then God is not truly the sovereign Master of all creation. On the other hand, if we assume things can enter and exit existence without God being "forced" to do anything, either something else is connecting and severing their Essences to existence, or Essences can be conjoined to existences "on their own," so to speak. That would obviate the Doctrine of Divine Conservation that Feser was supposed to be defending. The Doctrine of Deistically-Decreed Existential Inertia, in contrast to both those alternatives, provides an intelligible reason for how things can remain in existence without muddling into confusion over whether or not God must be involved in severing or conjoining existence to Forms due to human activity.

Perhaps Feser might say that God foreordains the creation and passing of all things, but that would imply He also foreordains when human beings create and destroy things, which would seem incompatible with free will. If I choose to destroy something, I am making the conscious decision to separate its Form from its act of existence. If only God is capable of such a thing, I am essentially forcing God to do it, unless He has actually determined that I should destroy the object. In that case, I am not actually freely choosing to do anything, I am merely acting as an instrument of God. Given that Feser is a Catholic rather than a Calvinist, I doubt he would find such an account very palatable.

Dr. Feser might say that human beings have free will in the same sense characters in a novel have free will. As he mentioned in *Five Proofs*,

> Consider once again the analogy with the author of a story. Suppose it is a crime novel and that one of the characters carefully plots the murder of another, for financial gain. We would naturally say that he commits the murder of his own free will, and is therefore justly punished after being caught at the end of the novel. It would be silly to say: 'Well, he didn't really commit the murder of his own free will. For he committed it only because the author wrote the story that way.' The author's writing the story the way he did is not inconsistent with the character's having freely committed the murder. It's not comparable to (say) some further character in the story hypnotizing the murderer and thereby getting him to commit the crime—something which would be inconsistent with the murder having been committed freely. If we got to a point in the book where such hypnotism was revealed, we would say 'Ah, so it wasn't an act of free will after all.' But we don't say that when we reflect on the fact that the story had an author. It is perfectly

coherent to say that the author wrote a story in which someone freely chooses to commit a murder.[1]

As you can imagine, there are several problems with this. First, to say that "characters in this novel only behave according to the will of the author" might be silly, but it isn't wrong. We call such a statement silly because most of us *already know* that all the characters in a novel are figments of the author's imagination and do exactly what the author says. Fictional characters and mere figments of the imagination cannot *truly* have free will, but we pretend they do—*suspend our disbelief*—in order to enjoy fiction. To say that fictional characters have free will *in the context of a story* is to admit they do not have free will *in reality*. But Feser isn't talking about fiction here, he is ostensibly talking about the world we live in. And if the real world is analogous to a story written by God, to say we have free will in the context of that "story" is to admit we don't actually have it in an objective sense.

This is easy to understand by looking at how we criticize novels and other works of fiction. Take *Star Wars,* for instance. The character Jar-Jar Binks was notoriously annoying, loathed by nearly everybody who watched *The Phantom Menace,* and George Lucas was excoriated for writing such a stupid alien. It would not have made any sense for Lucas to defend himself by saying, "It's not my fault! In the context of the story, Jar-Jar freely chose to act stupid and annoying, it wasn't like he was being controlled by a Sith or anything!" Nobody would take such a defense seriously, because regardless of how characters within a story might be expected to react to other characters in that story, as a matter of what is true in the real world, everything the characters do is ultimately determinate upon the author's will. The story might be constructed in such a way that its characters *seem* like they have free will, but by dint of being a story constructed by an author, that free will is ultimately an illusion. If it were not, no-one could ever criticize the

---

[1] *FP,* 200-215.

plotting or characterization of any novel or script because the author would be able to blame all of his mistakes on the characters.

Second, Feser's analogy makes God's power over His "story" rather difficult to make sense of. The human author of a story can change it as he wills. For instance, if a character dies in the first draft of a novel, the author can re-write it so she lives in the second draft. But God is apparently unable to do so, because such a thing would be a sort of change—that is to say, a first draft submitted to an editor on Monday would be different from a second draft submitted on Friday, and Pure Act cannot change. But this would seem to limit God in ways human beings are not. It would make the Author of the universe itself less powerful over His own creation, in a way, than mere human authors are over theirs. While perhaps not incoherent in the sense of being self-contradictory, this is certainly unintuitive, given God's supposedly unlimited majesty and power.

Third, Feser's analogy also vitiates his doctrine of Essences and final causes. In most stories, the characters inside it can never really be certain of the "true Essences" of anything they encounter—indeed, in many cases, the authors of such stories construct them in such a way that such knowledge is entirely inaccessible to the characters (and often to the consumer!). Was Rick Deckard a replicant in *Blade Runner*? He could never tell you in the context of the story, though Ridley Scott could. Was Childs an alien doppelganger by the end of *The Thing*? Only John Carpenter knows for sure. That being the case, wouldn't similar epistemic uncertainty attend to us, characters in God's "novel?" How can we be sure blacks or Jews or Catholics actually possess the Essences of human beings (and the moral rights and obligations entailed) as opposed to the Essences of doppelgangers God designed to merely resemble humans? How can we be certain the Essence of *anything* we encounter actually is what it seems to be?[1] Perhaps squirrels have some

---

[1] For an extended look at doppelgangers, or "p-zombies" and the problems they pose for theology, see Jonathan MS Pearce, "Heaven, Hell, and Philosophical Zombies," *A Tippling Philosopher,* September 6, 2013,

purpose beyond reproducing and eating nuts known only to God. And, of course, the million-dollar question—how can we be sure Christ actually did possess the Divine Essence as opposed to being a magician or trickster who only seemed as if He had died? It is not enough to say that God would not lie to us. Just as Ridley Scott and John Carpenter had reasons for keeping the truth about who was a replicant or doppelganger away from Rick Deckard and R.J. Macready, perhaps God would have reasons for permitting some sort of magician (as Celsus would say) to pretend to be Him.

Indeed, if we think about the implications of Feser's analogy, it seems as if Christ absolutely *could not have been* God Himself. If the world of our everyday existence is analogous to a story held in God's mind, then wouldn't the Incarnation of Christ be analogous to the author of a novel inserting himself into it as a character? But if you think about it, it is *metaphysically* impossible for an author to *literally* put himself inside a story. For instance, imagine if J.R.R. Tolkien wrote a story in which he was transported from his study into Middle-Earth and helped defend Minas Tirith. But Tolkien-the-author and Tolkien-the-character could not literally be the same person, because they are crucially different in both characteristics and actions. If they were the same, Tolkien-the-author would have to be yanked from his study at the *very same time* he was sitting down and writing about Tolkien-the-character being plunged into Middle Earth. Thus, we can conclude that Tolkien-the-author is *essentially different* from Tolkien-the-character, the latter simply being a *representation* of the former, a fictional character who might resemble in all particulars the author, but is otherwise a separate entity.

The exact same consideration applies to Jesus Christ: It is *impossible* for God to show up in His own "novel," because simply being part of a novel necessitates certain characteristics God must not have: God is timeless, but the events of His "novel" take place across and in

---

https://www.patheos.com/blogs/tippling/2013/09/06/heaven-hell-and-philosophical-zombies/ , last accessed July 5, 2020.

time, God is changeless, but His self-insertion obviously changes in a variety of ways, and so on. We could say Jesus *represents* God within the context of our story, but the doctrine of the Trinity demands that Jesus was not a mere "representation" of God but literally and essentially God Himself. Thus, while Jews and Muslims might find the Divine Novelist analogy to be useful, it deals a rather severe blow—to say the least—to the preferred religion of the Thomist.

6.6: Essence Is Existence

Even so, there is no reason for Jews, Muslims, and other more (apparently) traditional classical theists to get too cocky. The primary arc of this particular argument for the existence of a purely simple, purely actual God relies on Essence and existence truly being separate and distinct. So far, we have conceded this postulate to the classical theist, but now it is time to examine it critically. Why could it not be the case that at least some things have existence entailed by their Forms (obviating the need for God to conjoin the two, even by decree)? Feser thinks this is metaphysically incoherent and has provided several objections to the idea in *Scholastic Metaphysics* and *Five Proofs*. Once again, I find his objections unconvincing, and we will see why as I go through each of them in turn.

According to Feser as well as his Thomist friends such as David Oderberg, the Forms of various things and their existences *must* be distinct because it is supposedly possible to correctly understand the Form of something without knowing whether or not it exists. Feser gives us this example:

> Suppose a person had, for whatever reason, never heard of lions, pterodactyls, or unicorns. Suppose you give him a detailed description of the natures of each. You then tell him that of these three creatures, one exists, one used to exist but is now extinct, and the third never existed; and you ask him to tell you which is which given what he now knows about their essences. He would, of course, be unable to do so. But then the existence of the creatures that do exist must be really

distinct from their essences, otherwise one *could* know of their existence merely from knowing their essences.[1]

The key trick Feser is playing there involves his use of the term "detailed description." If our hypothetical interviewee wouldn't be able to tell whether lions, pterodactyls, or unicorns existed or ever existed, perhaps we have not actually given him a properly detailed description. Let us say the Form of a lion is a large cat that exists currently, the Form of a pterodactyl to be a flying reptile that once existed, and the Form of a unicorn to be a horned horse that never existed. If we just told our perplexed friend that lions were cats, pterodactyls were reptiles, and unicorns were horses, he would have a very incomplete grasp of the Forms of these things, since being large, flying, and horned are how we distinguish lions, pterodactyls, and unicorns from other cats, reptiles, and horses respectively. But since in this example, the existential status (presently-existing, previously-existing, and never-existing) is part of the Forms of each of these three creatures, our interviewee would not have been given a full description of those Forms if he still didn't know which ones exist, existed, and never did exist.[2]

Feser's response is that

> There is a crucial disanalogy between what is uncontroversially part of the thing's essence, on the one hand, and the existence of the thing on the other. Suppose you judge that a lion is a kind of animal but do not judge that it is a kind of cat. In that case, while you have only *incompletely* conceived of what it is to be a lion, you have not for that reason *misconceived* what it is to be a lion. By contrast, if you not only fail to judge that a lion is a kind of cat but judge that a lion is *not* a kind of cat, then you *have* misconceived what it is to be a lion. Now, if we suppose that you judge that lions don't exist—perhaps you think they

---

[1] *FP*, 118. Oderberg, *Real Essentialism*, 124.
[2] The philosopher Richard Carrier has made this same point somewhat more acerbically at his own blog. See Richard Carrier, "Feser's Five Proofs for the Existence of God: Debunked!" on *Richard Carrier*, February 20, 2018, https://www.richardcarrier.info/archives/13752 , last accessed on July 5, 2020.

have gone extinct like pterodactyls, or that they are creatures of fiction like unicorns—then while you have judged falsely, you have *not* misconceived *what it is* to be a lion. Yet if the existence of a lion were not distinct from its essence, this would not be the case. Judging it to be nonexistent would be as much to misconceive *what* it is as judging it to be a noncat would be.[1]

This strikes me as little more than an argument by assertion. Feser says that judging a lion to be an imaginary creature is just a false judgement, not a complete misconception of what it actually is. But why should we believe that? What, precisely, is the difference between a lion's cat-ness, large-ness, or any other essential characteristics and the fact of its existence? It is not made especially clear in *Five Proofs*, or Oderberg's *Real Essentialism* for that matter, and apparently, we are meant to just take the Thomist at his word when he tells us that such a disanalogy really does obtain. But unless he gives us a very specific, compelling reason to do so, we are under no obligation to believe him. And indeed, there may be good reasons to be very suspicious of him.

Recall Feser telling us that a thing's Essence, Nature, or Form is what "defines it and distinguishes it from everything else," or "that which makes it the sort of thing it is." If this is true, it would seem that traits that distinguish certain things from others are important enough to be considered essential traits, or characteristics which are important parts of a thing's Form. So, for instance, if we say that lions are a kind of reptile, or that pterodactyls are a kind of cat, we have gravely misconceived their Forms, or what it is to be a lion and a pterodactyl, because lions are distinguished from pterodactyls and other things by being cats, and pterodactyls are distinguished from lions by being reptiles. By the same token, we can distinguish between things based on whether or not they exist. Since we can, that makes existence a distinguishing characteristic. And since a thing's distinguishing characteristics are a part of (or "flow from") its Essence ("that which

---

[1] *FP*, 118-119. Feser makes the same point in *SM,* 243-244, as does Oderberg in *Real Essentialism*, 123.

distinguishes it from everything else"), existence would be such an essential characteristic, which means that any proper assessment of a thing's Essence or Form would also include its existential status. We can see how this is even more obviously true by returning to the example of a novelist in the previous section.

Let's turn from J.R.R. Tolkien to another aspiring author—myself. Let us say I'm working on writing the Great American Novel. I hope to become as well-regarded a writer as Herman Melville or Edgar Allen Poe, and I've already got an idea for the most sympathetic, compelling protagonist of any story ever penned by an American author. My tale is set in Los Angeles during the 2000s, and its main character, entirely a product of my muse, is a chubby white philosophy professor who teaches at Pasadena City College. Having just recently received his Ph.D. from the University of California at Santa Barbara, my hero is dismayed to find atheism, immorality, and bad taste in music running rampant among the benighted inhabitants of his city. Girding himself in the armor of his Catholic faith, he sallies forth against the forces of darkness, and my story details the course of his epic struggle. Thankfully, it has a happy ending, as he successfully publishes a book, *The Final Superstition: A Repudiation of Modern Atheism*, which convinces the entire world of the truth of Christianity and ushers in a worldwide era of peace and prosperity under the benevolent auspices of the Pope.

Oh, and I almost forgot one minor detail: The name of my story's protagonist is "Edward Feser."

Particularly alert readers will note that my entirely fictional protagonist is curiously similar to another famous person—namely Edward Feser, author of *The Last Superstition: A Refutation of the New Atheism*. Indeed, looking at Dr. Feser's website, it seems he's almost indistinguishable from the character in my novel—the picture there is of a nondescript middle-aged chubby white guy[1], and the "about" section notes that he received his Ph.D. from the University of California at

---

[1] I'm a chubby middle-aged guy myself, so this is hardly an insult to Feser.

Santa Barbara, currently lives in Los Angeles, and teaches at Pasadena City College.[1]

It seems as if we have found ourselves with quite a conundrum. How could we possibly distinguish Edward Feser, the protagonist of my book (let's call him Fictional Feser), and Edward Feser, the real-life professor of philosophy at Pasadena City College? Is it through their physical appearances? No, because Fictional Feser looks just like Edward Feser. Their life experiences? That can't be it either, because they both received their doctorates from the same institution and teach at the same place. Could it be the titles of their books? Perhaps, but since I'm the author of the novel in which Fictional Feser stars, I can deem that the name of the book he writes is *The Last Superstition* rather than *The Final Superstition*, making the two Fesers even harder to distinguish. Are we helpless, then? Must we assume that Fictional Feser and Edward Feser are the same thing, with no way to tell them apart?

No—we do have one hope, and we can see it in the moniker I have given my story's hero—*Fictional* Feser. Even if the two Fesers are the exact same in terms of appearance, psychology, background, and so on, Edward Feser exists in the real world while Fictional Feser does not. So we can distinguish them by their existential status. But remember, a Form or Essence is just that through which we can distinguish one thing from another thing. So if existence is the only way we can distinguish between Edward Feser and Fictional Feser, that would mean existence really is a part of Edward Feser's Essence, and that non-existence is really a part of Fictional Feser's Essence, and any "complete and comprehensive" account of their Essences must mention it. If that is true of the two Fesers, why should it not be true of everything else in the universe? This would mean that material things—squirrels, lions, Edward Feser, whatever—might be able to exist by virtue of their Forms, which would therefore mean that Mr. Pure Act, Whose Essence Just Is

---

[1] http://www.edwardfeser.com/about.html

Existence, might not be necessary to conserve them in existence at every moment.

Now, we cannot simply leave it at that, as there are some other considerations to take into account. For instance, one problem with saying that a thing's existence might be part of its Form is how to make sense of certain instances of certain Forms existing while others fail to do so. Another one of Feser's Thomist friends, Gyula Klima, has noted that

> If I know the essence of some thing which is of a certain kind, then I will know **a priori** [purely **deductively**, stemming from the essence] of any other thing of that kind which does exist, has existed, will exist, or could exist that it will have the attributes entailed by being a thing of that kind. But I will not know a priori whether any other thing of that kind in fact does exist, has existed, or will exist. I could know that only **a posteriori** [through **empirical** observation]. Now, this gives us a reason to think that knowing the essence of a thing does not entail knowing its existence, and it is a reason I could have whether or not it even occurs to me to ask about whether essence and existence are identical.[1]

Klima's argument seems to rest on the term "certain kind of thing," and if so, does not do much to put a dent in mine. I would argue that Edward Feser and Fictional Feser are simply certain kinds of things whose existence or lack thereof can be logically deduced from their Forms. If we were to say that Edward Feser and Fictional Feser were merely Rational Animals, then yes, Klima would be correct, existence would not be a part of either Feser's Essence or Form. We would need to empirically determine that Fictional Feser was a character in a book and Edward Feser really does exist in the real world. But I hold that Edward Feser is not just a rational animal but an *existing rational animal*, and that Fictional Feser is a *fictional rational animal*. They are different kinds of things. By virtue of the first Essence, Edward Feser belongs in the same category as existing human beings such as David Oderberg or

---

[1] *FP,* 140. The additions in brackets are mine for clarification.

Barack Obama, and by virtue of the second Essence, Fictional Feser belongs in the same category as Harry Potter, Sherlock Holmes, or other fictional human beings. Given their Forms, we would need to engage in no empirical inquiry at all to know whether or not they exist. Merely being an existing rational animal tells us "a priori" that Edward Feser exists, just like being a "rational animal" would tell us a priori that he can comprehend Forms and so on. By the same token, merely being a fictional rational animal is enough to tell us that Fictional Feser does not exist. Therefore, we have at least one less reason to assume that existence cannot be entailed by something's Form.

This conveniently addresses another objection Feser might raise. In *Scholastic Metaphysics* he contends that

> The essence of human beings, *rational animality*, has *rationality* and *animality* as parts. Suppose *existence* were another part alongside these. Then the existence of the whole human being would depend on this part. But that is no more plausible than saying that the whole human essence, *rational animality*, depends on *animality* alone. Now, if someone insisted that the whole essence really does depend on *animality* alone, with *rationality* being essentially derivative, that would make *animality* itself the true essence and *rationality* a mere property.... Similarly, if someone insisted that the whole human being depended on *existence* considered as a part of the human essence, then this would make *existence* the essence with the rest (*rationality* and *animality*) being mere properties.[1]

I freely admit to not being a classically-schooled philosopher, but I fail to see what, exactly, the thrust of Feser's objection here is. Yes, if we define the Form of a human to be a Rational Animal, we cannot say that Form depends on either one of its parts alone. But it seems obvious to me that the Form depends on both simultaneously. If something is an animal without being rational, it is simply a cat or bear or some other kind of non-human animal. If something is rational without being an

---

[1] *SM*, 246.

animal, it is an angel (Feser would say) or some other sort of non-human intelligence. Only something that is simultaneously rational and an animal can be a human being—neither part depends on the other, the whole depends on the both of them. But just as human beings can be distinguished from other animals thanks to our rationality, and distinguished from other rational beings thanks to our animality, can't human beings be distinguished among themselves by different ways? For instance, within the general category of human beings, can't we distinguish between real human beings like Edward Feser and imaginary ones like Fictional Feser? If that is the case, and I think I established it above, we can say that Edward Feser's Form is an *existing rational animal*, and Fictional Feser's is a *fictional rational animal*. This would mean that Edward Feser's Form depends on all three of those parts simultaneously—he would be something else, either an animal, an angel, or a fictional character, if any one of them did not apply to him. Given this view, there is nothing more obviously problematic in saying that being an existing rational animal entails existence, rationality, and animality than in saying that being a rational animal, whether fictional or not, entails both logical thought and a physical instantiation of animality.

One more objection Feser might have at this point is how to account for a thing going out of existence or coming into existence. To take Feser himself as an example, it would be absurd to say his existence is eternal in any sense. It isn't as if he always existed—he was born on a specific date. It isn't as if he has to exist—he is a contingent being, meaning that if things had been different (if his parents had never met, for instance) he never would have been born. And it isn't as if he will always exist—he will assumedly die someday, unless he's actually Connor MacLeod from the *Highlander* movies masquerading as a humble college professor. But if Edward Feser's Form is that of an existing rational animal—emphasis on the *existing*—wouldn't that seem to entail he necessarily exists, and could not possibly fail to exist under any circumstances, given that Form? I think even Feser might find that to be a little too flattering.[1]

Fortunately for both him and us, an even closer analysis of his Form reveals that we are not obligated to hew to this bizarre conclusion. The interesting thing about Forms is that their parts seem to limit each other even if (as established in the previous paragraphs) the Form as a whole depends on all of them simultaneously. Take, for instance, the Form of a Rational Animal. *Animality*, as Feser might put it, limits *rationality* in specific ways. Even though we are rational, the fact that we are animals means that immaterial activity of our rationality still inheres to a certain parcel of matter (our brains) and can be attenuated by damage or chemical imbalance within that part. Indeed, Feser would agree with the idea that simply by dint of being animals (material creatures by definition), we cannot be as rational and intelligent as angels, and infinitely less rational than God.[2] If we agree with Feser about this, then we also conclude that the same applies to existence. If one is an *existing rational animal*, one's animality limits one's existence in specific ways, just as it limits rationality, even if the Form does not depend on any one of those parts but all three of them simultaneously. And the ways in which animality limits existence would be this: Being an existing animal of *any* sort entails that one has not always existed but must have come into being at some point through whatever biological processes are appropriate to one's species, and will pass out of being after a given time appropriate to that species' lifespan. Thus, Edward Feser's Form does not entail he necessarily or eternally exists, but that he came into existence on whatever day he was born, and will leave existence on the date of his death. Given this, and all the above, we do not have any especially pressing reason to claim that even Subsistent Existence Itself is necessary for conserving everything else in existence. At the very most, perhaps we can say that God must have determined

---

[1] *TLS*, 103, *AQ*, 84-86, 97.
[2] Edward Feser, "Trinity Sunday," *Edward Feser* (blog), June 7, 2009, last accessed on July 5, 2020, http://edwardfeser.blogspot.com/2009/06/trinity-sunday.html

everything's Form and got the universe started, but it does very much seem like the Essences or Forms of things are a sufficient explanation for why everything in the universe continues to exist.

6.7: Act and Potency

If the existential argument is one of the stronger ones for A-T brands of theism, the supposed distinction between "actuality" and "potency" is its central one. As Feser has told us, "It is not for nothing that the very first of the famous Twenty Four Thomistic Theses is: 'Potency and Act divide being in such a way that whatever is, is either pure act, or of necessity it is composed of potency and act as primary and intrinsic principles.'"[1] Every A-T argument critiqued in the previous chapters ultimately comes from that first thesis. If we can call anything at all "good" or "bad," it must ultimately be because of something that just is Pure Act! If it is possible to solve the Problem of Universals, the solution must lie in Pure Act! If there is a distinction between Forms and the existence of the various things that instantiate them, Pure Act must be responsible for holding it all together! It would be no exaggeration to say that everything in the A-T philosophical tradition, ranging from ethics to metaphysics, falls apart if you do not accept their account of actuality and potency. Indeed, it falls apart even if you accept a *slightly* different assessment of those two terms than Thomists do. As you can probably expect, this section will tell you to do exactly that.

Let us bring together some arguments Feser has provided in both *Five Proofs* and *The Last Superstition*. According to *Five Proofs*, the argument for change, strangely enough, applies to un-changing things as well. Recall that any sort of change is just the actualization of potential; for instance, if a hot coffee cup becomes cold, we say the coffee's potential for coldness has been actualized, and actualized by something else—a cold breeze, for instance. But the breeze itself must be *actually* cold before it can actualize something else's potential for

---

[1] Edward Feser, "Act and Potency," *Edward Feser* (blog), May 7, 2009, last accessed on July 5, 2020, http://edwardfeser.blogspot.com/2009/05/act-and-potency.html

coldness, and must be made cold by an air conditioner. All well and good, but even things that are just staying the same can be said to be actualizing potentialities. Feser asks us to imagine a cup on a desk. There is nothing inherent in the cup that mandates it be, say, three feet above the ground. Rather, its potential to be above the ground is actualized by the desk. But the desk also has no potential to hold things up—rather, it must be supported by the floor on which it stands. The floor itself must be supported by the ground beneath it, which is part of the Earth. And while the Earth doesn't need to be supported by anything, it is reliant on the laws of physics and atomic bonds that ensure it doesn't simply disintegrate. So in that sense, the potential of the Earth itself to exist must be actualized by the attraction between atoms. As Feser says,

> Atoms have the potential to be bonded in other ways, and yet they are not so bonded. It is their potential to be bonded in such a way that [the Earth remains stable] that is in fact being actualized. Again, why? Appealing to the structure of the atom won't answer the question either, but merely pushes it back a stage. For why are the subatomic particles combined in just the specific way they are, here and now, rather than some other way? What is it that actualizes that potential rather than another?[1]

This line of thought becomes very curious when we compare it to what Feser wrote in *The Last Superstition*. There, he explained potentiality in this way:

> it might be said... that a thing is "potentially" almost anything, so that Aristotle's distinction is uninteresting. For example... we can 'conceive' of a 'possible world' where rubber balls... move by themselves.... But the potentialities Aristotle has in mind are the ones rooted in a thing's nature as actually exists, not just any old thing it might 'possibly do' in some expanded abstract sense rooted in our powers of conception. Hence, in Aristotle's sense of 'potential,' while a rubber ball could

---

[1] *FP*, 20-40.

potentially be melted, it could not potentially follow someone around all by itself.¹

If we give these two passages a few moment's thought, we can see how the latter undermines the former, and by extension the first Thomistic thesis upon which the argument for God rests. Feser tells us that the atomic particles which constitute the Earth (to take but one example) represent the actualization of a potential because there are ways they could otherwise be, not only at some point in the past but here and now. Their arrangement *could* be different, or the measurements of the forces holding them together *could* be something else. Crucially, however, Feser simply asserts this—he provides no independent reason this is true *in reality* as opposed to inside our minds. How can we be certain the Nature of atoms or the fundamental forces of physics actually could be different than what they are? Perhaps the alternate configurations of the atoms or measurements of the fundamental forces that Feser is thinking of belong in the same category as a rubber ball bouncing to the moon or rolling around by itself: figments of our powers of imagination and conception rather than any actual potentiality rooted in the Nature of these entities themselves. If that is the case, then it is entirely possible that such entities—the collection of fundamental particles, the physical forces, and so on—would be the "purely actual actualizer" or "unchanged changer" Feser says we need.

Now, Feser says such things cannot be "purely actual" because they can be differentiated from one another: "Even the fundamental particles—fermions and bosons—though they are not composed of other particles, still have parts in the sense that they have distinctive attributes. Furthermore, they exhibit potentiality insofar as they come into being and pass away."² In his second point, Feser is not quite correct—the law of conservation of matter would imply that the fundamental particles may change their relationships and arrangement,

---

¹ *TLS*, 54.
² *FP,* 199-200.

but not actually pass out of existence.[1] But even his first point is somewhat unconvincing, given the religion to which he himself is dedicated. Recall from Chapter 1 that all of God's apparently manifold attributes—Goodness, Power, Intelligence, Will, and so on—are not separate parts of God, but merely different aspects of the same thing. It's just sort of hard to understand due to our limited intelligence. Well, two can play at that game. Perhaps it is the case that the apparent differences between fermions and bosons are merely reflections of the same underlying reality, only appearing to be different things due to our lack of scientific knowledge. Would such a thing be impossible, because the particles are actually distinct? Not a problem for us. Recall the doctrine of mysterianism—that the three separate parts of the Christian Trinity are actually the same Being, despite at least one of those parts (Christ) walking around and changing in ways Pure Actuality shouldn't be able to do. We can fall back on the same doctrine—even if their characteristics seem to be distinct, fermions and bosons are the same thing, or reflections of a single reality, and we just can't figure out how yet.

Feser might then offer another rejoinder, this time taken from his book, *Philosophy of Mind*. According to him, there are two kinds of impossibility. The first kind of *physical* impossibility revolves around "the way the world works," and could conceivably be possible under different circumstances. The example of a rubber ball bouncing to the moon would be an example of such an impossibility: Given the laws of physics, rubber balls can't do that, be we can coherently conceive of

---

[1] Bruce Reichenbach, "Cosmological Argument", *The Stanford Encyclopedia of Philosophy* (Fall 2019 Edition), Edward N. Zalta (ed.), forthcoming URL = https://plato.stanford.edu/archives/fall2019/entries/cosmological-argument/ (last accessed on July 5, 2020). One thing I should mention here is that, as this article points out, if one holds that matter as a whole is a sort of "necessary being," then every arrangement of that matter becomes necessary, which is unintuitive if not self-contradictory. A possible solution "would be to invoke an indeterministic presentation of quantum phenomena, which would allow contingency of individual phenomena but not of the overall probabilistic structure."

different laws (gravity being half as strong as it actually is, say), under which rubber balls could bounce to the moon. On the other hand, "*no matter how different the world might have been,*" we cannot conceive of 2 and 2 equaling 5 or round squares. These are simply *metaphysically impossible*.[1] Feser might argue that since we can coherently conceive, without any apparent contradiction, of the basic laws of physics being different than they are, they could potentially be so, which means that what they actually are right now needs an explanation, which would be God.

This does not strike me as especially convincing. Recall the example at the end of section 3 of this very chapter. We can coherently, and without contradiction, imagine God not existing—if He did not exist, we would live in a world without final causality, meaning struck matches would produce tulips or elephants rather than flame. We can, without contradiction, imagine a world where God does not exist, which would be a world where morality would be an illusion and everyone just raped and murdered each other all the time. It would be a scary, ugly world, yes, but we can coherently imagine it, and there is nothing self-contradictory about such a dystopia. Thus, God's existence is only potential rather than actual, requiring some explanation for why it happens to be actual, which would obviously mean our God is not Purely Actual and thus not God.

Perhaps Feser would argue that it's merely *difficult* to see how a world without God would be inherently contradictory. It might be simple to see that is the case for worlds where squares are round or 2+2 = 5, but we just have to do a bit more work to prove that is also the case for God's non-existence, which is a "metaphysical" impossibility. The problem here is that I can do exactly the same for "physical" impossibilities. I can easily say that worlds with different laws of physics are actually inconceivable, and it just isn't immediately obvious.

---

[1] Edward Feser, *Philosophy of Mind* (Oneworld Publications, 2005), 23-25.

For instance, Feser might say "had...the gravitational pull of the earth been different, [it might have been possible to bounce a rubber ball to the moon]...we can give a description of such a state of affairs in a way that involves no contradiction."[1] But this is not true—there *is* a contradiction there, it's just not immediately obvious. The Earth's gravitational pull is a function of the gravitational force in general, and that affects *everything*. In a possible world where Earth's gravity was weak enough to permit a ball to bounce to the moon, gravity would also be too weak to keep the moon in its orbit, and it would have floated away long ago. The same applies to every other counterexample Feser might think of. A world where human beings run two-minute miles or jump fifty feet in the air (the ideas he came up with in *Philosophy of Mind*) would be so radically different from ours that such beings wouldn't really be human at all—fleamen, perhaps, but not *Homo Sapiens*.[2]

Feser might argue that we can imagine someone running a two-minute mile in a way we can't even imagine a round square or something similar. However, that the impossibility of such a state of affairs isn't immediately obvious doesn't mean it isn't there. For instance, ask someone to imagine a round square and they might think of a polygon with rounded corners. Feser would say they're just thinking of a semi-rounded shape, not an actual round square. But the same applies to Feser's example: If we think of someone leaping tall buildings in a single bound, we're not actually imagining a different world, we're actually thinking of a flea-human or a superhero like Superman rather than someone with the Essence of a human being doing such a thing. Thus, we return to the conclusion that the laws of physics are, in reality, precisely a sort of "purely actual" being. Whether they're descriptions of the Essences of the fundamental particles or something else, it is impossible to coherently conceive of them being different once you

---

[1] Ibid.
[2] Ibid., 23.

really understand what they entail, which means those laws have no potential—they're just pure, undiluted actuality, baby.

What of the distinction between Form and Matter, or Essence and Existence? We have already covered the problems with these supposed distinctions in the previous sections. Even accepting them, a Deistic sort of God who simply decreed they would remain together and then wandered off to do something else could still account for their unity. But we can go even further and critique this argument starting from its assumptions concerning actuality and potency. Feser believes that matter itself is simply potentiality—namely, the potential to accept or instantiate Forms. Thus, no material thing (such as fundamental particles) could possibly be purely actual.[1] But is this really true? Might it be possible that the Forms of certain things might entail their own materiality, which would mean their existence is necessary, in a sense, and therefore not the sort of thing that would need to be actualized itself? Let us say that the Form of the Boson, for instance, is this:

1: To follow Bose-Einstein statistics

2: To be a material object—a very tiny material object, but a material object nonetheless

3: To have existed eternally and to persist eternally

4: To give rise to all the manifold objects and forces we see in the universe around us via their interactions with fermions, who have the exact same Form except for property 1 (they follow Fermi-Dirac statistics instead).[2]

This Form would seem to satisfy all of Feser's requirements for a Purely Actual entity. Its existence is not a "potentiality" that needed to be actualized by something else, it is built-in (so to speak) by property 3 of its Form. The unification of its Form with the matter that comprises

---

[1] *FP*, 199-200.
[2] Andrew Zimmerman Jones, "What Is a Boson?" *ThoughtCo*, May 27, 2019, last accessed July 5, 2020, https://www.thoughtco.com/boson-2699112

it is also not a potentiality that needed to be actualized, because its materiality is entailed by its Form in property 2. If Feser wishes to claim that these 4 properties are separate and need an account for their unity, I can simply say that following Bose-Einstein statistics is the same thing as being a very tiny material object, which is the same thing as existing eternally, and so on—much like Feser would say that the various properties God seems to possess are really one and the same thing (His Goodness is His Power, which is His Intellect, and so on).[1]

    Might it be the case that this Form is, itself, a potentiality that is being actualized? Why couldn't the Form of fundamental particles have been something else? I would say that bosons and fermions *are simply not the kind of thing which, in reality, could follow any other laws or instantiate any other Forms*. For Feser to ask "What makes it true that things are governed by the laws of quantum mechanics rather than some alternative laws? What actualizes that potential, specifically?"[2] is as silly as asking "what makes it true that this rubber ball is not following me around by itself? What actualizes that potential, specifically?" A rubber ball simply does not have the potential to follow someone around, so its failure to do so does not represent an actualization of any potential and thus requires no actualizer. By the same token, fermions and bosons do not have the potential to follow any other kinds of physical laws other than the ones they do, and thus, the fact that they follow the physics we are familiar with does not actually count as an actualization of any potentiality, at least not any that requires an actualizer. Their Forms— at least the ones I have given them, which seem to be pretty close to the mark— are enough to entail that they could be no other way.

---

[1] A perceptive blogger by the name of Angra Mainyu has made a similar point, though his critique of Feser centers more on the fact that we seem to distinguish between things based on their *actualities* rather than their potentials. See Angra Mainyu, "An Aristotelian Argument: A Reply To Edward Feser," *Angra Mainyu's Blog*, February 27, 2018, last accessed on July 5, 2020, http://angramainyusblog.blogspot.com/2018/02/an-aristotelian-argument-reply-to.html

[2] *FP*, 55-57.

We are therefore left with a sensible, easy-to-understand answer to Feser's supposedly profound questions. Going back to Feser's example of the cup on the desk, we can say it is held aloft by the desk, which is held aloft by the floor, which is maintained by the earth, which is maintained by the atomic bonds that constitute the entire planet. But what maintains those atomic bonds? Well, their Form or Nature is such that they simply could not be any other way. It would be as silly to ask, "what makes it the case that the atoms which comprise the earth (or the particles constituting those atoms) stay in those particular configurations rather than others?" as it would be to ask, "what makes it the case that a rubber ball will stay still rather than following me around by itself?" Just like it is simply not in the ball's nature (entailed by its Form) to do anything other than stay still unless I pick it up, it is simply not in the Nature of the fundamental particles to be arranged in any other way than we see in the Earth as it exists, and it is simply not in their Nature to pop out of existence randomly.[1] In other words, the "purely actual" being Feser requires to actualize the potentiality of the desk to stay on top of the earth and the cup to stay on top of the desk just happens to be the Form of the fundamental particles, which also encompasses their materiality. If he wishes to call them or their interactions "God", he is welcome to, but there does not seem to be any logically necessary reason to postulate the existence of anything else, much less a deity with omnipotence, omniscience, and so on.

Now, perhaps we are still left with concerns about powers and intellect. One thing Thomists believe in very strongly is the **principle of proportionate causality**. This states that whatever exists in some effect must be located in some way or another in its cause or that "a cause cannot give to an effect what it does not have to give." For instance, say you want to start a fire in a forest (Smokey the Bear would be ashamed of you). In order to *cause* the fire, you would need

---

[1] Feser might say such particles *would* pop out of existence due to the Essence/existence distinction. Refer back to the previous sections to see why this isn't necessarily true.

something that actually possesses fire, or, in other words, *is actually on fire*, like a lit match.[1] By extension of this principle, Thomists believe that the root cause of everything, the Purely Actual Unactualized Actualizer that Actualizes Everything Else, must possess power and intelligence in some way because it is the root cause of those things elsewhere in the universe. Since the Fundamental Being is responsible for atoms and physical forces having whatever powers they do, that Being must possess power—indeed, all powers—in Himself. And since the Fundamental Being is responsible for things somehow exhibiting intelligence, He must Himself possess intelligence, indeed, all possible intelligence, making Him omnipotent and omniscient, and therefore God.

But, once again, Feser provides us a sneaky escape from this conclusion. As he also notes in *The Last Superstition*, a cigarette lighter or tinderbox can be used to start fires, despite neither of those things being on fire all the time (in the case of a lighter, which needs to be turned on) or at all (in the case of a flint and tinder, which produce sparks that can start a fire but no actual fire themselves). This would exemplify the difference between **formal** and **eminent** causation. A **formal** cause actually possesses the effect it produces, like a burning match actually being on fire as it sets other things on fire. **Eminent** causation, on the other hand, is when something merely has the power to produce an effect despite not actually having that effect itself, such as a tinderbox producing fire.[2] As Hugh Jidiette has asked, why wouldn't it be possible for God to be omnipotent and omniscient eminently rather than formally? Perhaps it is the case that He produces all the various powers we see in the universe, but does not actually exercise any of them in particular. And perhaps He produces intelligence in some way, but does not actually exercise any particular faculties of thought or conception Himself. Jidiette admits this may seem strange, perhaps even counter-intuitive, but the argument is not logically invalid. Given Feser's acceptance of eminent causality, he would have to explain why "Pure

---

[1] *TLS*, 67-68.
[2] Ibid.

Act" would have to be *literally* powerful and intelligent instead of merely being able to cause these things.[1] Considering the responses we gave him in the previous chapter—for instance, that unintelligent things like bees can apparently comprehend Forms and impose final causality on other things—I think we can agree with Jidiette that he'll need to work a little harder. And if that's so, we have an answer to how unintelligent particles can give rise to intelligent humans—the fundamental particles, in this view, would not possess intelligence formally, but they *would* have it eminently.

But even all this may be conceding too much to Feser, because the very ideas of "actuality" and "potentiality" as an account of change are dubious enough by themselves. There's one tremendously huge problem with the Aristotelian argument for God: You must first accept Aristotle's definition of change, and there seems to be absolutely no reason whatsoever to do so. It is true that only a fool (or a philosopher) would deny that change occurs, but there are a very wide variety of explanations for change that have nothing to do with "actuality" and "potentiality;" unless Feser can prove why every last one of those alternative accounts do not work, his preferred A-T argument for God is very far from binding or even especially convincing.[2]

Our friend the dictionary, for instance, says nothing at all about actuality and potentiality in its entry on change. Rather, change means "to become different" or "to undergo transformation, transition, or substitution."[3] Feser's favorite words do not appear once under any of

---

[1] Hugh Jidiette, "Edward Feser's Aristotelian Proof for God," *Hugh Jidiette*, January 9, 2018, last accessed at https://hughjidiette.wordpress.com/2018/01/09/edward-fesers-aristotelian-proof-for-god/ on July 5, 2020.

[2] Another blogger has extended on these points. See Jonathan Garner, "Five Proofs of the existence of God by Feser: Book Review," *Philosophy of Religion blog*, December 3, 2017, last accessed on July 5, 2020, https://jonathandavidgarner.wordpress.com/2017/12/03/five-proofs-of-the-existence-of-god-feser-book-review/

[3] "Change." Merriam-Webster.com. Accessed July 5, 2020. https://www.merriam-webster.com/dictionary/change.

the headings, at least not at the time of this writing. Feser, of course, might say the dictionary definition is (if not wrong) at least incomplete, and that *any* correct definition of change, regardless of the words used to describe it, can simply be boiled down to "the actualization of potentiality." But a closer look at alternative solutions to the problems Parmenides and Zeno posed can show this to be wrong.

Take, for instance, Zeno's caterpillar from Chapter 1. To paraphrase the mathematician Joseph Mazur, the caterpillar's task seems impossible because he "must perform an infinite number of tasks in a finite amount of time." Mr. Caterpillar must eat 50 leaves, but first must eat 25, and before that eat 12.5, and so on, ad infinitum. But is also true that "not all infinities are created equal." In mathematics, there are two types of infinite series—divergent and convergent. A divergent series is 1+2+3+4 and so on. That goes on to infinity. A convergent series, however, involves fractions rather than whole numbers, such as ½ + ¼ + 1/8 + 1/16 and so forth. Even if you were to extend this series infinitely, up to 1/128, 1/256, and so forth, the answer to it would eventually become 1. Thus, in our example, as long as our caterpillar is eating his leaves at a sufficiently fast rate, so that the fractions of leaves he is eating look something like 1/16th of a leaf plus 1/8th of a leaf plus 1/4th of a leaf, he will eat a whole leaf in a measurable amount of time, which would allow him to begin the process of change that Zeno said was impossible.[1]

My perceptive readers, of course, will note that this account is much different than Aristotle's and Feser's; both these men would say that Zeno "overlooks the difference between being-in-act and being-in-potency." They would say our caterpillar must indeed eat an infinite fraction of leaves between his first one and his fiftieth, but those fractions of leaves exist potentially rather than actually, so there is no

---

[1] Brian Palmer, "What is the Answer to Zeno's Paradox," *Slate*, March 5, 2014, last accessed on July 5, 2020,
http://www.slate.com/articles/health_and_science/science/2014/03/zeno_s_paradox_how_to_explain_the_solution_to_achilles_and_the_tortoise.html.

actually infinite number of leaves he must eat.¹ But Dr. Mazur has given an alternative solution based on the mathematical properties of certain kinds of infinite series. Mazur's theory does not seem to necessitate a "purely actual actualizer" or anything like that. So why should we prefer Feser's to his?

According to Feser in his most recent book, *Aristotle's Revenge*, Mazur's solution doesn't work because it relies on mathematics, and math is merely an abstraction—only the theory of actuality and potentiality explains how a convergent series can relate to concrete, material things. And even if such a connection could be made, the mathematics of convergent series would only "describe" how "an object really does get from A to B," but not "what it is about objective reality that could make it the case that an object gets from A to B."²

Curiously enough, it seems to me that *Aristotle himself* could provide an answer to that question. According to *Five Proofs*, Aristotle believed that mathematical truths didn't exist in a Platonic Realm apart from the physical world, but rather, they were entailed by the Forms/Essences/Natures of all things:

> It is also impossible for two men and two further men together to add up to twenty men, and necessary that they add up instead to four men. These truths are grounded in the natures not only of men but of every other thing too, and when the mind abstracts even more general mathematical features of things, it can deduce from them further mathematical truths.³

But if simple mathematical operations like addition or subtraction are grounded in the Nature of physical beings like humans (or leaves or the distance between points A and B or anything else Zeno might be confused about), so, too, can a more complex matter like convergent series. So when Feser asks us "what it is about concrete, objective reality

---

¹ *SM*, 33.
² *Aristotle's Revenge*, 206-208.
³ *FP*, 101-103.

itself" that enables change, we don't have to say "concrete reality includes potentialities and actualities."[1] We can instead say, "it is simply the Nature of these concrete real things (people, distances, whatever) that the infinite parts they're composed of add up to one finite sum."

Feser would probably respond by gloating about how an attempt to refute Aristotle still relies on Aristotle, and that, in any case, Aristotle's Natures, Forms, and Essences are themselves examples of actuality as distinct from potentiality. But it seems to me that the whole reason Aristotle came up with the act/potency distinction in the first place was that he didn't know any calculus, which would be invented centuries after his death. As implied throughout the previous chapters, we can be realists about Forms and Essences without believing everything Aristotle attached to them in terms of ethics. Why would the same not apply to certain parts of his metaphysics? Perhaps if someone traveled back in time to teach him calculus while he was responding to Zeno, Aristotle might have said, "Oh, we don't need potentiality and actuality at all to account for change! This would mean Form and Prime Matter aren't actually instances of 'actuality' and 'potency,' and I should modify my realist metaphysics!" Such an attempt would take too long to describe here (as I mentioned earlier, "prime matter" is a fairly abstruse concept better suited for analysis in a book of its own), but one can at least imagine him making the attempt, and perhaps meeting with success.

A similar alternative can also plausibly take care of Parmenides. Again, as we reviewed in chapter 1, Parmenides believed that change involved one thing becoming another thing, like a caterpillar becoming a butterfly. If the butterfly doesn't exist right now, at the moment it is nothing, and only when it emerges from the chrysalis built by its caterpillar forebear does it become something. But that would be a case of something coming from nothing, and that would be impossible, so Parmenides held that change itself is impossible. It seems to me

---

[1] *Aristotle's Revenge,* 207.

Parmenides was simply looking at the question in an entirely wrong-headed way. Why should we assume change involves something coming into existence rather than one *type* of existence transforming into another type? A caterpillar becoming a butterfly does not involve something entirely new simply popping into existence out of thin air. Rather, the elements that constitute the caterpillar rearrange themselves in such a way that they now express the attributes of a butterfly.

My explanation does not necessitate, or even mention, "actuality" and "potentiality." I am not saying the caterpillar has a "potential" to become a butterfly that is actualized by something else, I am merely stating the fact that its components can be rearranged in such a way that it can become a butterfly, rather than some "butterfly-ness" simply popping into existence. In this example, perhaps something else might be necessary to "actualize" the process or get it going (for the caterpillar, that would be eating leaves). However, since my theory does not define change as *only* the actualization of potential, but rather as rearrangements of components, it leaves the door open for many other kinds of processes that would not require any sort of fundamental being or "unactualized actualizer." For instance, if certain fundamental particles had Forms that entailed they would move around in certain patterns, all change in the universe could be accounted for in terms of the changing arrangements of those particles as they moved. Notably, this theory would not necessitate any "purely actual being" (i.e., God) either.

I just came up with this theory on the evening I was writing this chapter, but it seems like great minds really do think alike—what I have described is apparently the theory of "atomism" first formulated by thinkers like Anaxagoras and Democritus, who lived around the same time and place (ancient Greece) as Aristotle. Anaxagoras, like Aristotle, thought Parmenides was incorrect, but he accounted for change entirely in terms of varying mixtures of certain fundamental elements. As he is reported to have said, "The Greeks do not think correctly about coming-to-be and passing-away; for no thing comes to be or passes away, but is mixed together and dissociated from the things that are."[1] Unlike me, Anaxagoras also accounted for some of this activity by referring to a divine mind he called a *Nous*, but as Feser himself notes, the *Nous* is more similar to a deistic "watchmaker" type of God than an actively involved Unsustained Sustainer.[2]

Feser, as you can imagine, would still have problems with this. First, he claims that atomist theory would seem to deny the reality of Substantial Form (flip back to chapters 3 and 5 for a review of substance)—it implies that only the indivisible fundamental particles had Substantial Forms while everything else—trees, water, rocks, whatever—having merely accidental Forms, being mere relations between those fundamental particles.[3] Even if I, or my atomist friends, were to concede this, however, we would not have to concede that change was the "actualization of potency." We would simply say, "Well, when these particles enter into this arrangement—say, an oxygen and two hydrogen atoms coming together—that produces a change from the Substantial Forms of oxygen and hydrogen to the Substantial Form of water, rather than some 'potential' of the hydrogen and oxygen to become water being 'actualized.'" The change in question would rather be difference over time—a configuration of a certain number of particles at time A having such-and-such substantial form, and then at time B, that same group of particles having a different substantial Form due to being in a different configuration.[4]

---

[1] Patricia Curd and Richard D. McKirahan, *A Presocratics Reader (Second Edition): Selected Fragments and Testimonia* (Hackett Publishing, 2011), 103-104.
[2] Edward Feser, "Pre-Socratic Natural Theology," *Edward Feser* (blog), September 17, 2008, last accessed on July 5, 2020,
http://edwardfeser.blogspot.com/2008/09/pre-socratic-natural-theology.html
[3] *Aristotle's Revenge*, 30-31.
[4] Now, Feser would say that time itself is contingent upon the actualization of potency and therefore could not ground change—see *Aristotle's Revenge*, 233-269. But to address that would get us into the philosophy of time and involve issues such as A-theory versus B-theory, differences among A-theories, and even

Feser continues on to say that it is impossible for fundamental particles to exist in and of themselves. Since any particular particle has a particular size and shape as well as a particular location in space and time ("extended" is the technical term Feser uses), this implies that the particles possess potentiality—that is to say, a certain particle which is at location A could potentially wander off to location B, and so on. But as we have discussed earlier, only something that is "purely actual," with no potential whatsoever, could truly be immune from going out of existence eventually, and therefore so-called "fundamental" particles actually aren't.[1] I would say this is simply begging the question against the atomist. The whole point of our theory is to provide an alternative to actuality and potentiality; we therefore don't believe that whatever changes the fundamental particles might undergo indicate that they're "composites" of those two things because we reject the whole theory.

It does seem to me that there are good reasons to reject, or at least be suspicious of, Aristotle's act/potency theory anyways. When we take a closer look at some of Zeno's paradoxes, that theory starts looking less and less helpful. Let's review Zeno's Dichotomy Paradox: Movement is impossible because you have to traverse an infinite amount of smaller distances in a finite amount of time; the same applies to any other property (color, temperature, whatever) so *any* sort of change is impossible. Aristotle's theory of act and potency is supposed to have solved that because all the infinite subdivisions of that finite distance are only present potentially rather than actually, so while they do exist in a sense, "the *actual* distance that any movement would have to involve is finite, and the paradox disappears."[2]

Einstein's theory of relativity. That would require another chapter of its own! At the moment, I simply wish to prove that the atomist is not *immediately* inconsistent in acknowledging change while denying that it is the actualization of potency—the Aristotelian must first establish that his definition of time is the only one that works.
[1] *Aristotle's Revenge,* 31, 209-210.
[2] Ibid., 15.

The problem here is that the actualization of a potential—that is to say, the *process* of change, I'm not referring to the underlying stuff undergoing change, I'm talking about a verb rather than a noun, so to speak—itself falls prey to the issues the Dichotomy Paradox raises. This is a little harder to see when we're talking about change in the sense of moving from place to place, so let's go back to an example Feser used in *Five Proofs*: that of temperature. Rather than making coffee, let's say we're boiling water. Right now, the water is a lukewarm 40 degrees Celsius. We put it over a very hot flame that's over 100°C, and wait a few minutes for the water to get to 100°C as well. Feser would say that the water, which is actually 40°C, has the potential to be 100°C, and that potential is actualized by the flame, which is actually 100°C right now.

But wait a second. It's not as if the water instantly heats up to 100°C just by being close to the flame. It takes *time* to heat up, and more importantly, it does so *gradually*. The water goes from lukewarm to pretty hot (60°C), and then very hot (80°C) before reaching its boiling point. And those temperatures *themselves* are potentials that *also have to be actualized* before you can actualize the water's potential of being 100C. But that then necessitates the actualization of *even more* potentials! In other words, to actualize 40-degree water's potential to be 100 degrees, we must first actualize a potential that's halfway there, namely its potential to be 70 degrees. But to actualize *that* potential, we must actualize another one that's halfway there, namely the potential to be 55 degrees. And to actualize *that*, we must first actualize the water's potential to be 47.5 degrees. And so on, ad infinitum—the same applies to every other "actualization of potential," or any other change, whether in terms of motion (going from A to B requires you to actualize an infinite number of potential distances between the two points), or color (a yellow banana actualizing its potential to be entirely ripe and brown must first actualize its potential to be half-brown, a quarter-brown, and so on) or anything else.

Thus, I conclude that the division of being into act and potency doesn't actually (heh) do anything to solve the Dichotomy Paradox. In my boiling water example, it's no good to say that the 60 degrees, and by extension their infinite divisions, between the water's starting point of $40°$ and its end point of $100°$ are "merely potential," because each one of those degrees really does become *an actual part* of the process of change. The water is *actually*, not just potentially, $41°$, $42°$, $43°$, and so on at varying times in the process of being heated, and must therefore *actually* be the infinite points of temperature between its present state and its end state across the finite time it takes to reach that end state. Far from solving the Dichotomy Paradox, Aristotle only kicked it up a level, at least a far as I can tell.

But fine, let's leave all that aside. Maybe Feser has yet another pithy retort to all these reservations about Aristotle. Maybe Feser has a response to my point about the "actualization of potential" itself falling prey to the Dichotomy Paradox. Well, those aren't the only alternatives to and critiques of Aristotle out there. Looking at the ever-trustworthy *Stanford Encyclopedia of Philosophy*, Adolf Gruenbaum, Henri Bergson, and Alfred North Whitehead came up with their own solutions, but *Aristotle's Revenge* quotes only their criticisms of the purely mathematical solution.[1] Perhaps they are all wrong in some way, and perhaps Aristotle's response to Parmenides really is the only correct one. But for the reasons I have given above, it will take significantly more work than Feser has so far done, even in *Aristotle's Revenge*, to prove that Aristotle's metaphysics are the only game in town. And until that

---

[1] *Aristotle's Revenge,* 193, 263, 207, Huggett, Nick, "Zeno's Paradoxes", The Stanford Encyclopedia of Philosophy (Spring 2019 Edition), Edward N. Zalta (ed.), last accessed on July 5, 2020, URL =
https://plato.stanford.edu/archives/spr2019/entries/paradox-zeno/ Feser notes that Gruenbaum was unsatisfied with any mathematical solution that did not relate itself to the physical world, but it seems he himself believed there was a "correspondence between the physical and the mathematical continuum" that could be systematically analyzed. See Murray Code, *Order and Organism: Steps Toward a Whiteheadian Philosophy of Mathematics and the Natural Sciences* (SUNY Press, 1985), 55-57.

happens, the Aristotelian arguments for God's existence, and by extension those of the Thomists, remain more than a little suspect.

As we have seen, the very *metaphysical* foundations of Thomist thought in general seem more than a little suspect. Over the course of this chapter, we have explored the contradiction between the A-T thinker's response to Parmenides and his assertion of God's immutability: How can a changing world be contained in a Divine Mind that is supposed to be unchanging? That led us to look at the concepts of possible worlds, propositions, and final causality in general. A closer look at those subjects told us that possible worlds make it harder to tell if Feser's preferred religion is true, that God is not a sufficient "truth-maker" for some propositions, and the example of animals employing a sort of final causality makes it possible that God Himself might not be intelligent. We then turned to the famous Thomist distinction between Essence and existence, first noting how God could plausibly decree the two things remain conjoined rather than actively conjoining them forever as Thomists claimed, and subsequently examining how the Thomist conception of Essence raises serious epistemological problems. Finally, we took a good hard look at the most important doctrine Aristotle ever came up with (at least according to Feser): act and potency. We found out that even accepting Aristotle's idea, there are other candidates for "pure actuality" besides God, and in any case, the act/potency distinction isn't an entirely satisfying solution to the paradoxes of Zeno and Parmenides anyways, merely kicking the problems they raised up another level. Given all these issues with A-T philosophy, I hope, my dear readers, you have begun to suspect that Edward Feser's praise for this particular tradition might be somewhat excessive.

Even so, it is true that the Aristotelians and the Thomists deserve credit for one thing: They've endeavored to provide answers to the questions bedeviling philosophers for millennia, even if, as I hope I've shown, their answers are not very good. Sensitive readers might argue it is somewhat rude of me to spend so much time tearing down those who have made an effort without doing anything of my own. A fair charge, but one I believe I can easily meet. For the next and final chapter of this book, let's explore non-Thomist solutions to the philosophical quandaries discussed throughout all the reading we have done so far.

Chapter 7: Actual Alternatives

By this point, I hope I have managed to convince at least a few of you that the Aristotelian-Thomistic philosophical tradition does not actually solve any of the metaphysical or ethical quandaries it purports to. However, merely pointing that out is not enough. It would be in bad taste not to provide better alternatives, or at least equally good ones. The final chapter of this book will endeavor to do exactly that. Each of these alternatives will attempt to fulfill these three criteria:

1: They will offer an explanation of change that does not rely on "brute facts." The explanations I provide will also not contradict themselves; Feser will not be able to use the **method of retorsion** against them.

2: Starting from a realist position with regard to abstract objects, these alternatives will fulfill all 6 criteria the philosopher Greg Welty (whose work Feser enthusiastically recommends) has claimed are necessary for a comprehensive account of such things, along with one more from Feser:

A: Objectivity – Abstract objects must be mind-independent

B: Intentionality – These abstractions must be able to represent things

C: Simplicity – My alternatives must not posit any more entities than necessary (just a single being, no demiurges or mini-gods or anything)

D: Necessity – Under my alternatives, abstract objects must exist even if human minds did not

E: Plenitude – My alternatives must account for a sufficient number of abstract objects

F: Relevance – The alternatives must explain how immaterial abstract objects can affect our material world.[1]

G: Coordination – This is Feser's criterion not Welty's—to meet it, I must be able to explain how all abstract objects, as well as final causes, intersect and interact in harmony rather than self-destruction or chaos.[2]

3: Finally, my alternatives will explain how things can exist if there is any distinction between their Essences and their act of existence.

7.1: Deism

The most obvious alternative to classical theism, one we have touched upon several times previously, is Deism. Under a Deistic framework, an omniscient and omnipotent God exists, but He is separate from the universe aside from creating it and setting it into order, and does not actively interfere in human affairs. It is obviously incompatible with classical theism, both its religious variants (Christians, Muslims, and Jews all believe God interacted directly with human beings throughout history) and at a fundamental level (since classical theism holds God must actively maintain the existence of the entire material universe).[3]

But Feser's own Thomistic reasoning can also support Deism. It easily explains the existence of change: A Deist can say his distant, uninvolved God is Pure Actuality and purely simple (His Existence being the same as His Essence). This distant Unmoved Mover actualized the existence of the material world at the beginning of time, allowing for the elements created at the birth of the universe to interact and "actualize" the processes which gave rise to us, but He does not actualize them *constantly*, their behavior and their persistence in existence owing to a single decree instead of active participation. Thus, he can answer the paradox posed by Parmenides as easily as Aristotle. Things get a little

---

[1] *FP*, 107-111.
[2] *NSE*, 177.
[3] *FP*, 235-237.

more complicated when it comes to abstract objects, but not beyond a Deistic God's abilities. Such objects would of course be *objective* because they existed in the omniscient, human-independent mind of the Deist's God, and His omniscience would also satisfy Welty's *plenitude* condition, since He would know every kind of abstract object that exists. The objects would also be *necessary* because the Deistic God is necessary, *intentional* because His decrees would also obviously have intent behind them, and *simple* because the Deist is not positing any entity besides his distant God to explain them. Needless to say, we can also understand how all these Forms, along with the various forces in the natural world, can be coherently *coordinated* with each other because the distant Deistic God set them all up at the beginning of the universe.

Finally, in terms of *relevancy*, the Deistic God could simply decree that all of the Forms in His Divine Mind would appear within the material universe in all the particular ways they do. This approach would avoid the Platonic problem of how an inert Third Realm of abstract objects could affect the material world,[1] while still allowing for God to be entirely separate and aloof from the universe, since by decreeing that the objects in His mind be instantiated materially, it is not necessary for material things to be in contact with His mind constantly.

Now, Feser would say that this Deistic theism does not work because "nothing other than God possibly could exist even for an instant without God's conserving action…. To say that these things might exist without God after all would once again be like climbing a ladder and then blasting it out from under one."[2] But as described in the previous chapter, neither of these points is correct. The Deist would be perfectly happy to concede to Feser that there is a distinction between Essence and *existence*, both of which require God to put them together. However, he would say that the Deistic God simply decreed at the beginning of time that the material world's Essence should be conjoined

---

[1] *FP*, 107-109.
[2] *FP*, 235-237.

to its existence, rather than actively and constantly conjoining the two. As also previously described, this is in fact more keeping with the analogies Feser is so fond of, since the maker of a broom can leave or die and the broom's brush and handle will still remain together as long as its glue is good. And neither does the Deist undermine his own position, since he still agrees with Feser that a God was necessary *at the very beginning of things*. He will not fall into atheism, as an atheist would claim that God was never necessary *at any point*.

Deism also solves several of the problems with Thomism highlighted previously. Since the Deist's God does not directly interact with the world after setting it in motion, any given religious position is not necessarily true. Thus, there is no reason for Protestants and Catholics to kill each other over whether or not Jesus is present in the Eucharist literally or merely metaphorically, no reason for Muslims to fly planes into buildings, no reason for Jews to kill Arabs over some supposedly Holy land, and so on, and so forth.[1] On a philosophical level, a distant God is also compatible with the existence of evil—since He is not in constant contact with the world, He is not responsible for the existence of any particular evil. Similarly, this distance also solves several strange metaphysical issues Thomism causes. As described in the last chapter, if God is constantly conjoining existence and Essence, He must "conveniently" decide to sever the existence of things from their Essences whenever someone freely chooses to destroy something. If the existence of things is maintained by decree rather than constant conservational activity, freely chosen human decisions to destroy or create do not necessitate God Himself take or stop any action. Similarly, if God imparted Forms and other abstract objects to the material universe by decree rather than having material things participate in Forms contained in His Mind, it would not be necessary to posit a direct connection between that assumedly unchangeable Divine Mind and a

---

[1] Feser would, of course, point out that entirely Godless Communists racked up an impressive kill count without recourse to religion. But since, as described in chapter 4, the Commies were not quite as anti-Aristotelian as he would have us believe, such a retort is somewhat less cutting coming from him.

universe full of things constantly taking and shedding Forms (i.e., changing).

7.2: Lovecraftian-Aristotelian Realism

A stranger, but still coherent alternative to Thomism is what I call **Lovecraftian Theism**. This brand of theism is almost the same as Feser's. It holds that God is the ultimately simple and omniscient Purely Actual explanation for all things, fundamentally responsible for all the change in the universe, constantly conjoining the Essences of all material things to their existence, and holding all Forms and other abstract objects inside Its Divine Mind, organizing them in a sensible manner. However, Lovecraftian Theism holds that while God may have an intellect, It (to use the preferred Lovecraftian pronouns, for reasons we'll see shortly) does not have a will, meaning that It is not omnipotent in the same sense Feser's God is, and also more distantly Deistic in function than Feser would prefer.

To briefly explain Feser's reasoning, in the Thomistic view God must necessarily have free will for two reasons: First, God is intelligent, and since all intelligent things (beings capable of comprehending Forms, such as humans) have free wills, it follows that God has free will too. Second, recall from the previous chapters that God comprehends all Forms, possibilities, and abstract objects, including those that might have existed but do not in reality (such as unicorns and possible worlds). The only way to explain why some things actually do exist and others do not is that God chose to create the former and elected not to create the latter, which implies He has free will and can choose things of His own volition.[1]

Human experience, however, can show that Feser's inferences are not logically necessary, and that it is possible for an intelligent being to lack free will while still possessing the ability to grasp Forms and even

---

[1] *FP*, 223-225.

"choose" from among them.[1] We need only look at the mental activity involved in dreams, and particularly nightmares.

When someone is sleeping and suffers from a nightmare, it seems obvious that their mental faculties—their ability to grasp Forms—are still operational, but their exercise of free will has been suspended. Since dreams and nightmares are purely mental activities (they exist in dreamland, not out in the real world, of course), someone having a night terror about wolves or insects or tentacled monsters must comprehend (in some way) the Forms of wolves, insects, or the fictional creatures chasing her throughout her psyche. A completely unintelligent being, like a tree or an ant, would be unable to dream since it would not be able to hold those Forms in its mind while it slept. However, even though the Forms instantiated in a nightmare spring from the mind of their sleeper, that mind, while it sleeps, possesses no freedom to choose which of those Forms appears during the dream, or how they interact. If that were possible, the moment any of us started to dream of frightening monsters, we would only need to choose to dream about something else (like sheep or bunnies or other nicer Essences) to have a pleasant night. Since we cannot—we are forced to endure our night terrors until we wake up—the natural conclusion is that it is possible to have an intellect without having a free will.

Might it be possible that God (analogically) consists of just such an intellect? In order to satisfy Feser, the Divine Intellect must hold and order the Forms of everything in the universe, eternally and without undergoing change itself, and conjoin some of these Forms to *existence*, "actualizing their potentials," which produces *change*. But perhaps God does so unconsciously and without choosing to do so, in the same way one's subconscious psyche conjoins the Forms of monsters or axe

---

[1] Many Christian philosophers have made similar arguments, curiously enough. For a brief look at Protestant thinking on this subject, see Jonathan Pearce, "Does God Have Free Will? No.", *A Tippling Philosopher,* June 8, 2015, last accessed on July 5, 2020, https://www.patheos.com/blogs/tippling/2015/06/08/does-god-have-free-will-no/

murderers to existence within the context of a nightmare, even if our waking minds would choose not to do so (and would actually prefer not to). This would also explain things like the existence of evil, and solve the conundrum of how human beings can "force" God to conjoin or disassociate certain Essences from existence—It is not actually choosing among any of these alternatives, and all of us lower beings have lives of our own, so to speak, just like the phantasms in a nightmare have lives of their own that enable them to terrify and harass the dreamer that made them, regardless of what she would prefer.

This theory again satisfies Feser's other conditions. The Forms are *objective* because the mind of the Dreamer produces them. The Dreamer dreams of enough Essences to satisfy the *plenitude* condition, in the same way human dreamers conceive of enough Essences to keep themselves occupied at night. This explanation is *simple* because no other entities aside from the Dreamer are posited as explanations, and *necessary* because the Dreamer is a necessary Being—if It ever woke up (so to speak), we wouldn't be here. God makes the various Forms It dreams of *relevant* to each other the same way phantasms in our dreams interact with each other, and God's phantasms are obviously *intentional*, just like phantasms of centipedes, axe murderers, or other scary things represent fear and unease, even if an unfortunate person suffering from nightmares wishes they didn't.

Feser might point out some metaphysical problems with this position, but they can be dealt with. For instance, if God the Dreamer possesses no free will, why is it the case It dreams of certain things like horses and bluebirds and does not dream of others like unicorns and phoenixes? But the exact same question can be asked of human dreamers: Why do I have nightmares about centipedes and axe murderers when I could choose to dream about all the other things whose Forms I possess, like sheep or bunny rabbits? There seems to be something in my mind itself, lurking below my surface consciousness, that impels me to dream about those nasty Forms rather than anything else I might prefer. By the same token, there may be something about

God's Mind—we don't know what, exactly, and might never know for sure—impelling It to dream of the things It does rather than any other Forms that might exist.

If our universe is roughly analogous to a dream in God's mind, how can we explain its regularity, or the *coordination* of its Essences? After all, dreams and nightmares are well known for being very strange, capricious, and wacky. But on second thought, it is obvious that dreams are not entirely arbitrary. We can certainly dream of strange things indeed—worms the size of skyscrapers, talking cats, men with the heads of ravens, and so on—but we cannot dream of things that are logically impossible. No-one has ever had a nightmare about round squares or two and two making five. Thus, we can assume that whatever aspect of God's Mind (not a separate part of It, mind you) impels It to dream about existing things rather than non-existing ones also impels It to dream about sensible, well-ordered Essences that behave regularly rather than capriciously. Again, we may never know what, exactly, about God's mind necessitates that It dream in the particular ways It does, but then again, we never know exactly what about our minds necessitates we dream about the things we do. But if there is some intelligible reason behind our dreaming, there may well be one behind the Lovecraftian God's dreaming as well.[1]

Why would I call such an entity Lovecraft's God? As it turns out, the fellow from New England was well known for featuring similar beings in his numerous tales of terror. Indeed, the idea of utterly alien creatures who were not only far more powerful than man, not only utterly indifferent to his existence, but underlying the fabric of his reality as well, was what made Lovecraft's (hopefully) fictional cosmology so unspeakably dreadful. Many of Lovecraft's deities seem to operate in ways similar to my argument for a God lacking free will. In

---

[1] Benjamin Cain, "New Atheism and Edward Feser's Thomistic Gambit," *Rants Within The Undead God* (blog), February 3, 2015, http://rantswithintheundeadgod.blogspot.com/2015/02/new-atheism-and-edward-fesers-thomistic.html , last accessed on July 5, 2020.

Lovecraft's *The Haunter in the Dark,* for instance, Azathoth is described as a "blind idiot god," trapped in an endless stupor. The dread entity Cthulhu (the most well-known of Lovecraft's creations; his fictional universe is called the Cthulhu Mythos) supposedly lay "dead but dreaming" inside the submerged city of R'lyeh.[1] The idea of an unfathomably powerful being—the very Ground of All Being Itself—also being circumscribed in certain ways that seem befuddling to humans is an idea Lovecraft would find quite compelling. A mischievous philosopher could very well offer a slightly edited version of Lovecraft's most famous couplet as a rejoinder to Thomistic philosophy:

"That which changes not can eternal lie,

And with strange metaphysics even death may die."

7.3: Atheistic Atomism

While a Lovecraftian God might have an appeal for people who just really dislike the established monotheistic religions, postulating the existence of such a Dreamer might still seem like a cop-out. Most of the people reading this book (sympathetically, at least) are probably atheists. Even if I've managed to disprove Thomism, it might still be a little disappointing to see my alternatives so far are still vaguely religious. Worry not, as my next alternative to Thomistic metaphysics will in fact be an atheistic one. It does require more work to set its foundations than Deism and Lovecraftian Theism, but as we will see, the task is not impossible.

Let's review the Aristotelian argument for change. Change is when something that is potentially one way actually becomes that way, which can only happen through something else that is already actual in that

---

[1] As one of the pre-eminent contemporary scholars of Lovecraft's work has written, "the vast 'gods' and forces who ruled [Lovecraft's] universe (Azathoth, the 'nuclear chaos'; Nyarlathotep; Yog-Sothoth; Cthulhu) were designed as symbols for the eternal inscrutability of the boundless cosmos." S.T. Joshi, *Ramsey Campbell and Modern Horror Fiction* (Liverpool University Press, 2001), 23.

way. For instance, a cup of hot coffee that is potentially cold can change, or become actually cold, if it is cooled by a breeze that is actually cold itself. This also leads to the idea of a hierarchical series of changing things, where each actor depends on another here and now—again, the cup of hot coffee becoming cool depends on the cold breeze, and the coldness of the breeze depends on the air conditioner, which depends on electricity, which depends on atomic forces. Since all of these changing things are dependent, there must be one fundamental thing at the bottom of it all that they depend on, which is itself independent of everything else (if it weren't, it would be just another piece of the series rather than a true explanation for the series). Thus, Feser believes there is something "purely actual, an unchanged changer" which actualizes the potencies of the atomic forces so that electricity exists (which makes the air conditioner cool the breeze that cools the coffee) without having to be actualized itself, and this would be God.[1]

But is it possible the fundamental particles might collectively be a sort of unchanged changer, an eternal, "purely actual" actualizer that could carry out the metaphysical work required to avoid attributing the universe and everything in it to an inexplicable brute fact?

Feser would (of course) say no, but I believe I've addressed his objections in section 7 of the previous chapter. Let's quickly review those arguments, and then I'll build on them to provide a coherent metaphysical explanation of change and the persistence of the universe that does not rely on a conventionally divine foundation.

First, Feser has said that particles coming into and passing out of being mean they themselves are contingent, and therefore cannot be the eternal, non-contingent sustainers of contingent reality.[2] As I replied, since the second law of thermodynamics states that matter is neither created nor destroyed (merely shifted into different forms), that implies

---

[1] *FP*, 24-28.
[2] Ibid., 199-200.

that the fundamental particles themselves are not being created or destroyed, though of course the things they constitute are.

More directly, the "s" at the end of "particles" I've been using indicates why such things, in Feser's view, can't be purely actual. Since there are several different kinds of fundamental particles, they must be composed at least of metaphysical parts (even if they're not made of more fundamental particles) because they have characteristics that distinguish them in some way, and they must be "composites of act and potency" because all of them are actually at particular places in the universe at particular times in particular arrangements when they could conceivably be otherwise.[1] But as I replied, there are several reasons to think this is not true. As Feser has mentioned in *The Last Superstition*, simply because we can *imagine* something being different (i.e having a certain potentiality) does not mean it actually could be different or possess that potentiality.[2] Thus, it is possible that the various alternative locations or arrangements the fundamental particles seem to possess are merely products of our imagination, and in reality they could be nowhere else other than where they are, making them purely actual in that respect. By the same token, the apparent differences between them and the changes they seem to undergo might be illusions as well. God Himself seems to possess different, distinguishable characteristics (goodness, which is distinct from power, which is distinct from intelligence, and so on), but as Feser and other classical theists would tell us, those are all actually the same thing in God, and only appear to be different to us. God Himself appears to undergo change in the Bible (going from angry to pleased, undertaking certain actions within particular timeframes, and so on), but Feser would say that all this is change only from our perspective, and God Himself is not changing at all. Well, there's no reason the atomist couldn't play that game as well. The distinctions between the fundamental particles are merely apparent rather than genuine, as are the changes through space and time they

---

[1] *FP*, 20-40, *Aristotle's Revenge*, 31.
[2] *TLS*, 54.

seem to experience. This would also mean that there is no genuine (as opposed to apparent) distinction between the Forms of these fundamental particles and their existence, or their characteristics, or whatever. We might not understand how all this works at the moment, but perhaps we will as the progress of science (or the philosophy of science) marches on—unless Feser can see the future, he can't deny it's a possibility.

With all this established, we are now ready for an atheistic response to all the challenges Feser gives us in *Five Proofs*. The atheist can hold that the fundamental particles produced the universe and are responsible for all change in it, and also has an explanation that is not a "brute fact," accepts realism about Forms and other universals, and accounts for the existence of things separate from their Essences. The first and last criteria are easily addressed by the reasoning just provided in the preceding paragraphs: Since the fundamental particles are necessarily existing and not truly composites of actuality and potentiality, their Natures or Essences explain their existence—that is to say, they are not "brute facts" but necessary, self-explaining existences. By the same token, since these particles are not created or destroyed, they must have existed eternally and therefore there is no real distinction between their Essences and existence.

It's a little tougher for these little guys to account for universals like Forms, but still doable. In order to understand how, first consider the fact that certain kinds of Forms seem to entail or contain a selection of other Forms despite not necessarily being any one of those sub-Forms in particular. The Form of Triangularity, for instance, entails the Forms of Rightness (where one angle is 90 degrees), Acuteness (where all angles are less than 90 degrees), and Obtuseness (where one is greater than 90 degrees). This seems to simply be a necessary fact entailed by triangularity itself—even if all right, acute, or obtuse triangles were to go out of existence, the Form of Triangularity would entail that it was possible to create such things, despite triangularity itself being irreducible to any one of them. In other words, those sub-Forms seem to exist, in a sense, within the larger, over-arching Form of Triangularity.

Perhaps it is possible that the Forms and other Universals we experience in our daily lives are contained by, entailed by, or exist within the Forms of the fundamental particles in a similar way as Obtuseness, Acuteness, and Rightness are contained by triangularity. This would handily solve Welty's questions of *objectivity* and *necessity*, since if the Universals are grounded in indestructible, eternal fundamental particles, they would be necessary in the same sense and objective in persisting even in the absence of human minds. They also fulfill the criteria of *plenitude*—if triangularity can account for all the different varieties of triangle that could exist, no more and no less, perhaps the Forms of the fundamental particles (a subject far tougher to grasp than the Forms involved in simple geometry) could also account for the Forms of everything that is and could be composed of them (which also handily explains what grounds imaginary creatures and possible worlds). Those Forms would also be *coordinated* for that reason: Just as triangularity can encompass Rightness, Obtuseness, and Acuteness, but also coordinates those Forms in the sense that Triangularity also entails any individual triangle can be right, acute, or obtuse but not all three simultaneously, perhaps the nearly-infinite sub-Forms entailed by the Forms of the particles are coordinated and controlled in the same necessary fashion, so that (for example) the Form of Heat entailed by the interaction of certain particles is also kept by those particles from burning up everything chaotically.

Simplicity, intentionality, and relevance might be the most difficult to account for under this brand of materialism, but again, the challenge is steep but not impossible. It's hard to see how a collection of different particles could be entirely simple, but then again, it's also hard to see how a God with distinguishable characteristics (goodness, intelligence, and so on) who is also a Father, a Son, and a Holy Spirit could be simple. If Feser would say that God's goodness and intelligence are actually the same thing, or that we just can't yet figure out how a

Father, Son, and Spirit can be different things yet the same utterly simple Being, the atheist can say that the fundamental particles are just aspects of some single, simple underlying reality. Now, how could such mindless, material things account for intentionality and relevance? Well, flip back to section 6.4—recall that mindless (and entirely material, in Feser's view) bees and birds can exhibit intentional behavior that makes certain Forms relevant to the outside world. Again, there is no hexagonal structure in the tiny brain of a bee, but these little creatures are quite capable of imparting that Form to wax, which is not inherently hexagonal either. So perhaps the fundamental particles impart intentionality and relevance to the plenitude of Forms they contain, despite not being sentient or immaterial.[1]

Feser might not like this explanation, but perhaps he'd say my atheist readers wouldn't like it, either. As mentioned in Five Proofs:

> If the universe really were a self-explanatory, uncaused, necessary being, then it would have distinctively divine attributes. The resulting view would be pantheism, not atheism. The objection would not show that God does not exist, but rather that God does exist and is identical with the world. Many Hindus would happily accept this.[2]

Now, in this case it would be the fundamental particles rather than the universe itself that has these attributes, but the point applies to them as well: If I'm claiming that the particles are self-explanatory, eternal, responsible for all the Forms we encounter, and so on, haven't I just turned those particles into a God of sorts? I don't think so, and I suspect most atheists wouldn't think so either. Remember, according to Jews, Christians, and Muslims, God is not just necessary, self-explanatory, and uncaused, but also possesses will, intelligence, and goodness. I can't

---

[1] These particles could still *account* for sentience, by the by. Return to section 6.7 and re-read the quotations from Hugh Jidiette's blog: It might be the case that the fundamental particles possess sentience eminently, in the sense of being able to produce reason and rationality (or creatures that possess reason and rationality), even if they cannot reason themselves.
[2] *FP*, 262.

speak for Hindus, but they apparently believe in a whole raft of gods like Rama, Shiva, and so on. The attentive reader will notice that nothing in the description of fundamental particles I have given above necessitates them having any of those attributes, or giving rise to any multi-armed blue dudes. These particles are not sentient or aware, even though they can impart relevance and intentionality to certain Forms (as bees can with hexagonality or birds can with the Forms of their nests). They certainly don't demand worship. Given that most atheists claim not to believe in a deity that possesses intelligence, will, and desires pertaining to ceremony and worship, I doubt many would complain a whole lot about certain particles being eternal and indestructible but not much more than that.

A mindless universe (or most of the other alternatives discussed, such as a universe held in the mind of a dreaming God) would be metaphysically satisfying, as I hope I have proved. But perhaps Feser would say it's still missing something—namely, a solid foundation for ethics. "Even if we can explain abstract objects under non-Aristotelian frameworks," he might say, "then we'd lose any basis for morality!"

That would be a very troubling prospect, but fortunately, I don't think it's true. We have already seen from our discussion of Philippa Foot's work that an atheistic but still broadly Aristotelian ethics is quite plausible. Even that would be conceding too much to Feser, though. While an extended discussion of alternatives to Aristotle in the ethical realm would be out of the scope of this book, it should suffice to note that Feser's criticisms of utilitarianism, social contractarianism, and other non-Aristotelian moralities are not exactly ironclad. J.S. Mill, one of the nineteenth-century founders of the utilitarian tradition, addressed Feser's concerns about the objectivity of happiness in a letter to a contemporary, Adam Sedgwick.[1] Recent scholarship has found that the original social contractarian, Thomas Hobbes, believed civil society

---

[1] Henry R. West, "Mill and utilitarianism in the mid-nineteenth century," in Ben Eggleston and Dale E. Miller, eds., *The Cambridge Companion to Utilitarianism* (Cambridge University Press, 2014), 64-65.

itself provided an objective basis for morality, despite his loathing of Aristotle and Aristotelian metaphysics.[1] And that's not even going into debates between error theorists, moral skeptics, and (Nietzschean) nihilists, among many others! In the end, then, one just might conclude that "abandoning the classical tradition" might not have been such a terrible mistake after all. At the very least, Feser would have to do much more work to prove that we are entirely helpless in philosophical matters without the Stagirite's guidance.

---

[1] As David Boucher and Paul Kelly state, Hobbes believed "civil society unites otherwise morally unrelated individuals," in contrast to other thinkers for whom a "universal moral community of humankind [really constrains] the activities of states." See their edited collection, *The Social Contract from Hobbes to Rawls* (Routledge, 1994), 14, and Murray Forsyth's essay in that volume ("Hobbes's Contractarianism: a comparative analysis"), 35-51.

Conclusion

Edward Feser, to his credit, rarely minces words. At the conclusion of *The Last Superstition*, he succinctly lays out precisely what he believes he has accomplished:

> This book has, I think, established, (a) when rightly understood, the traditional arguments for an Aristotelian metaphysical picture of the world are powerful, (b) the modern philosophers criticisms' of that picture are no good and their own attempted replacements of it are fraught with various paradoxes and incoherencies, and (c) modern science is not only not inconsistent with that metaphysical picture but at least to some extent tends to point in its direction… By the time Aquinas and the other Scholastics were done refining and drawing out the implications of the Aristotelian system, it was evident it entailed nothing less than the entire conception of God enshrined in classical monotheism, the immortality of the soul, and the natural law system of morality.[1]

I think this is fair to say that this reflects Feser's thoughts on not only one of his books but most of what he has written. Though he is considerably less polemic in *Aquinas: A Beginner's Guide, Philosophy of Mind, Five Proofs for the Existence of God, Neo-Scholastic Essays, Scholastic Metaphysics,* and *Aristotle's Revenge*, all of those books spend a great deal of time defending traditional Aristotelian metaphysics against a wide variety of modern philosophers, scientists, and other thinkers. And while Feser has not written a full monograph specifically on Christianity or morality, very many of his essays, some in *Neo-Scholastic Essays*, most on his blog, are defenses of Catholicism and traditional Catholic morality (both sexual and otherwise), along with explanations of how those things constitute the fulfillment of the tradition began by Aristotle. If the defense of that tradition is the project

---

[1] *TLS*, 266.

to which Feser has devoted over fourteen years of hard work (since his first book was published in 2006), we can certainly applaud his persistence. However, I believe the book you are reading now has proven that, despite his best efforts, Feser was not successful.

I would not go so far as to say he has entirely failed. Given my lack of professional training in philosophy, it would be prudent to leave that judgment to the real experts. I would merely hazard that Feser has not come as close as he believes he has to the goals he laid out at the end of *The Last Superstition*.

Does the "Aristotelian system" really entail the "conception of God" Feser believes in? Just the opposite. Even if one believes in the *logical* elements of Aristotelian thought—the distinction between act and potency, the reality of Essences and final causes, and so on (and, remember, a nominalist or similar case completely eliminates such a distinction)—that offers no help in judging the historical, *inductive* claims of any religion. And given the notorious difficulty of claiming an immaterial, unchanging Purely Actual Being was somehow Incarnated into a material man who actually lived, actually died, and actually came back to life, the Aristotelian system would seem to prefer a very different conception of God than Feser's.

Does such a system entail a "natural law" system of morality? Perhaps not, or at the very least, not Feser's vision of a moral system. Is Catholicism the fulfillment of our moral duties? It's impossible to tell, given the aforementioned impossibility of proving a historically (that is to say, inductively) grounded religion to be absolutely, deductively true. Are masturbation, homosexuality, and contraception immoral? Even if we accept Aristotelian final causality, Feser has not shown that any of those things actually "frustrate" it in the specific, technical, and *philosophical* sense he claims. Does the "sexual act [point] beyond itself to marriage and family?"[1] Given the facts of human biology, we are more likely "directed towards" polygamy. Is abortion always murder? *Aristotle*

---

[1] Ibid, 267.

himself would not say so, and if we accept an *Aristotelian* view of sexuality as directed towards the higher metaphysical purpose of preserving the species, we shouldn't either. Is "natural law morality" even incompatible with various forms of murderous totalitarianism? That would come as a surprise to Russian Communists and American slaveholders, and to German Nazis as well, at least with regard to Plato.

Are the "traditional arguments" for Aristotelian metaphysics even that powerful on their own? One does not have to believe, or even defend, nominalism, conceptualism, or other forms of anti-realism to doubt that. How do we discern what Forms the things we encounter actually instantiate? What makes the definition of the word "good" as meaning "instantiating a Form" anything more than a bare assertion? Even if we accept that, why should instantiating the Form of a Rational Animal mean worshipping God as opposed to prospering materially through the use of rationality? And how well do Aristotle's original metaphysical arguments even hold up, anyways? If we can't deny that change exists, why are we obligated to believe it necessitates God as a "purely actual" unmoved mover? Feser's own words from the early parts of *The Last Superstition* undercut his arguments for the universe or the fundamental particles being anything other than purely actual.

It may be that modern philosophy is ridden with incoherencies and contradictions. But I hope this book has illustrated that the Aristotelian-Thomistic tradition suffers from the same problems, and that Feser has not warded off the many criticisms modern *and* ancient philosophers have leveled at the Stagirite. If there is no objective reason to accept the Aristotelian's definition of goodness, Hume's fact-value distinction remains in full force. If human beings will never be able to access the knowledge of God in this life, God's judgements of good and evil will always be as mysterious and arbitrary as Euthyphro claimed they are. Our lack of divine knowledge means that God could very well order us to torture babies for fun or hate Him, just as Ockham claimed. And Aristotle's vaunted act/potency solution to the paradoxes of Parmenides and Zeno isn't even that much to write home about if you really think about it. Maybe Joseph Mazur's calculus-based solution a is better one, albeit based on the Aristotelian Forms of the concrete things of our experience. And in any case, isn't the actualization of potency itself an infinite gradient that (as Zeno said) requires explanation?

Those are a small selection of the questions this book has hopefully raised in the minds of both supporters and opponents of the "natural law tradition." But I would go so far as to raise one more, perhaps the most important one of all: If the natural law tradition (and all the things it's associated with—monotheism generally and Catholicism specifically, "conservative" sexual morality, and so on) hasn't actually scored a knockout blow on its competitors, why should the rest of us take it all that seriously?

Such a question could have been asked by Thomas Aquinas himself. The very first pages of the *Summa Theologica* open with this discussion: "On the nature and extent of sacred doctrine," which is divided into several questions, the first two of which are, "Is it necessary?" and "Is it a science?" Aquinas concluded that the answer to both was yes—that "It was necessary for man's salvation that there should be a knowledge revealed by God besides philosophical science built up by human reason...because man is directed to God" and that "sacred doctrine is a science because it proceeds from principles established by the light of a higher science, namely, the science of God and the blessed."[1]

Aquinas spent much of the rest of that great work, along with much of his career, trying to prove that there was indeed a God and that we are indeed "directed" to worship Him, upon pain of irrationality. Centuries later, Edward Feser has embarked upon the same task, refining and enhancing many of the arguments Aquinas made. To refute Feser might not entirely do the same for Aquinas, or even the entire

---

[1] Thomas Aquinas, *Summa Theologiae*, first part, question 1, *NewAdvent.org*, 2017, last accessed on July 5, 2020,
http://www.newadvent.org/summa/1001.htm#article1

natural law tradition he represents. Aquinas alone wrote so much that refuting just one of his students would not be enough to demolish absolutely everything he stood for, and Feser himself would admit that the work of other modern-day Thomists, such as David Oderberg, provide even stronger defenses of the Angelic Doctor.

However, if this book has managed to cast at least some doubt on Feser's arguments, it has taught the reader that Aquinas, however great a philosopher he may have been, might have been wrong about both the existence and the necessity of God, and by extension many of his ethical positions. And if he was wrong, we can at least raise the possibility that the answer to his very first question was actually "no." The study of sacred doctrine might perhaps be a science. But if, as I hope this book has helped you understand, the actual existence of a personal God and an associated "law" based on Aristotelian essentialism, is not an absolute necessity, then such a study might just be an unnecessary science.

References

"Green," Dictionary.com, 2019, https://www.dictionary.com/browse/green (Accessed on July 5, 2020)

"Bat," *The Merriam-Webster.com Dictionary*, Merriam-Webster Inc., https://www.merriam-webster.com/dictionary/bat (Accessed on July 5, 2020)

"Change," *The Merriam-Webster.com Dictionary*, Merriam-Webster Inc., https://www.merriam-webster.com/dictionary/change (Accessed on July 5, 2020)

"Good," *The Merriam-Webster.com Dictionary*, Merriam-Webster Inc., https://www.merriam-webster.com/dictionary/good (Accessed on July 5, 2020)

"Human," *The Merriam-Webster.com Dictionary*, Merriam-Webster Inc., https://www.merriam-webster.com/dictionary/human (Accessed 8 December 2019)

"Mormons, Polytheism, and the Nicene Creed," *Fairmormon*, https://www.fairmormon.org/answers/Mormonism_and_the_nature_of_God/Polytheism#Question:_Are_Mormons_polytheists_because_they_don.27t_accept_the_Nicene_Creed.3F (Accessed on July 5, 2020)

"Round," Dictionary.com, 2019, https://www.dictionary.com/browse/round (Accessed on July 5, 2020)

"Thoughts on Slavery, by a Southern," *The Southern Literary Messenger*, Vol. IV, No. 12, Richmond, VA, Dec. 1838

Adams, Jimi and Light, Ryan (2015), "Scientific Consensus, the law, and same sex parenting outcomes," *Social Science Research*, vol. 53, September 2015, pp. 300-310, https://www.sciencedirect.com/science/article/pii/S0049089X1 5001209 (Accessed on July 5, 2020)

American Foundation for Suicide Prevention (2020), "Suicide Statistics," 2020, https://afsp.org/about-suicide/suicide-statistics/ (Accessed on July 5, 2020)

Alex SL (2015), "Euthyphro," *Phylobotanist*, March 12, 2015, http://phylobotanist.blogspot.com/2015/03/euthyphro.html (Accessed on July 5, 2020)

Ali, Abdullah Yusuf, trans. (2000), *The Holy Qu'ran*, Wordsworth Editions Limited

Alston, Richard, Hall, Edith, and McConnell, Justine, eds. (2011), *Ancient Slavery and Abolition,* Oxford University Press

Angra Mainyu (2018), "An Aristotelian Argument: A Reply To Edward Feser," *Angra Mainyu's Blog*, February 27, 2018, http://angramainyusblog.blogspot.com/2018/02/an-aristotelian-argument-reply-to.html (Accessed on July 5, 2020)

Aquinas, Thomas (2017), *Summa Theologiae*, NewAdvent.org, 2017, http://www.newadvent.org/summa/4043.htm (Accessed on July 5, 2020)

Arensb (2016), "The Last Superstition: Hedonism Killed Aquinas," *Epsilon Clue*, November 21, 2016, https://epsilonclue.wordpress.com/2016/11/21/the-last-superstition-hedonism-killed-aquinas/ (Accessed on July 5, 2020)

Arensb (2016), "The Last Superstition: The Unmoved Mover," *Epsilon Clue*, October 28, 2016, https://epsilonclue.wordpress.com/2016/10/28/the-last-superstition-the-unmoved-mover/ (Accessed on July 5, 2020)

Aristotle, *Politics*, trans. Baker, Ernest (1995), Oxford University Press

Arithmoquine (2012), "Universals and an Argument for the Existence of God: More on Edward Feser's The Last Superstition an Unpublishable Review, part 2," *The Unpublishable Philosopher*, July 27, 2012, http://currentlogic.blogspot.com/2012/07/universals-and-argument-for-existence.html (Accessed on July 5, 2020)

Augustine (1961), *Confessions*, (trans. R.S. Pine-Coffin), Penguin Books

Barron, Robert (2018), "An Evening with William Lane Craig," *Catholic World Report*, January 23, 2018, https://www.catholicworldreport.com/2018/01/23/an-evening-with-william-lane-craig/ (Accessed on July 5, 2020)

Beevor, Anthony (2012), *The Second World War*, Little, Brown, and Company

Besong, Brian and Furqua, Jonathan (2019), *Faith and Reason: Philosophers Explain Their Turn to Catholicism*, Ignatius Press

Bodeus, Richard and Garret, Jan, trans. (1992), *Aristotle and the Theology of Living Immortals*, State University of New York Press

Boucher, David and Kelly, Paul (1994), *The Social Contract from Hobbes to Rawls*, Routledge

Bourget, David and Chalmers, David J (2014), "What do philosophers believe?", *Philosophical Studies* 170 (3):465-500 (2014), https://philpapers.org/surveys/results.pl (Accessed on July 5, 2020)

Boyden, Aaron (2011), "Feser Chapter 5," *Neurath's Boat*, October 21, 2011, http://protagoras.typepad.com/adrift_on_neuraths_boat/2011/10/feser-chapter-5.html, archived at https://archive.is/4nOr6 (Accessed on July 5, 2020)

Bradley, Gerard V. and George, Robert P. (1995), "Marriage and the Liberal Imagination," *Journal Articles*, Paper 878, http://scholarship.law.nd.edu/law_faculty_scholarship/878 (Accessed on July 5, 2020)

Brakke, David (1995), "The Problematization of Nocturnal Emissions in Early Christian Syria, Egypt, and Gaul," *Journal of Early Christian Studies* (vol. 3, no. 4, 1995), 419-460

Brennan, Dan (2017), "Wet Dream FAQ," *WebMD*, December 5, 2017, https://teens.webmd.com/boys/wet-dream-faq#1 (Accessed on July 5, 2020)

Buss, David M., ed. (2015), *The Handbook of Evolutionary Psychology, Volume I: Foundations*, Wiley

Cain, Benjamin (2015), "New Atheism and Edward Feser's Thomistic Gambit," *Rants Within The Undead God* (blog), February 3, 2015, http://rantswithintheundeadgod.blogspot.com/2015/02/new-atheism-and-edward-fesers-thomistic.html (Accessed on July 5, 2020)

Callinicos, Alex (2012), *The Revolutionary Ideas of Karl Marx*, Haymarket Books

Carrier, Richard (2016), "No, Hitler Wasn't a Pantheist," *Richard Carrier Blogs*, December 16, 2016, https://www.richardcarrier.info/archives/13752 (Accessed on July 5, 2020)

Carrier, Richard (2018), "Feser's Five Proofs for God: Debunked!" *Richard Carrier Blogs*, February 20, 2018, https://www.richardcarrier.info/archives/13752 (Accessed on July 5, 2020)

Celsus and Hoffman, R. Joseph trans. (1987), *On the True Doctrine: A Discourse against the Christians*, Oxford University Press

Chapoutot, Johann (2016), *Greeks, Romans, Germans: How the Nazis Usurped Europe's Classical Past*, University of California Press

Chastek, James (2015), "Analogous to the Vestigial," Just Thomism, https://thomism.wordpress.com/2015/04/16/analogous-to-the-vestigial/ (Accessed on July 5, 2020)

CNN.com Law Center, "Attorney: Woman Thought God Told Her to Kill Sons," *CNN.com*, March 30, 2004, http://www.cnn.com/2004/LAW/03/29/children.slain/index.html (Accessed on July 5, 2020)

Code, Murray (1985), *Order and Organism: Steps Toward a Whiteheadian Philosophy of Mathematics and the Natural Sciences*, SUNY Press

Coontz, Stephanie (2006), *Marriage, a History: How Love Conquered Marriage*, Penguin Books

Craig, William Lane (2008), *Reasonable Faith: Christian Truth and Apologetics, Third Edition*, Crossway Books

Cueno, Michael W. (1999), *The Smoke of Satan: Conservative and Traditionalist Dissent in Contemporary American Catholicism*, Johns Hopkins Press

Curd Patricia and McKirahan, Richard D., eds. (2011), *A Presocratics Reader (Second Edition): Selected Fragments and Testimonia*, Hackett Publishing

Dabney, Robert Lewis (1867), *A Defence of Virginia: And Through Her, of the South, in Recent and Pending Contests Against the Sectional Party*, New York: E.J. Hale and Co

Dabney, Robert Lewis (1982), *Discussions of Robert Lewis Dabney, Volume III*, Southampton, Great Britain: Banner of Truth Trust

Davis, David Brion (2006), *Inhuman Bondage: The Rise and Fall of Slavery in the New World* (Oxford University Press, 2006)

Dobbs, Darrell (1985), "Aristotle's Anticommunism," *American Journal of Political Science*, Vol. 29, No. 1 (February 1985), pp. 29-46.

Dowd, Maureen (1991), "The Supreme Court: Conservative Black Judge, Clarence Thomas, Is Named to Marshall's Court Seat," *The New York Times*, July 2, 1991, https://www.nytimes.com/1991/07/02/us/supreme-court-conservative-black-judge-clarence-thomas-named-marshall-s-court.html (Accessed on July 5, 2020)

Eggleston, Ben and Miller, Dale E., eds. (2014), *The Cambridge Companion to Utilitarianism*, Cambridge University Press

El-Zein, Amira (2009), *Islam, Arabs, and the World of the Jinn*, Syracuse University Press

Evans, Richard (2000), *In Defense of History*, W.W. Norton and Co., 2000

Feser, Edward (2005), *Philosophy of Mind*, Oneworld Publications

Feser, Edward (2006), "Reply to Sullivan on natural law," *Right Reason*, October 31, 2006, accessed via the Wayback Machine on July 7, 2019, http://web.archive.org/web/20071014120434/http:/rightreason.ektopos.com/archives/2006/10/reply_to_sulliv.html#comment-29349 (Accessed on July 5, 2020)

Feser, Edward (2007), *Locke*, Oneworld Publications

Feser, Edward (2008), "Pre-Socratic Natural Theology," *Edward Feser (blog)*, September 17, 2008, http://edwardfeser.blogspot.com/2008/09/pre-socratic-natural-theology.html (Accessed on July 5, 2020)

Feser, Edward (2008), "Why Allow Abortion but Not 'Same-Sex Marriage?'" November 6, 2008, https://edwardfeser.blogspot.com/2008/11/why-allow-abortion-but-not-same-sex.html (Accessed on July 5, 2020)

Feser, Edward (2008), *The Last Superstition: A Refutation of the New Atheism*, South Bend, Indiana: St. Augustine's Press

Feser, Edward (2009), "Act and Potency," *Edward Feser (blog)*, May 7, 2009, http://edwardfeser.blogspot.com/2009/05/act-and-potency.html (Accessed on July 5, 2020)

Feser, Edward (2009), "Trinity Sunday," *Edward Feser (blog)*, June 7, 2009, http://edwardfeser.blogspot.com/2009/06/trinity-sunday.html (Accessed on July 5, 2020)

Feser, Edward (2009), "Trinity Sunday", *Edward Feser (blog)*, June 7, 2009, http://edwardfeser.blogspot.com/2009/06/trinity-sunday.html (Accessed on July 5, 2020)

Feser, Edward (2009), "Walters on TLS," Edward Feser (blog), January 14, 2009, http://edwardfeser.blogspot.com/2009/01/walters-on-tls.html (Accessed on July 5, 2020)

Feser, Edward (2009), *Aquinas: A Beginner's Guide*, Oneworld Publications

Feser, Edward (2010), "God, Obligation, and the Euthyphro Dilemma," *Edward Feser (blog)*, October 26, 2010 http://edwardfeser.blogspot.com/2010/10/god-obligation-and-euthyphro-dilemma.html (Accessed on July 5, 2020)

Feser, Edward (2010), "Happy Consequentialism Day!" *Edward Feser (blog)*, August 9, 2010, http://edwardfeser.blogspot.com/2010/08/happy-consequentialism-day.html (Accessed on July 5, 2020)

Feser, Edward (2010), "Pop Culture and the Lure of Platonism", *Edward Feser (blog)*, September 6, 2010,

Feser, Edward (2010), "Pop Culture and the Lure of Platonism," *Edward Feser* (blog), September ??, 2010, https://edwardfeser.blogspot.com/2010/09/pop-culture-and-lure-of-platonism.html (Accessed on July 5, 2020)

Feser, Edward (2010), "Trinity and Mystery," *Edward Feser* (blog), February 10, 2010, http://edwardfeser.blogspot.com/2010/02/trinity-and-mystery.html (Accessed on July 5, 2020)

Feser, Edward (2011), "Does Morality Depend on God? (Updated)," *Edward Feser* (blog), July 19, 2011, http://edwardfeser.blogspot.com/2011/07/does-morality-depend-on-god.html (Accessed on July 5, 2020)

Feser, Edward (2011), "Reading Rosenberg Part III," *Edward Feser* (blog), November 10, 2011, http://edwardfeser.blogspot.com/2011/11/reading-rosenberg-part-iii.html (Accessed on July 5, 2020)

Feser, Edward (2013), "Oerter on Inertial Motion and Angels," *Edward Feser (blog)*, January 7, 2013, https://edwardfeser.blogspot.com/2013/01/oerter-on-inertial-motion-and-angels.html, archived at http://archive.is/6diAL on February 24, 2019 (Accessed on July 5, 2020)

Feser, Edward (2013), "Oerter on Inertial Motion and Angels," *Edward Feser (blog)*, January 7, 2013, http://edwardfeser.blogspot.com/2013/01/oerter-on-inertial-motion-and-angels.html (Accessed on July 5, 2020)

Feser, Edward (2013), "Schliesser on the Evolutionary Argument Against Naturalism," *Edward Feser* (blog), January 21, 2013, http://edwardfeser.blogspot.com/2013/01/schliesser-on-evolutionary-argument.html (Accessed on July 5, 2020)

Feser, Edward (2014), "Pre-Christian Apologetics," *Edward Feser (blog)*, May 16, 2014, http://edwardfeser.blogspot.com/2014/05/pre-christian-apologetics.html (Accessed on July 5, 2020)

Feser, Edward (2014), "Signature in the Cell," *Edward Feser (blog)*, July 26, 2014, http://edwardfeser.blogspot.com/2014/07/signature-in-cell.html, archived at http://archive.is/bXg76 on February 15, 2018 (Accessed on July 5, 2020)

Feser, Edward (2014), *Scholastic Metaphysics*, Scholastic Editions - Editiones Scholasticae

Feser, Edward (2015), "Christians, Muslims, and the reference of 'God'," *Edward Feser (blog)*, December 28, 2015, http://edwardfeser.blogspot.com/2015/12/christians-muslims-and-reference-of-god.html (Accessed on July 5, 2020)

Feser, Edward (2015), "Christians, Muslims, and the Reference of God," *Edward Feser (blog)*, December 28, 2015, http://edwardfeser.blogspot.com/2015/12/christians-muslims-and-reference-of-god.html (Accessed on July 5, 2020)

Feser, Edward (2015), "Feyerabend on Empiricism and Sola Scripture," *Edward Feser (blog)*, July 13, 2015, http://edwardfeser.blogspot.com/2015/07/feyerabend-on-empiricism-and-sola.html Accessed on July 5, 2020

Feser, Edward (2015), "Should a Catholic vote for Ben Carson?" *Edward Feser (blog)*, December 11, 2015, http://edwardfeser.blogspot.com/2015/12/should-catholic-vote-for-ben-carson.html (Accessed on July 5, 2020)

Feser, Edward (2015), *Neo-Scholastic Essays*, St. Augustine's Press

Feser, Edward (2016), "Canine Theology," *Edward Feser (blog)*, January 3, 2016, http://edwardfeser.blogspot.com/2016/01/canine-theology.html (Accessed on July 5, 2020), archived at http://archive.is/eIOmJ on February 20, 2018.

Feser, Edward (2016), "Craig on Divine Simplicity and Theistic Personalism," *Edward Feser (blog)*, April 15, 2016, http://edwardfeser.blogspot.com/2016/04/craig-on-divine-simplicity-and-theistic.html (Accessed on July 5, 2020)

Feser, Edward (2016), "How to Go to Hell," *Edward Feser* (blog), October 29, 2016, http://edwardfeser.blogspot.com/2016/10/how-to-go-to-hell_29.html (Accessed on July 5, 2020)

Feser, Edward (2016), "Is Ancient Philosophy Still Relevant? Rediscovering Aristotle, Aquinas, and Classical Theism: an interview with Edward Feser," *The Dartmouth Apologia*, Spring 2016, http://augustinecollective.org/rediscovering-aristotle-aquinas-and/ (Accessed on July 5, 2020)

Feser, Edward (2016), "Mind-Body Interaction: What's the Problem?" *Edward Feser (blog)*, September 17, 2016, http://edwardfeser.blogspot.co.uk/2016/09/mind-body-interaction-whats-problem.html (Accessed on July 5, 2020)

Feser, Edward (2017), "Cartesian Angelism," *Edward Feser (blog)*, July 29, 2017, http://edwardfeser.blogspot.com/2017/07/cartesian-angelism.html, archived at http://archive.is/vE3Hz (Accessed on July 5, 2020)

Feser, Edward (2017), "Foundations of Sexual Morality," *Edward Feser* (blog), February 7, 2017, http://edwardfeser.blogspot.com/2017/02/foundations-of-sexual-morality.html (Accessed on July 5, 2020)

Feser, Edward (2017), "The Problem of Hume's Problem of Induction," April 9, 2017, https://edwardfeser.blogspot.com/2017/04/the-problem-of-humes-problem-of.html (Accessed on July 5, 2020)

Feser, Edward (2017), *Five Proofs of the Existence of God*, Ignatius Press

Feser, Edward (2018), "Carrier on Five Proofs, *Edward Feser* (blog), February 24, 2018, https://edwardfeser.blogspot.com/2018/02/carrier-on-five-proofs.html (Accessed on July 5, 2020)

Feser, Edward (2018), "Caught in the Web," *Edward Feser (blog)*, October 1, 2018, https://edwardfeser.blogspot.com/2018/10/caught-in-web.html (Accessed on July 5, 2020)

Feser, Edward (2019), *Aristotle's Revenge: The Metaphysical Foundations of Physical and Biological Science*, Editiones Scholasticae

Feser, Edward (2020), "Adventures in the Old Atheism, Part IV: Marx," *Edward Feser* (blog), January 23, 2020, http://edwardfeser.blogspot.com/2020/01/adventures-in-old-atheism-part-iv-marx.html (Accessed on July 5, 2020)

Feser, Edward (2020), "Theology and the Analytic a Posteriori," *Edward Feser* (blog), June 10, 2020, http://edwardfeser.blogspot.com/2020/06/theology-and-analytic-posteriori.html (Accessed on June 20, 2020)

Feser, Edward (2020), "The Socialist State as an Occasionalist God," *Edward Feser* (blog), February 15, 2020, http://edwardfeser.blogspot.com/2020/02/the-socialist-state-as-occasionalist-god.html (Accessed on July 5, 2020)

Foot, Philippa (2003), *Natural Goodness*, Clarendon Press

Forti, Simona (2006), "The Biopolitics of Souls: Racism, Nazism, and Plato," *Political Theory* 34, no. 1 (2006), pp. 9-32

Fortin, Denis, Moon, Jerry, eds. (2014), *The Ellen J. White Encyclopedia*, Review & Herald Publishing

Foster, Michael Dylan (2015), *The Book of Yokai: Mysterious Creatures of Japanese Folklore*, University of California Press

Garner, Jonathan (2017), "Five Proofs of the existence of God by Feser: Book Review," *Philosophy of Religion Blog*, December 3, 2017, https://jonathandavidgarner.wordpress.com/2017/12/03/five-proofs-of-the-existence-of-god-feser-book-review/ (Accessed on July 5, 2020)

General Conference of Seventh-Day Adventists Administrative Committee (1997), "How Seventh-day Adventists View Roman Catholicism," Adventist.org, April 17, 1997, https://www.adventist.org/en/information/official-statements/statements/article/go/0/how-seventh-day-adventists-view-roman-catholicism/24/ archived at http://archive.is/poQnJ on February 24, 2018 (Accessed on July 5, 2020).

Gigot, Francis (1911), "Moloch," *The Catholic Encyclopedia*, Vol. 10, New York: Robert Appleton Company, http://www.newadvent.org/cathen/10443b.htm (Accessed on July 5, 2020)

Guenther, Hans (1928), *Plato: The Guardian of Life*, J.F. Lehmann's

Haldane, John and Lee, Patrick (2003), "Aquinas on Human Ensoulment, Abortion and the Value of Life," *Philosophy* 78, no. 02 (2003)

Haldane, John and Lee, Patrick (2003), "Rational Souls and the Beginning of Life (A Reply to Robert Pasnau)," *Philosophy* 78 no. 4 (2003)

Hare, John (2014), "Religion and Morality," *The Stanford Encyclopedia of Philosophy* (Winter 2014 Edition), Zalta, Edward N. (ed.), https://plato.stanford.edu/archives/win2014/entries/religion-morality/ (Accessed on July 5, 2020)

Harper, William, Dew, Thomas Roderick, et. Al (1968), *The Pro-Slavery Argument: As Maintained by the Most Distinguished Writers of the Southern States*, New York: Negro Universities Press, 1968

Hart, David Bentley (2019), "The Exemplary Clarity of the Five Proofs of the Existence of God," *Church Life Journal*, March 1, 2018, https://churchlifejournal.nd.edu/articles/the-exemplary-clarity-of-the-five-proofs-of-the-existence-of-god/ (Accessed on July 5, 2020)

Hennessey, Richard E (2015), "Universals in Feser's The Last Superstition. A Neo-Aristotelian Alternative to Realism in the Theory of Universals," *After Aristotle*, January 21, 2015, https://afteraristotle.net/2015/01/21/universals-in-fesers-the-last-superstitution-a-neo-aristotelian-alternative-to-realism-in-the-theory-of-universals/ (Accessed on July 5, 2020)

Hitler, Adolf and Ralph Manheim, trans. (1943), *Mein Kampf*, Houghton-Mifflin

Hood, John Y.B. (1995), *Aquinas and the Jews*, University of Pennsylvania Press

Horn, Laurence R. (2018), "Contradiction," The Stanford Encyclopedia of Philosophy (Winter 2018 Edition), Edward N. Zalta (ed.), https://plato.stanford.edu/archives/win2018/entries/contradiction/ (Accessed on July 5, 2020)

Hudson, Valerie M. and den Boer, Andrea M. (2004), *Bare Branches: The Security Implications of Asia's Surplus Male Population*, MIT Press

Huggett, Nick (2019), "Zeno's Paradoxes," The Stanford Encyclopedia of Philosophy (Spring 2019 Edition), Edward N. Zalta (ed.), URL = https://plato.stanford.edu/archives/spr2019/entries/paradox-zeno/ (Accessed on July 5, 2020)

Hursthouse, Rosalind (2012), "Philippa Ruth Foot, 1920-2010," *Biographical Memoirs of Fellows of the British Academy*, XI (2012), https://britac.ac.uk/sites/default/files/11_07-Philippa_Foot.pdf (Accessed on July 5, 2020)

Jidiette, Hugh (2018), "Edward Feser's Aristotelian Proof for God," *Hugh Jidiette*, January 9, 2018, https://hughjidiette.wordpress.com/2018/01/09/edward-fesers-aristotelian-proof-for-god/ (Accessed on July 5, 2020)

Jones, Andrew Zimmerman (2019), "What Is a Boson?" *ThoughtCo*, May 27, 2019, https://www.thoughtco.com/boson-2699112 (Accessed on July 5, 2020)

Joshi, S.T. (2001), *Ramsey Campbell and Modern Horror Fiction*, Liverpool University Press

Kamenka, Eugene (1963), "Philosophy in the Soviet Union," *Philosophy*, vol. 38, No. 143 (Jan., 1963), pp. 1-19

Kenny, Anthony (1980), *The Five Ways: St. Thomas Aquinas' Proofs of God's Existence*, University of Notre Dame Press

Kenny, Anthony (2001), "We Have All Been Here Before," *The Times Literary Supplement*, July 22, 2001, https://www.the-tls.co.uk/articles/private/we-have-all-been-here-before/ (Accessed on December 9, 2019)

Kershaw, Ian (1999), *Hitler, 1889-1936: Hubris*, W.W. Norton

Kershaw, Ian (1999), *Hitler, 1836-1945: Nemesis*, W.W. Norton

Kreeft, Peter (2017), *Catholics and Protestants: What Can We Learn from Each Other?* Ignatius Press

Lawler, Dan (2014), "Medieval Times (are here again!)," Amazon.com review of the Kindle edition of The Last Superstition, October 19, 2014, https://www.amazon.com/gp/customer-reviews/R2RETCY4TFAQ5D/ref=cm_cr_getr_d_rvw_ttl?ie=UTF8&ASIN=1587314525 , archived at http://archive.is/GPrh3 (Accessed on July 5, 2020)

Levine, Samuel (1980), *You Take Jesus, I'll Take God: How To Refute Christian Missionaries*, Hamoroh Press

MacIntyre, Alasdair (2012), *After Virtue*, 3rd ed., University of Notre Dame Press

MacIntyre, Alasdair (2016), *Ethics in the Conflicts of Modernity: An Essay on Desire, Practical Reasoning, and Narrative*, Cambridge University Press

Maimonides, Moses and Halkin, Abraham S., trans. (2019), *The Epistles of Maimonides: Crisis and Leadership*, The Jewish Publication Society

Maitzen, Stephen (2009), "Ordinary Morality Presupposes Atheism," *European Journal for Philosophy of Religion* 2 (2009), pp. 107-126.

Martin, Paul (2004), *Counting Sheep: The Science and Pleasures of Sleep and Dreams*, Thomas Dunne Books

Marx, Karl (1976), "The German Ideology," *Karl Marx and Friedrich Engels, Collected Works*, vol. 5, New York: International Publishers

Mazower, Mark (2008), *Hitler's Empire: How the Nazis Ruled Europe*, Penguin Books

McCarthy, George E. (1990), *Marx and the Ancients: Classical Ethics, Social Justice, and Nineteenth-Century Political Economy*, Rowman and Littlefield Publishers, inc.

McCarthy, George E. ed. (1992), *Marx and Aristotle: Nineteenth-Century German Social Theory and Classical Antiquity*, Rowman and Littlefield Publishers, inc.

Mike D (2015), "Metaphysical Bigotry," *The A-Unicornist*, April 16, 2015, https://www.theaunicornist.com/2014/09/metaphysical-bigotry.html (Accessed on July 5, 2020)

Morson, Gary Saul (2018), "Among the Disbelievers," *Commentary Magazine*, September 2018, https://www.commentarymagazine.com/articles/among-the-disbelievers/ (Accessed on July 5, 2020)

Murray, Anthony (2014), "When Judges Believe in 'natural law'," The Atlantic, January 27, 2014, https://www.theatlantic.com/national/archive/2014/01/when-judges-believe-in-natural-law/283311/ (Accessed on July 5, 2020)

Oderberg, David (2007), *Real Essentialism*, Routledge

One Brow (2009), "Review of TLS – Problems, problems, problems," *Life, The Universe, and One Brow*, December 24, 2009, http://lifetheuniverseandonebrow.blogspot.com/2009/12/review-of-tls-problems-problems.html (Accessed on July 5, 2020)

Oppy, Graham, ed. (2015), *The Routledge Handbook of Contemporary Philosophy of Religion*, Routledge

Paddock, Catharine (2014), "Prostate cancer diagnosis may be more accurate with semen test," *Medical News Today*, June 9, 2014, https://www.medicalnewstoday.com/articles/277949.php (Accessed on July 5, 2020)

Palmer, Brian (2014), "What is the Answer to Zeno's Paradox", *Slate*, March 5, 2014, http://www.slate.com/articles/health_and_science/science/2014/03/zeno_s_paradox_how_to_explain_the_solution_to_achilles_and_the_tortoise.html (Accessed on July 5, 2020)

Pearce, Jonathan MS (2015), "Does God Have Free Will? No.," *A Tippling Philosopher*, June 8, 2015, https://www.patheos.com/blogs/tippling/2015/06/08/does-god-have-free-will-no/ (Accessed on July 5, 2020)

Pearce, Jonathan MS (2019), "Easter Round-Up: Everything You Need To Know About The Resurrection (Skeptically Speaking)," *A Tippling Philosopher,* April 20, 2019, https://www.patheos.com/blogs/tippling/2019/04/20/easter-round-up-everything-you-need-to-know-about-the-resurrection-skeptically-speaking/ (Accessed November 1, 2019)

Pearce, Jonathan MS (2013), "Heaven, Hell, and Philosophical Zombies," *A Tippling Philosopher*, September 6, 2013, https://www.patheos.com/blogs/tippling/2013/09/06/heaven-hell-and-philosophical-zombies/ (Accessed on July 5, 2020)

Pearce, Jonathan MS (2016), *Did God Create the Universe from Nothing? Countering William Lane Craig's Kalam Cosmological Argument*, Onus Books, Kindle Edition

Pearce, Jonathan MS (2019), "God's Morality or Meaning Is Merely Subjective," *A Tippling Philosopher*, December 6, 2019, https://www.patheos.com/blogs/tippling/2019/12/06/gods-morality-or-meaning-is-merely-subjective/ (Accessed on July 5, 2020)

Pigliucci, Massimo (2013), "Plantinga's Evolutionary Argument Against Naturalism," *Rationally Speaking*, July 15, 2013, http://rationallyspeaking.blogspot.com/2013/07/plantingas-evolutionary-argument.html (Accessed on July 5, 2020)

Pike, Jonathan E. (1999), *From Aristotle to Marx: Aristotelianism in Marxist Social Ontology*, Ashgate Publishing, 1999

Plato and Grube, G.M.A., trans. (1992), *The Republic*, 2nd Edition, Hackett Publishing

Rabinbach, Anson and Bialas, Wolfgang, eds. (2014), *Nazi Germany and the Humanities: How German Academics Embraced Nazism*, Oneworld Publications

Reeve W. Paul and Parshall, Ardis E., eds. (2010), *Mormonism: A Historical Encyclopedia*, ABC-CLIO

Reichenbach, Bruce, "Cosmological Argument," The Stanford Encyclopedia of Philosophy (Fall 2019 Edition), Edward N. Zalta (ed.), forthcoming URL = https://plato.stanford.edu/archives/fall2019/entries/cosmological-argument/ (Accessed on July 5, 2020)

Roche, Helen and Demetriou, Kyriakos, eds. (2017), *Brill's Companion to the Classics, Fascist Italy, and Nazi Germany*, BRILL

Rose, Devin (2014), *The Protestant's Dilemma: How the Reformation's Shocking Consequences Point to the Truth of Catholicism*, Catholic Answers Press (Kindle Edition)

Rosenthal, Andrew (1991), "Marshall Retires from High Court; Blow to Liberals," *The New York Times*, June 28, 1991, https://www.nytimes.com/1991/06/28/us/marshall-retires-from-high-court-blow-to-liberals.html (Accessed on July 5, 2020)

Ruse, Michael (1988), *Homosexuality: A Philosophical Inquiry*, Blackwell

Rydecker, Timothy (2008), *Hitler's Private Library: The Books That Shaped His Life*, Alfred A. Knopf

Savage, Rachel (2019), "Suicides fall with gay marriage in Sweden, Denmark as stigma fades," Reuters, November 19, 2019, https://www.reuters.com/article/us-nordics-lgbt-health-trfn/suicides-fall-with-gay-marriage-in-sweden-denmark-as-stigma-fades-idUSKBN1XO010 (Accessed on July 5, 2020)

Seidman, Michael (2002), *Republic of Egos: A Social History of the Spanish Civil War*, University of Wisconsin Press

Service, Robert (2000), *Lenin: A Biography*, Belknap Press

Skalko, John (2019), *Disordered Actions: A Moral Analysis of Lying and Homosexual Activity*, Editiones Scholasticae

Smolkin, Victoria (2018), *A Sacred Space is Never Empty: A History of Soviet Atheism*, Princeton University Press

Snyder, Timothy (2010), *Bloodlands: Europe Between Hitler and Stalin*, Basic Books

Steedman, Marek D. (2012), *Jim Crow Citizenship: Liberalism and the Southern Defense of Racial Hierarchy*, Routledge

Swinburne, Richard (2003) *The Resurrection of God Incarnate*, Oxford University Press

Tismaneanu, Vladimir, Howard, Marc, and Sil, Rudra eds. (2006), *World Order after Leninism*, University of Washington Press

Tooze, Adam (2006), *The Wages of Destruction: The Making and Breaking of the Nazi Economy*, Viking Press

Tribe, Lawrence (1991), "Clarence Thomas and 'natural law'," *The New York Times*, July 15, 1991, https://www.nytimes.com/1991/07/15/opinion/clarence-thomas-and-natural-law.html (Accessed on July 5, 2020)

Trotsky, Leon and Eastman, Max, trans. (1937), *The Revolution Betrayed: What Is the Soviet Union and Where Is It Going?* Pathfinder Books

Weaver, Mary Jo and Appleby, R. Scott, eds. (1995), *Being Right: Conservative Catholics in America*, Indiana University Press

Weinberg, Gerhard L. (2005), *Visions of Victory: The Hopes of Eight World War II Leaders*, Cambridge University Press

Whitman, James Q. (2017), *Hitler's American Model: The United States and the Making of Nazi Race Law*, Princeton University Press

Wiedemann, Thomas (1981), *Greek and Roman Slavery*, London: Routledge

Wilkins, John (2012), "Plantinga's EAAN," *Evolving Thoughts*, January 31, 2012, https://evolvingthoughts.net/2012/01/31/plantingas-eaan/ (Accessed on July 5, 2020)

www.ingramcontent.com/pod-product-compliance
Lightning Source LLC
Chambersburg PA
CBHW050543170426
43201CB00011B/1546